# The Darker Side of Samuel, Saul, and David

## Narrative Artistry and the Depiction of Flawed Leadership

—⚭—

G. D. Vreeland, Ph.D.

# The Darker Side of Samuel, Saul, and David

Narrative Artistry and the Depiction of Flawed Leadership
## Volume 1

—∿—

## G. D. Vreeland, Ph.D.
Associate Professor of Semitic Languages and Biblical Literature
Northwest Baptist Seminary

Xulon PRESS

*THE DARKER SIDE OF SAMUEL, SAUL AND DAVID:*
*Narrative Artistry And The Depiction Of Flawed Leadership. Volume 1*
by G. D. Vreeland, Ph.D.

Printed in the United States of America

ISBN 978-1-60266-211-7

www.xulonpress.com

Dedicated to His Royal Majesty
on behalf of His choice servant,
my wife, Donna.

# Table of Contents

—⁂—

# Acknowledgements

—∿∿—

I would like to thank my publisher and copy editors from Xulon Press: without whose tireless work, this volume would have had many more and serious errors and probably not lived to see the light of day. I am reasonably certain that martyrdom points accrue to those several English Bible and Hebrew Bible students who have survived classes specifically devoted to the Samuel Narratives—as well as those who had to suffer a disproportionate emphasis and nerdy enthusiasm on the Samuel Narratives while sledding through Old Testament survey courses. Special thanks go to those several churches that had me as a guest speaker for a series in the Samuel Narratives—they paid twice.

Special thanks also go to the leadership of my school, Northwest Baptist Seminary, for allowing me to use their students, teach their courses, and abuse their equipment in the production of this volume and its sequel. Strong thanks go to inspirational friends Robert E. Longacre for his help on a related subject in my doctoral dissertation, Robert D. Bergen and his commentary in the NAC series along with the best article ever written on Saul, "Evil Spirits and Eccentric Grammar" and my former student Steve Mathewson (*The Art of Preaching Old Testament Narrative*). I also need to thank my associate, Karen Pease, for her tireless work in poring over these pages looking for mistakes great and small. These were non-family encouragements.

Finally, my warmest and most heartfelt appreciation goes to my immediate family. First, thanks to my children—who also often paid twice by having to read and listen to these words in multiple formats. Secondly, thanks and blessings to my wife, Donna, who paid for this work and its sequel in many ways: subsidy, reading, and listening to the manuscripts multiple times, and encouraging me to follow through. In all ways she lives what I have called her on several continents: "The best English Bible scholar in the modern era."

And to you my friend, may you find provocative thought, warning, encouragement and blessings!

G. D. Vreeland, Ph.D.
Commencement Bay
Valentine's Day, 2007

# Notes on Style

—⚬—

Translations of Hebrew words and phrases will be by the simplest manner possible to avoid unnecessary ambiguity at the location in question.

Unless otherwise noted, all translations will be the author's own.

## Main Abbreviations

BDB Brown, Driver and Briggs: *A Hebrew and English Lexicon of the Old Testament*

BHS Biblia Hebraica Stuttgartensia

ESV English Standard Version

JSB Jewish Study Bible

HALOT: *Hebrew and Aramaic Lexicon of the Old Testament*

NASB New American Standard Bible

NIV New International Version

(Other Bibles will be noted where they appear.)

The Darker Side of Samuel, Saul and David:
Narrative Artistry and the Depiction of Flawed Leadership
Volume 1

# General Introduction to the Darker Side of Samuel, Saul and David

—⟋ⱴⱴ⟍—

## The Title

First, why have I entitled these volumes *The Darker Side of Samuel, Saul and David*? Reasons are myriad, but foremost among them is that I am not under the influence of pietistic literature, the Puritans, or devotional commentaries whose authors seem to feel the need to find heroes in the Old Testament. While doing my doctoral work, I remember reading volume after volume that painted a picture of Joseph as a paragon of virtue. How that is even possible after Robert Alter's exposure of the themes and ideas of the Joseph Narrative is impossible for me to see.[1] Yet each year, it seems, I see a couple more in the genre of what I call sugar-coated Joseph books.

Be that as it may, I believe, and think I can prove, that the people whose stories unfold in the older testament of the Bible were people with many of the same human failings as people of today. In this alone is some of that which transits the testaments, indeed the eons, to our day. That they were persons of faith is also evidenced to varying degrees and at different times. That there is nothing that is disproved in the newer testament of the Bible, will also be demonstrated.

Beyond that, we have to remember that historically, Israel was attempting to extricate itself from its own dark ages, the period otherwise known as that of the judges. If these people knew the law and tried to keep it, they ought to have known better at some points. However, there were movements; cultural, political, and military, that may have kept them from complete compliance. This will not impress the "all or nothing" folks; but theologically, I do not believe that perfection is possible in this life. *Everything* done at any point is merely an approximation and perhaps the lesser of multiple evils. Nothing in history has proven to me that humans are innately good or potentially perfectible—nothing has even indicated the possibility. In this, we must remember that one man's cynic is another man's realist: I style myself a realist; you may style me a cynic. We will have to get that squared away at the outset, no? What about the characters themselves?

Saul is a pretty dark character at points and nobody seems to get in a snit if you paint him in the light that he finally ends up in. I hope to demonstrate that, superficially at least, Saul was not always such a loser. Where people start to get a bit tense is when we go out of our way to show one of the great prophets of Israel as a mere mortal. This is no more true than with Samuel. However, should you have had to interact with him on anything of a regular basis, I am willing to wager that there would have been conflict—perhaps you would have found that you did not even like the man.

Where people get downright irritated, is when David, supposedly "the man after God's own heart" and the self-styled "sweet psalmist of Israel," is painted in anything other than glowing tones. Yet the literature recently is replete with discussions of his treatment of women, outlanders, and domestic opponents. Some try to make excuses—based upon ignorance, culture, philosophy, etc.—for his actions. I will not: I will show that there was a distance between what he was, said, and did and that he should have known better if he was as devoted to the law and his court prophets as he said he was. I will also attempt to balance the equation by trying to paint him in the light of a man of faith as described in Hebrews 11. There were some things that David did very well; there are some things that I would have had to go on record as opposing.

**Shape of the Commentary**

The following two volumes are designed to be a commentary on the Samuel Narratives. However, they have several peculiarities. These are: the author—very peculiar indeed—the overall format of the volumes, and the design of each subsection. We will look at these in reverse order.

**First, let us examine the design of each subsection.**

The design is unique in that it is proposed that each section be complete in and of itself. Of course, coming down to specific cases this will be more or less true. Regardless, this format becomes awkward for a couple of reasons. It requires either a lot of internal referencing or a good knowledge of the biblical text on the part of the reader. Although it may be something of an assumption, I am going to presume upon quite a bit of both. The second major setback is that there may be quite a bit of repetition. For instance, there will only be so many times that one can complain about David's treatment of outlanders and women; but it might be so many times as to be tedious should the reader allow it to be so.

However, there are some major advantages to such a format; first is that the reader gets a complete thought at each given locus. That is, if you pick up on the section entitled "Abishag: The Prop of Contention" in the "Epilogue" to Volume 2, for instance, you will get a pretty complete thought on the little bit of time that she appears in the narrative. There will, however, be other sections that tangentially mention Abishag in reference to the ancient treatment of women in general and the leading characters' treatment of women in particular. A less politically volatile example? In 2 Samuel 4, I go off on the trail of biblical brotherhood in a section entitled "When Brothers Are Not Friends." In that section, I attempt to show that the usage of the word brother/brothers is more restrictive in the Samuel Narratives (including the "Epilogue" of 1 Kings 1 and 2) than in the larger expanse of biblical literature.

The second advantage is that if I do not happen to deal with the particular problem or point of interest that you have in mind, you can quickly switch off and go find another volume that will be more helpful. Yes, I am actually asking you to read mine and anybody else's that addresses your particular concerns. My hope is that you will find these pages such a delight (call me arrogant should you wish; but these pages have been field tested with good results) that you will save mine for last to get just the right spin on the facts and data given to you by other more eminent scholars.

**Secondly, there is the distinction of format.**

The overall format of these two volumes is as follows: Introduction (In 1 Samuel 9-31 there will also be, Reading from "Saul: A Life Suspended in Doubt"), Textual Observations, Textual Problems (in some cases this section will have been completely ignored), Textual Applications and Anecdotes and finally the Conclusion. I suppose at the point of a sword I might confess that others have approximated this design. However, wishing to become all things to all persons—and while attempting to avoid becoming nothing to anyone, I want to include things from fields as diverse as text-linguistics, compositional analysis, and narrative interpretation (see the more detailed "Introduction" relegated to the appendix of the first volume) as well as literature, philosophy, ethics, and practical application.

I begin with an "Introduction," attempting to tell the reader where we have been and where we are going. Necessarily, some introductions will say more than others. For instance, in regard to the "Epilogue" in volume two, the introduction to 1 Kings 1 will be more involved and there will be no conclusion; the conclusion to 1 Kings 2 will be more involved and there will be no introduction. This will be followed by a section on "Textual Observations." Here, I will attempt to describe what I see and its ramifications to studies narrative, historical, literary, theological, and pragmatic. I am attempting to go from the data of the text—both from literary theory and linguistic theory—something I have been told is relatively incompatible. I will attempt to prove that through the vehicle of compositional analysis, both may be brought together (again, see the more technical introduction in the appendix of the first volume).

The next section has to do with "Textual Problems." Although there are textual problems in each chapter, some do not merit much consideration and so the section will be absent. If I do not hit your pet problem, I apologize; but I do think these texts are readable and really quite lucid. The problems I enjoy have to do with the semantic games lexicographers play and the problems entailed in bad text joins. Some of the worst text joins are due to where the ancients decided—oddly in some cases—to change the chapter. Part of that problem is merely the difficulty of certain episodes being much more involved than others and hence longer. Chapter divisions can be a bit arbitrary and forced at times. The problems that I do not enjoy are those with no compelling solution; hence, I tend to avoid them or to refer the reader to others who have written on the matter. Perhaps it is one of those paths that I should have taken, for instance, with the number of years commentators feel compelled to assign to Saul's reign in 1 Samuel 13:1. But just like many before me—and I will assume after me—I will waste an inordinate amount of space merely to prove the rather creative solution to the problem posited by the English Standard Version,[2] vis. leave it blank. In my opinion, any solution arrived at is theory laden and not compelling. More later.

The next section will be where I attempt to offer "Anecdotes and Applications." In this section, there will be everything from proverbs to witticisms, the design of which is merely to make the reader think. Earlier in my career I had the goal to make a principle from each verse of the Bible. Yeah, I know, I was young. As it turns out, there is something you can say without moralizing from almost every verse of the Bible: lists are tedious, however. For instance, I abandoned the effort at the list of thirty of David's mighty men (2 Samuel 23:24-38). But, there are lots of ideas you can infer from the last unit in the list (about Uriah the Hittite).

The final section is, I suppose fittingly, the "Conclusion." In this section, I attempt to sum up what has gone before and occasionally abstract the lessons I have derived from the preceding text. I have tried very hard not to moralize; but I am afraid that, like everyone else, abstraction on ethical/theological texts lends itself most readily to such vices. In this section, I have also often attempted to give a hint of what is to come in the following chapter. In that way, themes and ideas are kept in the reader's view (despite sections that may seem a bit choppy).

### Thirdly, these two volumes are anecdotal.

I am told that this is a problem in formal writing. I hope to prove that to be erroneous. I managed to slip a couple of living-language, linguistic anecdotes into my doctoral dissertation (only one was caught and questioned, but it stood the test). This helps me to know that some serious scholars do not consider anecdotes invalid as long as they can be corroborated with other research. However, here I would wish to fall from a new height.

There will be times where I insert illustrations from personal experience or personal philosophy of life. We in Christendom are often confronted with our conservative politics (should we possess them) and told that we ought to keep our mouths and word-processors quiet. It would be pretty easy for me to develop a persecution complex: I'm white, male, straight, conservative, Protestant, etc. However, I learned something way back in 1983 on a plane from Nairobi to Amsterdam that had started in Johannesburg. You will recall that this was in the era when we in the west were being schooled with respect to the evils of apartheid by the leftist media. I sat between two white guys, one from the military and one from the business world. The guy from the business world said it best: "I'm an auditor from Price-Waterhouse: everybody hates me anyway." The lesson? We have to assume that people will dislike us not so much for what we say, but for what we are or what we represent. We have to let the chips fall where they may. I even had one student go so far as to say I had a persecution complex. Fun stuff! The problem with his perception of my life description is that I really do not care what people think about me—I am oblivious to my own insecurities! Be that as it may, we remember that "fools boldly go where angels fear to tread" and the only difference between the hero and the fool is the consequences of his action. I will thus go into action here.

We know, in advance, that everything we do with respect to the interpretation of the biblical text has ramifications personal, political, religious, economic, moral, and ethical. To stifle the ethical voice of either the Bible or its interpreter is a matter of either taste or prejudice, not a matter of truth. If you disagree with my assessment, fine; but know that there are multiplied millions of educated people who do agree with me—even if my opinions are in the minority. The last time I checked, truth was not a majority proposition.

And so there might be about three reasons you do not like this volume. The first is that it might not meet your preconceived expectations as to what an expository commentary ought to be. Every day is a new day. New perspectives and methods are revealed daily and perhaps this is only the trough of an important, cresting wave. There is certainly something authentic about an anecdotal approach: it acknowledges the fact of the subjective nature of interpretation. I have no preconceived notions, assumptions, and presumptions about objectivity; but beyond that, I do not think anyone else ought to have them either. Along with Hirsch, I really think that interpretation is a subjective matter and that we all need each other even to make a movement toward truth—even should you believe it to be *proven* that such a quest for truth is ultimately a quest for the illusory.

The second thing you might not like about these volumes is that they are my anecdotes. It is my firm conviction that over the years too much deference has been paid to the old theological research model of writing. I have a research degree; but I do not think that is all there is to say about it. A Ph.D. is supposed to be a doctor of philosophy degree and that means, if it means anything, we are supposed to deal with the validity of ideas. We are to be doctors of philosophy—the true lovers of wisdom. With that in mind, I have endeavored to interface with the text of the Samuel Narratives and show you how it is that I have reflected upon them. You may disagree with my conclusions, but you will know exactly how I have approached the text and what it is I see when I look at them. This is just fine; I should most certainly feel free to disagree with your writing, yes? Even so, my desire is to interface with the text and expose my reflections upon it. Do not worry; when I get scared, just as do other authors, I will check with and note people I respect.

The third thing you may not like about these volumes has more to do with my philosophies on matters political, economic, and religious. Let us look at these in reverse order. Out of the closet, I am what you might call, *charisbaptarian*. That is, whereas I deeply respect the work of the reformers, I do not believe that the reformation is over, nor do I believe it should have frozen with the Westminster documents. Secondly, I am baptistic in that I believe in a couple of things that drive most clerics to the sacramental wine: I view the New Testament as my creed and as the final and authoritative commentary on the Old Testament. I am also a firm believer in such things as congregational church polity (certainly a dinosaur from another era, no?) and the sovereign autonomy of the local church. But those are battles for another day. I am also charismatic (small "c") in that I view my brief stay with the International Church of the Four Square Gospel as a period of incubation in respect to my philosophy of worship. Neither do I believe that Pentecostals, Charismatics or the Signs and Wonders people are inherently of inferior intellect. They have their approach to the biblical text and others have their own. So, if you do not like what I have written because of my faith, fine—I have painted myself into a corner. But when you write your book, if you have any intellectual honesty, you will paint yourself into just as small a corner and people will still read it.

Additionally, in the matter of economics, I make it a point to rarely associate with tax-and-spend liberals. I do not like the tax structures in this country; but I have lived in other parts of the world where it is worse. It is axiomatic, like the weather in the Pacific Northwest, no matter how bad it gets, wait a few minutes and it will get worse. This spills over into politics, I think you will agree. I do not think that laws should be made by people who make their money off the legal system. I view it as a conflict of interests when, for instance, people who can afford bodyguards—whether paid for by themselves or my tax dollars—make laws restricting my ability to defend my wife and children. Mice know about cheese; do you want them guarding the cheese factory? Lawyers—prosecutors in particular—know about law; should they make laws that unnecessarily restrict law abiding or otherwise virtuous citizens and increase their own ability to make money and hence have power over those they prosecute? Interestingly, police unions and guilds are often at loggerheads with lawyer associations as to which candidates they will back.

Finally, when it comes to politics, I would not make a very good federalist. I like Adams better than Jefferson as a person and with regard to foreign policy, but I like Jefferson's domestic policy better than Adams'. I am a firm believer in the Constitution, but not as a document subject to change. I am also a firm believer in states' rights; but I do think that the federal government needs to rein in these weird left and right coastal states a bit. I am what you might call a conservative, epithets being what they are. I do believe that change is a given; but I do not believe the maxim that all change is good. I believe that some change is just plain evil and that the political processes that support it need to be reversed. I also believe that when elected officials go out of their way to hurt the people of a region or country, they should be censured. Part of that has to do with failure to be reelected. Part of that has to do with being removed from office by the body he or she claims to serve. Part of it has to do with bodies having the courage to put into effect the consequences of censure.

There are many more things that might be added here; but time is short and we need to get on with how it is I am going to present the commentary and how we read a text. But before we go on, I would like to supply a good anecdote. The last church I pastored was in what they would call a progressive denomination. It was, in fact, politically, religiously, and economically liberal; again, epithets being what they are. Oddities abounded in such a place. The chairman of the board was politically conservative and theologically liberal—he did not like me at all. Fine! Another leading member of the council was theologically conservative (a post-millennial theonomist). and politically conservative—although he had completely abdicated on the subject of secular education. Although he did not like my theology, he remarked that he liked me because he always knew where I would stand on issues political, economic, and religious. I am predictable and from that, even if you do not like what I have written—or even like me for that matter—you should be able to profitably reflect upon my work and derive some benefit. I will have to pass on to you a blessing for trying.

**Theory on Reading the Biblical Text**

As an unabashedly Christian thinker, I am moved by Jesus' words to "a certain lawyer" in Luke 10:26. He asked him, "What is written in the Law? How do you read?" It proved to be pretty self-evident to Jesus that the lawyer could read and cull the simple meaning of a text. "You have answered correctly. Do this and you will live" (v. 28). Where push came to shove had to do with significance and reference: "And who is my neighbor" (v. 29). And this brought forth the parable of the Good Samaritan—two words of which could not be held in the same sentence, in their minds—without having them on opposite sides of adversative clauses. The point at issue is that the master teacher Himself is interested in how we read and thinks it is a relatively simple process to arrive at a fairly unified field theory of meaning. He did not even get too stressed about the issues of significance and reference; he simply illustrated it.

I believe it was Noam Chomsky who said humans were "hard-wired for language." For whatever we might think of his political opinions, he has certainly given us an interesting notion here! Hence, there is something we share with every other human being currently and throughout history. We have an ability to communicate, to possess thought (thinking in words) and to transfer that—with some line-loss, admittedly—to another human being. Secondly, I learned a lot about language when I taught Hebrew to graduate students the first couple times because I had two year olds at home. I discovered that every human child has the ability to learn any human parent's language and with greater facility than that of adults. In addition, although there are variations in abilities, each culture seems to be able to produce adults proficient in its linguistic medium. Thirdly, I theorize that the ancients wanted to communicate with subsequent generations and were not trying to be particularly opaque when they did so. Never have I found this more so than in my study of Middle Kingdom Egyptian hieroglyphics; I am astonished that it took so long for a Champollion to come along and break the code.[3] Be that as it may, it seems to be true as well with biblical Hebrew. That there is ambiguity is a known fact. The meanings of some words have been lost through the years—and even that may be due more to over-study than to neglect. Much of what passes for ambiguity in the literature seems to me to be artificially inserted into the text. And so, fourthly, I start with what everybody starts: the text. I am an out-of-the-closet phenomenologist, and I am reflecting upon the text that I read, as are you. I simply have no pretenses about objectivity—other than that it may be possible to achieve it. As you read and reflect upon the text and as I do so, we may achieve a passing approximation of the truth. It is my hope that we do so together—and enjoy the ride!

## Rules of Engagement

As I said earlier there will be several viewpoints combined in these pages. I wish to look, sometimes all at once and sometimes one to the exclusion of the others, at modern narrative interpretation, text-linguistics, and compositional analysis. I do not wish to entirely ignore matters historical; but they will certainly arrive as a fourth priority.

With regard to *narrative interpretation*, I wish to look at things like plot, characterization, and use of artifacts. I will take Robert Alter, Robert Polzin, and others fairly seriously, even when I disagree with their methods and conclusions.[4] And so I will look at such things as type-scenes, convention, the difference between narrative and discourse, what to do with repetition, the ghosts of reticence, and dancing between narrative and knowledge (see my analysis of Robert Alter in the appendix).

One of the things that I will not look at too often is the current chiasm craze. People seem to want to find chiasms, envelope structures, inverted parallelism, and verbal bracketing everywhere. Fine, they are welcome to; but once you say that all of your A, B, C, D, D', C', B' and A's line up, what have you said? Nothing! But you ask, exasperatedly, "How can you possibly say that, with all the literary emphasis placed upon it recently?" Want anecdotes? Here comes one: The other day, after church, I was putting away my keyboard and all its attendant accoutrements. As I was folding up the monitor cords, I had an epiphany: all stories are the same. Either they go out and come back as when the monitor cord is folded double or they go around and come back as when it is rolled up or it starts, proceeds, and ends as when it is laid out end to end. Convolutions (twists and/or knots in the cord) notwithstanding, there are only so many ways to tell a story. In addition, I am also an avid novel reader and I have found that—apparently regardless of the time period or the particular sub-genre—there is a sameness as to how we tell a story. Whether we are working through time, geography, or ideology, we either go and retrace our steps, go around and come back by a circuitous route, or we start, proceed, and finish in a line (it might be a "snake's back," but it is linear nonetheless).

Another thing that has bothered me about the hunt for inverted parallelisms is the lack of balance. That is, it is pretty easy to show that an A matches an A' and so on; but having said that, why is it that the number of verses, sentences, phrases, and words does not regularly balance? Hence, the analysis is suspect, in my opinion, of ramming post-Enlightenment, Romance Period literary categories back into ancient literature. There is an artificiality that plagues the practice and that throws ideas at the text and winds up with texts out of balance. Perhaps that does not bother literary theorists; but the rabbis tended to find more symmetry in the text. As we will repeatedly demonstrate below in regard to the difference between the episode initial position and where tradition has placed the chapter breaks; however, symmetry may be just as artificial. Perhaps the whole thing is misguided and the quest for structure is merely something to help us avoid what the text is trying to communicate. And so, in this, it will be assumed that the text proceeds in a linear fashion and builds upon and adds enrichment to that which has preceded. To that end, it yields its cognitive content initially in a linear fashion and then more multi-dimensionally (see the appendix for clarification).

I will also look at the Samuel Narratives in the light of modern *text-linguistic theory* and how it does or should affect our reflection upon the story. I will at times look at things so fine as clause-analytical considerations and sometimes so broad as discourse analysis. In the appendix, I discuss the tests for textuality and what is the syntactical hierarchy for the various kinds of discourse. For instance, when in narrative, we will expect to find preterites (simple past tense) reigning supreme in pushing the story along, whereas we will find other verb types for the discourse, episode, and paragraph initial forms. We will also find other verb forms when we are looking for the backgrounded material. When we discover discourse (e.g., hortatory, expository, procedural, or predictive) imbedded in narrative, we will find different kinds of verb structures yet that will, combined with the other three, tell us what the message of the story is. We will talk about macrostructures foregrounded and backgrounded (see the appendix on the analysis of Robert Longacre). Briefly, foregrounding is deduced from the string of narrative tense verbs that propel the story forward. This *is* the story. Backgrounding is deduced from the constellations of other verb forms in discourse. This is the *message* of the story.

And finally, I will attempt to look at these texts in the light of modern *compositional analysis theory*. Following the work of Bar-Efrat (see the appendix), I will examine how a story chains its episodes together using four major means. First, at the verbal level, things are held together by shared words and phrases. Secondly, I will attempt to demonstrate this cohesiveness through an examination of the narrative technique and, for instance, the balance between report and dialogue. Thirdly, there will be the larger consideration of a shared narrative world describing, for instance, the same characters and events. Finally, there will be the overarching technique of sharing conceptual content with all of biblical writing including the New Testament. In this there will be a more genetic and yet global examination tracing themes and ideas throughout the paragraph, episode, discourse, the so-called "deuteronomistic history," and biblical thought as a whole.

Throughout the journey that follows, it is my sincere hope that you will enjoy the flight. Reflect on the text of the Samuel Narratives and experience the joy of reading it. Where I drive you to the text—either for an epiphany or to prove me wrong—I will have considered it energy well spent. I hope you receive not only the author's blessing for your part in the effort but a blessing from reading the text and more importantly, a blessing from the Senior Editor of the text Himself.

# Special Introduction to the Books of Samuel

—⟋⟍—

## I.  Authorship

A.  The books are anonymous. The Talmud ascribed 1 Samuel 1-25 to Samuel and the remainder to Nathan and Gad (1 Chron. 29:29).[5] The name Samuel (שְׁמוּאֵל, *Š'mû'ēl* means either "asked of God,"[6] (The folk etymology, 1 Sam. 1:20) or, according to the spelling, "name of *'ēl*," or "*His name is 'ēl*."[7]

B.  The two books were originally one; they were divided into two by the LXX. This division was then followed by the Latin Vulgate and subsequently into all our modern versions.

## II.  Historical Setting

A.  Historical Setting

The events of the books of Samuel run from the last days of Eli (c. 1050 BC) to the close of David's reign (c. 970). The birth of Samuel was c. 1120 BC; Saul's accession was c. 1050.

B.  Religious Setting

The low state of religion at the beginning of this period can be seen in the evil conduct of the sons of Eli who were religious functionaries. Yet a faithful remnant still kept the feasts, worshipping in sincerity, as seen in the parents of Samuel.

As this period begins, the ark is at Shiloh (having been moved there from Gilgal by Joshua; Joshua 18:1). After its capture by the Philistines, it was returned to Kiriath-Jearim (1 Sam. 7:1) and finally brought to Jerusalem by David (2 Sam. 6).

C.    Political Setting

The books of Samuel begin with the final judgeship of Samuel, the priest-judge, and end with the establishment of the theocratic kingdom. Samuel's headquarters was in Ramah, though he went in a circuit from Bethel to Gilgal to Mizpeh, judging Israel. He was the first nationwide judge. Saul reigned from Gibeah and Gilgal. David reigned first at Hebron over Judah and later at Jerusalem over all Israel.

The primary external opposition during this period is that of the Philistines (fought by both Samuel and Saul and finally defeated by David) and the Ammonites. Under David the countries of Edom, Moab, Ammon, and Syria were put under subjection to Israel; most of Philistia was conquered and a peace treaty was made with Phoenicia.

## III.    Purpose and Theme of the Books of Samuel

A.    The unified *theme* of the two books is *establishment of the Kingdom of Israel* progressing from a loosely connected disorganized group of Hebrew tribes, existing in practical anarchy, to a solidified kingdom under David, its greatest king. It shows the transfer of the crown from the tribe of Benjamin to Judah.

B.    A further *theme* underlying both books is *the overlordship or kingship of YHWH* over the theocratic state of Israel. He sets up, deposes, and commands the rulers of Israel. When obedient to Him, they win their battles and achieve prosperity; when disobedient, they are defeated by their enemies and confounded in their domestic affairs.

C.    The purpose of both of the books of Samuel is *to catalogue the events from the defection from the faith during the priesthood of Eli to the sunset of the reign of King David.* The books of Kings then expand upon this historical purpose with the transfer of kingship to David's elect son, Solomon. Then we once again see a history of spiral (cultural disintegration) as in the period of the judges.

## IV.  Outline for the Book of First Samuel

| | | |
|---|---|---|
| I. | The Rise and Rule of Samuel | 1–8 |
| | A.  The Birth of Samuel | 1:1–2:11 |
| | B.  The Growth and Call of Samuel | 2:12–3:22 |
| | C.  Philistines and the Ark | 4–7 |
| | D.  Israel's Demand for a King | 8 |
| II. | The Rise and Rule of Saul | 9–15 |
| | A.  The Selection of Saul | 9–10 |
| | B.  The Victory and Confirmation of Saul | 11 |
| | C.  The Final Address of Samuel | 12 |
| | D.  The Rejection of Saul | 13–15 |
| III. | The Rise and Early Role of David | 16–31 |
| | A.  David's Rise as a Shepherd | 16–17 |
| | B.  David's Service as a Courtier | 18–19 |
| | C.  David's Training as a Fugitive | 20–31 |

Theme: The Establishment of Israel As a Theocratic Kingdom

# 1 Samuel 1-3
# Introduction to Samuel the Prophet

—⁓—

## Introduction

How do you tell a story? In the Samuel Narratives, there is one overarching, indeed global mode, that must be mentioned. You frame a good story with lyric poetry. Observe the positioning of the three major songs in the Samuel Narratives. Resist the temptation for a moment to view them as two separate books—it would be just as easy to see them as three. Note the position of Hannah's song: the front bracket. This song sets the pace for what is to follow—her words culminating in "he will give strength to His king, and will exalt the horn of His anointed." So the whole focus of the what follows is the anointed king, which, of course, she has never met! It does make one ask the question whether or not there might be a choir of voices singing for different reasons.

The second song is at the beginning of Second Samuel. It is the lament David offers upon the occasion of hearing about the death of Saul and Jonathan from the Amalekite. After killing the messenger, David offers a song that at once conceals as much as it reveals about David himself. There are words about their statecraft and their warfare; but mostly things that everybody would have known. David feels something deeply about Jonathan— but again it is immortalized in something that indicates more how Jonathan treated David than how David felt about him. Nevertheless, this is about kingship, and at this point, its abrupt termination. In view of the fact that the song reveals little of the author, we are left to speculate as to the motivation. The writer does infuse the narrative with a dramatic irony that has been replayed over and over again in the stories of leaders who publicly mourn the passing of the individual whose crown they wear and in whose fate they privately rejoice. Concerning such transfers of power, it is often impossible to establish how often and to what extent public grief masks secret conspiracies or unexpressed joy.[8]

It is not my purpose to be quite so cynical about David's motivations—but the silence screams at us, I think. With respect to Jonathan, I think we have some grounds for hope. Saul? I am not as optimistic. Again, the song is about kingship as is the whole of Old Testament biblical history. This is how David wants—indeed, demands—to be treated (publicly, at least): with the respect and dignity befitting the office.

Chapter 22 would, of course, be the third song if we were counting noses. However, since it is a text that is inserted into the Samuel Narratives from Psalm 18 (virtually without revision), our only necessary point of contact has to do with the last lines which again echo the words of Hannah: "[The LORD] is a tower of salvations to His king,[9] and doing lovingkindness to His anointed, to David and his descendant(s) forever."[10] Never let it slip from memory that this is about kingship and the manner the Davidic dynasty is to be treated—from David's perspective—and the ruination of the monarchy from the historian's perspective.

And so the third song is "The Last Words of David." This also is about rulership: "He who rules over men righteously, who rules in the fear of God is . . ." (Several images indicating that he is a really good guy.) Then we are given the argument that David's house is that way. The reason is, "Because He has made an everlasting covenant with me, ordered in all things and secured; for all my salvation and all my desire, will He not indeed make it grow?" So, although it is left in the form of two questions, really, there is little doubt in David's mind. The bad guys mentioned and imaged for us in verses 6 and 7 are probably as much the rabble of the kingdom as they are the bad kings who came along all too frequently in Israel's history. And so the songs are about the proper comport of kingship. It is also about the way properly comported kings are to be treated by their constituency as well as the way improperly treated kings are to visit retribution upon those not acknowledging their exalted position. These are David's words, perhaps shaped to the text by the narrator, to show the way the whole story is going to go. The monarchy, the nation, and the people are doomed from the outset. Saul, David, and Solomon are only symptomatic and paradigmatic paragons of everything that will go wrong and be done wrong in the future and the consequences of those wrongs.

# 1 Samuel 1
## "A Child Was Born, Just the Other Day
## He Came to the World in the Usual Way"[11]

—⟋⟍—

## Introduction

(See introduction to chapters 1 through 3 above.) Because of the names of these books, we are automatically programmed to be looking for a protagonist by the name of Samuel. He does not appear immediately—and when he does, it is not in the usual manner of heroes. He is but a new-born baby when he arrives safely in verse 20.

## Textual Observations

## Introducing the Players

Although not universally true, many of the major players in the text of the Bible are triply introduced. We get one very thorough introduction to Elkanah in the first verse (which, by the way, looks very much like Judges 17:1; 19:1 and even Ruth 1:1—although you have to hunt for "man" down the line: "Now it came to pass that there was a man"). Even so, it is hard to get a handle on who he is. Is he an Ephraimite (NASB)? An Ephrathite (as per Hebrew)? From the hill country? From Bethlehem? Is he a Levite living among them? Questions abound, but we know he had two wives and that sets up the story.

Note that, using an A, B/ B, A structure, the wives are introduced twice for us in verse 2: first, their names are given and secondly, their productivity is noted—this is of cultural importance in case you think I'm being sexist.

We also get the first of several introductions to the wicked priesthood of the day. In verse 3, Hophi and Phineas are named—they will be excoriated and condemned in the very near future. I will make a major expansion of this topic when we get to chapter 2, so hang on. In any case, we probably ought to mention that they are the officiating priests at Shiloh and are the sons of the "high-priest," Eli. The boys will fill the roles of antagonists; Eli, first introduced here, is a foil against which Samuel will prevail. More about that below, as well.

In the second mention of his name, we learn that Elkanah is a religious man and, like the patriarchs of old, he plays favorites (vv. 4-5). Note that Elkanah gives Hannah the double portion (reserved for heirs, or the heir producer?). Then twice we are told that the LORD Himself had closed her womb. This is the narrator's voice coming through and so we must believe it since, as we have seen in the general introduction, the narrator is sovereign over his text. First, it is merely noted (v. 5) but then it is noted as the cause for Hannah's rival's crass behavior. I have always found it fascinating and a real knot in the stomach that religious occasions bring out the very best in rivals.

At the second mention of her name (v. 5), we learn that Hannah is barren, the Lord is the cause of it and that she is the favored wife. Because we have read this kind of story before, we know that when the narrator has the cause of barrenness being the Lord Himself, the end will be rather more glorious than the seemingly interminable condition to which we are early on introduced. At the third mention of her name (v. 8) it is in the mouth of her husband. He says, "Hannah, why do you weep and why do you not eat and why is your heart sad? Am I not better to you than ten sons?" Although I hear no echoes of the monarchy, Polzin does at this point. He hears Elkanah's questions in God's words: "Given the equations of sons and kings in the introduction to the history of royal Israel in 1 Samuel 1-7, Elkanah's voice dissolves into God's, who can be heard chiding Israel in similar terms: God asks Israel throughout the history, "Am I not worth more to you, O Israel, than ten kings?"[12]

So, expanding: "Israel why do you weep, and why do you not eat and why is your heart sad over your desolation? Am I not better to you than ten kings?" Of course, the answer will be, "no." And Israel, through Samuel the king-maker, will find themselves a Saul who is certainly a king such as all the other kingdoms have. And so, in something of a multivalent form, the single utterance of Elkanah becomes at once indicative of matters domestic, monarchical in the near future, and a harbinger of the final doom of the nation in the distant future. But, back to our story: at this, Hannah eats and drinks and rises. We know that she is functional; we know little else except that she is going to appeal to God to alleviate her heretofore childless condition.

At verse 9, we get the second introduction to one of the players on the national stage, Eli. Remember, Hannah is not mentioned by name after 2:21, Eli will be; but it won't be positive. Verse 2:19 indicates that Samuel's mother might have had a longer life than Eli: "And his mother would make him a little robe and bring it to him from year to year when she would come up with her husband to offer the yearly sacrifice." I would imagine that the "little robe" got a little bigger each year. But, back to Eli: remember that Hophni and Phineas were the officiating priests at Shiloh (v. 3) and we do not know much about their relationship other than that they are father and sons. Most of the time we meet Eli; he will be sitting, lying in bed, or finally breaking his obese neck. Here (v. 9, in case you had lost count), Eli is sitting "by the doorpost of the temple of the LORD." The Bible is replete with seers who do not see very well and Eli is no exception. He thinks Hannah is drunk and is pretty indignant about her behavior—and he tells her as much! In the category of "straining out a gnat and swallowing a camel" we will have much more to say about Eli's own two sons in a bit. Regardless, Eli and Hannah get their cognitive dissonance harmonized and she leaves in peace with a blessing and a wish for the fulfillment of her prayers. A final note: Hannah is a fiery Yahwist, she prays to the LORD and she talks about the LORD (vv. 10-16). She has God on her mind and in her heart. Her lips are replete with "God-talk." Conversely, Eli is much more reserved at this point and says, "may the God of Israel grant your petition" (v. 17). Although he will know revelations from God, his is a God more distant and his is a faith more opaque and yet fatalistic (cf. 1 Sam. 3:18).

In verse 19, both Elkanah and Hannah are named; but not by way of introduction this time. They are named by way of reintroduction and clarification for the only thing they do that blasts the story forward—producing a son. Since the LORD had made her barren, it is only fair that the narrator note that the LORD remembered her. She conceived and went through a normal gestation and gave birth. There is nothing abnormal about that, women have been doing this sort of thing for millennia! However, what is different is the naming. She calls him "Samuel." And she says that this is "Because I have asked him of the LORD." That is her folk etymology and it bears up with what she says in verse 27. Now wait just a minute! Who is she naming? It sounds for all the world like she is naming Saul, not Samuel.[13] Even this early, before we are ever introduced to Saul, he is the great question mark of 1 Samuel. This is because "Saul" is really a passive participle from the root meaning "to ask." Her etymology of the name "Samuel" requires perhaps the juggling of letters and at the very least the insertion of a glottal catch—which is not impossible. If you add the letter *ayin* after the "u," you would get something like "heard by God." And yet other suggestions have been given for Samuel's name as it sits. Some possibilities are: *name of El,* or *his name is El.*[14] Hannah seems to be saying, "Requested of God." There may be something she knows about the "u" vowel that we are not so clear on.[15] Nevertheless, it does make an interesting contrast between Samuel "requested of God" and Saul "asked, requested or questioned" of *no one*! Even the words in verse 27 only add to the enigma. Both the word petition and request are more closely related etymologically to Saul than to Samuel. So although I have no definitive answer as to the meaning of Samuel's name, at the outset, the book is about the failed monarchy under Saul. Of course, that is easy for us to agree on since we know the end of the story.

Samuel is not introduced so much by the title of the book (a later intrusion) than by the narrator's documentation of his birth. We are told that everything went rather normal and after normal gestation, a baby boy was born. We are told that she named him Samuel and that is his debut on the scene of biblical history (vv. 19-20). Apparently, she did not want to follow through on the letter of her vow any sooner than necessary. She kept him at home for a while—until she weaned him. That would make the boy something over two or perhaps three years old. All this was with the complicity of her husband (vv. 21-23).

Having fulfilled his time at home he is brought to Shiloh and introduced to Eli but here he is referred to merely as "the boy." This will be the case severally until our biblical debutant, Samuel himself, becomes a real player in chapter 3. We are also lead to suppose, upon his dedication, that he is also introduced to the LORD whom he will be serving. Not much is said about that, however; Samuel is, after all, a very young boy. We also know that he "did not yet know the LORD, nor had the word of the LORD yet been revealed to him" (3:7).

His second introduction is really in chapter 2 verse 18 where he is reintroduced and named as a little boy wearing a linen ephod. We also know that little boys play and grow and wear out clothes—at least mine does! So, "his mother would make him a little robe and bring it to him from year to year when she would come up with her husband to offer the yearly sacrifice" (2:19). Instead, however, of merely leaving in peace along with a well-wish, she now leaves with Eli's blessing. It looks as though Samuel has a distinguished service record even as a boy in matters levitical and priestly. I really have no idea what his collective responsibilities could have been. With religious and ceremonial defection being so acute (2:12-17, 22-25), he could have been doing anything he was physically large enough to do—under the supervision of the high priest, of course, along with his decadent and depraved sons.

Samuel's third introduction is the bread slices of an indictment sandwich regarding Eli's sons. Whereas Eli had done miserably in raising his own two sons, Samuel, Eli's "adopted son" performed valiantly— until he, too, has to raise his own sons . . . fatherhood doesn't get very good press in the Samuel Narratives. Be that as it may, in 2:21 we are told that Hannah had more children and then that is the last we will ever hear of her in the pages of Holy Writ. However, of her firstborn it is said, "the boy Samuel grew before the LORD." Then we have the implication against Eli's sons for turning Israel's religion into yet another fertility cult—and his weak-kneed attempt to curtail the boys' adventures. This is then followed by what I view as part two—and the most important part—of the third formal introduction of Samuel. Remember, he is still little more than a child: "Now the boy Samuel was growing in stature and in favor both with the LORD and with men." Those of us with New Testament roots will of course hear its echo loud and clear; for it has been said of Christ: "And Jesus kept increasing in wisdom and stature, and in favor with God and men" (Luke 2:52). We know that Jesus was about twelve at that time (v. 42) and so it is a good bet that the lad, Samuel, is not much beyond this, if that far along. Nevertheless, the similarities are quite striking and the New Testament reader should understand the tacit implications: Jesus is and will function both as priest and prophet on behalf of men. When we next meet Samuel, it will not be by way of introduction, as a debutant, but as a real player: as priest, as prophet and as king-maker. Basically, all the players have had proper introductions. We will talk more about Hophni and Phineas, the antagonists over which Samuel will prevail, when we get to the next chapter.

## The Joys Biblical Narrative Reflects Regarding Polygamy

Whoever thought polygamy was a good idea never read the Bible. There is not a single positive presentation of the institution in its pages. After having lived in East Africa for a while, I am not convinced that there is a positive presentation of the institution in history, ancient or modern. As is so often the case in the Patriarchal Narratives of Genesis, plants will sprout out of the seedbeds of polygamous conflict—if that's not too base an image. With respect to polygamy in Samuel and Kings, you have to ask yourself, "Did they never hear the patriarchal stories?" Ah, well, fools boldly go. . . . Perhaps it was due to male attrition caused by constant warfare, or so we are told. Be that as it may, as we begin, we see that one wife has children and the other is barren. We automatically call to mind such heroines of the faith as Sarah, Rebekah, and Rachel who had difficulties in production, the assembly line being temporarily interrupted, as it were. And so we know that this, like those other stories, is going to have a bittersweet ending. That is, Hannah will get her child, maybe several; but there will be trouble along the way.

Provocation is the word of the day. I am not really sure what Elkanah was thinking when he married two of them. I am pretty certain that if he were a righteous man, they were not sisters. Leviticus 18:18 seems to preclude that particular aspect of the institution of polygamy. "And you shall not marry a woman in addition to her sister as a rival while she is alive, to uncover her nakedness." This says several things that may lead us in several directions. Historically, however, this text has usually been understood to mean: "Do not take your wife's sister as a rival wife and have sexual relations with her while your wife is living."[16] So, their family is not all in the family; this is good. However, it is good literary game to note that the word rival (*tzarar*), literally "adversary," is the same in Leviticus 18:18 and 1 Samuel 1:6. And so, out of an adversarial relationship, the great prophet known from Dan to Beersheba (3:20) and the great king-maker (10:1, Samuel's words are in the interrogative), Samuel is born.

With respect to the idea of rivalry, we want to be thinking more of the story of the biblical "love triangle" of Rachel and Jacob and Leah. We will recall that there is an adversarial relationship between the two women that began on what became Leah's wedding night. Every now and again we get a window into their conflict: "Is it a small matter for you to take my husband?" (Gen. 30:15) says Leah, who normally suffers her unloved status either in the deafening silence of the narrator's report or in the folk etymologies that surround the naming of her children. In 1 Samuel, at the highest level of authoritative discourse, the narrator tells us that there is rivalry. In fact, in verse 6, Peninnah is not even given the dignity of her given name but merely introduced by epithet as the subject of the verb "provoke" with the title "her rival." Nevertheless, and like our Hannah here in 1 Samuel 1, Rachel's condition is divinely imposed, "Now the LORD saw that Leah was hated and He opened her womb, but Rachel was barren" (Gen. 29:31). And later on in nearly the same words as those with respect to our Hannah, "Then God remembered Rachel (*wayyizkōr 'elōhîm eth-Rāchēl*), and God gave heed to her and opened her womb" (30:22). "And the LORD remembered her (*wayyizkᵉrehā YHWH*). And it came about in due time after Hannah had conceived. . . ." The stories are similar and we might expect similar outcomes: Hannah will have to give up Samuel to the ministry just as Rachel had to give up Joseph when she died.

**Textual Applications and Anecdotes**

1 Samuel 1:
vs.
1. Some introduction to the characters is necessary.
   Some people are well known; some require a listing of relatives.
2. Nowhere in biblical literature is polygamy painted positively . . . there is always rivalry.
   In biblical narrative, focus will be upon the unloved or unproductive wife.
3. The picture at the beginning of 1 Samuel as with the story of Ruth is that during the period of the judges there were tiny oases of fidelity amidst huge oceans of infidelity and corruption.
4. The biblical protagonist often does what is proper for the antagonist.
5. The biblical protagonist often does what is generous for the heroine.
   The biblical hero loves the heroine despite culturally determined liabilities.
6. Polygamy entails rivalry and conflict in the biblical picture.
   God is viewed as the ultimate cause of or withholder of children in biblical narrative.
7. Rivalry and provocation end at death in polygamy.
   Such provocations produce behaviors that are self-destructive ("she would not eat").
8. The hero encourages the heroine in biblical narrative.

9. The heroine receives encouragement from the hero in biblical narrative ("Then Hannah rose after eating and drinking").
10. Out of deep provocation comes fervency in prayer.
11. Out of deep provocation comes the solemn vow.
12. Devotion from deep provocation will be noticed—it may be misunderstood!
13. Talking to one's God or oneself may be viewed as drunkenness or insanity.
14. Position is no guarantor of correct understanding.
15. The respectful response to position is the correct manner of response.
16. The plea for significance awaits a response expectantly.

17.    There is relief in the release from indictment by one in position of authority.
18.    Acknowledgment from authority may remove an element of sadness.
19.    The timeless request is answered in time.
20.    In ancient Israel, there was a memorial in the name of the child; we in the post modern West should have something that corresponds.
21.    The faithful man is predictable.
22.    The faithful woman plans for the keeping of her vow.
23.    The faithful man recognizes and acknowledges the plan of his faithful wife.
24.    In ancient Israel they weaned a child at an older age than we often do in the modern West; but we should still present our best with our best to God.
25.    Dedication and commissioning should be accompanied by culturally appropriate celebration.
26.    When the events surrounding a promise are known, celebrate the fulfillment with those who know by relating the details.
27.    Acknowledge the details of a promised fulfillment and a blessing.
28.    The dedication is attended by celebration and worship—indeed, worship should be a celebration!

## Conclusion

(See conclusion to chapter 3 below.)

# 1 Samuel 2
## Hannah Serenades the King
## Samuel Dedicated

—⋙—

**Introduction**

(See introduction to chapters 1 through 3 above.)

**Textual Observations**

**Hannah's Song of Praise — The King She Had Never Met**

By way of review: When you tell a story, in the Samuel Narratives, there is one overarching, indeed global mode that must be mentioned. You frame a good story with lyric poetry. As you observe the positioning of the three major songs in the Samuel Narratives, note the position of Hannah's song: the front bracket. This song sets the pace for what is to follow, her words culminating in "he will give strength to His king, and will exalt the horn of His anointed." So the whole focus of what follows is the anointed king — which, of course, she has never met! It does make one ask the question whether or not there might be a choir of voices singing for different reasons.

We must always make the effort to remember that when a quote is introduced into the text, there are two voices speaking. In this particular case there may be an entire choir. But for the purposes of this discussion, we will merely acknowledge Hannah and her editor. Hannah, out of the conflict of her rivalry with Peninnah, is writing on the occasion of her great personal victory. Samuel, the long-awaited son (Peninnah had at least two, that takes time; is Elkanah's offhanded mention of being better than ten sons a reference to Peninnah's productivity?) has been born. He has been weaned and he has been presented to the high priest and to the LORD. Hannah has won this round and Peninnah's provocations will ring more hollow in the future. The adversarial dog has become more toothless. The inclusion of matters of child production amidst images of warfare and economics are striking. "Even the barren gives birth to seven, But she who has many children languishes" (1 Sam. 2:5). However, the next words blaze up like a warning flare: "The LORD kills and makes alive; He brings down to Sheol and raises up" (v. 6). What is she saying here? Is she offering a warning to her rival? Is this a threat of divine or not so divine retribution should Peninnah get out of line again? It is difficult to know.

Comparisons may be made with Mary's Magnificat in the first chapter of Luke. I do not want to go there at this time. However, the military and economic images in the Magnificat as well as the Song of Hannah are intriguing to me. Why—and we will probably need to hear the prophetic voice for the answer on this—why does Hannah paint so many military and economic pictures? Why are they included at this point? The journey to the end starts at the beginning. The end is the picture of the king she has never met. Getting there requires a population, economic development, and most likely military conflict. She begins with praise to the LORD and the claim of speaking boldly in the presence of her enemies (Peninnah and unknown others). Salvation here might have polyvalence: personal temporal salvation from the humiliation of childlessness, to the ability to keep her promise to God, or some kind of subjective understanding that she was in God's will, one of God's people, and thus heiress to eternal salvation (after all, she does mention the netherworld in verse 6 and the possibility of resurrection from it). The claims she makes on behalf of God are astounding for one locked in the dungeon of Israel's dark ages. First, she says that God is the most Holy Being; second, she make a profoundly monotheistic claim to God as the only Being worthy of the title; and third, she states that this only holy God is the only worthy basis for anything (v. 2).

In verse 3, Hannah reverts to her diatribe on rivals and enemies real and imagined. She tells Peninnah—and the narrator tells his readership—that there is no ground for boasting and arrogance in the presence of a sovereign and omniscient God. In verse 4, Hannah begins to catalogue reversals in the expected order of things with a warfare image. In battle, "The bows of the mighty are shattered, but the feeble gird on strength." Then in verse 5, she chronicles the issue of economic reversal as well as that of childbirth versus bereavement. In verse 6, she speaks of the LORD's sovereignty even over matters of life and death—even to the point of reversals in the order of nature. Repeating the general notion of verse 5, Hannah again talks about the LORD's sovereignty in the reversal of economic fortune which she follows for both verses seven and eight. This culminates in the notion that these less fortunate that are raised up by the LORD become the wealthy, honored nobility.

In a more surprising turn of events, Hannah's song now turns to God's preservation of the godly. In the fashion of Psalm one, the ends of the righteous and wicked are contrasted and their own fate is not in their own hands (v. 9). Back at the original theme of the conflict Hannah has been in, it is as though she indicts Peninnah for fighting against the LORD because she has provoked Hannah. But then in a rather surrealistic shift of focus, we see a move from Hannah's personal conflict and her victory and preservation to that of the coming king and anointed. The song has evolved from one of the personal conflict of two rival women to proportions that can only be described as cosmic.

Often you can tell something about lyric poetry, indeed, quotes in general, by the way it is framed in text. I am afraid that Hannah's song is something of an exception and only the most wispy inferences are possible. In 1:24, we do not even see the mention of Elkanah, whereas in verse 2:11 we see that it is he who returned to Ramah. At the front cover of the song in chapter 1, it is all about Hannah and at the back cover it is about Elkanah and leaving the boy behind. Maybe this is a picture of the exhilaration of Hannah in fulfilling her vow in contrast to the desolation of the father leaving his first and only son—so far—from the favored wife. We certainly have no knowledge and I doubt that Elkanah could have had any that there would be other children until we are so told in 2:21. Fatherhood is rough in Samuel!

Again, on the front cover of the song, we see that "she brought him up with her when she had weaned him" (1:24). The subject of these feminine verbs is of course, Hannah. Elkanah is nowhere to be seen from verse 23 through the end of the song. Hannah is the one who brings the sacrifice to go with the dedication. Then the verbs go plural and "they slaughter it" and "they bring the boy to Eli" (1:24). Elkanah becomes little better than the presumed subject of a pair of plural verbs. Then Hannah's mouth speaks and it is her mouth and her words that address the high priest with the answer to the prayer and the fulfillment of the vow. We know that she has Elkanah's permission to do all this because of his words in 1:23, "Do what seems best to you . . . only may the LORD confirm His word." Does anybody but me hear the pathos of a man about to be bereft of his only son?! Elkanah could be asking for something on the order of a sign from heaven to verify that this boy is to go to and remain in Shiloh and not stay at home in Ramah. But the back cover is merely the man going to his place perhaps a bit desolate. It is as though Hannah's presence on the return trip is inconsequential. He is better to her than ten sons; but she has separated him from his only son.

Participant reference often shifts in these first two chapters of 1 Samuel. However, by the end, we begin to see that there is a way in which the narrator handles Elkanah and another manner in which Hannah is handled. Peninnah is left at the level of narrative report and so hardly more than a foil or antagonist for Hannah. Hannah is named at the introduction to her prayer in 2:1. After that she becomes a creature of relationship. In 2:19 she is called "his [Samuel's] mother" and is said to come to the annual sacrifice "with her husband." Eli then blesses Elkanah and "his wife" (2:20) and calls her "this woman" with respect to her future childbearing. She is given reference to her personal promise with a mere pronoun "she dedicated." Then in the final mention of her name it is said the "the LORD visited Hannah [a euphemism, no doubt]; and she conceived and [she] gave birth to three sons and two daughters." Then the focus goes right back to Samuel.

Where is Elkanah in all this? He is not really a man of many words (note his barrage of questions in 1:8 and his reply about her absence from the annual festival in 1:23). However, he is a man of action. He has children (1:3); he goes to the annual sacrifice (v. 3); he demonstrates his generosity in general and his favoritism in particular toward Hannah (v. 5); his words motivate his wife to action (vv. 8-13); he is part of the "they" that arose, worshiped, and returned home (v. 18); he is the one who had relations with his wife when she conceived Samuel. Elkanah goes to the yearly sacrifice with or without the accompaniment of Hannah (vv. 21-23). Although we are told that she took the boy to the festival after she had weaned him and that she brought the bull for the sacrifice, and it was she who had brought him to present him to Eli, it is "they"—Hannah and Elkanah—who slaughter the bull and they who bring the boy to Eli (vv. 24-25). After her song, she is eclipsed again and it is Elkanah who goes home to Ramah. The boy is mentioned; but his mother is merely assumed to have accompanied her husband (2:11). It is the mother who accompanies the husband who demonstrates his devotion annually by going to the yearly sacrifice (v. 19). It is Elkanah who is named when he and "his wife" receive the priest's blessing (v. 20). In view of the referents, it is clear that Eli is addressing Elkanah directly and Hannah indirectly: "May the LORD give you [Elkanah] children from this woman [Hannah] in place of the one she dedicated to the LORD" (v. 20). And then Elkanah is part of the "they" that returned home. Although the LORD "visits" Hannah, we must presume natural processes as well and imagine that the same one who fathered Peninnah's children also fathers Hannah's children (v. 21).

Another thought that strikes me has to do with a man of few words who is a man of action and yet is passive with respect to his family. Elkanah is hardly a passive-aggressive type; but there are two obvious places where he backs down to his wives. The first is, of course, with respect to the internecine rivalry between Hannah and Peninnah. Because Hannah is the clear favorite, it would make sense for Elkanah to extend a stern rebuke to Peninnah rather than slapping Hannah in her despair. I do not personally know men who are polygamous. However, I know several children of polygamous marriages. One universal in these families is that the reigning patriarch puts up with a minimum of infighting. Order, in these families, is more important than affection. To them, order is the environment within which affection may be nurtured—indeed, often the first wife helps select the second and so on. When the first wife helps to select the second, she knows that culturally this second wife will become the favorite wife. She is the playmate and she is the companion. When there is hostility, the man merely appeals to the selection process and separates the combatants. In a Qur'anic manner (Sura 4:34), there will be the withholding, shall we say, of the rewards of a conjugal nature for frolicsome participants, then more corporal punishments should dissonance persist. I have no idea which is the first or second wife in respect to the biblical text before us. My suspicions are that Peninnah is not confronted due to her status as first wife. Coming from an East African context, I have to continually fight my predilection to view Hannah as the second wife due to her favored status; but that is the conclusion to which I arrive nevertheless. Peninnah has pride of place as child producer and this makes her gloating either all the more heinous or more mysterious. She is either attempting to overemphasize her superiority or the situation is akin to the competitive nature of the second child—she is trying to assert her real superiority despite secondary status. It is difficult to choose; but, I go with Hannah as the second wife.

Elkanah's response to Hannah's depression (disconsolate weeping and not eating) shows a couple of things. First, it seems that Elkanah knew at least something about his favorite wife. After he asks what to some might seem a barrage of questions (four, depending upon how one counts), she is at least motivated—"encouraged" is more than the text demands—to action: she eats and drinks and goes to prayer. However, even her focussed prayer life still includes bitterness of soul and intense weeping (1:10). Secondly and perhaps based upon the above inferences, Elkanah's questions may have a more gentle tone to them than their stark translation indicates in English. To us they look abrupt. Either Hannah is extremely tough mentally, which her response to Peninnah's provocations does not seem to indicate, or Elkanah's tone is less a rebuke, however gentle, and more pleading. I think Elkanah really loved her and cared about her. I think the text indicates that he attempted a response in as understanding a way as their awkward triangular situation would permit. I also think that, unlike Rachel's rather random explosion (Gen. 30:1), Hannah was not embittered against her husband. That there is a rivalry between her and Peninnah is mentioned a couple of different times and a couple of different ways by our Omniscient Narrator. There is no reason to believe the antipathy was not bi-vector.

The fact that Peninnah is not mentioned after verse 7 may indicate several things: first, she could have died; but second and more likely, she simply ceased to be a factor. The romance in this story is between Elkanah and Hannah; Peninnah is merely the velvet upon which the gem is displayed. We are programmed to view polygamy as evil, and rightly so. However, in their world of violence, corruption, and perversion, any form of convention—however deviant—would be considered stability. Both Peninnah and Hannah are provided for by Elkanah and the society that both gave them birth and license to be what they are: married. When chaos reigns supreme, even the oddest form of structure seems comforting by comparison.

So my conclusion is that Elkanah is more a man of action than a man of words. His two little speaking parts are critically important, but not more so than who he is as demonstrated by where he goes and what he does. The narrator may even be viewing him as the vehicle that transports our protagonist, Hannah. Because he is the one who goes and does, because he is the one with the predictable religious practices, he becomes the logical choice as a vehicle to move Hannah into the place of God's will and the place of God's blessings. This, then, will have trickle-down effects to any children she might produce. It does raise the question as to whether the focus is Elkanah or Hannah. We are programmed to see these first two chapters as an introduction to the boy, Samuel; yet, there is more here. Because of the often shrill dissonance between narrative and discourse in biblical history, I would wish to distinguish carefully between what each is saying—even, as is usually the case, when they are moving us in the same direction. However, my inclination at this point is to view the Elkanah material as more a part of the foregrounded macrostructure—what the story is—and to view the Hannah material as a part of the backgrounded macrostructure—the message of the story. Elkanah moves the story forward as do story-line preterites; Hannah tells us, in her discourses in prayer/praise and those with her husband and with the high priest, about Israel's king and Israel's king-maker, Samuel. Elkanah is history in action; Hannah is history in document. She is the text; he is the event. As such, he dies and is buried along with Israel and her monarchy and other institutions; she lives on in moving testimony of faith in the dark and prophetic faith as well. She may be one who, in Hebrews, "performed acts of righteousness, obtained promises . . . experienced mockings . . . having gained approval through their faith" (Hebrews 11:33-39).

## Meanwhile, Back at Antagonistic Introductions

Let us go back and take a closer look Hophni and Phineas. As you have noticed in the treatment of 1 Samuel 1, Hophni and Phineas are given the barest introduction (1:3), little better than an aside. In Hebrew they are introduced in the form of a nominal sentence, there is no "to be" verb. As such, this is backgrounded material of the deepest nature—almost subliminally we are introduced to those who will be foils or antagonists to Samuel (really including Eli). Nothing is stated about them except that they served as priests and that they were related to Eli as his sons. It is as if the narrator is saying, "see below for details."

In their second appearance (2:12-17), Hophni and Phineas are not introduced by name; they are rather introduced by their relationship to their father Eli as in half of the introduction in the paragraph above. Several striking things are said about them in this paragraph: first, the obvious facts that they are Eli's sons and that they are engaged in sacrilege. Their crime is described on two levels. They are taking select portions of the sacrifices for themselves that are not part of their allotted portion as officials of the temple. In addition, when they are questioned with respect to their priorities and procedures they respond with threats of violence and force (v. 16).

Secondly, their description includes something that might not leap off the page at us. They are called "worthless men" (NASB). These are "sons of Belial." Some translate this "worthless men."[17] This reintroduces a sub-theme in the writing of the Samuel Narratives. These "sons of Belial" will miraculously reappear at several points when the narrator needs a descriptive term for the boorish ignoramuses (jerks, schmucks—pick your favorite epithet!) that surround antagonists and help them to plague our protagonists, our heroes. The word in the dictionaries tends toward an abstract noun, e.g., "worthlessness,"[18] or "uselessness," or "wickedness" with an adjectival usage of "good for nothing."[19] It has been my sometime observation that stupidity and wickedness are not so separate in the wisdom literature of the Bible as they are in Western thought. It seems that stupidity is a wicked choice in many cases.

Be that as it may, I would like to trace the usage of the term Belial (*beli'al*) through the text of the Samuel Narratives so that we might see the additional freight each subsequent usage bears. I do not think this will produce an illegitimate totality transfer as much as broader understanding of what kinds of people can be jerks in the Samuel Narratives. As here, a son of Belial can be the son of a priest—in case you were not up on several of your more frequently used modern epithets, think what that does to their father. That makes Eli correspond to Belial! They were sacrilegious, they were perverted, and they are going to get killed doing something stupid.

Remember, I specifically used the word "reintroduced" with respect to Hophni and Phineas being called "sons of Belial." The initial usage is in Hannah's personal denial to Eli that she was a daughter of Belial in 1 Samuel 1:16. Since she was accused of drunkenness, her articulate speech was all that was needed to exonerate her of the crime. Nevertheless, it is not lost on the reader that she is addressing Belial himself, if Hophni and Phineas are his sons! As we will explore below, Samuel has a couple of seers who do not see well.

In 1 Samuel 10:27, we see that there were certain persons with lives greatly at risk (11:12), who were considered "sons of Belial" because they did not support the new king, Saul. They did not believe that Saul had any of the virtues necessary to deliver them in their current plight, neither did they bring him any tributary gift. We will leave it a point of the ironic as to whether or not they were right in their initial assessment.

Speaking of the vested aristocracy, we find that chief of all fools, Nabal (whose very name means "fool" according to his wife Abigail), in 1 Samuel 25:17 is called a "son of Belial." This is stated by Nabal's own employees—fearing for their lives, not from him but from David—in a very candid conversation with his wife, Abigail. Both parties know him well. A son of Belial in this case is one who is so frequently drunken and self-absorbed as to be cognizant neither of the winds of change nor the storms of impending disaster.

Adopting the stance of the hired help, Abigail attempts to placate David and 400 bitter hearts in 1 Samuel 25:25, by referring to her husband, that boorish ignoramus, as a "man of Belial." She knows her husband, the fool, and she knows that he is a dead man if she does not roll back the tide.

Such talk must have spread among David's men because in 1 Samuel 30:22, after the recovery of no less than Abigail and everybody else that had been taken captive by the Amalekites, "all the men wicked and Belial" demanded that the recovered spoil be divided only among those who went into battle. In this case, the rear guard that stayed with the baggage would not only have been denied any part in the spoil, they would have been denied the return of their own possessions including potentially their own wives and families. This resulted in a new bit of case law in Israel (*hoq*) in that the people who went to battle and those who guarded the van were to share equally in the fortunes of war. The upshot of this discussion is that these rapscallions are also greedy, selfish materialists.

We know that, despite the domestic problems David had as monarch of Israel, he is still the legitimate king. In 2 Samuel 16:7, David is on the run from his son, Absolom, who has usurped the throne. One disgruntled subject of the deposed regent then decides to hurl abuse at the humiliated David. Shimei yells—from a relatively safe distance, no doubt—"Get out, get out, you man of bloodshed, and worthless fellow" (man of Belial)! When things go against Shimei, he quickly admits guilt and begs forgiveness (19:19-20). Despite the counsel of Abishai, David gives an uneasy remission to Shimei (vv. 21-23) Of course, when Solomon is instructed as to how to consolidate his empire, David makes specific mention of Shimei (2 Kings 2:8) and how to dispatch him. This is acted upon with all patience and stealth by Solomon (2:36-46), who sets up impossible boundaries of Shimei's movements and when they are conveniently transgressed, Shimei is executed.

Psalm 18 is inserted nearly intact into 2 Samuel 22. It is difficult initially to determine whether David is talking about circumstances that afflict him or persons. But in 2 Samuel 22:5, David moves to a more human image of this "water" that overwhelms him. "For the waves of death encompassed me; the torrents of Belial overwhelmed me." There were so many of them that he viewed them as a flood and as waves one on top of the other that beat him down and threatened to drown him. Sons of Belial seem to swim in large schools.

In a contrast between David's "faithful" house and those of lesser virtue, in 2 Samuel 23:6, David calls up the contrast by way of the "worthless." "For all my salvation and all my desire, will He not indeed make it grow? But the worthless, every one of them will be thrust away like thorns, because they cannot be taken in hand." So the worthless are the unsaved; the worthless are the rejected; the worthless are not related rightly to David. And so we conclude that the sons of Belial were boorish ignoramuses that achieved infamy by being persons of note in opposition to God's program and in violation of His laws. They were sacrilegious, perverted, self-interested bullies, and traveled in overwhelming numbers. These are the character traits that can be ascribed to Hophni and Phineas.

Third, Hophni and Phineas are described with the epithet: "they did not know the LORD" (v. 12). In itself, that would not be the epitaph upon their tomb because Samuel will be introduced in the same manner (3:7). The differences are at once subtle and stark: in 3:7 the subtle application of the modifier "yet" tells us that Samuel's spiritual condition will improve. But the stark fact that Hophni and Phineas are dubbed "sons of Belial" means that things will most likely remain in that same sorry, hopeless condition. Indeed, following David's pictures painted above in his last two poems in 2 Samuel, we might say that they were hopelessly incorrigible.

The third introduction to Eli's sons is also performed through their relationship to their father. It is said that "he heard all that his sons were doing to all Israel and how they lay with the women who served at the doorway of the tent of meeting" (1 Sam. 2:22). Eli addresses the issue in a rather pathetic manner and to no effect (vv. 23-25). His logic is sound, humanly speaking. They will hardly avoid disaster by offending a sovereign Lord. It is also somewhat prophetic in that they soon receive their just desserts. Eli himself is doubly confronted: first, by "a man of God" who predicts the fall of not only Hophni and Phineas, but the near eradication of the whole line. Secondly, the prophecy of the man of God is confirmed in the night revelation to Samuel. Eli takes something of a stoically detached stance to this announcement.

This brings us finally to the main event, the culmination of the expenditures of all the energies of Hophni and Phineas—their death. In 1 Samuel 4, Israel is initially defeated in battle against the Philistines. Without going through proper channels and consultation of the Lord, the people send to Shiloh for the ark of the covenant as something of a protective talisman for the upcoming counterattack. It had been a point of custom for the ark of the covenant to go into battle (Josh. 6:6), but that was only by God's direct statement. Hophni and Phineas go with the ark as would have been their duty. In the battle, the Philistines show themselves mightier against a godless Israel and defeat them. Hophni and Phineas are killed in the melee and the ark is taken captive to Philistia. In the aftermath, "a man of Benjamin" (an interesting introduction to the Saul material to follow), delivers the bad news to Eli. At that time, he falls over backward and breaks his neck. Finally, when Phineas' wife hears about the death of her husband, she goes into early delivery and dies in childbirth (4:19-22). It looks as though the midwife names the baby boy. His name is Ichabod, meaning approximately "no glory." This is said to be because of the death of Mrs. Phineas' husband and father-in-law and the loss of the ark. This, then, is the beginning of the fulfillment of the prophecy of the man of God (2:27-36). It continues with the slaughter of the priests of Nob (1 Sam. 22) and concludes apparently with the dismissal of Abiathar by Solomon (2 Kings 2:26-7). He is placed under virtual house arrest and dies in oblivion.

This is the end of Hophni and Phineas. They lived badly, died violently, and left virtually no legacy. It is also not so tacit proof of the fact that fatherhood gets rather poor play in Samuel. Eli raised sacrilegious degenerates; Samuel raised those who did not walk in his ways but were corrupt and recipients of bribery (8:3); David raised a brood of vipers that were constantly detrimental to his rule. This is one aspect of leadership that rarely looks good in biblical narrative. Fathers tend to pass on their bad traits to their children but rarely their good ones. Perhaps that is why the apostle Paul was adamant about leaders proving to do well on the domestic front before they tried their hand on the church (1 Tim. 3:4-5; Titus 1:6).

## Textual Applications

1 Samuel 2
vs. (1-10 in Hannah's words)

1. In biblical narrative, the story well told ends with a song and an epilogue.
   The positively answered prayer naturally bursts forth in thanksgiving.
   Thanksgiving to the Lord and boldness against adversaries often go together.
   "Salvation" can be different things at different times.
2. Proper praise acknowledges God's holiness, His uniqueness and His reliability.
3. Boldness against adversaries includes the indictment against pride and arrogance.
   The adversary's arrogance runs up against God's knowledge and discernment.
4. Those making an arrogant claim to might are broken.
   Those making a humble claim to reliance upon God are strengthened.
5. Reversals in the normal order of things are the prerogative of a sovereign God:
   The full are hungry; the hungry are filled. The barren produces a clan; the clan mistress is bereft.
6. It is the Lord's prerogative to begin or terminate life; to condemn or to exonerate.
7. It is the Lord's prerogative to enrich or impoverish; to elevate or to humiliate.
8. It is the Lord's prerogative to determine—against all expectations—who will rule, because He rules the world.
9. The proviso is that those who would be kept safe must be godly.
   The wicked have no hope but silence and darkness.
   Against all expectations, the strong, if they are wicked, will not prevail.
10. Fighting against a sovereign God is stupidity ending in eternal disaster.
    The proper praise of the Old Testament saint includes statements about the Messiah-King.
11. The epilogue: the hero and heroine go home, the protagonist goes to work.
12. Introduced the first time, described the second time; villains do not know the LORD.
13. The explanation of custom is for the reader's benefit.
14. The explanation of sacrificial custom is more valuable as time distances us from them.
15. Breach of protocol in sacrificial custom is a direct affront to God.
16. Breach of protocol in sacrificial custom will become known by man.
    Breach of protocol will be covered by lies and intimidation.
17. This first set of sins for Hophni and Phineas were of a cultic nature; more are coming.
18. Oddly, the boy ministers when not yet of age in a spiritual vacuum.
19. The vow made, the promise kept: the annual vigilance of mother for a growing son.
20. The religious man remembers his close encounters of the divine kind.

       The religious man is always quick with a blessing, a curse, or an admonition.

21.     The LORD often proves Himself to be more generous than we could have ever hoped.

22.     Villains who do not know the LORD are introduced, described as worthless and depicted as perverted.

23.     The religious man confronts evil to no effect.

24.     The religious man relies upon second-hand information.

25.     The religious man knows well the stupidity of affronting a sovereign God.
       When marked by the heavy hand of God, the perverted and sacrilegious are soon removed.

26.     Good boys will receive honorable mention.
       Good boys are specially favored (graced?) by God.

27.     The *ad hoc* office of the prophet confronts the *de facto* office of the priesthood.
       The prophet reminds the priest of divine revelation.

28.     The prophet reminds the priest of sovereign choice.
       The prophet reminds the priest of priestly responsibilities.

29.     The prophet indicts the priest for breaches in protocol in sacrificial custom.
       The prophet indicts the priest for favoring familial relationships over proper respect for God.

30.     The true prophet declares the facts of the case.

31.     The true prophet declares those events that will transpire.
       The true prophet declares an end for the corrupt priesthood.

32.     The true prophet does not hide behind either the veil of eons or that of verbal ambiguity—it will shortly and obviously take place.

33.     The punishment of God is not without mercy.

34.     Introduced, described as worthless and doomed on a single day: villains who do not know the LORD.

35.     The future includes a faithful priest and an enduring Messiah.

36.     Those who survive the demise of the corrupt priesthood will come to the faithful priest for a livelihood.


## Conclusion

(See conclusion to chapter 3 below.)

# 1 Samuel 3
## The Calling of the Boy Samuel
## and the Horrific Prophecy Concerning Eli's Family

—ɯ—

## Introduction

One of the most loved texts of 1 Samuel is this, the third chapter. It encompasses a couple of important things: the calling of Samuel as a young boy and the prophecy he is required to relate to Eli about the imminent demise of his family. The story is told in a realistic style and is striking to the new reader only in that then as now "word from the LORD was rare . . . visions were infrequent" (3:1). So, the events are surprising to those unaccustomed to a God who breaks into His creation to talk to small boys and tell them of the future. Anyone who has read the story knows its power to charm its reader. Anybody who has had the opportunity to use this text for an oratory occasion knows how it captivates audiences of all ages. It is often said that if you want the parents' attention, talk to or about their children. Samuel comes to us as a little boy and leaves the chapter as a prophet of renown.

## Textual Observations

### Samuel as a Headliner

Although properly introduced in the customary and expected threefold manner, Samuel has been conspicuously absent for several verses. After the profound statement about him growing in favor with everybody including God, he is not mentioned during the diatribe from the man of God (2:27-36). He must, therefore. be properly reintroduced since now he will be center stage. Picking up on the language from 2:11, it is said, "Now the boy Samuel was ministering to the LORD before Eli." The disjunction at the beginning of the verse is correct. We have an entirely new pericope here; however, we are pulling forward threads from 2:11 and 2:26 so as not to get lost in the flow of thought.

One of the fascinating discoveries afforded us by participant reference studies is with respect to Samuel's changed role in the story. Notice that in the first two chapters of 1 Samuel, Samuel is spoken about: he is the prayed for, promised, and devoted son of Hannah and Elkanah. He is also involuntarily moved about here and there: he comes into the world in the normal manner and is kept in Ramah for one scene and transferred to Shiloh for another. In addition, he is involved in service to the Lord and Eli. Finally, he is described along with all this as characterized by the growth customary of little boys. However, he never speaks! Like Benjamin in the entirety of the Joseph story, Samuel is a human prop in the first two chapters. Unlike Benjamin in the Joseph story, Samuel is now elevated from the role of human prop to that of central interest. This is done by giving the boy voice in chapter 3.

However, his meteoric rise to centrality is short lived, since he will live in the exile of the reader's mind and away from the text from 4:1b until 7:3. When the Philistines are victorious, Samuel is absent. When Samuel is present in 1 Samuel, the Philistines are defeated. This appears to be true right up to the point of his death. How could things turn around so quickly?! In the first place, we must never confuse narrative distance (how long it takes to tell a story) with historical distance (the duration of the events themselves). When we left Samuel in chapter 3, he was a boy; when he reappears in chapter 7, he has a much more commanding presence and may be an adult. The discussion of his itinerant ministry (7:15-17) makes it appear that he was nationally respected. The discussion about his age and the decadence of his sons (8:5) makes it appear that quite some time has elapsed since chapter 3. In the events of the capture of the ark and its return and the turning of the tables on the Philistines, there is no clear demarcation of historical time. Half to two-thirds of the man's life could have slipped by us and we would have no way of knowing—like Moses losing forty years of his life in Midian in just a few verses (Ex. 2:15-22). Regardless, all this is to state the fact that Samuel is now a player and soon to be the headliner.

### Sight, Insight, and Foresight

Light and sight go together; indeed, it is difficult to have one without the other. This is true when the literal become metaphorical. When sight, insight, and foresight become terms with spiritual overtones, perception of the divine realm, understanding of the same, and prophecy become the order of the day. In an environment where reciprocal relationships between the spiritual and material world are infrequent, the surprise of it bursting upon the scene brings with it new dynamics: curiosity, fear, hope, and/or hope dashed. Eli, the spiritual dolt[20] of chapter 1 does not perceive that Hannah is a woman much troubled; he thinks she is a woman much inebriated. When he figures out the facts of the case, it is not due to spiritual perception but rather to the fact that her speech is not slurred. His response is professional, cool, and distant. Later on, he warms up to Hannah and Elkanah as they fulfill her vow. Whatever vision Eli has at this point is pretty much cash-and-carry.

Little boys grow up despite the bullies in their lives—or maybe because of them. When next we see Samuel, he is ministering to the Lord at Eli's behest and apparently doing a fine job. We have no idea how old he is in chapter 3, only that he is considered a boy. Like Hophni and Phineas (2:12), Samuel does not know the Lord (3:7). Because of the strategic deployment of the tiny modifier "yet," we know that the die is not cast for Samuel as it is for Eli's sons. Nevertheless, he still has no spiritual insight—but he is about to get some sight and that will lead to foresight. When the light dawns in Eli's mind and he realizes that Samuel is being called by the Lord, he instructs the boy rather carefully as to how to respond. One of the more fascinating omissions in all of the Bible is the result. Eli tells him, "Go lie down, and it shall be if He calls you, that you shall say, 'Speak YHWH, for Your servant is listening'" (v. 9). Remember, Samuel does not know the LORD yet and addressing deity by His name might be a bit daunting to the boy. So when he is called, he responds, "Speak, for Your servant is listening" (v. 10). At once, his response is more abrupt and less presumptuous. But the LORD speaks to him in any case.

When Samuel gains some small amount of sight he is able to recount the Lord's words to Eli. Samuel is afraid—of whom, the Lord, of Eli?—and reluctant to give his recitation. But when threatened with an oath by Eli—an indication of the old man's teaching the boy superstition?—Samuel is able to tell Eli everything. The result of this was the beginning of Eli's protégé as a prophet. It is said that the LORD was with him (like Joseph, does he really know? [Gen. 37; 39]) and that God let none of his words fall (1 Sam. 3:19). Samuel then achieved a certain level of fame and subsequent revelation. It might then be granted that because of the wording in verse 21, Samuel must now know the LORD because it is the resumption of the language used in verse 7. However, despite this obvious advantage, Samuel will not always perform at an optimum level as a seer.

## Lamp as Material and as Symbolic

In what can be hardly called anything other than the most pregnant of clauses, the narrator tells us: "and the lamp of God had not yet gone out, and Samuel was lying down in the temple of the LORD where the ark of God was" (1 Sam. 3:3). Samuel has become a player and the most significant prop of his absence in the next three chapters, the ark of the covenant, is nearby. What is this lamp? Is it the golden lampstand described in detail in the law of Moses? Is it the light of revelation, illumination, understanding, and instruction given to the priesthood of Israel? (Deut. 33:10). Is it both? Because we think of light (illumination) as necessary for sight or "vision," and because we have already been told that "word from the LORD was rare . . . visions were infrequent" (1 Sam. 3:1), we are really set up for both to be true. That is, it is night, Samuel is sleeping in the sanctuary, and the lamp has not run out of oil yet; it is spiritual night, and there is about to be a new breaking in of God into His universe, to His people, via His prophet elect.

Some scholars have split these words up due to allegedly alternate spellings—for the sake of discussion *nēr*, here or perhaps *nîr* in Psalm 18:29. My editions of BHS (1st, 5th and 6th) do not have the difference and neither does my copy of Snaith. However, they do differentiate between *nēr*, and *nêr* in contrast to Polzin's discussion.[21] Regardless, Polzin's point is well taken. As we have seen from the beginning, the Samuel Narratives are about the monarchy at several levels. In 2 Samuel 22:29, "my lamp" is a cover term for the monarchy. There is the slightly altered spelling in Psalm 18:29 for lamp. Both say, "For Thou are my [King David's] lamp, O LORD; and the LORD illumines my [King David's] darkness" (2 Sam. 22:29). Be that as it may, by the end of the Narratives, we are conditioned to see more of the metaphorical meaning than the literal meaning when we see the word "lamp." And so lamp may become a cover term for dynastic light and darkness.

## Seers Who Cannot See

Besides fathers who know nothing about fatherhood, the Samuel Narratives also portray seers who do not see very well. In some cases that myopia is physical and in some cases it is spiritual or both. Eli gets a couple of things figured out by the end of his life; the evidence that Samuel came around comes during his posthumous appearance in 1 Samuel 28. Spiritually speaking, of course, the reason seers cannot see is because there is nothing to look at. Again, verse 1 sets up the background conditions. "And word from the LORD was rare in those days, visions were infrequent [or precious]" (3:1). If there is "no vision spread abroad," there will be nothing to see. However, since we already know how biblical narrative works, we will see by the setting of the table that the prophetic dish will be served and our suspicions are that it will be delivered cold by a little boy to a doddering old fool.

A second problem has to do with physical sight. The second verse notes by way of deeply backgrounded material that Eli's "eyesight had begun to grow dim; he could not see well." This reminds of the setting of the stage in Genesis 27:1 where Isaac has visual acuity problems—he was blind as a bat and could not tell his macho outdoorsman son from his houseplant mama's boy son. What was the upshot of that scenario? A bad decision was made and a ruse was perpetrated by the disenfranchised. By reading the patriarchal narratives, we are pre-programmed to read that a bad decision is going to be made; there will be bad judgment; there will be a problem rectifying the problem.

This brings us to the third problem: when we finally get a vision, we do not recognize it as such because we are not accustomed to having God break into our universe in such a manner. I should think this were rather true in your current universe, no? However, the frequency of the revelatory is going to increase and these seers are still not going to do very well. They are too accustomed to seeing with their physical sight. Later on in the book, Samuel will receive a gentle backhand in regard to this when he is very much mid-career and should know, or should know better. Samuel, looking at the surface says to himself, "Surely the LORD's anointed is before Him" (1 Sam. 16:6). But the LORD has a different opinion, "Do not look at his appearance or at the height of his stature, because I have rejected him; for God sees not as a man sees, for man looks at the outward appearance, but the LORD looks at the heart" (v. 7).

This will be important material later on; but for now, it will serve as illustrative material for Eli. The old prophet does not go down in three swings but the count is full. Each time he tells the young boy to return and lie down until the third time when the light (this is our image, not theirs this time) finally dawns in the cobwebs of his mind and he "discerned that the LORD was calling the boy" (3:8). When the morning dawns, Eli confronts the boy who confirms the predictions of the man of God in the previous chapter. Eli resignedly sighs, "It is the LORD; let Him do what seems good to Him" (v. 18). Then he does what he is supposed to do: he nurtures Samuel until the time that he dies suddenly at the news of the death of his sons and the capture of the ark of the covenant. In Eli's words we hear the echo of Elkanah from the first chapter who says to his wife, Hannah, "Do what seems best to you . . . only may the LORD confirm His word (1:23). And in both cases, the Lord confirmed His word. In both cases, Samuel was the vehicle for the confirmation and in both cases, Eli and Elkanah play their part flawlessly.[22] However, it is difficult to know how to read Eli's response. As I have read him here, is he resigned to God's will? Is he indignant as a subordinate to an indifferent superior whom he feels has taken away both his rights and his voice? Does something click in his mind that resonates with the man of God's prophecy? Is Eli merely saying: "this is right"? These questions and others might haunt us as we see the obstacles cleared out of the way for Samuel's ascendancy. Peninnah, Elkanah and Hannah, Hophni and Phineas, Eli, the Philistines, and the nationalistic spirit of the Israelites might all be viewed as obstacles through which Samuel must wend his way. Before he is done, Samuel will have functioned as priest, prophet, and viceroy in Israel's attempts at theocracy. But by way of summary, let us remember that seers cannot see due to the rarity of the revelation, the problems with their own physical sight, and their spiritual myopia including expectations or some combination of the three.

## Light Where There Is None

Part of the reason there is no sight is because there is no light. We can assume the obvious: Samuel was lying down in the sanctuary because the sun had set and he wanted to sleep. What the words on the page say comes through the window clearly enough; however, a second look reveals more. "The lamp of God had not yet gone out" (1 Sam. 3:3). Why not just say, the "golden lampstand?" Surely, the narrator knows the terminology. Why, this particular collocation? My best bet rests with the notion that there is here a desired intrusion of the divine into the mind of the reader on the part of the narrator. We know that lamp can have to do with the monarchy (see above: "Lamp As Material and As Symbolic"). But a lamp, as nearly extinguished, also seems a fitting notion to attach to the matters described for us in verse 1: "And word from the LORD was rare in those days, visions were infrequent." When will the "lamp of God" be extinguished? In the same breath we ask, "When will there be the light of vision"? We find both light and vision in this prophetic call to the boy Samuel.

However, this will also cause us to reflect when we get to chapter 4. The lamp in chapter 3 had not yet gone out; but in chapter 4 the ark is taken by the Philistines; Eli and his sons are dead, and there is an absent Samuel from our text. Is the light then out for these several chapters then to reappear in 7:3? Have both the physical golden lampstand and the light of revelation been extinguished? We cannot know these things reading forward. We can only gather that a small flickering flame is allowed to burn by the statements that look over their shoulder with respect to Samuel's itinerant ministry (7:15-17). The light is about out; vision is rare: who will carry the torch? It will be a small boy who becomes a man and conducts the most subversive campaign his Philistine overlords could ever hope to uncover: he is educating and administering justice in a circuit in the highlands.

## Eli and the Double Oracle

In a bowl of critical alphabet soup, the question might arise as to why the double oracle. Certainly it seems to be an unnecessary repetition. Is it two sacred traditions woven together in a haphazard manner? Is it awkward redundancy? Perhaps because of the ties between Elkanah and Eli mentioned above, it is neither but rather the skillful weaving of a prophetic tapestry. Elkanah says to Hannah, "only may the LORD confirm His word" (1:23). Hannah had prayed about a child and vowed to dedicate him to God's service. I would certainly need some kind of independent confirmation to that effect if my favorite wife were to dedicate our only child to the priesthood. Elkanah needs that as well. One of the things that reticence teaches us is that when there is repetition we need to be on the alert for those few things that are added. In this particular case, conspicuous by its absence is a response by Eli to the prophetic promise by the man of God. Perhaps Eli just doesn't get it yet. The man has told him that he has honored his own sons above God. Eli has attempted to cajole them into behaving with better decorum but they are two noncompliant children. What is an old man to do? With the second version of the oracle against Eli's family, he gives assent, at the very least. What the tone of his response is, I can only venture a guess: provisionally, it looks as though it was merely a sigh of acquiescence.

Finally, we must remember that if we follow Elkanah's confirmation notion, this is a statement confirming everything said by the man of God. Some rather profound things were said: "I will raise up for Myself a faithful priest who will do according to what is in My heart and in My soul; and I will build him an enduring house, and he will walk before My anointed always" (2:35). What this means at the very least is that Eli is not considered "a faithful priest." But what it bodes is even more ominous: there will be a faithful priest who will have an enduring house. That house will walk before the anointed forever. The anointed, we have come to understand since Hannah's prayer, is Israel's king par excellence. That Eli was an anointed priest may indicate that God's indictment includes Eli's supererogation to the point of the unification of all the offices into one person: prophet, priest, and monarch. The thing that is truly arresting is the way God will have to deal with Samuel in this same manner in chapter 8, specifically in verse 7. The text there indicates that Samuel was about to or already had crossed the theocratic line.

## Forever

Chapters two and three contain a fine repeated combination punch to Eli. It comes in the form of a 2 + 1 formula including the word "forever" and another set of terms meaning the same thing. In chapter 2, the man of God tells Eli, "I did indeed say that your house and the house of your father should walk before Me *forever*; but now . . ." (1 Sam. 2:30). But since Eli's family has been irreverent, He says, among other things, "And you will see the distress of My dwelling in spite of all that I do good for Israel; and an old man will not be in your house *forever*" (v. 32). He and his family are to be deposed and defrocked and God says, "I will raise up for Myself a faithful priest who will do according to what is in My heart and in My soul; and I will build him an enduring house, and he will walk before My anointed *always*" (lit. "all the days," verse 35). Just a point of curiosity: I wonder how much of this the boy Samuel had heard? If he had heard any of it and understood any of it, it makes the next pericope very engaging.

This is because, in chapter 3, Samuel becomes the messenger, the mouthpiece—the very "man of God" himself! Although a reluctant voice, when threatened (1 Sam. 3:17), Samuel comes out with terminology that in both form and content would have resonated in Eli's tingling ears (1 Sam. 3:11). First, God says, "In that day I will carry out against Eli all that I have spoken concerning his house, *from beginning to end*" (v. 12). Rehearsing what He had said previously, God then says, "For I have told him that I am about to judge his house *forever* for the iniquity which he knew, because his sons brought a curse on themselves and he did not rebuke them" (v. 13). And then God reiterates: "And therefore I have sworn to the house of Eli that the iniquity of Eli's house shall not be atoned for by sacrifice or offering *forever*" (v. 14). And so in a nice neat envelope structure we have the indictment, case, and sentence on Eli and his family. The repetition of the terminology of unending duration powerfully draws the two texts together into a single confirmatory assault upon the priest's house. The usage of terminology throughout that backreferrences the oratory of the man of God from chapter 2 betrays the text's omniscient self-consciousness and at the same time offers no room for some sloppy redactor, some haphazard editor merely splicing two divergent traditions together.

## Behold!

This word, "behold" (*hinneh*) appears at a strategic location in both chapters 2 and 3. In chapter 2, verse 31, it appears as the transition between the historical protocol of the priesthood along with the indictment against Eli's house and the execution of sentence. *Hinneh* has long been known be a macrosyntactic sign and to have a deictic function,[23] but here it is a classic. Sometimes it has been called a particle of immediacy. We always translate it with some adverbial expression or some imperatival expression "behold" or "look" or "see." But what it does is to slap us in the face with the realities and the gravity of the situation at hand. It will also do this in chapter 3. Although it is fronted in God's discourse rather than at a transition point, the locus is effectively the same: it introduces the execution of sentence on Eli's family and the impact that it will have on "both ears of everyone who hears" (1 Sam. 3:11). This particle indicates vividness, immediacy, the acute nature of the situation, and the horrific consequences of the discourse to follow. In other places its use becomes almost redundant (e.g., the Joseph story, Genesis 37 and 41 in the dream locations); here, it is a shrill text pointer to the horrific messages that follow.

## The Teacher's Task: When History Becomes Prophecy

Anyone with any kind of gifting in teaching will be called upon at some point to "read the handwriting upon the wall." That is, because of the nature of the game, the teacher knows what has happened in the past when various sets of occurrences have pertained. Teachers look at a grid of historical data and recognize points in the present or near future when the data will no longer fall through the grid and the correlations and analogies will be shrill enough to sound a warning. That is when the teacher becomes the prophet. This is what happens to the man of God and to the boy Samuel in 1 Samuel 2 and 3.

Although the man of God is little better than a voiceless prop used by God, that voice still informs Eli of what he should already know as a teacher. The things of history related to his ancestral vocation are handled briefly before the indictment and the passing of sentence. The reminder of lessons of the past becomes the vehicle through which the prophecies of the future are conveyed.

With regard to the boy Samuel, the events of history are all more in the recent past and have to do with people yet alive who will not be in the near future. Samuel, as was the case with the man of God in chapter 2, will then be eclipsed and be the vehicle through which this confirmatory address is delivered by God to Eli. Samuel, even though only a boy and even though he will not receive his own personal relationship with the Lord until later (vv. 21-22), takes the lessons of history, some of which he has seen and all of which Eli knows, and turns them into the prophecy of the imminent doom of Eli's family—even the extended family that will die long after Samuel himself is gone (cf. 1 Sam. 25:1; 1 Kings 2:27).

## Divine Soliloquy Versus Divine-Human Conversation

One observation that might cause us to reflect for a moment is the changes in the description of the communication between God and His prophet or between those two and the target of His discourse. One of the annoying things we have to deal with along the way is that there are things left out that would be immensely helpful to us. They are consciously omitted by our Omniscient Narrator no less! Every oracle of God is not recorded for us—and that should prove riveting were it available. So, our narrator extracts bits and snippets for us and weaves them in with dialog and narrative so as to tell his story, his way. There are, therefore, some things included and some things glaringly left out.

One of the noisier absences in chapter 2 as we have already observed has to do with Eli's response to the prophecy of the man of God. What we get is a "Thus says the LORD" (2:27) formula and we are off to the races. But God adopts the mouth of the prophet and speaks the oracle in first person. It is hardly deniable that first person is the strongest manner in which to present such an oracle. However, it is probably the reason the messengers' guild coined the phrase: "Don't kill the messenger." Depending upon the receptivity of the recipient (see the appendix under "Text-linguistics"), it could go badly for a messenger of doom. Notice also that the "man of God" has no exit. He arrives safely at the end of his diatribe—we must assume! But, there is no notation that he finished, he left, he fell over dead, or anything—he just disappears! Not so with the boy Samuel.

Some things are missing from the story in chapter 3 as well. You have already noticed that Samuel "did not yet know the LORD" the same as Eli's sons (2:12; 3:7). You have already observed that when Eli instructs his novitiate as to how to address the Deity, Samuel leaves out the name—because, well, he "did not yet know the LORD." But when the initial introductions and pleasantries are concluded (amounting to: "'Speak, for Thy servant is listening.' And the LORD said to Samuel, "Behold. . . .'"—abrupt, to say the least—God launches into round two of His sentencing of Eli. As before, the narrator makes no conclusion or exit for God; He merely stops talking. This is all told to the boy Samuel. Samuel is then threatened in kind by the prophet himself and apparently divulges the information. We are lead to believe that the information is related verbatim, though we cannot know for certain. "So Samuel told him everything and hid nothing from him" (v. 18). Was it verbatim? Was it paraphrased? Was it crystallized and synthesized? Whatever it was, it was confirmatory and Eli swallows the bait hard, acquiescing to the inevitable. He is an old man at this point and probably expects what is coming to him in any case. However, the stiff upper lip for his sons is a curious twist. He was a bit detached with Hannah earlier; but the situation must have gotten so out of hand with his sons that he becomes stoic. But notice, in conclusion, that both statements are rather unilateral. They are monologues: the first, the man of God is the mouthpiece of God; the second, Samuel is addressed without the boy's comment and he conveys God's message.[24]

Later on in Samuel, the relationship becomes one of dialogue. Revelation being anything but predictable, we see that Samuel and God have what would be called at home a domestic dispute in chapter 16. This comes in conjunction with the final rejection of Saul and the transfer of the "anointing" to David—but, I'm getting ahead of myself. God rebukes Samuel, "How long will you grieve over Saul, since I have rejected him from being king over Israel? Fill your horn with oil, and go; I will send you to Jesse the Bethlehemite, for I have selected a king for Myself among his sons." Samuel does not take this new direction very well and responds by covering his indignation-masked remorse by a thinly veiled strata of fear: "How can I go? When Saul hears of it, he will kill me." And so God gives him a legitimate—He is, after all, God—alibi: "Take a heifer with you, and say, 'I have come to sacrifice to the LORD.' And you shall invite Jesse to the sacrifice, and I will show you what you shall do; and you shall anoint for Me the one whom I designate to you." For the moment, we shall have to forego discussions about the countermanding of the centralization of the cult. I suppose that was never strictly in force until the time of the temple in any case. Regardless, this is hardly subterfuge: God is giving a temporary, time bound command to His prophet, regarding His projected anointed monarch.

Then things get even more interesting: at first blush the oldest son of Jesse looks the part of the monarch; but, we are not looking for a king such as all the nations have at this time. We are looking for someone who has God's interests in mind. Samuel thinks or says, literally "Surely the LORD's anointed is before Him." One wonders if he says this out loud or only in his thoughts. Whether responding to Samuel's exclamation or reading his mind, God says, "Do not look at his appearance or at the height of his stature, because I have rejected him; for God sees not as man sees, for man looks at the outward appearance, but the LORD looks at the heart" (1 Sam. 16:7). Interestingly, the language is nearly the same as the rejection of Saul—even stronger in that the full writing of the object pronoun adding another syllable is used in the case of Eliab. It is abbreviated in the case of Saul in 16:1.

We may assume from that point forward that there are a series of conversations going on that are reduced to the public statements from the seer momentarily struck blind: "Neither has the LORD chosen this one" (vv. 8-10). After they go through all the sons minus one, David is referred to in verse 11 and subsequently makes his appearance in verse 12, although he is not named until verse 13. The conversations become decidedly one way at this point and God says, finally, "Arise, anoint him; for this is he." Then we have the spiritual turning point of verses 13 and 14—to David and from Saul. This describes the dialog manner of revelation.

David himself, at various times, will have these dialogues with God. This is the case in Keilah on two levels: directly and with the Urim and Thummim. In the initial decision to attack the Philistine garrison, David engages in dialog with God (1 Sam. 23:2-4). Later in the decision to escape to the wilderness from Saul, it looks like the priest with vestments and oracles does a "yes" or "no" divining of God's will. This should show adequately the contrast between the unilateral oracles and the dialog revelations. I think it might be added that these things seem to show a progression in the degree of intimacy between God and His man (prophet or king). Indeed, both progress and regress may be seen to the point where Saul receives nothing via the accepted means and gets the revelation of the age by calling Samuel back from the dead (1 Samuel 28).

## When Eyes Cannot See But Ears Certainly Tingle

First Samuel 3:11 has a very deuteronomistic ring to it. In fact it is a ringing in the ears that goes clear to those who risked their lives prophesying to Manasseh (2 Kings 21:12) and Jeremiah's prophecies at the end of the kingdom of Judah (Jer. 19:3). Samuel is a book where seers do not see clearly; but it is also a book where the oracles of God are dreadful in their scope. Unless we acquiesce slavishly to the spirit of the age that says there cannot be predictive prophecy; unless we serve naturalistic masters who would have the story be *vaticinium ex eventu*, we will find a foreboding message here. Our ears will tingle when we realize that our business is with a God who can not only tell us what the future is going to be but then removes any vestige of so-called free will we might have thought we had and can condemn us to an incontrovertible future that He makes happen. To know a prophecy, in some way or another, requires us to be subservient to it. Either we will do as Eli does and acquiesce to it, or we will expend enormous amounts of physical and mental energy attempting to avoid the inevitable as does Saul. Regardless, both know they are running into the jaws of destiny. They cannot avoid it; it is a mark of maturity for Eli, I think, that he falls silent.

## Textual Applications and Anecdotes

1 Samuel 3
vs.
1.  There are the times when God is silent.
    Times of God's silence are usually times of deep spiritual defection.
    God never leaves Himself without a witness.
    That witness may be an unlikely person in an unlikely position.
    That person will be taking care of his or her responsibilities.
2.  Often in biblical narrative, there are comparisons and contrasts between physical and spiritual vision.
    The supervisor sleeps while the worker works . . . .
3.  Often in biblical narrative, there are comparisons and contrasts between physical and spiritual light.
    God's man or woman will intuitively stay close to that which is holy.

4.     Acknowledge a call.

5.     Research a call.
        Check with the local authority.

6.     Acknowledge each call.
        Check your references again.

7.     There is some information we will not be able to assimilate.
        There is some information we will not even be able to apprehend.

8.     Acknowledge every call.
        Check your references repeatedly.
        Eventually, the light will come on in the mind of the local authority.

9.     At that point, listen carefully to the directions of the local authority and modify only with conscious wisdom.

10.    Answer the understood call.
        If you are not sure, be careful on names.

11.    Hang on for dear life: the message may not be pleasant.
        There are not many pleasant messages during times of spiritual defection.
        Ears burn at the revelation of the decimation of a clan.

12.    When a clan is doomed, those we care about go along with those who have hurt us (Eli and Abiathar as over against Hophni and Phineas).

13.    The father—right or wrong—bears the reproach of the sons.
        To confront, question, and challenge is not to rebuke.
        There comes a point in wayward behavior when one brings a curse upon oneself.

14.    Some things are broken beyond remedy.
        Some things that are ruined cannot (will not?) be forgiven.

15.    Terrifying words from God and the faithful one has a sleepless night.
        Terrifying words from God and yet the faithful one still performs his/her tasks.
        Terrifying words from God and the faithful one may keep silent until confronted.

16.    Answer the call of the local authority.

17.    Some local authorities have the right to know.
        Some local authorities merely claim the right to know.
        Some local authorities will manipulate the weak using disincentives like guilt and fear.

18.    There is the truth; there is the whole truth; and there is nothing but the truth.
        Hands often fall slack at the prophetic confirmation of a previous revelation.
        Identical information received from independent sources is a powerful motivator to belief.

19.    When the LORD is with someone, they will grow (multiple sense), and their words will not fall.

20.    When the LORD is with someone, people will hear about it.

Prophetic confirmation is at the least of national proportions.

21.    The prophetic office and the knowledge of the Holy are not necessarily inclusive terms in biblical narrative (contrast vv. 7 and 21).

When the LORD reveals Himself, appearances are not deceiving.

When the LORD reveals Himself, His voice is known.

## Conclusion

After the initial verses of chapter 4, Samuel will now disappear from the pages of biblical narrative until he reappears full grown and full of authority in chapter 7. Indeed, the sequel will prove that the ark of the covenant will disappear from the occupied land of Israel for a while! All things, themes, and players suitably introduced, we are ready for a bit more development of some themes and ideas prior to the first dance as Israel begins her romance with the idea of monarchy. We will now explore the idea that both historically and literarily Israel is helpless and hopeless without Samuel (or proxy, or successor). Subliminally, we will also explore the notion that Israel makes a serious mistake when she turns her artifacts and institutions into talismans. I should suppose that in that there will be the lesson concerning dead and blind orthodoxy and ideology that transits the testaments and the eons to our day. We will also see that God does not really need any help from the legions of Israel to decimate a foreign adversary. The ark can take care of itself, thank you!

As we now explore the conclusion to the period of the judges, we will see that Israel still needs a charismatic leader to free her from her self-inflicted bondage to idolatry, ethical transgression, and external oppression. Samuel will be the last of those and ushers in the period of the monarchy, anointing the first two but only living to the coronation of one king, Saul. Let us follow one of the last great disasters of the judgeships of Israel and follow that with the reappearance of Samuel and a moment when Israel "serves the Lord alone."

# 1 Samuel 4-6
## The Odyssey of the Ark

# 1 Samuel 4
## The Events in Samuel's Absence (Part 1)
## The Philistines Capture the Ark
## Eli and His Sons Die

—ɯ—

## Introduction

Samuel bursts on the scene in chapter 3 and exits as a boy wonder. He will be absent for the better part of three chapters. During this time, Israel will endure many humiliations. Let us follow the trail of the ark of the covenant as God, apart from human help, defends Himself from the irreverence of men.

## Textual Observations

God must rid Himself of several loathsome and unnecessary obstructions to His program. He must get remove Hophni and Phineas from the priesthood, the hard way. He must remove Eli from the priesthood and from his virtually agnostic influence over Israel. Oddly, he must remove Phinehas' wife, as pertains to the narrative; she is worth more for her final words than she is for the child she gives birth to—destined to fulfill the prophecies: "there will not be an old man in your house . . . an old man will not be in your house forever . . . I will raise up for Myself a faithful priest who will do according to what is in My heart and in My soul; and I will build him an enduring house . . . everyone who is left in your house shall come and bow down to him for a piece of silver or a loaf of bread and say, 'Please assign me to one of the priest's office so that I may eat a piece of bread'" (1 Sam. 2:31-36). Mrs. Phinehas says, "Ichabod . . . the glory has departed from Israel . . . the glory has departed from Israel for the ark of God was taken" (1 Sam. 4:21-22). And God must put Samuel away and protect him for later use.

## Samuel's Absence Indicates Israel's Failure

It might be a silent indication as to who is responsible for the composition of this section of biblical history. Because Israel is in complete failure here, we must look for scapegoats. The priesthood has likely been decimated. As pertains to the story, at least Hophni, Phinehas, and Eli are known to have perished ignominiously. But, where is Samuel? He exits after 1 Samuel 4:1a—which might be better kept with the epilogue material at the end of chapter 3—and does not reappear until 7:3. Even there, he does not come or go or arrive; he merely speaks. His words are heard without recourse to his appearance. They are heard with intrinsic authority and obeyed. It is as though he has been there all along going through Israel's trials with her and yet he is noticeably absent from the narrative. Why is this? It may be because he is doing his job in a rather unobtrusive manner. We do not find any evidence to this fact until late in chapter 7 when we discover what his customary practices were. He seems to have doubled his duty as a circuit court judge and itinerant preacher: "And [no disjunction] Samuel judged Israel all the days of his life. And he used to go annually on circuit to Bethel and Gilgal and Mizpah, and he judged Israel in all these places. Then his return was to Ramah, for his house was there, and there he judged Israel; and he built there an altar to the LORD (1 Sam. 7:15-17).

But while Samuel is gone from the story, Israel suffers a major defeat and one with long effect. When we left Samuel in chapter 3, he is but a boy. When he returns, he is full grown and in command. Let us review. The Philistines engage Israel twice in battle and Israel is finally overwhelmed. The ark is taken and the priesthood suffers significant losses. Then the ark begins doing its own damage to the enemy. Where is Samuel in all this? Is he just a small boy, too insignificant for the corrupt priesthood to bring along to the army of Israel? Is this another of the many evidences of the sovereign protecting hand of God in keeping Samuel out of the fray until Israel's humility is complete and Samuel can guide them to do something about their predicament? In the meantime, is he mourning the loss of his mentor Eli? Boys grow up! We should not miss the fact that in these three chapters Samuel did and was going about doing his work as assigned in Torah. We should also not miss the fact that a lot of water is going to go under the bridge in Samuel's life. Where is mention of his wife? Where is mention of his two sons? Samuel is going to get old, according to Israel's standards for leadership by chapter 8 (v. 5). The indictment on Samuel by the elders of Israel was that "your sons do not walk in your ways." The growth and maturity process that culminated in their rejection by Israel and apparently by God began in these three silent chapters. As so often in the Samuel Narratives, fatherhood does not get very good press and neither does the ending of good men (see especially my "epilogue" on 1 Kings 1 and 2, in volume 2).

### Ebenezer, Memorial of Defeat, and Victory

We have noticed from time to time that characters are often given triple introductions in biblical narrative. There is a fascinating triple introduction or foreshadowing of a positive nature in these chapters. Samuel is absent, but his words reach back into these chapters. This, of course, has to do with the memorial site, Ebenezer.

First, it is said after the introductory or epilogic note about Samuel, "Now Israel went out to meet the Philistines in battle and camped beside Ebenezer while the Philistines camped in Aphek" (1 Sam. 4:1). This might be viewed as an anachronism by a Westerner with a critical mind; however, it is doubtful that the ancients would have even noticed the tension. Even for us, it is not really much of a problem since the ancient writer would merely have given the common place name to his ancient audience. This would have been the case despite the fact that perhaps as long as a generation later, Samuel would give it its formal name.

Secondly, in the aftermath of Israel's calamity, the ark is reintroduced in its location by resumptive reinsertion into the text: "Now the Philistines took the ark of God and brought it from Ebenezer to Ashdod" (1 Sam. 5:1). The focus has now shifted to what God will do to the Philistines apart from any Israelite military presence. Again, this being perhaps the same day as the verses above, there is the historical anachronism, I maintain, for a profound literary effect.

Finally, in chapter 7 with the reappearance of Samuel, Ebenezer finally gets its place as a headliner: "Then Samuel took a stone and set it between Mizpah and Shen, and named it Ebenezer, saying, 'Thus far the Lord has helped us'" (1 Sam. 7:12). Etymologically, the word itself means approximately, "stone of help." That is, it was erected as a memorial of the assistance given against Israel's enemies by God, Himself.

So why do we have the apparent historical anachronism? Of course it may not have been an anachronism at all. In the same manner as a new generation of the patriarchs might rename places in the book of Genesis (cf. Gen. 21:31; 26:33), Samuel might simply have been making something special of a name that had already existed. Fine, but what purpose would that serve in the story? It is my contention that the real reason for the two portentous and somewhat prevenient usages of the word "Ebenezer" are to herald the return of Samuel and the eventual subduing of the Philistines (1 Sam. 7:13)—at least during the lifetime of Samuel.

"So the Philistines were subdued and they did not come any more within the border of Israel. And the hand of the LORD was against the Philistines all the days of Samuel. And the cities which the Philistines had taken from Israel were restored to Israel, from Ekron even to Gath; and Israel delivered their territory from the hand of the Philistines. So there was peace" (1 Sam. 7:13-14).

Of course, hostilities will heat up after the death of Samuel in 1 Samuel 25:1; however, for the time being it will be "all quiet on the western front." Nevertheless, it is indicative as to who is probably responsible for these sections, however. It would seem that Samuel could have easily sat down and edited a final edition of his memoirs before his death including this statement about his absence, his critical importance to Israel's spiritual well-being, unification, and power—his essentially irreplaceable quality—and this clever intrusion foreshadowing his return and the memorial of a great national victory. That it was left in the final edition, may be indicative that either it was viewed as sacred or that the heirs to the prophetic, scribal task agreed that Samuel was irreplaceable.

## Textual Applications and Anecdotes

1 Samuel 4
vs.
1. Epilogue may serve as prologue.
   Meeting the enemy on his own turf is not always the best idea.
   Indication of a place before it is named is not necessarily an anachronism to Israel; but it is a foreshadow of how things will eventually go (cf. 7:12).
2. The foreshadowing of the "stone of help" indicates that this loss is not the final statement.
3. Usage of sacred furniture as a talisman does not please God and accomplishes nothing.
4. The supervisors of folly are doomed to failure.
5. When superstition and pagan worldview reign supreme, people are moved by the presence of objects.
6. When one side is encouraged, the other side falters—however briefly.
7. Dread of the superstitious is a powerful disincentive.
8. When something momentous happens, the pagans recognize or blame the gods.
9. The opposite of war and battle may be slavery—either literally or slave to fear.
10. A great disaster does not mean that a greater one cannot befall us . . . neither does it mean that we cannot look to the future.
11. When we rely on relics and artifacts we are demoralized when they are taken. What is it when the most significant thing one can do is die? (Hophni and Phineas).
12. Ever beware the besmirched Benjamite with news.
13. Old men ever watch the horizon when their relics and artifacts are taken.
14. Old men are disturbed over commotion.
15. Old men are disturbed over commotion they cannot see.
16. He who escapes the battle lives to escape and tell the bad news.
17. Bad news? Tell it all.
    Bad news? End with the worst.
18. Old fat judges fall and die.

Blind seers eventually fall.
19.    Bad news causes shock.
20.    The wives of evil clerics eventually perish.
21.    In times of defeat it is easy to think that God has forsaken us.
       In times of spiritual defection it is easy to think that God has forsaken us.
       In times of defeat and spiritual defection, God will attempt to use severe means to restore us.
22.    When superstition reigns supreme, the stolen relic is all that is left of the glory that once was.

## Conclusion

(See conclusions to chapters 5 and 6 below.)

# 1 Samuel 5
## The Events in Samuel's Absence (Part 2)
## God Vindicates Himself in the Temple of Dagon

—⁓—

## Introduction

(See introduction to chapter 4 above.)

## Textual Observations

### Israel Cannot Protect Her Artifacts, But God Protects His!

God will not allow His things to become talismans. Ultimately, this will be true even with regard to the temple. Israel thought that God would not allow Jerusalem and the temple to fall to the Babylonians because of the presence of the holy site. This was, perhaps, a mistaken sense of false security brought about by the miraculous rescue from the Assyrian hordes at their doorstep in an earlier generation. False senses of security are not foreign to Israel. But when the ark is taken by the Philistines, it begins to have a life of its own.

First, it wreaked havoc on the idol next to which it was placed. This started a brand new superstition in Ashdod: "Therefore neither the priests of Dagon nor all who enter Dagon's house tread on the threshold of Dagon in Ashdod to this day" (1 Sam. 5:5). Unfortunately, I doubt that this means that the people suddenly stopped patronizing the temple and impoverished its priesthood. That merely seems to indicate that they stepped over this zone of Dagon's trouble. Be that as it may, I have long wondered why the mention of this particular damage to the statue of Dagon: "and the head of Dagon and both the palms of his hands were cut off on the threshold, only Dagon [a fish body?] was left to him." I wonder if the Omniscient Narrator is making a statement here. It could be that, like the religions of the indigenous peoples around the Philistines, they too have gone off into practices that are too abhorrent for God to countenance any longer. Several of the Baal cults included the religious ritual of child sacrifice. It is said that the Phoenicians would later spread this cult to Carthage and then to the Islands, most notably, Sardinia. We know of an earlier era when Baal worship was in the northeastern Mediterranean basin at Ugarit. There are representations of the idol that include hands upon which the sacrificial infant victim are laid until it rolls off into the fire. I wonder if this is a not so subtle indication by the author that God was not pleased either with the conceptual apparatus (head) of Ashdodite religion, or of its most hideous ritualistic practice (infant sacrifice). The more obvious message is that God cannot be put into a box: He does not need the legions of Israel to fight His battles or Israel's battles for that matter; He does not take second place to any piece of carved stone (or other medium); and He can influence people to act positively toward Him without Israel's influence. But in addition, I think that the narrator is also indicating that God will not long tolerate other ideas of divinity or their more savage practices.

Secondly, we do not know how the Philistines treated this artifact plundered off the battlefield. What we do know is that God did not treat Israel very well for having lost it or the Ashdodites very well for having kept it. And so the people of Ashdod and its environs were plagued with tumors. At this point, matters are so bad that they call the warlords and ask them what to do. Superstition being what it is—and this being quite a prize—the warlords counsel the people of Ashdod to send the ark away to the southeast to Gath rather than relinquish it to Israel.

The third thing that happens is that the people of Gath become host to the same kind of tumors with which the people of Ashdod had been afflicted. So we might score one for the warlords: they have now potentially decimated the populations of two of their five principalities. Fourthly, the same thing happens when they send the ark north to Ekron. And the warlords are called to account again. "And the men who did not die were smitten with tumors and the cry of the city went up to heaven" (v. 12). With respect to the "outcry," this is very similar language to the discussion between the Lord and Abraham with respect to Sodom and Gomorrah (Gen. 18:20-21; cf. 19:13). Regardless, God is taking notice and He will use some rather unusual means to return the ark to Israel—but not before a measure of calamity is shared by the people of Beth-Shemesh.

Despite the huge hole in the life of Samuel—somewhere—indicated above, what we have is a mere seven months that God is decimating the Philistines because of their misappropriation and ignorance of and disrespect in regard to the ark (6:1). In the next scene, it will be proven that Israel is no better. Perhaps they were a mixed group of Israelites and other nations and were paganized. Perhaps they just let their curiosity get the better of them. Regardless, God has a way He will be treated and people of all nations had better be called to account.

### The Warlords Make Their Grand Entrance; Their First Terrible Appearance: The Tyrants' Terror Is Their Own!

Special focus on the Philistines is the order of the day. Their grand entrance on the stage of history is not one that makes them appear very terrifying. In something of a cartoon fashion, they run around from city to city dealing out disease and death with each directive regarding the ark. Who are these warlords of the Philistines (*sarnê p*<sup>e</sup>*lishtîm*)? They appear on the scene as though the reader knows them well. This is the first mention of them in the Samuel Narratives, but they are introduced in related literature that would be an expected antecedent. Through studies in intertextuality we might ascertain that all we really need to know about the five lords of the Philistines is given to us in the biblical books of Joshua and Judges. Historical mentions include their presence in the land that remained yet to be taken in Joshua's day (Josh. 13:3). These five lords are said to be from Gaza, Ashdod, Ashkelon, Gath, and Ekron. No further mention is made of them in Joshua's day. In the days of the judges, there is an historical review of the nations that Israel had not yet conquered. The five lords of the Philistines are included among those whom Joshua and Israel did not eradicate (Judges 3:3). Their cities are not given at this time.

Finally, we have the well-known Samson cycle. Although Samson's entire life was dedicated to being an impossible thorn in the side of the Philistines, Samson does not meet up with the five warlords until near his demise in chapter 16 of Judges. After ripping the very gates of the city off their hinges, Samson walks from a very exposed Gath up the mountain to Hebron. The lords of the Philistines here, as in Samuel, are fairly powerless so they attempt to get at him through subterfuge. They apply their energies to his only—and now regionally famous weakness—women. So when the lords of the Philistines appear they address Delilah: "Entice him, and see where his great strength lies and how we may overpower him that we may bind him to afflict him. Then we will each give you eleven hundred pieces of silver" (Judges 16:5). Of course, the story dips and twists over several abortive attempts to bring Samson to heel (16:8-17). When the truth of the matter is revealed, Delilah "called the lords of the Philistines, saying 'Come up once more, for he has told me all that is in his heart.' Then the lords of the Philistines came up to her, and brought the money in their hands" (v. 18). So the Philistines take a sightless Samson to Gaza, the scene of the gate crime and gather to sacrifice to their God, Dagan—apparently the God of subterfuge. As the story goes, Samson's public display is viewed by thousands of Philistine notables including the five warlords themselves (v. 27). Samson is given back his strength in answer to his final earthly prayer and he knocks out the main supports for the temple, killing the five warlords of the Philistines and many of their guests. This is the picture that is generally painted of the Philistine warlords. They are a comical lot, an expendable enemy which Israel must gradually come not to fear. In the days of David's monarchy they would be all but pushed into the sea.

There is another angle from which to pursue the five warlords of the Philistines. It is thought that due to the unusual spelling of the word "lords" (*has-s*<sup>e</sup>*rānîm*, e.g., Judges 16:30), that it is a loan word from another language. One noted lexicon has it as "tyrant, lord (Philist. loanword) only of tyrants, lords of the Philistines, five in [number]. . . [apparently], one ruling each of the five cities . . . ."[25] Others go so far as to indicate that it has some phonic similarities to the Greek for tyrant (τύραννος).[26] Some have seen this as an indication of an Aegean origin for the Iron Age Philistines.[27] Regardless of the etymological derivation of the word, its place in the story in 1 Samuel 5 is rather more comical than either lordly or tyrannical. Every time they give a command, it ends in the withering death of more of their countrymen. Perhaps this is the view that Samuel came to have of the Philistine warlords. Because they had been quieted in his own day, he felt that they could finally be eradicated in that of Saul. Again this is a very dark shroud pulled over the head of Saul—before he is even king. Saul and the armies of Israel cannot defeat the nearly cartoon-like characters. Only God in His sovereignty can—and David will be the agent of that destruction, not Saul.

## When Warlords Have to Settle Domestic Disputes

We expect Alexander to hack the Gordian knot apart! Since Somalia, we readers of biblical narrative have come to view warlords as, well, warlords. Part of the cartoon-esque thing that happens to them upon their grand entrance in 1 Samuel, surrounds their impotence as effecting anything good on behalf of their own people. The domestic disputes they settle are on two levels. First, they must settle the disputes between deities: their own and one more powerful. This they will finally do when they elicit the support of the soothsayer priests in chapter 6 and finally wave goodbye to the ark as it heads toward Beth-Shemesh. In the meantime they must settle domestic disputes among their own people. One might wonder at the level of complicity the lords of the Philistines engage in when they take the ark from the battlefield at Ebenezer to Ashdod. Regardless, they are responsible for holding it for the next seven months as they bumble from one disaster to another.

That the ark cannot remain in Ashdod is self-evident. It will kill everybody there if not removed. So, the lords of the Philistines are called and their counsel sought. To alleviate the suffering of the people of Ashdod, they inflict similar suffering on the people of Gath. One more round of this happens as the ark goes from Gath to Ekron and the warlords are again consulted to get the thing out of Philisia proper. The warlords are unable to settle disputes between their own people without getting people killed. This is another illustration of how gifting for generals and diplomats differs. By the time they are done, the warlords look like fools and must call in even greater buffoons than themselves, the priesthood, to remove the ark. When this course of action finally proved successful in ridding them of the plague producing ark, "they returned to Ekron that day" (1 Sam. 6:16). The return to Ekron was undoubtedly thought to be a return to a safe haven. However, with so many of the people of the northeast sick, dying, and dead, I will always wonder if their return was not met with more regret than relief—perhaps both on the part of the people and of the warlords themselves. Regardless of their intentions, the ignorance and arrogance of these warlords, like those the world over and throughout time, was responsible for the death of many of their people. If they would have just left the religious art; if they would have returned it directly from Ashdod; If . . . Pride *is* our undoing.

## When Bad Things Happen at the Winepress (Gath)

Meanwhile back at Gath: Gath figures prominently in biblical literature. It is the seat of one of the warlords. It has its own king, known to us as Achish, a name apparently also of Aegean origin.[28] It is the hometown of the famous giant, Goliath, and his several gigantic sons and relatives. It is the place where David will attempt to defect, apparently bringing Goliath's sword with him and have to feign madness to escape. Later, David will successfully defect to Gath while all Philistia, it seems, is blinded to the ramifications of his presence.

"Gath" means "winepress." One wonders at the imagery of trampling out the vintage of the grapes of wrath in "Winepress." It seems that Gath is the starting point for some of the calamities of the tribe of Judah. In this case, the ark will be arriving soon—just in time to kill many of its citizens. The first words of the warlords in the Samuel Narratives are "Let the ark of the God of Israel be brought around to Gath." Exactly why that would make a difference is unclear. Perhaps there was another storage place rather than the temple of Dagon there. Perhaps it was the least offensive and most agnostic of the towns. Perhaps these three most northern and eastern towns were particularly the target of an offended God who wished to weaken substantially the military might of the people closest to Judah. In any case, Gath gets the second appearance of the ark in Philistia. Chaos reigns supreme: "And it came about that after they had brought it around, the hand of the LORD was against the city with very great confusion; and He smote the men of the city, both young and old, so that tumors broke out on them. So they sent the ark of God to Ekron" (1 Sam. 5:9-10). The thing we see about Gath is its independence. The people of Ashdod and Ekron seem to be much more in communication with the warlords. The people of Gath, who will be first suspicious of David and later blinded to him, seem to operate more independently. When bad things happen at the winepress, it is a bet that its citizens will act independently and quickly and be hurt badly.

## Textual Applications and Anecdotes

1 Samuel 5
vs.
1.  The relic may be gone; but follow it anyway!
    It is not a good idea to steal someone else's property—especially if that property belongs to God.
2.  We know the story, but it seems odd and perhaps arrogant that pagans put captured artifacts in the temples of their own gods.
3.  Circumspection tells us that it is the subject of lampoon to reposition idols after they have fallen over.
    All the idols fall on their face before God.
4.  Pay attention! The second fall breaks the statue.
5.  The superstitious create new superstitions and the mythology snowballs down the hill to destruction.
6.  When God is angry with a foreign nation there will be some serious physical repercussions.
7.  The pagan mind finds it easier to believe that their god is merely inferior rather than non-existent—after all: they would have to change their theology and their clerics would be out of work.
8.  If in Ashdod you don't succeed, try, try, try again in Gath.
9.  If everybody got tumors in Ashdod, why would it be any different in Gath?
    This is evidence of the superstitious, pagan mind.
10. Paganism, superstition and hysteria: they all go together.
    When pagan countrymen do anything wrong, their fellow countrymen take it personally.
11. Evidence of the pagan mind: when plague breaks out, call the generals.
    Death is the great equalizer; in it, even the pagan mind might recognize the sovereign hand of God.
12. The cry goes up to heaven: even stupid people are cared for by God.

## Conclusion

When the warlords appear in history, such notices as their cities and their number are all that is given. When they become confrontational with Israel, they should beware. In the case of Samson, after having gained their desire they are destroyed in a moment in one of the most amazing reversals in biblical narrative. In the case of 1 Samuel, they look like ignorant, barbarian tyrants who can do nothing beneficial for their own people. During the times of Samuel and David, they will not even be able to mount much of a military threat against Israel. Yet as bad as they are, as inept as they are, as impotent as they are and as comical as they are, they are seen to be the ones who finally finish the monarchy of Saul. Apart from David, Jonathan, and Abner, Saul is useless before the five great Philistine buffoons.

# 1 Samuel 6
## The Events in Samuel's Absence (Part 3)
## The Ark Returns to Israel

—⁓—

**Introduction**

(See Introduction to chapter 4 above.)

**Textual Observations**

**The Twofold Return of the Ark (The Sixes of Samuel)**

The ark returns first to Israel in 1 Samuel 6; but it does not come to rest at its desired locus in Jerusalem until one book later—2 Samuel 6. In our text, the ark remains in the land of the Philistines for a period of seven months, wreaking havoc, and then returns by rather unusual means to territory more formally controlled by Israel. However, even there, a bit of impropriety causes the Lord to get irritated and kill thousands of curious, irreverent, and sacrilegious people. At that point the people from Kiriath-Jearim are invited to try their hand. If any lore went along during this odyssey of the ark, I doubt that certain of the people would have been thrilled to bring it back up. When you handle the holy, you want to abide by the rules. Then we are told that it remained in Kiriah-Jearim for twenty years. It may be here that Samuel grows up and has a wife and sons who do not follow in his ways.

The ark makes one brief appearance during the reign of Saul, about which not much can be said. It appears for a moment in the custody of one of Eli's condemned relatives—the "brother" of another condemned relative of Eli. Saul apparently wants to use it as a talisman very much like it had been used a generation earlier in the charge of Hophni and Phinehas. In "talking to the priest" Saul apparently ascertains that this is not such a good idea. None of the details are shared; but we might surmise that the priest said: "This turned out to be a disaster in the days of my uncles . . . maybe we shouldn't risk it again." The king would then have agreed and then suggested that he "stay his hand" (1 Samuel 14:18-19).

Much later, David will bring the ark back to Jerusalem—but a lot of history happens between this scene of the ark in Kiriath-Jearim and that of David dancing before an ascending ark. Saul will be anointed king; Samuel will die; the Philistines will vanquish Israel; Saul and most of his sons will fall on the battlefield; there will be internecine struggle between the north and the south; David will consolidate the kingdom; the Philistines will be pushed back to the sea; the ark will ascend and then preparation will be made for its final resting place.

## A Pagan Priesthood Propitiates an Unknown Deity

What do you do when a lot is at stake and the rules are suddenly changed? This is the question that faced "the priests and the diviners" (1 Sam. 6:2). The stakes were high: plague had broken out in Ashdod, Gath, and Ekron and this was not a God who played by Dagon's rules. "What shall we do with the ark of the LORD? Tell us how we shall send it to its place" (v. 2). Notice first the progression: back in chapter 5 the men of Ashdod said, "The ark of the God of Israel must not remain with us, for His hand is severe on us and on Dagon our god" (5:7). At that point, the "men of Ashdod" do not even dignify the "God of Israel" with a name. He is just one among many—and right now, He is beating up our god. This follows with the question: "What shall we do with the ark of the God of Israel"? This is followed by the answer from the cowardly warlords, "Let the ark of the God of Israel be brought around to Gath" (v. 8). The narrator all along knows the power of the ark of God (the true God). But even the people of Ekron initially refer to it in terror: "They have brought the ark of the God of Israel around to us, to kill us and our people" (v. 10). And the people of Ekron command the ignorant, impotent warlord tyrants, "Send away the ark of the God of Israel and let it return to its own place, that it may not kill us and our people" (v. 11). But after seven months, someone has figured out that it is the ark of YHWH (6:2), dignifying the God of Israel with a proper name—from Philistine lips!

The soothsayer priests "divine" that an expiatory guilt offering is the order of the day (6:4). That would have been their custom for an offended deity in any case. Perhaps there is something universal amongst humankind in the matter of guilt/expiation. In any case, they decided at that point that the guilt offering must represent several things: It must be something of value, to expiate their ignorance and irreverence; it must represent the five warlords and their territorial domains; and it must be something representative of the punishment inflicted upon them for their impudence (v. 4). They choose to put golden representations of tumors and mice, five each, in a box and set it next to the ark in a cart to send it home. In doing this it is said that "you shall give glory to the God of Israel; perhaps He will ease His hand from you, your gods, and your land" (v. 5). It would sound for all the world that the priests and diviners are making a distinction between their (perhaps, newfound) belief system and that of the warlords! The pronouns are instructive: "you, your gods, and your land." We hear echoes of Joshua's words: "As for me and my house, we will serve the LORD" (Josh. 24:15). Throughout the Old Testament, Israel's faithlessness is rewarded by foreigners' conversions to her faith. As we often say about Jonah, Jonah had more conversions by default than by design. Whatever the case, these out-of-the-closet

Yahwists now propose some rather unusual means toward the desired end of returning the ark to its rightful and somewhat perturbed owner.

## Magic Carpets and Other Unusual Oxcarts

From time to time in the *Arabian Nights,* a convenient *ifrit* or carpet appears for the purpose of transporting the protagonist astonishing distances in infinitesimal amounts of time—technically the collapsing of narrative time and space. Nothing so in violation of the laws of physics appears here. But something in violation of the laws of nature and mother-hood does. When the ark is placed upon a cart, it is to be drawn by two new mother cows that have been bereft of their calves. Of course, the cows set out straightaway to return the ark to Israel, because in biblical narrative, never is an animal disobedient to the will of God. Humans try their best to disobey and defy the sovereign will of God, but animals never do. There are a few lessons here somewhere: animals always obey God, people rarely do. Animals may even be called upon to act contrary to their nature as animals (donkeys speaking; cows leaving calves; hungry ravens leaving perfectly good food for prophets, etc.). Whereas humans sometimes receive blessings—sometimes even despite their obedience—animals suffer the abuses of humankind. The sacrificial system is only one illustration of this—they die for the sins of humanity. In this particular case, after the cows, acting contrary to their maternal instincts (and vocally expressing as much) and in obedience to their commission to return the ark, arrive at their destination in Beth-Shemesh, they are slaughtered and burned as sacrifices (it looks like peace offerings to me) to the God to whom the narrative indicates they have been obedient. Again, animals suffer for the excesses of humanity. I was once lecturing on the book of Revelation at a theological seminary in Nairobi. I asked the students whether they believed there would be animals in heaven. One unusually sharp lady responded that "At least we could apologize to them for eating them." And we would have all eternity to do it. N.B.: decisions on that question remained suspended.

## The Sacred Profaned in Beth-Shemesh

But once back within the confines of Israel's control, things do not fare much better. We have not really had an episode with a stolen and returned ark yet. So this may yet fit within "Jerry's law of the first offense." We know that when Nadab and Abihu "offered strange fire" in the tabernacle, they were scorched to a cinder (Leviticus 10:1-7). Exactly what it was they did is not clear to us: "using the wrong incense" is a frequent interpretation. It was, however, a first offense and God showed us exactly what it was He thought of similar acts of disobedience that culminated in desecrations of the holy. In the present case, however, the men of Beth-Shemesh start well and end poorly. They begin by offering as victims, as peace offerings, those poor unfortunate, calf-bereft but obedient cows. Possibly things would have gone well had the story ended here. What happened next is where curiosity got the best of some people and they acted in an irreverent manner. God "struck down some of the men of Beth-Shemesh because they had looked into the ark of the LORD. He struck down of all the people, 50,070 men, and the people mourned because the LORD had struck the people with a great slaughter" (1 Sam. 6:19). See below for the number problem. To us, the punishment does not fit the crime; but to the ancient audience, there was a certain decorum expected of people in contact with the holy. For the eyes of faith and devotion, there is a tacit acquiescence to the need for that which is holy to be treated with respect. Others will find this harsh in the extreme. They will also find it inconsistent that it does not happen at every desecration of the holy—as though that argument from silence proves the non-existence or indifference of God. However, if God treated every such affront in the extreme, it is an open question as to whether or not there would be humans populating this planet. Perhaps that would vindicate those abused animals mentioned above. In any case, this story is an indication in biblical thought how God is viewed as thinking about irreverent behavior: "Then Moses said to Aaron, 'it is what the LORD spoke, saying, "By those who come near Me I will be treated as holy, and before all the people I will be honored"'"(Leviticus 10:3).

**Textual Problems**

Of course, criticism has always had problem with the numbers: in the first place, fifty thousand plus does not sound like "some of the men"; secondly, the larger number seems too large for a village. After having lived next to the largest slum in Africa (estimates range from two-thirds to a million in an area one-half by three miles), arguments based on having fifty thousand people in an area the size of a postage stamp no longer affect me. It might seem pretty mindless from a western standpoint; however, the western point of view is probably neither the only view nor the correct one. In the rest of the world, people live in closer proximity to each other than here. After having examined the confines of Iron Age I Beth-Shemesh, it does not seem much of a reach to have that many people in the urban confines or at least in the immediate vicinity—without demanding final decimation of the entire Asian population!

## Textual Applications and Anecdotes

1 Samuel 6

vs.

1. Long absence, fading memory, fading reliance on talismans.
2. It seems absurd to ask pagan priests about how to treat God or His artifacts.
3. The principles of placation and expiation may be universal.
4. Whatever the gift—and it may seem odd—it should be something of value, something indicating sacrifice in the giving.
5. The pagan mind easily shifts its allegiance from its gods in times of disaster. Recognition of God's sovereign hand in disasters is even possible for the most entrenched pagan cleric.
6. "History became legend, legend became myth"—until there is a disaster, an act of God; then the history is recalled.
7. Wholesomeness is considered valuable, even to the pagan mind.
8. Give the offering and send away the artifact.
9. Pagan priests and diviners do not really know what they are talking about; they are merely open to the possibilities.
10. The pagan mind searches for the paradoxical (calfless cows acting contrary to their nature) for in it he thinks he has found the divine.
11. Follow through, what do you have to lose but your dignity or your pride.
12. There is no case of a disobedient animal in Scripture. Perhaps it is the case that when an animal acts contrary to nature, the hand of the Almighty is at work.
13. Despite its long absence, people recognize and welcome back the relic.
14. Animals have a horrific price to pay for their obedience in the Bible; usually, the problem has to do with their human fellow sojourners upon this earth.
15. When the artifact is returned, rejoice in God—instead of the relic.
16. The pagan watches God work and goes home in silence.
17. The offering is given; there is the presumption of expiation of guilt.
18. The offering is given; there is the hope that it will pay the debt of both individual and group.
19. Irreverence is often avenged quickly in the Bible—and often severely! Irreverence meets God's retributive justice.
20. Respect, fine. Curiosity can lead to impropriety. To God it is irreverence.
21. Bring the relic back to its place.

## Conclusion

We have concluded our Samuel-less sojourn in the biblical narrative of 1 Samuel 4-6. When we left him, he was but a boy, known "from Dan to Beersheba . . . confirmed as a prophet of the LORD" (1 Sam. 3:20). When he returns from his textual exile in 1 Samuel 7:3, he will be a grown man and thunder with the authority of command—immediately obeyed command. While he was gone, Israel was defeated. When he returns, Israel will be victorious. His absence demonstrates his essential role in maintaining Israel's spiritual and geopolitical existence. The design of this text of three chapters, whether written by Samuel or one of his successors, is to show that Samuel either viewed himself or was viewed as indispensable to Israel's existence as a nation. What the ark narrative actually shows is that God could take care of Himself and His artifacts just fine without Samuel, and that foreigners would come to know Him and use His name. However, Samuel's presence will prove that there is a truth to his importance . . . but only on a certain level. He was a failure as a husband; he was a failure as a father; and he failed to win the confidence and devotion of the nation at a crucial point in its development. His was to be the last of the charismatic leaderships that characterize the period of the judges.

# 1 Samuel 7
# The Indispensable Samuel Returns to the Text:
# When Good Players Get Out of Bounds

—⟋⟋⟍—

## Introduction

S amuel has now returned to the stage of history. He left us as a small child—at least in the narrative of his childhood—renown from Dan to Beersheba. He will now return as a full-grown man. We know what he has been involved in because of the notation at the end of the chapter. He has been a circuit judge and teacher in an area in the highland of Ephraim. However, he left us seemingly as a boy and by chapter 8 he will be an old man. The only temporal notations we have are the seven months that the ark was in the land of the Philistines (1 Samuel 6:1) and the twenty years that it was in Kiriath-Jearim (1 Samuel 7:2). From the time of the boyhood of Samuel along with this twenty years and seven months to his old age in chapter 8, there are hardly enough years to advance his life. That is the place that 1 Samuel 7:15-17 fills. Be that as it may, during this entire time Samuel is absent from the text. He now returns to the text to act as the preacher of a doctrine of repentance from polytheism. He acts as the intermediary in prayer on behalf of the repentant nation. He acts as the judicial representative of God among His people. And he acts as the last vestige of the old charismatic judgeships of the previous era. Soon he will play his last role—that of the king-maker of ancient Israel. He will play that role begrudgingly, abortively, and terminally. He will never live to see the right king on the throne. Let us see how his story plays out on these pages.

## Textual Observations

### Other Gods: Baalim and Ashtaroth in Narrative

In reading the so-called "deuteronomistic history," one cannot help but see how readily the Jews fell into the practice of idolatry. Why they would do that, I have no idea—until I consider materialistic western pragmatic thought. To people from the United States, idolatry is lampoonable. We have that heritage from Isaiah:

Those who fashion a graven image are all of them futile, and their precious things are of no profit; even their own witnesses fail to see or know, so that they will be put to shame. Who has fashioned a god or cast an idol to no profit? Behold, all his companions will be put to shame, for the craftsmen themselves are mere men. Let them all assemble themselves, let them stand up, let them tremble, let them together be put to shame. The man shapes iron into a cutting tool, and does his work over the coals, fashioning it with hammers, and working it with his strong arm. He also gets hungry and his strength fails; he drinks no water and becomes weary. *Another* shapes wood, he extends a measuring line; he outlines it with red chalk. He works it with planes, and outlines it with a compass, and makes it like the form of a man, like the beauty of man, so that it may sit in a house. Surely he cuts cedars for himself, and takes a cypress or an oak, and raises *it* for himself among the trees of the forest. He plants a fir, and the rain makes it grow. Then it becomes *something* for a man to burn, so he takes one of them and warms himself; he also makes a fire to bake bread. He also makes a god and worships it; he makes it a graven image, and falls down before it. Half of it he burns in the fire; over *this* half he eats meat as he roasts a roast, and is satisfied. He also warms himself and says, "Aha! I am warm, I have seen the fire." But the rest of it he makes into a god, his graven image. He falls down before it and worships; he also prays to it and says, "Deliver me, for thou art my god." They do not know, nor do they understand, for He has smeared over their eyes so that they cannot see and their hearts so that they cannot comprehend. And no one recalls, nor is there knowledge or understanding to say, "I have burned half of it in the fire, and also have baked bread over its coals. I roast meat and eat *it*. Then I make the rest of it into an abomination, I fall down before a block of wood!" He feeds on ashes; a deceived heart has turned him aside. And he cannot deliver himself, nor say, "Is there not a lie in my right hand?"

Isaiah 44:9-20 NASB

Perhaps this is why so many, and not merely the first, instances of idolatry were punished so severely in biblical narrative. So how is it here in the Samuel Narratives?

After a couple of notations about the ark of the covenant, we must be content to leave it in Kiriath-Jearim for decades until David haltingly brings it back up to Jerusalem in 2 Samuel 6. Back in this period of time, the people of Israel mourned the absence of the Lord in their lives—mostly due to a lack of security, I should suppose. Then, out of the blue, with respect to his reinsertion into the narrative, Samuel blasts through the silence: "If you return to the LORD with all your heart, remove the foreign gods and the Ashtaroth from among you and direct your hearts to the LORD and serve Him alone; and He will deliver you from the hand of the Philistines." This is followed by the surprising notation—surprising, because we know how Israel has behaved historically—that "the sons of Israel removed the

Baals and the Ashtaroth and served the LORD alone" (1 Sam. 7:3-4). How has this played out in the mind of the historian?

We do not need to believe in a "Deuteronomist" writing on the eve of the temple's destruction or later to understand these words in Samuel. What we do need is to understand the various prohibitions against idolatry (e.g., Exodus 20:1-6; Deut. 5: 6-10) and Moses' prophecy of Israel's defection from the faith and turning aside to idolatry (Deuteronomy 31:16-18). God says to Moses:

> "Behold, the time for you to die is near; call Joshua, and present yourselves at the tent of meeting, that I may commission him." So Moses and Joshua went and presented themselves at the tent of meeting. And the LORD appeared in the tent in a pillar of cloud, and the pillar of cloud stood at the doorway of the tent. And the LORD said to Moses, "Behold, you are about to lie down with your fathers; and this people will arise and play the harlot with the strange gods of the land, into the midst of which they are going, and will forsake Me and break My covenant which I have made with them."
>
> Deut. 31:14-16 NASB

This indicates that the battle with the people of Israel was lost before it was begun. That is, on the eve of the crossing of the Jordan, the people are told of their impending defection. It would only be a generation or two before that would come to pass.

At the end of the next generation, Joshua's speech goads Israel into making a promise she will never be able to keep as a nation. There would, of course, be individual exceptions. He says: "You will not be able to serve the LORD, for He is a holy God. He is a jealous God; He will not forgive your transgression or your sins. If you forsake the LORD and serve foreign gods, then He will turn and do you harm and consume you after He has done good to you" (Joshua 24:19-20 NASB).

We all know that history is a better teacher than the prophet—because we can independently verify what the historian says, we have to take a wait-and-see attitude with the preacher. And so we examine the words of the angel of the Lord and the deuteronomistic historian in the early sections of the book of Judges.

"I brought you up out of Egypt and led you into the land which I have sworn to your fathers; and I said, 'I will never break My covenant with you, and as for you, you shall make no covenant with the inhabitants of this land; you shall tear down their altars.' But you have not obeyed Me; what is this you have done? Therefore I also said, 'I will not drive them out before you; but they shall become *as thorns* in your sides, and their gods shall be a snare to you'" (Judges 2:2-3 NASB).

"Then the sons of Israel did evil in the sight of the LORD, and served the Baals, and they forsook the LORD, the God of their fathers, who had brought them out of the land of Egypt, and followed other gods from *among* the gods of the peoples who were around them, and bowed themselves down to them; thus they provoked the Lord to anger. So they forsook the Lord and served Baal and the Ashtaroth" (Judges 2:11-13 NASB).

So we see that Samuel has fallen heir to the legacy of the spiritual heritage of Israel throughout the period of the judges. The fact that Israel has agreed—on the face of it—to put away their idols indicates that Samuel's reappearance at this strategic point in the narrative signals an end to the period of the judges more formally. However, we see more clearly than ever perhaps that it also signals a beginning to the judgment of the king in chapter 8. Perhaps Samuel the king-maker views himself as Israel's first regent and that is why he feels so badly about the idea of the monarchy. We will have to watch Samuel stumble and bumble his way through the next sixteen chapters or so before we can come to a definitive conclusion, but this has not begun as well as it looks.

Is Samuel a ne'er-do-well? Certainly not. He knows that he is to officiate in matters pertaining to the reunification of the federation at strategic points. He does that by functioning as the leader at the most central shrine in the country. Here, he offers sacrifice and guides them in prayer and fasting. He also does this by speaking to a large group of people whenever possible, exhorting them to do the right thing. Finally, he is engaged in and has apparently been so disposed to perform his function as teacher, legal advisor, and judge in a circuit throughout the highlands. His is a leadership of renown; as a prophet, his is a leadership of the power of the clairvoyant; his is the influence of cases well decided and lessons well taught. But he has become and now is also the imperious end to the charismatic leadership given in the period of the judges.

## The Threefold Notation of Mizpah

Places take on a life of their own in biblical narrative. Mitzpah is no exception. Where Israel is at the time Samuel preaches to them the gospel of repentance from polytheism is unknown. However, Samuel's desire is for the people to adopt a resolute monotheism and apparently, for the first time, they do so. The people mourn after the Lord (1 Samuel 7:2), and then after the demand for repentance and the adoption of Yahwistic monotheism, the people "removed the Baals and the Ashtaroth and served the LORD alone" (1 Samuel 7:4). Then Samuel told them to "Gather all Israel to Mizpah" for the purpose of prayer (v. 5). Apparently there was a cult site at that place, as was the case with the site at his hometown of Ramah (v. 17), and they would offer sacrifice and seek the Lord there.

First, they are ordered to gather to Mizpah (v. 5). Then we are told that they "were gathered to Mizpah" for various ceremonies (v. 6). And then we are told that this is the national "gathering themselves together at Mizpah" that inspires the aggression of the Philistine warlords (v. 7). This threefold introduction of the site prepares us for the central role the town will have in the revelation of the power of God and the subsequent deployment of the armies of Israel against the Philistines (v. 11). When the list of towns included on the highland circuit of Samuel's itinerant ministry is given (v. 16), we expect it to be named along with sites of prominence such as Samuel's hometown of Ramah. The city of Ramah is where the next events occur. But Mizpah features as the memorial of the deployment before the rout ensuing in the memorial and monument of Ebenezer.

## Samuel's Itinerant Ministry

Much has been said about Samuel's ministry already. He was presented as a boy, both to Eli the high priest and to the Lord. He apparently had something of an unusual meeting with God as a boy. Although he had not known the Lord previously (1 Samuel 3:7), he came to know the Lord in a very intimate way (1 Samuel 3:21). He had a flawless record as a prophet (1 Samuel 3:19), which would have been required according to the clear stipulations in the Law (e.g., Deuteronomy 18:20-22). He has abandoned the text for three chapters; but apparently he has not abandoned either his people or his ministry. We are told that "Samuel judged Israel all the days of his life" (1 Samuel 7:15) and then we are told of the parameters of his circuit court ministry (vv. 16-17). We know from later on that he offers sacrifice for the people (e.g., 1 Samuel 7:6, 9) and that he will be engaged in the ministry of prayer for the people and educating them (1 Samuel 12:23).

By the time we reach him in chapters 8 and 12, we find him an old man. That he is an old man with a history is commented upon by the narrator (1 Samuel 8:1-3), the elders of Israel (v. 5), and by Samuel himself (1 Samuel 12:1-3). When he attempts to clear himself of responsibility for hypothetical crimes against the people, he will name some of the same sins of which his sons are guilty. Fascinating! He did a remarkable job in respect to getting the nation temporarily back on track; and yet, he did a rather abysmal job with respect to his own family. There is probably a lesson there for all of us: Leadership is in all ways taxing; we need to be extra careful and expend extra time and energy with respect to our family. Whether or not the direction taken by our families disqualifies us from ministry or even undermines our authority as leaders, such faults, lapses, and family problems will be perceived as being detrimental. Like Israel of old, people may even ask for a regime change.

## Textual Problems

Just a brief note: I feel something of a moral obligation to document whenever I feel that the chapter breaks are wrong. Using even the most bland definitions of textual linguistics, there is absolutely no reason to break the text at verse 1. The text continues with the same preterite (simple past tense) sequence that it had in 1 Samuel 6:21. The text breaks more naturally at verse 2 with the usage of the preterite from the "to be" verb. This appears to be more often a break point at the paragraph, episode, chapter, and discourse initial points of the text. I view it as nearly equivalent to the discourse initial perfect in narrative.

## Textual Applications and Anecdotes

1 Samuel 7

vs.

1.  Sometimes the best place for relics is out of the way places.
    A spurious priesthood becomes the nation's antiquarians.
    Sanctification of a spurious priesthood means nothing to God.
2.  When the artifacts are quarantined, the religionists mourn.
    When the religionists mourn after their relics, the people of the land mourn after God.
3.  Mourning after God should include divesting oneself of all his or her accumulated pseudo-gods.
    Singular devotion to God most probably includes deliverance from enemies.
4.  Removal of all the other pseudo-gods is indicative of their worthlessness.
5.  There are times of corporate, national prayer.
6.  Corporate, national prayer includes corporate, national repentance.
    Times of intense prayer may include fasting—though not necessarily so.
7.  A national gathering gives the nation's enemies a national target.
    The knowledge that the national gathering is a national target provokes national fear.
8.  In the trepidation of a repentant nation there is the recognition that only God will suffice for deliverance.
    Sometimes we sense that there are the prayers of particular persons that are efficacious.
9.  Devotion, sincerity, and unusual sacrifice seem to go together.
    Some people get "yes" answers to their prayers.
10. The Lord has reserved the tempest for the day of battle (Job 38:22-23).
    Storms confuse the armies of the enemy.
11. If we sense that God is on our side, the tempests do not confuse us.
12. Great victory? Great monument or great memorial!
13. A major tactical victory can, in the right circumstances, become a major strategic victory.
14. Dual ownership of cities is evidence of a power pendulum.
    Victory in war can be a path to peace—unfortunately, because of human nature, it is all too short-lived.
15. There are those who serve for life—and there are those who live to serve.

16.  In the mention of the tour of duty is the tacit admission of the fact that someone is not caring for the home front.
17.  In the mention of the tour of duty is the tacit, wistful admission of the desire to be home.
18.  Home is where the heart is.
     Home is where the altar is.
     Home can be where the unnamed wife is.
     Home can be where the unruly children are.

## Conclusion

Samuel is back in the text after a long break. He has been on the scene all the way along. However, and as we shall see in the coming chapter, Samuel has been doing the work—prayer, sacrifice, inquiring of the Lord, administration of justice and teaching—but has been unable to keep some things in line with his boys. This was the legacy of Eli before him and will be the legacy of David after him. However, for a man to stand in the gap as Samuel has done and to aid the nation out of its period of the dark ages, Samuel will stand as a beacon to future generations. In any case, the next chapter will prove that no matter how good a job you do, things can go wrong and you will grow old. Samuel will begin to be replaced in his high office in the next chapter by a younger man, more commanding in appearance, selected by God to occupy the position of supreme leader or king. We will have to see how the elderly Samuel will take the change in the status quo.

# 1 Samuel 8
## The *Mishpat Hammelech* (The Custom of the King)
## Samuel Explains Political Despotism to Israel

—ᴍ—

## Introduction

In what has to be one of the most revealing of texts with respect to the state of the people of ancient Israel, Samuel is subjected to perhaps the most humiliating adventure of his life. First, the narrator will tell us that, for whatever reason, Samuel's sons were guilty of white-collar crimes against the state and cult. Then the in-group leadership (elders) will remind Samuel of this fact and will demand another form of government. Because he is hesitant to comply, he must address the issue to God directly—He will confirm their wish, but not for their reason. Samuel must then obey God and comply with a request that he suspects is doomed to failure. Throughout the process, Samuel may be accused of dragging his feet—that assessment is open to certain criticisms. Be that as it may, Samuel will tell the people what it is going to be like under the leadership of a king and then send them home. Let us begin with a few observations.

## Textual Observations

## Intertextuality

It is my opinion that a correct understanding of the "custom of the king" in particular and the deuteronomistic history in general requires an understanding of the rules laid out for us in Deuteronomy 17. That will be supplied here:

When you enter the land which the LORD your God gives you, and you possess it and live in it, and you say, '*I will set a king over me like all the nations* who are around me,' you shall surely set a king over you *whom the LORD your God chooses, one from among your countrymen* you shall set as king over yourselves; you may not put a foreigner over yourselves who is not your countryman. Moreover, *he shall not multiply horses* for himself, *nor shall he cause the people to return to Egypt to multiply horses*, since the LORD has said to you, 'You shall never again return that way.' *Neither shall he multiply wives for himself*, lest his heart turn away; *nor shall he greatly increase silver and gold for himself*. Now it shall come about when he sits on the throne of his kingdom, *he shall write for himself a copy of this law* on a scroll in the presence of the Levitical priests. And it shall be with him, and *he shall read it all the days of his life*, that he may learn to fear the LORD his God, by carefully observing all the words of this law and these statutes, that *his heart may not be lifted up above his countrymen and that he may not turn aside from the commandment, to the right or the left*; in order that he and his sons may continue long in his kingdom in the midst of Israel

Deuteronomy 17:14-20,<br>NASB; emphasis added

The first point is that it will happen; Samuel is wrong on these grounds to challenge it. The problem on Israel's side is that they want a king for the wrong reason (to lead in battle) and the wrong kind (like the nations have). In effect, they get what they want—and what they deserve! They get a king like all the nations around them and they get one like Saul.

The second point is that the king must be chosen by God from among their countrymen. This is not like California where an immigrant might be the governor/viceroy. That being done, the nation state is off to a good start. However, there is a series of prohibitions that come to the fore here.

The third point and the first prohibition is that the king is not to multiply horses for himself. As is the case today, horses were a symbol of power and wealth. Unlike today, horses were a strategic force deployed in offensive wars (less so in defensive battles, where the home field advantage might include very broken terrain and guerrilla warfare rather than pitched open-field battles involving chariots and cavalry). By way of illustration: Solomon is clearly guilty of an infraction on this because he not only multiplied horses, he drew them out of Egypt to sell to the Syrians (1 Kings 10:26-29). David, by contrast, went to the other and rather cruel extreme: he hamstrung most of the horses so that they could not be used in warfare—by either side (2 Sam. 8:4). It would seem that a happy medium might be to keep the horses without breeding them or to let them run free on the range in the Golan—or even sell them to diffuse buyers.

The fourth point and second prohibition is that the king was not to multiply wives for himself. David's numerical addition is suspect; but all bets are off with Solomon and his 700 wives and 300 concubines (1 Kings 11:3). And in fact, Solomon proves the point of the rule of the monarchy in Deuteronomy 17: "For it came about when Solomon was [or grew] old, his wives turned his heart away after other gods; and his heart was not wholly devoted to the LORD his God, as the heart of David his father had been" (v. 4).

The fifth point and third prohibition is that the king was not to multiply silver and gold for himself. Saul and David had little problem with this seemingly, for different reasons: Saul could never amass enough wealth, apparently due to constant warfare in which the outcome was always in question. David seems to have had interest in different things of a more or less tangible nature: houses and women. Solomon, again, is proof of the wisdom of the injunctions in Deuteronomy 17. Although even here, he cannot be proven to be literally guilty: "Now the weight of gold which came in to Solomon in one year was 666 talents of gold" (1 Kings 10:14). "None was of silver; it was not considered valuable in the days of Solomon" (v. 21).

The sixth point presupposes, perhaps, a kinesthetic learner: he is to write for himself a copy of the law. There is the attendant set of checks and balances, that the Levitical priest was to be there to maintain quality control. The temptation would have been to add cases and illustrations and to leave out particularly tedious and threatening material. I once read a feature article on a mosque that housed a copy of the Qu'ran written in the blood of Saddam Husein. I doubt that he wrote it himself, since he only acted on some matters of it. The point is that one will have one more chance to learn as they pour over writing it. I often tell my Hebrew students at the beginning of the year that the choice is theirs: they can buy the flashcards for their vocabulary exercises or they can write their own; but I firmly believe that some learners will short-circuit the learning process if they do not go through the motions of creating their own cards. But the point is to be conversant in it. He was to read it (the word *qārā'* being "to call out" or with preposition *b<sup>e</sup>* to read—perhaps, out loud). The idea was to read it, perhaps for all at court to hear and to know it well. The design was to avoid a couple of major pitfalls to leadership in general and monarchical government in particular: that he might not become arrogant, think himself intrinsically superior to his countrymen, and that he might not deviate from the statutes as written in the law. The writing of the law seems somewhat haphazard to us perhaps; but it is the charter and constitution for the theocracy of Israel. Any king worthy of the title and desirous of keeping the position had better stand respectfully before it.

## Turning Aside to the Right or to the Left

This idiom is of interest due to how it appears in the remainder of the Samuel Narratives. Israel is told not to turn aside either to the right or the left. It is an idiom that is common in respect to biblical literature as a whole. Let us merely look at the idiom at the covers of the Samuel the king-maker narrative. First, we are told that Samuel's sons "did not walk in his ways, but *turned aside* after dishonest gain and took bribes and perverted justice" (1 Samuel 8:3). This is the occasion—not the cause—of Samuel having a king demanded of him. This is the front cover of the narrative and sets the tone for its usage throughout the Samuel Narratives.

At the end of the king-maker narrative, Israel is told by Samuel "do not turn aside from following the LORD, but serve the LORD with all your heart. And you must not turn aside for then you would go after futile things which can not profit or deliver, because they are futile . . . if you still do wickedly, both you and your king shall be swept away" (1 Samuel

8:20-21, 25). There are, of course, several voices here: one is the voice of Samuel offering a warning to the people of Israel. The other voice is the voice of the narrator who at once indicts Samuel's sons as paradigmatic of the nation's sins as a whole and hints that such a destruction may, in fact, be inevitable in the words "shall be swept away." Historical hindsight is 20/20 and we have the luxury of seeing over the centuries. Like armchair prognosticators we see that Israel's collapse was inevitable as would be the case with any human governmental system. Yet, was it necessarily so from Samuel's perspective? Perhaps the negative spin he puts on it indicates that the fall was inevitable from his prophetic perspective as well. Perhaps.

Does this necessitate the postulation of a single author, a Deuteronomist, writing on the eve of the destruction of Jerusalem and the temple, or from Babylon, or after the exile in the sixth or fifth centuries BC? No, I do not think so. The Jews always called them the "Former prophets" and *vaticinium ex eventu* (prophecy after the fact or pious historical retrojection) was the invention of a much later, more anti-supernaturalistic and cynical age. But it does require us to think that people who read and knew Deuteronomy well were responsible to both pass the tradition on to us as they received it and indicate where they were successes and failures at their point in history. How they did that is the subject of our inquiry.

## The Custom of the King

This is the diatribe that Samuel concocts for Israel; a casual glance will indicate that it is not so far from the mark—neither is it incoherent when read next to Deuteronomy 17.

> This will be the procedure of the king who will reign over you: he will take your sons and place *them* for himself in his *chariots* and among his *horsemen* and they will run before his *chariots*. And he will appoint for himself commanders of thousands and of fifties, and *some* to *do his plowing and to reap his harvest and to make his weapons of war and equipment for his chariots.* He will also *take your daughters* for perfumers and cooks and bakers. And he will *take the best of your fields and your vineyards and your olive groves, and give them to his servants.* And *he will take a tenth* of your seed and of your vineyards, and give to his officers and to his servants. *He will also take* your male servants and *your female servants* and your best young men and your donkeys, and use *them* for his work. *He will take a tenth* of your flocks, and *you yourselves will become his servants.* Then *you will cry out in that day* because of your king whom you have chosen for yourselves, but the LORD will not answer you in that day.
>
> 1 Samuel 8:11-18, NASB;
> emphasis added

When it all goes badly, even when it all goes according to the law of the monarch (Deut. 17), the people will be exasperated with the form of government they have chosen. Even were we to have the perfect system and the perfect environment, it would not go well apart from perfect subjects of a perfect monarch. Not much has changed. We live in an imperfect world, with imperfect people subject to imperfect statutes written by imperfect statesmen and effected by imperfect executors over imperfect populations. The only variable is time as to when inertia finally kicks in and the system collapses to chaos. Socrates was right, democracy collapses to chaos and then a despot substitutes order. What he was wrong about is that so do all forms of government, including his beloved benevolent oligarchy. It will only be perfect when Messiah comes to rule over a perfect kingdom—even then, there will be rebellion simmering in the hearts of some of the subjects. When the perfect benevolent monarch and the perfect rule are combined with perfect subjects and the perfect environment, only then will government be perfect—characterized by both peace and justice.

## Textual Applications and Anecdotes

1 Samuel 8
vs.
1. Sometimes old men do not make the wisest of appointments.
   Sometimes the nepotistic appointments of old men prove to be unwise.
2. Unjust judges: names that will live in infamy.
3. Corruption, bribery, and distortion of justice render the judge fit for the halls of infamy.
4. Unjust judges will become known.
   Unjust judges will be reported.
5. Old men can be held accountable for sons who do not follow their ways.
   Old leaders can be requested to change the rules when sons do not follow in their ways.
   Wanting the same kind of a government as other heathen nations is wrong headed— and hearted!
6. Old leaders will be resistant to change.
   Old leaders should pray about change in any case.
7. Rejection of a leader's leadership may actually entail a rejection of God's leadership.
8. If there is a history of rebellion and the rejection of God's leadership, we should expect more of the same.
9. Change? Fine! One form of human government is as bad as another; but the leader shares the responsibility to inform the people of the weaknesses of a particular form of government.

10. Monarchy was in God's program from its inception (Deuteronomy 17).
    However, what kind of a king are we looking for?

11. Government abrogates the rights of the individual in place of the corporate body.
    Government will conscript young men for the military.

12. Government will train officers for the military.
    Government will conscript people to take care of its own food production.
    Government will manufacture weapons for the military.

13. Government will provide services for itself that may be extravagant in the estimation of the people (e.g., perfumers).
    Government will provide goods and services for itself at the expense of the constituency.

14. Because of its economic power, government will be able to provide itself with the best of
    arable land and the best people to tend it.

15. Taxation of a tenth was considered exorbitant in Samuel's day.
    Any taxation beyond a ten percent flat rate income tax should be considered exorbitant.

16. Government can and will use its right to conscription and government employment—in some cases at the expense of the family who donated the persons.
    Government thinks nothing of double indemnity; hence checks and balances are necessary.

17. Ten percent taxation is only the beginning when government takes you as its servant.

18. Watch out what you want (especially in terms of regime change); you may get what you asked for.
    If you want a government to act in place of God, watch out, it may just do that.
    If you want a government to act in place of God, He will allow you to reap the harvest you have sown in rejecting Him.

19. Resolute request for regime change will be answered.

20. Watch out for those who want to be "like all the nations."
    Watch out for those who want leaders to be judges and military commanders—keep the offices separate.

21. The godly leader will rehearse the words of his constituency in the hearing of the Lord.

22. The godly leader will obey the Lord even when it is not in his own best interest.
    The godly leader will obey the Lord even when it hurts.
    The godly leader will obey the Lord even when he does not understand the reason.
    The godly leader will obey the Lord instantly.

**Conclusion**

Samuel has now delivered his address on the custom of the king. There will be something of a reprise given in chapter 12. When we arrive there we will see that Samuel, a seer who is sometimes surprised by the future, will think that he has accomplished the will of the people and obeyed the command of God. Things will not go as smoothly as he thinks they will. Now we proceed to acquire the king. That appointment will be more of a surprise to Samuel than it should be to us because of how chapter 9 begins. We see that at major junctures in the so-called deuteronomistic narrative, we begin with, "Now there was a man" That is how we begin chapter 9 and how we will be introduced to the king. Samuel is only told that at "about this time tomorrow I will send you a man from the land of Benjamin, and you shall anoint him to be prince over My people Israel. . ." (1 Samuel 9:16). That text provides a fascinating rollercoaster ride, replete with surprise. We will have to wait and see how it is that the seer regains his sight.

# 1 Samuel 9 (and 10)
## The Quest for the King
## The Threefold Introduction of Saul

## Introduction

How are you on leadership issues? One of the best lessons we can learn is that, among other things, leaders are human beings as well. Too bad, too! Sometimes we take our focus off Christ and elevate them to the point of heroes. Bad idea! We are planning for disappointment and failure when we do that. It really does not matter if we talk about Disraeli or Jim Bakker. To a greater or lesser degree we all have the abilities to be both king and king-maker and to share in Humpty-Dumpty's great fall! In 1 Samuel chapters 9 and 10 we have a point-counter-point, a narrative with its dynamic tensions between characters. We have a narrative universe with its power struggles, pathos, and ideals that gives us something of a window into leadership issues.[29]

## Reading from "Saul: A Life Suspended in Doubt"[30]

As I lie here and agonize over my life, I wonder how it all came to be this way. I was always the "dark horse." After the civil war with the rest of the tribes of Israel, our people, Benjamin were never a numerous people. My family was not really all that significant among our people. I guess we were never more than one of the least of the surviving six hundred. Rumor had it that my grandfather kidnapped a wife for himself at a festival. I guess, despite what I looked like, being the youngest son, I never had the respect of my family, much less my people.

My earliest memories of the events that culminated in today are enshrouded in the paradoxical. I was wandering around looking for my father's donkeys. I had taken one of the brighter of the family servants. It seemed that we covered half the land of Israel when we decided to head back for home. My servant indicated that we ought to talk to the seer and see if he could give us some help locating the donkeys. We had nothing for a gift except a few cents in silver. We decided that the worst that could happen was a laugh or a rebuke. It was in this context that I was to meet the prophet, Samuel. What a blow hot, blow cold relationship! If I had it to do over again, I would handle this one with a bit more delicacy. In any case, by the end of it all and through some bizarre selection process of which I know nothing of the details, I was anointed king of God's people Israel and embraced by the prophet of God. Be assured, when I got home, I told no one of these things! I have never been so confused in all my life. The prophet had told me that at least two signs would come to pass on my way home and they did. The most alarming was when I rather lost control of myself for a while in the company of the prophets. I still have no idea what happened there. The memoirs of Samuel himself say that I was changed into another man. Something certainly happened to the more retiring side of me. I am by nature a shy person. I now recall that at some meeting or another, or so my father told me, the people of Israel had asked for a king since Samuel's sons had gone the way of Eli's sons into corruption. If only the people could have waited another 40 years! (1 Samuel 9, 10)

## Textual Observations

### Verbal Focus

Several of the themes and ideas that are initiated here will be developed throughout both volumes and I am generally thankful to Meir Sternberg and Robert Alter for their exposure. Some of these themes have to do with vision, including the seer and the prophet. Others utilize the verbs hear, see, and what you might see should you look at something or somebody. There is also the emphasis on that which is good. Some people are noted for their good looks and perhaps their stature. We might cite, initially, such examples as Saul, David, and Absalom, who will be singled out not only for their appearance but for the calamities that later befall them.

### Textual Structure

In his commentary, Robert Bergen has illustrated some thematic replications that occur at the level of the text. A reproduction of his chart follows.[31]

| Saul informed of donkeys' return (9:20) | Saul informed of donkeys' return (10:2, 9) |
|---|---|
| Saul receives the food of sacrifices (9:24) | Saul receives the food of sacrifices (10:4, 9) |
| Saul receives the holy anointing in the presence of a prophet (10:1) | Saul receives the Sprit of the LORD in the presence of prophets (10:6, 10) |

In this we can see that there are repetitions of ideas both theological and mundane that appear in such configurations as to indicate not only narrative artistry, but are also indicative of the texture of the text itself.

## Dialogues

Robert Polzin indicates some ambiguity expressed, not only in the words themselves, but at the level of syntax.[32] He indicates that four of the dialogues, each of which begin with a question, become progressively more prophetic/revelatory. Each is answered below:

Saul with his servant: "perhaps."
Saul and Servant with water-drawing maidens: "you will."

The LORD and Samuel: "tomorrow at this time."
The question ("Is this the man?") is implicit in "answered" (v. 17).

Samuel with Saul (more antecedent revelation): "Today you will eat with me."

And so we see that there is more information and more certitude in each dialogue.

Additionally, I have noted that although God finally calls the office "Make king a king" (8:22), God never calls him "king" in this section of the narrative. God calls Himself the kingly ruler *mimmeloch*. He is called ("declared," *nagad* by narrator and speakers elsewhere) "prince" (*nāgîd*) and it is said that he will "*rule*" (no word there) "over" the people and "deliver" (*hôshîa'*) God's people. The people demand that a king *melech* be appointed for them, given to them, and just plain "be" over them. In fact, God even tells Samuel that Saul is the man who will constrain/restrain *'atsar* His people (9:17). Most translations have some word for "rule" in the text at 9:17.

We might also note that finally, the LORD tells Samuel—adopting the people's language—"you shall make king for them a king." Notice that at the beginning of chapter 10, Samuel's conversion is not so complete: "Is it not that the LORD has anointed you over his inheritance as a ruler?" First, the "declaration" is a question—just like Saul! Second, he is called *nagid* instead of *melech*.

An additional observation is that causal clauses abound in the water girls' explanation to Saul and servant. There is so much explanatory material that the girls seem to be falling all over themselves. They say, "because he has come . . . because the people have a sacrifice . . . because the people will not eat until he comes, because he must bless the sacrifice . . . because you will find him at once" (1 Samuel 9:12-13). As with servants throughout the Samuel Narratives and biblical literature in general, their material is not only superabundant, they prove to be perfectly accurate in their assessments of reality.

Samuel is called "man of God," "seer," and "prophet" but never "Samuel" until verse 14. Why the delay if he is to be seen in the best light? For three chapters he was not mentioned; then he has this diatribe *mishpat hammelch* and then silence for fourteen verses. This is similar to the manner in which David is introduced in chapter 16. He is brought in with pronouns from the sheepfold and anointed by Samuel and then the Spirit of the Lord comes upon "David." As in that reference, this is hardly some sloppy cut-and-paste action of a crude redactor. It is narrative art that reintroduces a character for dramatic effect.

What is this dynamic tension between the *mishpat hammelech* and the *mishpat hannabi'*? That is, might we infer that there is some tension between *the custom of the king* and *the custom of the prophet*? We are never really certain that Samuel is a hundred percent behind God's acquiescence to Israel's demand for a king. We are never really certain that he knows exactly what is entailed in the custom of the king. We are never really certain that he backs the first monarch of Israel until, after being deposed by God, he mourns over Saul (1 Samuel 15:35-16:1). Perhaps by that point Samuel had poured so much emotional energy into Saul that he was grieved as much over his own wasted efforts as he was in the failure of the first king of Israel.

After chapter 8, there are certainly more questions than answers. After the *mishpat hammelech* of chapter 8, we see that Samuel sent everybody home (v. 22). Why is there this delay if the people's decision is to be seen in a positive light? In view of this delay, can Samuel be seen in the best possible light? God commanded him to appoint (make a king—e.g., the king-maker) a king for the people. And yet he immediately sends them home—no public declaration here!

**Textual Applications and Anecdotes**

1 Samuel 9
vs.

1. It is a good idea to know who you're talking about.
2. In biblical narrative, initial statements of beauty are portents of impending disaster.
3. With respect to this story, one often asks: "Will the real [jackass] donkey please bray?"
4. It is no mystery that we search a wilderness of unknown one-horse towns for lost jackasses.
5. Family realities may be of greater concern than lost possessions.
   Predictive discourse is not necessarily prophetic discourse.
6. A real "man of God" has a high level of correspondence between what he says and what happens.
7. Real leadership does not necessarily respond to every answer with a question.

Protocol can be very important at times.

8.    I doubt that the man of God is much interested in "chump change."

A shekel was about 11.5 grams of silver so—< 3 grams—not much (Archer, ZPEB).

9.    Historical context matters.

It is a good idea to know not only what you are talking about but when.

10.    Good idea? Proceed!

11.    In biblical literature, often the best information comes from Mr. or Ms. Anonymous.

Check your communication sources: women at the wells of life know an awful lot.

12.    Good information? Good procedure!

13.    If you've got good advice, don't be ashamed to encourage people to take it.

14.    What you're really looking for is always in the last place you look.

15.    In biblical narrative, antecedent action tells you things at the thematic level.

In biblical narrative, God is in session and revelation is afoot.

16.    Don't be surprised if revelation is a bit unconventional (from the tribe of Benjamin?!).

God is not in the business of accommodating our sensitivities (reversal of primogeniture, beauty, size and skill) but of accomplishing His will.

17.    When even the prophet is clueless and the seer blind, God "answers."

18.    Meet the prophet and walk directly into your destiny.

19.    A true prophet can tell all that is in the mind.

20.    Put donkeys in one hand and the kingdom in the other and who weighs the most.

21.    Some things that are seemingly insignificant don't initially make much sense on a grand scale.

22.    Being a servant of the big guy (king elect) may get you a front row seat.

23.    Being the big guy gets you the best eats.

24.    Being the big guy often brings about confusion as to who is really important.

25.    Closed-door meetings happen.

26.    There is a time to go back home.

27.    Privacy is important.

## Conclusion

(See conclusion to chapter 10 below.)

# 1 Samuel 10 (And 9)
# More Introductions to Saul

—ɯ—

**Introduction**

(See introduction to chapter 9 above.)

**Reading from "Saul: A Life Suspended in Doubt"**

Anyway, a little later on, Samuel called all Israel together at a particular place. Because I was the youngest, I was pretty much assigned the task of watching our family's possessions. I was a little on the large side to tangle with for a single thief, so our things were pretty safe. What I didn't realize was that this Samuel the prophet had called all Israel together to give them a king. Samuel, the Kingmaker! The really alarming thing—the thing that I had almost forgotten and really wanted to forget was that I was the object of his, and subsequently everybody else's attentions! When a group of men came to collect me from the baggage depot, I first thought that they were a bunch of robbers and adopted a defensive posture. However, I quickly came to recognize that they were respected leaders and military officers—that I'd only seen from a distance before—that had come to get me to present me to the nation. What a head rush! Despite my natural slouch, my stature was at least 8 inches above the tallest of them. There was no place to hide. Samuel went through some ritual and read something to the people—what was it? I cannot remember—the "custom of the king" or something. I don't remember anything other than that I became something I wasn't before. All of a sudden, I had life and death authority over people whose names I didn't even know. Suddenly, I had gone from the youngest son of the smallest family in the least tribe—to king of all the families, clans, tribes, and nation of Israel. (1 Samuel 10)

## Textual Observations

### Revelatory Dialogues . . . Round Two

Polzin again notes how the dialogues betray the messages within the text in chapter 10. There are three such revelatory dialogues. These begin, oddly, with the string of prophecies indicating a future that has been heretofore rather opaque to the myopic prophet. In the conversation between Samuel and Saul, as it is continued in the first eight verses of chapter 10, we see that Saul is absolutely bombed with personal prophecies. We might note in passing that not every detail in their fulfillments is explicated by our Omniscient Narrator. That does not mean that it did not happen according to the overarching point of view; but it certainly opens the possibility that not everything that Samuel spoke was correct. It is a sometimes tedious point of narrative interpretation for us to remember that when the narrator tells the story or when the narrator inserts discourse from the mouth of God, understanding and truth are much closer together than when the fallible characters speak. With respect to Saul, no one doubts this; but when such a statement is made about the prophet, some people are incensed.

The second dialog is between Saul and his uncle in verses 14 through 16. Here, we see how easy it is to dance between the truth and the whole truth. Saul certainly declares to his uncle that which is independently verifiable, vis. the donkeys have been found. That is clearly true. However, he did not tell his uncle about the prophecy that he would become king. I cannot really blame him: one would run the prospect of either being part of a campaign for a kingdom or a laughingstock. I do not really like to put myself into the position of being mocked and in the present case it would be rather hard, before the fact, to independently verify Saul's claims. There is another possible illumination to such a glaring absence of Samuel's words as well—or darkness, as the case may be—and that has to do with Saul's temerity. Possibly this throws light on the next section where Saul is hiding by the baggage in the hope of escaping notice. Finally, it is also possible that Saul, despite the immediate fulfillment of so many of Samuel's short-term prophecies (vv. 2-8, did they all come true?), does not really believe that he will become king. It is a difficult call; but we can certainly guess at why he does not tell his uncle about the main prophecy.

The third dialog is one in which we see that Samuel is discussing the kingdom with the people in verses 18 through 24 as something of a reprise of the *mishpat hammelech*. In it, lots are drawn and we discover what we have known since 1 Samuel 9:1, that someone from the tribe of Benjamin will be taken. In what has been called the "seize the culprit" motif, Saul's draft number finally comes up and he is nowhere to be found. The last time this happened in biblical narrative was in the events surrounding the sin of Achan in the book of Joshua (7:16-26). At that place we see that the motif is not really something viewed as positive. Achan and his family have died for their transgression regarding the proscription of things taken from Jericho. One wonders if at this early stage in the story, the die is already cast for Saul *and his family*, as well.

Again, Samuel concludes his discourse and this scene with a question: "Do you see him whom the LORD has chosen, because there is no one like him among all the people?" Samuel is a slow convert to the monarchy program—in fact, it may be argued that he never comes on line until it is too late (15:35; 16:1). This sparks at least three questions: What was Samuel really grieving over? Was it Saul's failure or his own? Or was this grief merely masked anger with God? And so at the end of this chapter, we are left with many more questions than answers as we ponder Saul (*Shaul*) the great question mark of 1 Samuel.

## There Are Prophets and Then Again There Are Prophets

Polzin reminds us that Saul is absent at the roll call for Benjamin. He is not often called king but yet he is a prophet or is said to prophesy.[33] We might initially ask about a prophetic turf war. It is enough that Saul will now have the supreme civil office, removing the judge, Samuel, from his eminence. Now, it would appear that Saul runs the risk of stepping over the line in respect to the prophetic office. When he usurps the position of the priest, Samuel will find the situation intolerable. Another thing that may hint at trouble ahead has to do with the form of the verb used when Saul "prophesied." Although I will detail more of this when we come to it again in chapter 19, I will note here that the *hithpa'el* form of this verb often, if not usually, indicates "rave" elsewhere. Whatever the case, that is what he will be doing at the end of chapter 19.

## A Treasure Trove of Words—A Veritable Thesaurus

There are wordplays throughout biblical literature, none more striking than those in the Samuel Narratives. Also called paronomasia, it is "to call with a slight change of name." It is a play on words. It has the synonym "PUN" according to *Webster's Ninth Collegiate Dictionary*. Here are some we might examine.

We will recall that most of what Saul says in chapters 9 and 10 is interrogative. Indeed, for these two chapters, Polzin calls him "a traveling question mark."[34] If Saul (*Shaul*, "asked") is the great question mark of 1 Samuel, we might look at the answer or answers. The Hebrew word *'anah* is "to answer." Throughout, we will want to know, what question did the LORD answer? What questions did the players answer? Does Saul himself ever come to anything of a resolution as to his place as the great question?

One of the great puns alluded to above is the relationship between revelation and that which is revealed. The wordplay between the words "to declare" and "leader" (*nagad nagid*): *nagid* is used at 9:16, "you shall anoint him to be a prince [*nagid*] over my people." Again it is to be noted that God seems to have an aversion to calling the new leader, "king."

Following the standard word for declaration, Samuel says, "I will declare [*agid*] to you [Saul] all that is in your heart" (9:19). Despite the morphological problem of the *n* falling away in the incompleted action tense, professionals and first languages people will immediately see that some delightful expressions are herein used.

Another bit of wordplay we might examine has to do with the sounds *b-o* or *n-b-o*. They appear as *bo', nabi', nabo', yabi'u,* and *yabo'*. These can mean "come, go, enter" and "prophet," "we will go," "we will bring," or "he will go" respectively. Look at how this might be played out. At 1 Samuel 9:7, we might have either "What shall we bring to the man" or "What is a prophet to mankind" (9:7). A simple question becomes one of cosmic importance depending upon how the words are translated. Because of who the servant is (inerrant), we are tempted to take the more philosophical route. However, due to the nature of the situation, context drives us to the more simple reading.

Another is to look at some presumed words of the sons of Belial at the end of chapter 10. Perhaps they said *lo'-* or *ma-nabi'* and thought, "We will not bring" [him any gift] since he cannot save Israel or "[he is] no prophet" since he cannot be of the line of old charismatic military commanders.

Another repeated phrase that is used at the beginning of the episode is *wayhi 'ish* meaning, "Now there was a man. . . ." We have seen this at the episode initial position five times before. After the customary editorial beginning to a cycle in the book of the judges, "Now Israel again did evil. . . ," the Samson cycle begins with "Now there was a certain man from Zorah. . . ." Similar clauses to this reappear in Judges 17:1, 19:1, Ruth 1:1, 1 Samuel 1:1, and here at 1 Samuel 9:1. In view of the fact that Samuel passes historically from the scene in 1 Samuel 25:1, it is possible that this is a subliminal note of who is writing. I have a colleague who believes that Samson and Eli, at least, if not Samuel, were contemporaries.[35] Hence, it is not out of line to believe that Samuel was responsible for the final editing of the cycles and the addition of the two Dark Age episodes along with those matters that could have fallen within his purview. Other writers, before and after, do not usually begin stories in this way.

Because of Saul's status as the question mark of the Samuel Narratives, we might wonder what kind of anxieties rear their ugly heads in the story. Sometimes they show up as events, like worrying over donkeys, and so they use the word *da'ag*, "to be concerned," "anxious," worried; "to worry" as in 1 Samuel 9:5 and 10:2. Worry is indeed a multi-headed hydra and can rise to bite you in other ways. Another nuance of the word is adjectival and it can mean "concerned," "anxious," or "worried." Here is part of the English definition from *Webster's Ninth Collegiate Dictionary*: "to harass by tearing, biting, or snapping esp. at the throat (as in packs of wolves [we recall the episode in the Mowgli stories called "Red Dog" by Rudyard Kipling]) . . . to assail with rough or aggressive attack or treatment: torment . . . to afflict with mental distress or agitation: make anxious. . . ." And so it does not take a literary critic to point out that there is a little literary foreshadowing on the name of our least favorite assassin Doeg (*do'eg*) the Edomite, whose name would then mean "worried" or "worrying."

## Monarchy Doomed at the Outset?

One of the genetic questions pertaining to the Samuel Narratives that we will have to ask ourselves is whether or not this whole adventure of the quest for a king is a fool's errand. Is the monarchy wrongheaded? Is the monarchy merely poorly managed? Or, is the monarchy mis-timed? Should we have waited for David to be born and grow up; or are we doing the right thing at the right time with failing human beings to demonstrate what a good king might look like when David arrives? Such has been the conclusion of some conservative interpreters. However, Polzin notes that despite the fact that kingship is provided for (Deut. 17:14-20), "Saul, as Israel's first king, is singled out as a personification of kingship's sinfulness."[36] Because the monarchical experiment is provided for in Deuteronomy, and because I do not consider Torah as having been written late, it would seem that there is some reason behind the conservative interpretation. However, it would seem that Polzin's point is well taken—Saul, at the very least is doomed to failure because that is the way the narrator paints his portrait. However, we can wax Platonic (*The Republic*!) and assume the somewhat skeptical position that any human government is doomed to failure.

What I really think on this matter has more to do with Saul's fall being illustrative of "Jerry's Law of the First Offense." That is, in biblical narrative (e.g., Adam and Eve, Cain, Nadab and Abihu, Achan, Ananias, and Sapphira, etc.) there is a sense in which the perpetrator is singled out, not necessarily for cruel and unusual punishment, as much as sudden punishment. Whatever the case, it shows what God and the Omniscient Narrator think of the matter at issue. They are then held up as an infamous example for coming generations (e.g., Sodom and Gomorrah).

So what is manifest and what is opaque in regard to Saul's character? We do not see him in these early chapters doing much more than asking questions. He does not seem to know anything. Indeed, nobody seems to know anything except the servants (Saul's personal attendant and the water girls). So, other than his ignorance and the withholding of information to his uncle, what do we know of Saul's character? What does his hiding by the baggage during the roll call of Benjamin mean? Some have seen this as a sign of timidity. Some have seen it, as in the case of the withholding of information from his uncle, as a sign of shrewdness. Can we really be certain? Polzin says: "shrewdly or timidly we cannot tell."[37] It is God who the narrator reports as telling Samuel that "Behold, he is hiding himself by the baggage" (1 Samuel 10:22). Hence, we are led to believe, because of the word "hiding," that he is afraid of something. However, it could be merely a coy ploy by the monarch-elect to make something of a more grand exposure of the monarch-elect. Be that as it may, head and shoulders taller, Saul looks every inch a king,[38] as the people acknowledge; but, we do not learn until much later (1 Sam. 16:7) that, "God sees not as man sees, for man looks at the outward appearance, but the LORD looks at the heart." There is something that is not right about the man, and we are led to believe, early on, that it will go no better for this king than it did for the abortive monarch, Abimelech (Judges 9).

The "worthless ones" or "*sons* of Belial" (*bene-belial*) of 10:27 may also be seen as a verbal and conceptual tie to those of Eli in 2:12. The image is patent and loaded: Eli becomes, therefore, *belial!* Remember that this is the man who practically raised Samuel. Fatherhood will not get very good press in the Samuel Narratives. Another good argument for Samuel writing Judges 17 through 1 Samuel 24 or so is that Eli's sons and Saul's adversaries are called *bene-belial*; but despite the fact that the same general descriptions are given for both Eli's sons and Samuel's sons, these latter are never called *bene-belial*. That would rather indict the author—or at least one who might be viewed as the hero. Samuel, like Eli before him, would then become Belial.

Warnings and Disclaimers Dept: We see the actions of the players on the stage of scripture; we hear their public and private declarations; but access to their internal states is rare. Hence, we would do well to limit our psycho-linguistic assessments. Application is also more difficult in narrative, no?

## Textual Applications and Anecdotes

1 Samuel 10
vs.

1.   Sometimes questions are more powerful than declarations.
     Cultural conventions are sometimes a bit slippery.
2.   Tradition and history strike an uneasy balance (re: Rachel's tomb).
     Though it may be obvious by now, the prophet knows the worries of fathers.
3.   Pilgrims take gifts with them.
4.   Pilgrims tend to be generous.
5.   The faithful have always been musical . . . to some degree.
6.   When the Spirit of the LORD moves a person, he or she will be different.
7.   Within the prophet's imperatives there is the sense of freedom.
8.   Within the prophet's imperatives there is the sense of constraint.
9.   One tends to depart the true prophet differently from how one approached.
10.  Prophets of a feather prophesy together.
11.  When the Spirit of the LORD moves a person, it will be evident to bystanders.
12.  Momentous events tend to become slogans.
13.  Worship rightfully goes at the end of the prophecy.
14.  Watch for the question following the question.
15.  When the prophet speaks, people want to know.

16.     Often the elect will dance between the truth and the whole truth.
17.     When the prophet calls a meeting, it is best to be in attendance.
18.     Historical memory is short; refresh it often.
        A good historical memory may cover a multitude of transgressions.
19.     Bitterness turns the truth into a tirade.
20.     Watch out: when someone is taken by lot, a bad end is in store (Achan, Saul, Jonathan).
21.     When the lots are cast, be someplace else!
22.     If you hunt through enough baggage, you might just find a king.
23.     Big guy? Big fall!
24.     Questions and exclamations are not declarations! (Samuel's doubts and bitterness.)
        It is, however, an open question as to whether a live king or a dead one is the aim of Samuel.
25.     After the *mishpat hammelech* comes the *mishpat hannibi'* and finally the *mishpat hammelukah*. When warning is adequate, do your job faithfully and conclude with the constitution.
26.     God will surround the leader of His people—any leader with valiant men.
27.     There is no shortage of *bene-belial*, hold your tongue and pick your battles carefully.
        Those *bene-belial* plague the leadership of all generations and times (cf. 1 Sam. 2:12).
        Sometimes it is best just to be silent for now and act later.

## Conclusion

Remember that leaders are human and that in several senses of these words you will be both leaders and humans. Leaders come with their own individual idealism; yes, but they also come with their own limited abilities, attitudes, and tragic character flaws. We would do well to remember that when God chooses leaders—whether we are that leader or the channel through which God's selection is delegated—God chooses human beings. Perhaps we will be at once more understanding and more circumspect in our relationships with them.

# 1 Samuel 11
## Saul's Victory over the Ammonites
## Things Begin Well

—∿—

## Introduction

What with Samuel sending "all the people away, each one to his house" (1 Samuel 10:25), it would seem like a perfectly good place to begin a new chapter in the life of Saul. However, not before we introduce those ubiquitous "bad boys of the Bible" the *Bene-Belial*, the "worthless ones" in verse 27. They will live—surprisingly—to prove that the movement to make Saul king was nearly national—but not quite (see "Textual Problems" below). We have talked about these worthless ones elsewhere and so we need not elaborate on them here except to say that they are rude, crude, and out of step with the mainstream. They are everywhere leadership is and they intend to gain power for themselves. However, by the end of the story, we might wonder if they were not right in that "they despised him and did not bring him any present" (v. 27). Because, as we have said at the outset, all the indicators are that Saul is going to go down hard and go down for the count.

This chapter (1 Samuel 11) presents several positives in the life of Saul. As we shall see, things really did start out well and we might expect them to continue unless we read the signs given to us in the text. There is the report of atrocity; Saul responds quickly and passionately. He includes the king-maker (Samuel) in his designs and he extends clemency to his internal enemies—those *Bene-Belial* that will prove to be more right than wrong. Let us follow Saul in what began well.

## Reading from "Saul: A Life Suspended in Doubt"

Things really did start out well. There was a crisis in the eastern part of our country. The men of Jabesh Gilead reported that they were being harassed and threatened with partial blindness by the Ammonites. This was an old song, the first verse of which was sung even before the days of Jephthah. As with his days, there would be something of a harbinger of ominous things to come. My response, of which I'm somewhat embarrassed today, was nothing short of an emotional tirade. I cut up a yoke of oxen and sent the pieces around to the people of Israel. It was a threat; I'm not sure how much teeth I could put behind it. Time would tell. In any case, this was almost exactly what they had done when they nearly annihilated us many years before—except that the pieces sent to the tribes of Israel were the remains of a servant girl! Anyway, when all was said and done, we had amassed an army of about 330,000 men. Such forces had not been seen in Israel since the days of Joshua. We pretty well swept the Ammonites and then got together to celebrate. Because I had made one rather minor tactical decision and it had resulted in a rout of Ammon, there was an undercurrent of hostility toward those who had opposed me politically at the inception of my monarchy. Although I kept things very much in the back of my mind for later reference, in an act of uncommon latitude, I decided that there would be no executions that day. Whether or not I believed it at the time, the LORD had, in fact, given Israel the victory that day and brought liberation to the people of Jabesh Gilead. That relationship may play itself out on the stage of history soon. (1 Samuel 11)

## Textual Observations

### Beginning in the Middle—Again

Unless we admit some of the evidence rejected below in the "Textual Problems" section, we must first observe that there is no break between 1 Samuel 10 and 11 at the traditional point. The preterite verb presupposes a narrative dance in motion. We should not just arbitrarily cut in on a whim. I would maintain that this is all part of the "Rise and Fall of Saul" begun in the first verse of chapter 9 (with the same narrative formula as Judges 17:1; 19:1; Ruth 1:1; and 1 Samuel 1:1) and concluding at 15:35a or b. The history of interpretive thought does have several centuries of momentum on me though and so the present chapter breaks are probably with us to stay.

Speaking of the middle of things, let us briefly discuss the man, Samuel. With everything going so well, what role does Samuel play? Samuel has sent everybody home (10:25) and then has to do a quick boomerang to Gibeah because of Saul's bovine explosion. Because he does not speak until the end of the chapter (11:14) and the first verse of chapter 12, Samuel functions as little better than the hood ornament on an Iron Age Buick for this episode. That is, like Benjamin in the Joseph story (Genesis 37-50), Samuel is a human prop. Samuel's home is in Ramah, not Gibeah; although the distance is not great. I personally doubt that Saul conferred with Samuel before sending bovine bits around to the territory of Israel. This might make his edict seem somewhat presumptuous. He says, "Whoever does not come out after Saul and after Samuel, so shall it be done to his oxen" (1 Samuel 11:7). If Samuel does not know about this beforehand, it is presumption to include the great prophet of Israel and Israel's king-maker in this scheme. Apparently, Samuel silently goes along with it.

That he is there in the mix is indicated later on in verse 12. In drawing the *Bene-Belial* envelope to a close (1 Samuel 10:27; 11:12), the men of Israel say after the victory over the Ammonites, "Who is he that said, 'Shall Saul reign over us?' Bring the men, that we may put them to death." Again, this is directed to Samuel; but before the old prophet can get a word in edgewise, Saul butts in and speaks for him, "Not a man shall be put to death this day, for today the LORD has accomplished deliverance in Israel" (v. 13).[39] Things went well on this day and Samuel is apparently mollified with this statement. He is given the last word of the episode. Rather than contest Saul's public statements as he will do repeatedly in the next few chapters, Samuel sends everybody to Gilgal for kingdom renewal. After that, Samuel will make his second and final state of the monarchy address, but that is for the next chapter.

### Hacking Things to Pieces—Parcel Post and Show and Tell

What Saul has done here in hacking a yoke of oxen to pieces and sending them "throughout the territory of Israel" (1 Samuel 11:7) is not without historical precedent. In fact, this display of what we might call pathological emotion is very similar to that which decimated Saul's own tribe. In one of the earlier "Now there was a man" books (beginning in Judges 19:1), there was a concubine who was raped to death. This was considered so horrid that the man, her owner/husband cut her in twelve (why twelve and not eleven?) pieces and sent her around "throughout the territory of Israel" (19:29). This caused all Israel to gather together, in the same words, "as one man" (Judges 20:1; 1 Samuel 11:7). The result of the earlier display was that war was declared upon Benjamin and the evil purged from the midst of Israel.

In the second case, our present case, Israel gathered together to defeat a common enemy, the Ammonites, and deliver their relatives, the men of Jabesh-Gilead, from oppression. Messengers carried the oxen parts around with the threat that if their warriors were not sent to Saul, it would not go well with their own herds. The threat was graphic enough and most probably individualized enough—farms being separated enough from each other that each set of messengers confronted a rather small number of farmers at any given time—that each man felt compelled to come out. In retrospect, it is observed then that they all came out "as one man."

Apparently the image caught hold because later on Samuel will use Agag the Amalekite as a similar object lesson. Since all Israel's warriors are present, it is unnecessary to send the parts to the four winds. Israel apparently got the point—Saul may not have—that when God says to annihilate the enemy and put their goods under the ban, He means business. It must have been some show to see the old grizzled prophet become a berserker with respect to the Amalekite king. It was something you would not soon forget and something you would want to be certain to tell the family back home.

**Threefold Introductions Vs. Threefold Presentations:**
**Samuel, Saul and David: A Comparison of Participant Introduction**
**and Character Presentation in 1 Samuel**

Although I have discussed some of these matters before, one of the more interesting observations the reader can make is how a story is told in ancient Israel. Part of that has to do with the introductions of subjects and characters. It would appear that there are two levels of triplets. I am certain that both can be proven to be relevant to some literary category, but these will clearly be shown to be at different levels. My theory is that at the textual level there is a threefold introduction of the subject (person or perhaps place, e.g., threefold introduction of Gath and Rammah).[40] In addition and more at the story level, there will be a threefold introduction of the subject by way of formal presentation to various persons in the story. The chart below indicates some comparisons and notable contrasts between and within categories of participant introduction and the more global issue of character presentation at the thematic level.[41]

| | **Introduction** | **Presentation** |
| --- | --- | --- |
| **Samuel** | Baby | Presented to Eli |
| | Presented to Eli; Yahweh | Serving in the temple |
| | *Heirodule* (temple servant) | Effects of the battle |
| **Saul** | Donkey chaser | Anointed < prophet |
| | Meets prophet | Presentation -> Israel |
| | | Saul at the baggage counter |
| | Anointed -> prophet | Victorious over the Amalekites |
| **David** | Referred to (pronouns) | Anointed |
| | Present (described) | Servant at Saul's court |
| | Picked (anointed & named) | Warrior—victory over Goliath |

This, of course, shows similarities and differences, but the patterns are intriguing and demonstrate that the narrator understood that there is a way both to tell a story and a way to get across an overarching message. It introduces subjects as names into the discussion at the micro-level and introduces subjects as characters on the stage of the story at the macro-level.

At the story level in our current context, it is important because Saul has first been anointed by Samuel in 1 Samuel 10:1. Then secondly, Saul is divined amidst the baggage and presented to the nation in 10:20-24. Third and finally, Saul gets his own pride of position due to the military victory against the Ammonites and the deliverance of the kinsmen in Jabesh-Gilead.

## Why the Text Makes Sense as It Is

It seems that many people want to amend this text because of the confirmatory material of Josephus' old expansion of the introduction by the Qumran material. You can read the "Textual Problems" material below to explore that more thoroughly. Robert Polzin has an extended treatment on the matter and you may consult him.[42] However, I am not going to approach the issue that way. In the first place, as already indicated above, the story does not begin at verse 1. It began back in chapter 10 or earlier. The story makes perfectly good sense because of the fact that when things are done "Samuel sent all the people away, each one to his house" (1 Samuel 10:25).

Also, part of the issue involved here has to do with the deception of the monarchy, or the seduction of Israel. The nice bracketing effect of the *Bene-Belial* problem (10:27 and 11:12) is indicative of the fact that the seduction of Israel in respect to its monarchy has now become complete. We have the best of all possible worlds: we have a king who will defeat our enemies for us and yet shows clemency when the dissonance is not treasonous. Be that as it may, after the battle to liberate Jabesh-Gilead, Israel will be hopelessly entangled in her monarchy. Only the Babylonians will be able to cut that Gordian knot.

## The Alpha and Omega of Saul's Rectitude

Saul did several things well here and he should be congratulated for them. First, he did something about a problem. We might argue that his passion was a bit overwrought; we might argue that he was presumptuous in including Samuel in his schemes without first—to our knowledge—notifying him; but in the long and short of it, Saul gave credit for the victory to God. Like David after him, we might recoil from what could be just another public statement designed to make the new monarch look good, but we cannot know that with certainty from this side of the story. We must read on. Again, Saul showed clemency to his internal adversaries. Their offense was merely that they were skeptical of his abilities. That is hardly treason and Saul correctly lets it pass. Finally, Saul won this skirmish. He will live to lose some in the future. He will prove that he has no clue as to the faithfulness of his cabinet ministers. He will prove himself less than competent in matters religious, political, economic, civil, military, and interpersonal. However, for now, Saul shows himself to be the king for which Israel is looking. It will be a couple of disasters down the road before Bergen's dagger-under-the-fifth-rib quip will be true—that Israel indeed has "a king 'such as all the other nations have.'"[43] But we know it is coming.

## Textual Problems

## Long Introduction

There appears to be a manuscript tradition that indicates a rather extended end to chapter 10 or beginning to chapter 11. The material appears to be introductory to chapter 11 and so I will treat it as though it were. I will quote the translation used in the footnote *ad loc.* of the NLT:

> Nahash, king of the Ammonites, had been grievously oppressing the Gadites and Reubenites who lived east of the Jordan River. He gouged out the right eye of each of the Israelites living there, and he didn't allow anyone to come and rescue them. In fact, of all the Israelites east of the Jordan, there wasn't a single one whose right eye Nahash had not gouged out. But there were seven thousand men who had escaped from the Ammonites, and they had settled in Jabesh-gilead.

BHS (editions 1–5) makes no mention of this; however, it does show up in the commentaries and the JSB margin *ad loc.* takes it as a datum along with a statement from Josephus. It seems odd that no other tradition aside from Qumran contains it. To me, it almost looks like something the Habakkuk Pesher might do. In any case, I defer to Robert Bergen:

> The standard Hebrew text, and therefore all but the most recent of Bible versions, presents what is possibly an abridged version of the original account of Saul's encounter with the Ammonites. The Qumran manuscript 4QSam[a] as well as Josephus (*Ant.* 6. 5. 1.) add a short paragraph of information now found in several modern versions (10:27- 11a).[44]

At the inception of the discussion, it would be difficult to say whether one account is abridged (MT) and another complete (Q), or one complete (MT) and another embellished (Q). However, I think we will be hard pressed to determine a reason for the addition. As we shall see, the Vulgate shows independence at verse 8, and thus may be used as something more than a confirmation of the Septuagint. And so I have one strong voice (Qumran) and a weak voice (Josephus) against two strong voices (MT and LXX) and a weak voice (Vulgate, a little stronger in this case). There is no reason to amend the reading of the MT.
And so Bergen concludes:

> The information contained in this paragraph is irrelevant to the central purpose of the story and may introduce a chronological problem into the narrative flow

(cf. 10:8; 13:8-14). Especially in view of its omission from the standard Hebrew text, it may be safely ignored.[45]

At this point, I will have to agree with Bergen. It would appear that it is not only irrelevant to the central purpose and runs the risk of chronological/sequential problems, it may also inject material that is disruptive to the end of getting Saul from national acceptance to national success. Bergen references Gordon as the final voice of reason on the discussion:

> Cf. Gordon's useful discussion on the appropriateness of including this passage in modern versions. After surveying modern scholarly opinion, he concludes that "the wise course for the present . . . is to reserve judgement on the status of these additional lines in QSam[a]" (I and II Samuel, 64). Baldwin favors its inclusion in modern versions but notes that "it will not add substantially to the meaning of the text" (I and II Samuel, 96).[46]

Since, according to Baldwin, nothing of substance is gained if the text is inserted into our Bibles, nothing will be lost if we leave it out. Since that best represents the course taken by the broadest scope of the manuscript textual evidence, there is no harm in taking the text as it is and regarding Qumran and Josephus as *pesher* (commentary).

In conclusion, since it does not show up in the Septuagint or other versions and only in Qumran and Josephus (apparently), and since MT is both the shorter reading and the reading that best explains the other, I opt for the reading of the older Bibles. That is, following the ceremony with Saul, it became known that Nahash was harassing the people from Jabesh-Gilead. Bergen is right: the addition is disruptive to the narrative flow. The shorter reading moves Saul quickly from ignominy to his (one?) good deed for the people of Jabesh and the shadow cast beforehand of their part in his burial.

## Introductory Clause

The Septuagint has "And it came to pass after about a month." It is in the Qumran text and the old Latin. However, it is not in the Hebrew. It is starting to show up in modern translations (e.g., NLT) and notes (e.g., NLT). Because of the above discussion, it is tempting to ask: about a month after what? Are we talking about those who fled to Jabesh, or are we talking about the events surrounding Saul's public presentation as king of Israel? It makes sense either way. However, if the Qumran addition is chosen, the introductory clause becomes redundant. If not, the Septuagint addition makes sense; but it becomes an explanatory gloss. Since nothing is lost or gained either way, I recommend we stay with the shorter reading of the MT.

## Judah's Numbers: Representative or Representative of Dissent

At verse 8, the numbering of the tribe of Judah differs: it is thirty thousand in Hebrew; it is seventy thousand in Qumran text and the Septuagint. The Vulgate, rather independently reverts to the thirty thousand of the Hebrew. Mixed bag! Which to choose? This would be indicative of a choice made by Jerome in the fourth century. He must have known of both traditions and consciously chose the lower number. Apparently, he did not feel that the tradition represented by the Septuagint (and Qumran, if that were known) was something to be eschewed. Apart from the seemingly fantastic "600 thousand from Israel" of the Septuagint, it is a coin toss either way for the numbers of Judah. I defer:

> The LXX offers much higher counts: 600,000 for Israel and 70,000 for Judah; Josephus (*Ant.* 6. 5. 3.) suggests 700,000 for Israel. The text of 4QSamᵃ, though fragmentary, supports 70,000 for Judah. Nevertheless, these numbers probably are not the ones in the autographic text: well-meaning transcribers in antiquity probably corrupted the numbers.[47]

It would be difficult to know how or why, since the numbers are so different: 300K, 600K, 700K for Israel and 30K or 70K for Judah. There is really no reason for such confusion. There must have been a scribal error along the way that found its way into three living first-century traditions (that of Qumran, that of Josephus, and that ultimately adopted by Jerome).

What is lost and what is gained? As compared and contrasted with the two censuses in the book of Numbers, either count for Judah is disproportionately low. What could this mean? It might mean that the king never really had the backing of the south. The larger the count in the north and the smaller the count in the south, the more graphic the disparity. Judah will later only offer up ten thousand to the muster (as in Saul's half-hearted assault on the Amalekites in 1 Samuel 15:4). It would look as though Saul's popularity in the south is on the wane and that makes his thanks for the treachery of the Ziphites all the more shrill (1 Sam. 23:19-21; Ps. 54 superscription) since almost nobody down there liked him at that point.

## Textual Applications and Anecdotes

1 Samuel 11
vs.
1. Besieged? Best to consider your options. Sometimes terms of peace are better than slavery, mutilation, and annihilation!
2. A one-eyed society is a handicapped society.
   Negotiations can be painful.
   A big mouth makes a big mess.
3. Predicament? Send for help.
   If no help comes, accept your fate.
4. When one member of the family suffers, we all suffer.
   Sometimes emotional expression is cathartic.
5. Often the leadership is clueless.
   Often the leadership is in need of a briefing.
   Brief the leadership with some tact.
6. When the Spirit of God comes upon someone mightily and they get angry, we might want to ask some questions.
   The discussion of Saul and spirits is one fraught with difficulty.
   Whichever way we go, "The anger of a man does not accomplish the righteousness of God" (James 1:20).
7. Sometimes a rather graphic illustration will get the point across.
   Sometimes a rather graphic illustration, broadly disseminated, will get a universal response.
   Sometimes dropping a name (Samuel, in this case) along with graphics and marketing will help to gain the appropriate universal response.
8. Big numbers help us see disparity.
   Judah is disproportionately low.
   Disproportionately low numbers indicate any of several things: either the population had been decimated or there is a reason for disinterest.
   Disinterest evokes the question, Why?
9. Good news of deliverance comes on bad days: vis. you needed deliverance!
   Good news with timing provides opportunity for action—or retaliation.
10. If you are the bait, how well you set the trap is directly proportional to how much you smell like bait.
    Trap-spring delayed is trap-spring relished!
11. Wisdom or a shrewd maneuver will surround your adversaries.
    Adversaries should not be given quarter until there is "no two of them left together."

12.  Vengeful attitudes sprout on days of overwhelming victory.
     Watch what you say (10:27); it may be used as evidence against you.
13.  Public proclamations of clemency on a day of victory will be transparently wise to the shrewd ruler. It is capital banked for later.
     Victory? Blame God.
14.  Victory? We should talk about government and justice.
     Victory? We should talk about leadership and constituency.
15.  Victory? Acclaim the king!
     Victory? Celebrate God.
     Victory? Celebrate with your compadres.

## Conclusion

This was the great day in the life of Saul. We cannot know how long it took all Israel to gather 330 thousand strong. However, one cannot help sensing that Israel moved with some haste. With such overwhelming odds, a workable strategy and a well-baited trap, Saul could hardly help but win. With Samuel along for the ride—silently this time—Saul may have felt invincible. Saul will not live to have another day as successful as this one. Because of this, he rightly shows it as a time for clemency for internal adversaries and for acknowledging God as the One who gave a great deliverance in Israel. After Samuel's speech in chapter 12, things will spiral very quickly for Saul and that makes us ask a few questions. When Saul slaughtered the oxen, was that indicative of something that was not right in the man himself? When Saul presumptuously included the prophet Samuel in his scheme, was that something of a misunderstanding of the roles of the two men and the place of Israel's faith, religion, and God in the grand scheme of things? When Saul showed clemency to those who were less than enthusiastic about his place at the head of the monarchy, was Saul merely biding his time and using it as an excuse to watch people and their associations—to see how deep the treason really was? Was he really that smart? When Saul gave credit to God for the great deliverance (of the army? of Jabesh-Gilead? of Saul?), was it merely a public statement, opaque as to the real internal states of the monarch himself?

Because we know how all this is going to end, Saul will not be able to sustain such a scrutiny of his character. He will fall to such a cross examination; but it is a good lesson for us. When we forgive people, do we forgive them in earnest or do we merely use it as an opportunity to bank capital for later? When we make loud acclamation of God's greatness, are we doing so to be noticed by the political, religious, and economic notables, or are such sentiments true reflections of our internal states? When we publicly include others in our schemes, are we certain that they would be included, or are we being presumptuous? Have we had the courage and courtesy to consult with them first? Even if it ends well, the end does not justify the means; such presumption could merely be manipulations masked.

Finally, when we fly off the handle—even if it ends well and great things are accomplished—does the end justify the means? Could it be that this shows something deeply flawed in our character? Could it be that the same mission might be accomplished without the rage? I think so.

# 1 Samuel 12
## Samuel's Warning
## The King's Confirmation

—⁓—

## Introduction

After such a howling victory for the Israelites—and perhaps a stunning reversal of expectations for the aging prophet, Samuel—it might seem unusual to have a chapter entirely devoted to snatching defeat right out of the jaws of victory. But that is precisely the way chapter 12 reads. The celebrations of chapter 11 are given to us by the narrator: "So all the people . . . made Saul king before the LORD in Gilgal . . . and there Saul and all the men of Israel rejoiced greatly" (v. 15). But by the end of the day, "all the people greatly feared the LORD and Samuel" (1 Samuel 12:18). It would seem that any fear or "reverence" diverted from the Lord Himself is misplaced and we might wish to say that Samuel has overstated his case. But that is a point for another discussion. What is at stake here is the final statement of the prophet Samuel with respect to the monarchy. Samuel does not like the idea of monarchy and will express that here in several ways. Remember, monarchy was built into the system as far back as Deuteronomy 17. When God laments Israel's rejection, it is not so much the idea of monarchy as the spirit in which the demand is made. God said, "They have not rejected you [did Samuel supererogate himself to the role of or style himself as regent?], but they have rejected Me from being king over them" (1 Samuel 8:7). The sentence itself allows for the ideas of Deuteronomy 17 if Israel had been willing to view their king as a leader (*nagid*), a viceroy, rather than with the sole and final life-and-death authority of a despot. Something has gone terribly wrong here, but I do not think Samuel has a good grip on it. Follow along in the text and discussion.

## Reading from "Saul: A Life Suspended in Doubt"

As part of the festivities of that day, Samuel made a speech. Part of it involved an excursus concerning the history of Israel and events in the life of Jacob and Moses and so on. Those history lessons always left me cold. It just never seemed that anything of value came out of them—although I guess I did get the idea of a three-pronged attack from the story of Gideon. If only I could have realized then that I was merely a cog in the much larger historical wheel of the life of the nation of Israel, perhaps this could have ended differently. Nevertheless, part of Samuel's address did concern me directly and he called to heaven for a sign of approval at a confirmation service in my honor. In the middle of what is usually a dry harvest season, we had a thunderstorm and it seemed at the time a sign of approval. It has always seemed to me, though, that thunder and lightning were more a sign of God's anger than approval. With all Israel, I feared greatly! However, unlike some around me, my fear was genuine terror rather than reverential awe.

As part of the conclusion to his message, Samuel announced the obvious: that he was an old man and that he would not be with us much longer. How I wish I could talk to him today in a manner other than that of last night. I would try to make things right between us . . . before it was too late. As the final statement of the party, Samuel committed himself to a life of prayer for the nation of Israel. He told us to obey the Lord and prognosticated that if we didn't, both the nation and their king would be swept away. As he said the word "king," he glanced over in my direction—a look I will never forget. He knew even then, didn't he? (1 Sam. 12)

## Textual Observations

## Samuel Cleared of Culpability

One might sense in this chapter that some of the fire evident in Samuel's diatribe in chapter 8 has been extinguished. Facts are facts: things went well in the new monarch's first call to action. We have described Samuel as a seer who does not always see well; this may be a case wherein God has intimated to His prophet nothing of what is to come. Literarily, in Bible we should always be wary of good beginnings; but that is of no pressing concern at this point. Samuel's goal at this point is to clarify his relationship with the people he has served for all these years. Remember, Samuel left the text at the beginning of chapter 4 as a boy; returned at the beginning of chapter 7 as a grown man with a history of service and now, already, he is "old and grey" (12:2). He calls the Lord, the Anointed (king, here), and the nation to witness that he has done nothing outside the bounds of professional propriety. They agree and in the customary single syllable ('*ed*, witness), a lifetime of work is given a positive review by the nation. We should be reminded that this is the way the book was written. Those of us with a New Testament view to the text will be reminded of Luke 2:52 in the words of 1 Samuel 2:26: "Now the boy Samuel was growing in stature and in favor both with the LORD and with men." That is the narrator's evaluation on the front cover and this is Israel's evaluation toward the close. Things will get a bit ticklish with respect to the latter days of the monarch and arguably, Samuel will not finish the race as well as he ran the better part of it. But for now, Samuel is exonerated of any guilt, perceived or real, in the esteem of the nation he has served. That we might do as well.

## On Beginning a Sermon with a History Lesson

Throughout biblical literature, the best messages are begun with a history lesson, early (Moses in Deuteronomy 1:6-3:29) and late (Stephen in Acts 7). Samuel's message here is no exception; however, it is sameness with distinctiveness! Because, of the particular sin that Samuel mentions and the manner in which he mentions it, it is a historical prologue with punch. He begins with the commissioning of Moses to bring the people out of Israel. We have, as it were, the nation born in a day. We also have the mention of the nation's sins during the early and late period of the judges—Sisera of Canaan and the Philistines, respectively. Then deliverers are provided, but not before the national repentance described by Samuel: "We have sinned because we have forsaken the Lord and have served the Baals and the Ashtaroth; but now deliver us from the hands of our enemies, and we will serve Thee" (v. 10). This was, of course, a bi-lateral agreement that was evidenced by only one lateral. That is, God kept His part of the bargain, repeatedly. Israel only kept her part partially or temporarily—at the best for only a generation at a time over the hundreds of years.

Now at the end of Samuel's days, he reminds them that in view of the Ammonite scourge, Saul was chosen as king. This is an interesting spin on the events as described in the text. It is also part of the reason why criticism has viewed the text as composite. It does, however, make sense as it appears here; although it does so only as the culmination of a sequence of events resulting in the confirmation of the king as it was the day that Samuel spoke. Historically, however, it might be viewed that the incident with Jabesh-Gilead was merely the capstone on a much longer oppression of the Ammonites against the trans-Jordanian peoples of Israel. So far as the critical problem is concerned, it evaporates under the slightest scrutiny. Literarily, though, the problem develops nicely into full bloom. Because this was to be the capstone of Samuel's life work, the gravity of the event is to be portrayed as such. That is, all this ancient history and all these current events culminated in one thing: the Israelite monarchy—for good or ill. And so they are admonished to fidelity to the Lord, complete with the very real threats recalled in Samuel's history lesson in verses 6-11.

Meanwhile back at the beginning, notice how the history lesson begins. It seems that after acknowledging that he (begrudgingly?) installed the new monarch, Samuel then confesses his chronologically challenged status just before one of the most pregnant clauses in biblical narrative. He says, "and behold my sons are with you" (1 Samuel 12:2). The word "behold" (*hinneh*) or "look" or "see" is a text pointer that draws vivid attention to the oration of the speaker. It is sometimes called the particle of immediacy and is virtually untranslatable. The closest thing I can come up with is the positive attention-grabber of the youth culture of the early millennium, "Check this out!" But behold, this "behold" is a two-edged scimitar, because the memorial of Samuel's sons and Samuel's failure as a father is anything but positive. Samuel may be trying to put a positive spin on something that received a scathing review from the narrator. In chapter 8, we read:

And it came about when Samuel was old that he appointed his sons judges over Israel . . . they were judging in Beersheba. His sons, however, did not walk in his ways, but turned aside after dishonest gain and took bribes and perverted justice (vv. 1-3).

Israel knows this to be the case and perhaps they do not want another Eli and sons type of judgeship. So they convene and request a king with the antecedent conditions: "Behold, you have grown old, and your sons do not walk in your ways. Now appoint a king for us to judge us like all the nations" (1 Sam. 8:5).

Samuel says they "are with you." Is this a somewhat less than tacit admission that they are incorrigible and that they are Israel's problem now? Perhaps. Regardless, this whole sentence goes in the category of "confessions of a failed leader." If you win the war against the Philistines and lose your family, what have you accomplished? History will prove that another Philistine war is imminent and that one will go the other way. Net gain: negative. Leadership is people in the public eye. Leadership simply must be successful on several fronts simultaneously. We know that Samuel's work took him away from home and that it included matters judicial and educational (1 Samuel 7:15-17; 12:23). However, if such matters prove to be a failure at home, can it ever be said that the man was a good teacher? In Samuel's School of Law, two of the alumni proved to be immortalized as failures. There is much more that can be said.

## On Continuing a Sermon with a Sound and Light Display

I have always wondered where the contemporary music scene would have gotten to had it not been for pyrotechnics and laser-light shows. Although it is the medium in which I grew up, it had nothing of sophistication—neither has it yet. However, some of the events themselves were of high visual interest. Before selling out to some Islamic cult, Cat Stevens had one of the most interesting shows going, with a magic act and all the bells and whistles necessary to sell the "Peace Train" and "Moon Shadow" product. Here, Samuel punctuates his message with a sound and light show of cosmic proportions. As a punctuation to the warning uttered in verse 15, Samuel foretells of meteorological events out of place for the season. There will be "thunder (sounds) and rain" (v. 17) in the harvest season. Samuel paints the sky for Israel as a picture of their disobedience: "Then you will know and see that your wickedness is great which you have done in the sight of the LORD by asking for yourselves a king" (v. 17). Events transpire as Samuel has foretold and the proper response is recorded by our Omniscient Narrator: "all the people greatly feared the LORD and Samuel." I wonder if it is right to "fear" a prophet in the same sense as one is to fear God. Be that as it may, the people ask for the prophet's intercession because of their presumption—if it was ever merely that—and the prophet informs them of their absolution. I still have problems with Samuel's spin on the whole problem with the monarchy due to the provision for it in Deuteronomy 17. That Israel initially chose the wrong king is a luxury we biblical historians can impose upon them. That the whole thing was wrong headed, may not necessarily be the case. In Samuel's mind the whole adventure is wrong headed and that brings in notions of ulterior motives. Samuel has been dethroned from his position as supreme judge — that is the position of the monarch. What with "Saul among the prophets" and his soon-to-be-usurped role as "sacral-king" (well, officiating priest), it is pretty easy to see how Samuel might be a bit testy about the whole thing.

Exactly what God was saying with the thunder and rain in harvest, might be another matter. The people ask Samuel to pray for them and yet he provides verbal absolution. He says, "Do not fear. You have committed all this evil, yet do not turn aside from following the LORD, but serve the LORD with all your heart. And you must not turn aside, for then you would go after futile things which can not profit or deliver, because they are futile. For the LORD will not abandon His people on account of His great name, because the LORD has been pleased to make you a people for Himself" (1 Samuel 12:20-22). So the people ask for intercession and the prophet gives them absolution. Only later does he say, "Moreover, as for me, far be it from me that I should sin against the LORD by ceasing to pray for you; but I will instruct you in the good and right way. Only fear the LORD and serve Him in truth with all your heart; for consider what great things He has done for you" (vv. 23-24). In the context those things could be the events described in the historical prologue to Samuel's message, deliverance by the monarch from the Ammonite oppression, the kingship itself, or the meteorological display. There are several points at which the prophet injects pending judgment into his discourse; but none are so pointed as the last verse.

## On Concluding a Sermon with a Word of Doom and a Word of Comfort

Not necessarily in that order — the word of comfort is that Samuel will pray and teach. The word of comfort is that Israel should reflect upon God's greatness, in character and in deed. The warning, on the other hand, is directly related to Samuel's agenda in the preceding message: "But if you still do wickedly, both you and your king shall be swept away" (1 Samuel 12:25). Samuel's last words are directed at the people's desire for a king and at the king himself, there listening. However, the Omniscient Narrator's selection of these words for the text indicate something larger in scope. In the general introduction to this work and in the introduction to the life of Samuel, we have discussed the notion that the selection of a quote entails two voices — that of the orator/writer and that of the person who edited his or her work into his larger text. In this case, it is pretty easy to assume with those of the deuteronomist school that we have a historical retrojection from the standpoint of the eve of the fall of the city of Jerusalem and the burning of the temple. However, it is just as easy to see a teacher (1 Samuel 12:23) doing his job. Samuel has seen a lot of history and lived a lot of bad national ideas. He can read the handwriting on the wall and he knows that if Israel continues along the pagan path, both she and her king "shall be swept away." It is a job begun by Moses and carried on by the prophetic voice throughout the history of Israel and on into the modern day. Disaster casts a shadow before it. National disaster casts an ominous shadow! Because of the lessons of history (vv. 6-11); because of the nature of current events (vv. 12-15); because of the kind of God YHWH is (vv. 16-18); because of the fickle nature of God's people (vv. 18-24); it is possible to predict with comparative accuracy that the nation is headed for ruin—the only contingency is the timing. They "shall be swept away."

### Reprise: Baalim and Ashtaroth

Since the issue has been addressed before, not much more than a review and summary statement is in order. Should you wish to see more on the subject, turn to my section on 1 Samuel 7 or look at Polzin's treatment of the subject.[48] First, if it could ever be proved that there was any such a thing as a deuteronomist, it might be noticed that this appearance of spurious deities and their consorts is at something of the thematic level for the whole piece. They were to be rejected and in their place a resolute determination to specific monotheism was to be substituted. Sufficiency and necessity are interesting discussions at this point. That the reappearance of these false deities is a sufficiently intriguing correlation for the premises of the deuteronomistic history is apparent; however, that it might be cited as evidence for a historically recurring problem is indicative of its failure as necessary evidence to sustain the argument. In short: the textual reappearance of these idolatrous practices might merely reflect the historical tendency—indeed the appeal—for a fallen people to resurrect the practices of a fertility cult. It might have nothing to do with the establishment of a single author or editor—the "dueteronomist." Apparently, only in the humanities does correlation equal causation. Anyway, where do these spurious deities and their consorts appear?[49]

In the law, we are told that such practices are to be eradicated (See all the references in Deuteronomy in the footnote below along with the indictment of the angel of the LORD in Judges 2:1-5). And so in Judges 2 we are told that: "There arose another generation after them who did not know the LORD nor yet the work which He had done for Israel. And the sons of Israel did evil in the sight of the LORD, and served the Baals, and they abandoned the LORD . . . and followed other gods from among the gods of the peoples who were around them, and bowed themselves down to them; thus they provoked the LORD to anger. So they abandoned the LORD and served Baal and the Ashtaroth" (vv. 10-13). This, early and late, becomes the bone of contention between God and His people. They are to be singularly Yahwists and they have become syncretistic at best and polytheistic at worst. And so we begin the cycles of the judges beginning with religious defection and ending in oppression. After deliverance, again, Israel went right back to her defection in Judges 2:13. We are told, "And the sons of Israel did what was evil in the sight of the LORD, and forgot the LORD their God, and served the Baals and the Asheroth" (note the difference in spelling). Toward the middle of things—and the way things would be by the time Samuel arrives on the scene, Israel again defects and becomes fodder for the Philistines: "Then the sons of Israel again did evil in the sight of the LORD, served the Baals and the Ashtaroth, the gods of Aram, the gods of Sidon, the gods of Moab, the gods of the sons of Ammon, and the gods of the Philistines; thus they left the LORD and did not serve Him" (Judges 10:6). This is not just polytheism—this is selective polytheism! Anybody *but* the one true God, the only one with an historical claim to be Israel's God.

As we have discussed formerly, in 1 Samuel 7:3, as the prophet reappears on the scene to deliver (in the style of the judges) Israel from the Philistine oppression, he tells them to prove their allegiance to YHWH: "If you return to the LORD with all your heart, remove the foreign gods and the Ashtaroth from among you and direct your hearts to the LORD and serve Him alone; and He will deliver you from the hand of the Philistines." Which they apparently did *en masse* for the first time: "So the sons of Israel removed the Baals and the Ashtaroth and served the LORD alone" (7:4). This goes as we have come to expect: Israel repents, serves the LORD, and He delivers them from their oppressors. Be that as it may, revivals do not usually last very long in ancient Israel and it will not be too long after Solomon before one generation's revival becomes another generation's defection. As mentioned above, Samuel gives a historical prologue to set the tone for his message and the application to Israel's request for a king. Samuel reminds them of the front cover on the history book that many of them were participant in before its close. With reference to the period of the former judges, "And they cried out to the LORD and said, 'We have sinned because we have forsaken the LORD and have served the Baals and the Ashtaroth; but now deliver us from the hands of our enemies, and we will serve You'" (1 Sam. 12:10). Of course, God was the only one who kept any part of this bargain.

Though it will not rear its ugly head again for some time, it seems fitting that in the context of a Philistine uprising, Saul's end to his terrestrial existence is as a display. In 1 Samuel 31:8-10, our Omniscient Narrator tells us that "they found Saul and his three sons fallen on Mount Gilboa; and they cut off his head, and stripped off his weapons and sent them throughout the land of the Philistines . . . and they put his weapons in the temple of Ashtaroth, and they fastened his body to the wall of Beth-Shean." The significance of headlessness and bodies and heads coming to separate resting places will be discussed below. However, and for the time being, it should be indicative of the fact that Saul did not keep his head, his focus, and did not eradicate these practices and places from everywhere within the purview of Israel—including the Canaanite city states.

## Textual Problems

### No Good Place to Break the Text

You have to go backward to verse 11 of chapter 11 and forward to the end of our chapter break to find the full section. It would appear that the chapter break was based upon the change in location. However, this is the concluding episode of "Saul the king and Samuel the king-maker." Things will be on the slide after chapter 12. Indeed, chapter 12 may herald the slide of Saul into the abyss of failed leadership.

### Textual Applications and Anecdotes

1 Samuel 12

vs.

1. The majority will either rule or eventually overrule.
   The admission may be tacit and begrudging.
2. The realist calls events as they are (enthroned king).
   The realist calls conditions as they are (age).
   Failure elicits denial (Samuel's sons).
   Public occupation forces the issue of public analysis.
3. Leadership has the right to demand its own accountability from its constituency—it will be a matter of utmost courage for it to do so.
   Leadership's self-accountability may include restitution.
   The restitution proviso proves either courage or innocence.
4. The people make the statement; but apart from the oath it has no force.
5. Calling God and the king to witness against oneself entails risk.
   The tension of risk is alleviated when the people testify in the affirmative.
6. National history best begins at the beginning of the nation.
   The mention of the founding fathers tacitly places us in a respectful position to them.
7. The prophet pleads for the people based upon historical precedent.
8. God answers the plaintive cry for deliverance—in His timing.
   God gives lands, times, and seasons.
9. Neglect God and our enemies will become powerful.
10. A proper cry to God for help should include contrition and repentance.
    Proper repentance should include a resolute determination to obey God.
11. God provides deliverers and security—however, it is an open question as to whether or not His people abide by their half of the agreement (obedience).
12. History spun, is history tendentious (monarchy begun on the Ammonite issue?).

It is always good for us to ask, "Who is the real king?"

13. It is the Lord who provides leadership—that may not always be a comfortable fact.

14. Continuation of any people and government is dependent upon willingness to obey and follow the Lord.

15. Disobedience and rebellion "force" God's hand to act against us.

16. "Take your stand" and watch what the Lord will do.

17. A miracle is something that happens out of season when called by the prophet.
    A miracle may be a confirmation of sin.

18. It is good to fear the Lord always.
    It may not be good to fear His servant on the same terms.

19. Confession must be properly directed (king? or the rebellious reason for one?).
    The people's repentance and request for forgiveness should be answered immediately.

20. Fear the Lord and follow the Lord are good ideas—if from right motives and a good heart.

21. Futile things are powerless.
    Idolatry is futility.

22. The Lord's relationship to His people is based upon His own character—not theirs.

23. The prophet's job description: prayer and instruction—in that order.

24. The wholeheartedly obedient will see great things from God.

25. Wickedness sweeps away both people and leadership.

## Conclusion

Samuel has spoken his final words on the monarchy as a system. Israel will henceforth romance the monarchy for several centuries before its final collapse . . . well, the condition pertains at least up to the present. We have seen the manner of his delivery, the issues at stake, and the meteorological witness of the Lord as to the gravity of the situation. As to whether or not the people confessed to the right sin, I am dubious. Had the issue with the monarchy gone according to the rules laid out in Deuteronomy 17, perhaps the whole party would not have been a silver lining on such a dark cloud. Israel wanted a king instead of God, not a vice-regent. The sins were sins of the heart and not sins of form. That the messianic view styles the coming ruler as a monarch should be proof enough that there is nothing inherently evil in the notion of monarchy.

With respect to leadership, Samuel has confessed his capitulation to the will of the people despite his dislike for the people's chosen institution, his failure as a father, and strikingly, a spiritual defection. The people ask for intercession at that moment and he deflects their request with platitudes "far be it from me that I should sin against the LORD by ceasing to pray for you; but I will instruct you in the good and right way." In effect, he is saying, "Don't bother me with your perceived spiritual condition, I will be the judge of that and I will tell you what you need to know."

It was a great day in the history of Israel that was turned dismal by her prophet of gloom, Samuel. Fine! We have been warned, but what of the aftermath? Textually, henceforth, the story of Saul will be negative. Saul will fail, as had Samuel's sons before him. Could that be a reflection on the abilities of his mentor? Could that be because the teacher was somewhat less than competent? Could it be that the teacher's lessons were never really able to generate more than the people greatly fearing the LORD and Samuel (v. 18). But I wonder about the day itself. Saul will be characterized by fear working its way out alternately in rage and indecision. Could that have been begun today? Could it be that there is no way he could win? Saul is the king; Samuel dislikes monarchy; therefore, Saul is not in a very good position to curry favor with the king-maker. Because Samuel has now been deposed as top authority in Israel, the only place where he can finally hold Saul accountable is in respect to religion (usurping the priesthood, disobedience to the divine injunction regarding Amalek, necromancy). Could it be, though, that the fear that characterized Saul's life was begun this day? "All the people greatly feared the LORD and Samuel" and that would include Saul. I wonder if this is the best approach to the monarchy. I should think that a healthy respect for the office was required; however, a paranoid monarch will prove in the coming chapters to lead the people to death, ruin, and nearly national dissolution. Had Samuel provided a more positive and forward looking leadership (not just the obedience/disobedience issues), perhaps the monarchy might have begun on better footing. Had he drawn as his text for the "custom of the king" the verses in Deuteronomy, the foundation would have been at once more biblical and concrete and less moralistic and abstract. But because of the way Samuel begins and ends this chapter, it is clear that he is more interested in exculpating himself and distancing himself from the institution than in being the intellectual (ideological and pragmatic) guide for the inception of this new epoch in the history of the nation.

# 1 Samuel 13
## The Impending Strategic War and Saul's Cosmic Blunder

—ɯ—

## Introduction

This section begins with a textual problem (see below) and proceeds with several problems in the sense of unanswered questions. We read backward and so we know that several occasions of King Saul's failures will be the occasions against which David will be chosen. However, and along the way, several questions remain unanswered. The first question is, what exactly was Saul's failure? Others include: When did Samuel know that Saul would be replaced? How will Samuel take his first failure as king-maker? What will be the failed monarch's term of office? How will he be removed? In chapter 13, more questions are asked than answered. In this section, Samuel will make a move away from the monarch; but we wonder about the communication between the prophet and God. Saul will overstep his bounds; but would he have known the gravity of the situation beforehand? The context is a raid on a Philistine garrison. Let us follow the text through the first of Saul's several failures as a leader. His failure will be with respect to the holy and the text will not betray any indications of his repentance.

## Reading from "Saul: A Life Suspended in Doubt"

There was a lot of movement and excitement at the inception of my monarchy. I began to gather about myself a group of elite guard which was comprised of the best fighters and military strategists in the region. We finally solidified the group at about 3,000 men. I kept 2,000 with me and my first-born son Jonathan kept 1,000 with him. Since he held the royal house at Gibeah, he needed a sizable guard; but, I wonder if my apprehension of political intrigue and military coup got the best of me. Jonathan was clearly the better administrator—and how he could garner the hearts of real men! Looking back, it amazes me that he never really wanted to be anything other than number two. The world needs more like that one: real men with real integrity.

We had problems in the acquisition of military armament. It seems that the Philistines had something of an economic stranglehold, a monopoly on all metallurgical activities in the region. Clearly, they had brought sophisticated iron technology with them from the Aegean that we could only marvel at from a distance.

However, their industrial activities had threatened our forests. Our Tabor Oak stands were being depleted to heat their smelting furnaces and carburize their iron.[50] We needed to regain the passes in order to keep them to the low countries. We also needed to keep them out of the woods and somehow gain access to their metal technology. Strategic matters of this nature, naturally, all fell to me. I really sensed the powerlessness of the people. They paid inflated prices just to get their tools repaired and sharpened. They had no defense against the raiding bands of the low country people either.

Samuel, the ancient prophet, had called us all together to Gilgal to offer sacrifice before our offensive mission. There was a lot fear in the ranks and attrition was at an all time high. We did not have to worry about defection because our people risked the grossest kind of torture imaginable should they defect to the Philistines. Our people ran away and hid in the bush and in caves. I was terrified and after the seven days in which Samuel was supposed to show up, I took matters into my own hands and offered the whole burnt offering. There was always something repugnant to me about the sacrificial system of the Mosaic injunctions. It just always seemed that there had to be a better way to maintain fellowship with God. In any case, I knew that what I had done had been wrong; but, I proceeded with the ritual to the best of my memory and with as much dignity as the occasion demanded. The other kings in the region would have admired my piety, I suppose.

When Samuel arrived on the scene, he was livid—but not as angry as I would live to see him. He called me a fool and then he fired off a salvo about my presumption; then he blasted me about disobedience to the Mosaic injunction. When he finished his diatribe he had all but removed the kingdom from me—and he had assured me that there would be no descendants upon the throne of my kingdom. Apologies never worked with Samuel so I kept my mouth shut . . . this time. I never could see what Samuel's problem was. If there was a religious event, he was the center of it. I had done exactly what anybody in my station would have done. I am not really certain of what statute of the Mosaic law I'd violated anyway. According to one legend, Samuel himself was not even a Levite: he was adopted into Eli's family from a clan of the people of Ephraim. He was supposed to take the place of Hophni and Phineas because they were—just like Samuel's sons—corrupt, twisted, and as dangerous as a puff adder.

He left and we moved off, following at a distance, to where Jonathan was garrisoned at Gibeah. What was to happen next was the kind of thing that the Aegean refugees used to spend their time late into the night telling stories about. I've always said that the only difference between a hero and a fool is the results. In what could variously be called a selfless act of bravery or mindless tomfoolery, my son,

Jonathan, was to remind us of some very important facts—a battle can be won by many, or by few. (1 Samuel 13)

## Textual Observations

### "At the Appointed Time": What Happens When the Boss Is Late

In the recasting of "The Fellowship of the Ring," in reply to Frodo's comment as to the wizard's lateness, Gandalf states, "A wizard is never late, Frodo Baggins; nor is he early. He arrives precisely when he means to."[51] Grammatical abominations notwithstanding, we might say that old prophets are never late, they arrive precisely when they mean to. Because of my seminary training and who I had for a mentor, I was taught to always be five minutes early for a meeting. Because of my tenure in East Africa, I came to understand that only the servants arrive early—and that I was considered cheap labor! Needless to say, this put my universe into some rather dynamic tension until I noticed something of the universals and stopped feeling the particulars of the case. In the main, the white and Korean missionaries worked from sun up to sun down (which is really an insult to the Koreans who started their day much earlier and ended it much later and humiliated us all by their work ethic!), while most usually, our indigenized bosses worked somewhat less than bankers' hours. Of course, when confronted with their conspicuous absence and lavish lifestyle, they would merely say that they were taking work home (as were we) or copying their imperialist mentors—we all learned so much from the British! Regardless, any way you lose, you lose. When the thin veneer of my idealism wore through, and I came to the realization that I was building the wrong kingdom, I packed for America.

Be that as it may, in the power struggle between the political and the religious, we see Saul trying to feel his way around the whole burnt offering on the altar and getting his fingers burned. The situation is bleak: the Philistines are coming, the Israelites are deserting or defecting and there is no spiritual leadership to tell us what the future bodes (1 Samuel 13:1-7). What is a new monarch to do? And so Saul takes it upon himself to offer the sacrifice and ask the favor of the Lord. Well, that is the way he casts the story to Samuel.

The narrator tells us that "he waited seven days, according to the appointed time set by Samuel" (1 Samuel 13:8). He requests the burnt offering and peace offerings and then the narrator tells us, "he offered the burnt offering. And it came about as soon as he finished offering the burnt offering, that behold, Samuel came; and Saul went out to met him and to bless him" (vv. 9-10). The narrator does not paint the picture of a malevolent, scheming Saul here. He paints the picture of a clueless Saul. He is like a dumb puppy that does not know where to go or what to do and piddles on the carpet. Either that, or the narrator masks an unusually surreptitious bravado in the new monarch. Because of the way the narrator has Saul speak, I am going to follow though as Saul plays the dumb puppy role. I also think that in the rest of the story, Saul will be clueless with respect to the Philistines, his servants, David, God, and Samuel. But more on that later.

Then comes all the trouble! No question is as threatening as, "What have you done?!" (1 Samuel 13:11). The narrator follows the results by allowing the two characters to vie for the status of protagonist/antagonist. As it will turn out, perhaps neither wins. Saul ruins the monarchy and Samuel fails initially as king-maker and never lives to see the fruit of his work. Saul responds: "Because I saw that the people were scattering from me, and that you did not come within the appointed days, and that the Philistines were assembling at Michmash, therefore I said, 'Now the Philistines will come down against me at Gilgal, and I have not asked the favor of the LORD.' So I forced myself and offered the burnt offering" (1 Samuel 13:11-12).

This would seem like a great answer. He has covered all the bases: desertion/defection, the prophet's apparent truancy, the enemy's advance, the religious aspect of the problem, and the compunction against his better nature (if that is not just an excuse).

We should probably notice that Samuel's response is not really to Saul's statements. Samuel answers some other set of questions: "You have acted foolishly; you have not kept the commandment of the LORD your God, which He commanded you, for now the LORD would have established your kingdom over Israel forever. But now your kingdom shall not endure. The LORD has sought out for Himself a man after His own heart, and the LORD has appointed him as ruler over His people, because you have not kept what the LORD commanded you" (1 Samuel 13:13-14).

So, Saul is left standing there with his teeth in his mouth and either has no response or it is merely omitted by the narrator. Then Samuel leaves for Gibeah of Benjamin and apparently Saul follows like a whipped pup at his heels (1 Samuel 13:15; 14:2 does "outskirts of Gibeah" indicate some spatial distance between king and monarch?). But what do we make of Samuel's words. Saul has given a reasoned response to an exclamation phrased as a question. He is apparently hoping that somebody might reason with him as to what exactly it was he did wrong. Samuel does not reason with him (maybe the rabbis were right, Saul was like a one-year-old—however there was more than a couple of people in these narratives who act like toddlers). Samuel's response is from the security of prophetic authority. He does not have to respond to the king: he has the power of the knowledge of the future with him. So, Samuel calls Saul a fool; indicts him for not keeping the commandment (as the narrator has already told us) and then informs him of a forthcoming replacement and that person's spiritual qualifications for leadership (which the narrator has *not* already told us). Is this fair to Saul? Probably not, but it fits with Jerry's (my) Law of the First Offense. First king? Like late innings in league softball, you go to the plate with a full count and strike one, you're out!

We have to ask ourselves why the prophet was late in the first place. Gandalf's response initially indicates something of a self-important air. Is that the case with the aging prophet?

Is he pushing his weight around? Was he merely delayed? Is he, in fact, really late? The narrator comes out sounding as though he was on Saul's side: "Now he waited seven days, according to the appointed time set by Samuel, but Samuel did not come to Gilgal" (1 Samuel 13:8). When Saul attempts to defend himself, he says much the same thing, "Because I saw . . . that you did not come within the appointed days" (v. 11). However, Saul asked for and sacrificed the burnt offerings and peace offerings on the seventh day and as he had finished offering the burnt offerings (was he about to begin with the peace offerings?), Samuel arrives (vv. 9-10). Perhaps we might fault Saul for being a bit impatient. Perhaps he had forgotten the stories about Gideon and his three hundred men and his worries about defections and desertions were misplaced. We have no window into Saul here except that he is afraid of the loss of his men and the (spoken) need for propriety with regard to Israel's religion.

The narrator's description of the events and his recording of the conversation indicate that the aging prophet did come late on the appointed day. We might ask ourselves whether Samuel had planned to offer the evening sacrifice along with the burnt offerings and the peace offerings. We might also ask whether or not the whole thing was a test. Was Samuel testing Saul to see if he would abide by the prophet's time schedule or not? Was he testing Saul to see if Saul understood that the directive was actually from God and that the prophet was merely His mouthpiece? Was Samuel privy to a lot more information—as perhaps indicated in the statement of deposing (1 Samuel 13: 13-14)—including such early knowledge as that Saul was to be deposed and that there was another one more worthy of the office? We cannot know much about the communication between the prophet and God except where the narrator informs us. Be that as it may, Saul apparently got ahead of himself in time and stepped outside his bounds. He should have waited and not transgressed the jurisdiction of the priesthood. The fact that the narrator gives him no voice after Samuel's authoritative rejoinder is indicative that this is how matters are to stand. Saul has been deposed and he is now the de-legitimized monarch of Israel. He is fallen and waiting to hit the ground.

## Dwindling Numbers: Defections and Desertions from the Army of Saul

This problem of defection and desertion is the occasion, not the cause, of Saul's altercation with Samuel. We are told that they hid themselves (1 Samuel 13:6); we are told that they ran to far territory (v. 7); we are told that they were scattering (v. 8). We are also told in Saul's words that he perceived that his forces were decimated due to attrition (v. 11). There is a very real threat as indicated in the numbers of the Philistine forces given to us by the narrator (1 Samuel 13:5).[52] The men and Saul perceive it as a real threat. The men scatter and Saul acts inappropriately.

We are told that some hid themselves. This would be memorialized by the Philistines themselves, "Behold, Hebrews are coming out of the holes where they have hidden themselves" (1 Samuel 14:11; cf. 13:6). We are told that some of them went across the Jordan (1 Samuel 13:7). We are told that this was a cause of fear for Saul (1 Samuel 13:8, 11). What we will not find out until later is that the "scattering" (v. 8) also included defections. In chapter 14 we are told, "Now the Hebrews who were with the Philistines previously, who went up with them all around in the camp, even they also turned to be with the Israelites who were with Saul and Jonathan" (1 Samuel 14:21). At this point, they double defected, back to the side of Saul and Jonathan his son. Apparently, they came to realize that Jonathan had the home field advantage and they were really on the home team.

This business of defection is going to plague Saul throughout the rest of his (de-legitimized) reign. David will attempt defection (1 Samuel 21) and finally succeed at it (1 Samuel 27-31). Double defections being what they are—defecting back to the original home team—we find that allegiance among the Hebrews was a matter of the situation. Loyalty was not automatic; loyalty had to be earned. We are all here for the Ammonite war; the Philistines are another matter altogether. More later as David defects.

### The Pen Is Mightier Than the Sword—Especially If You Cannot Find a Sword . . .

. . . And Israel was unable to find a sword. "So it came about on the day of battle that neither sword nor spear was found in the hands of any of the people who were with Saul and Jonathan" (1 Samuel 13:22). There is an old saw, reduced to bumper sticker logic, that goes as follows: "Politicians want unarmed peasants." The Philistines were good students of that proverb. Be that as it may, we find ourselves in the latter third of Iron Age IB (1150–1000).[53] And there is a fundamental gap in metallurgical technology. The text says that "no blacksmith could be found in all the land of Israel, for the Philistines said, 'Lest the Hebrews make swords or spears'" (1 Samuel 13:19). This is a fundamental reality in the political science of overlordship. One simply must control any resources and skills of a strategic or tactical nature. The Philistines apparently knew that well and they controlled the trades in such a way that even the manufacture and servicing of farm implements was strictly controlled. They had, in effect, a monopoly on all iron trade at the time. Perhaps this explains why the Philistines threw so much of their military might at the Battle of the Pass of Michmash. They viewed it as maintaining their control over the use of iron.[54] They also viewed it as reducing the chance of attack from the high ground at their back on the east.

In controlling strategic metal production, the Philistines were also controlling the servicing of industrial metals. "So all Israel went down to the Philistines, each to sharpen his plowshare, his mattock, his axe, and his hoe" (1 Samuel 13:20). What this means is that there is a sense in which Israel's vassalage extends to her agricultural practices. If Israel had to go to the low country to have their tools serviced, she could hardly have independent farming. This controlled the amount of time farmers were at their crops and how much time they would have to allocate to travel.

In keeping strategic and industrial metal production and servicing to themselves, the Philistines could exploit another resource. "And the charge was two-thirds of a shekel for the plowshares, the mattocks, the forks, and the axes and to fix the hoes" (1 Samuel 13:22). The Philistines could control Israel to a degree economically. If the Israelites were forced to outsource their tool production and servicing, the money that should have been building their own economy would then have been building the economy of her most mortal enemy. In short: the Philistines had a stranglehold on Israel and she needed to be free of it. Jonathan is about to lead the charge.

## Textual Problems

Apparently nobody knows exactly what to do with the number problem in the first verse. The Hebrew text reads literally "A son of a year was Saul when he ruled; and two years he ruled over Israel." Pretty obviously, something is missing. However, this is the form one might expect, according to the other enumerations,[55] if numbers were added: "A son of X [plural] year [singular] was Saul when he ruled (inception in view here); and two + Y years he ruled over Israel." Well, what to do? Here is a partial survey of the evidence:

1.  Biblia Hebraica Stuttgartensia (BHS, Codex Leningrad) and Snaith are the same as the text given above.[56]
2.  Septuigint (LXX *Codex Vaticanus* at least) has no verse one.[57]
3.  BHS marginal notes indicates that Saul reigned thirty years following LXX Lucianic Recension ("partly," they say [?]).[58]
4.  BHS marginal notes indicate that the Syriac has that he reigned twenty-one years.[59]
5.  A Targum indicates regarding the first number that "Like a one-year-old who has no sins was Saul when he became king."[60]
6.  Bergen notes Josephus' inconsistency: "Josephus variously declared the length of Saul's reign to be twenty (*Ant.* 10.8.4) and forty years (*Ant.* 6:14.9)."[61]
7.  In Acts 13:21, Luke records Paul's speech indicating that "they asked for a king, and God gave them Saul the son of Kish, a man of the tribe of Benjamin, for forty years."
    This at least indicates a tradition with which Paul was familiar.[62]
8.  The NIV has that he was thirty years old when he became king and that he reigned forty-two years. The marginal notes *ad loc.* indicate "A few late manuscripts of the Septuagint; Hebrew does not have *thirty*," and "See the round number in Acts 13:21; Hebrew does not have *forty-*." Actually, this is an attempt to flatten the text.

The editors of the NIV are able to include the words from Luke's recording of Paul's speech in Pisidian Antioch *and* to insert Paul's numeral next to the "two" of the Hebrew text.

9.   The NASB has italics for the numerals forty and thirty respectively (the NIV often, as here, reversing the assessment of the NASB) without notes.

10.  The Latin Vulgate is of no help here because it follows the seemingly odd textual tradition of the Hebrew.

11.  Bergen's hesitating suggestion is as good as any. In answer to the solution of the NIV, he says: ". . . yet it may contradict the writer's intentions at this point. Perhaps the writer purposely used the small number to indicate that Saul reigned only two years before the Lord disqualified him from kingship (cf. 15:26); Paul's larger number would then represent the number of years Saul functioned as king, in spite of his rejection by the Lord."[63]

There is a decision we have forced upon us: we must assume that the text is deficient (in a place or two) and attempt to solve the problem; or we must assume that the text is not fractured and attempt to explain why it looks so strange to our eyes. And so there are about three options one can take here:

Assuming that the text is fractured here and that a couple of significant things have fallen out, we can, first, be obscurantists and say that there is no solution with the data we have at hand and consequently suspend judgment. One side of my head says that this is the way we ought to go.

Secondly, we might flip historical coins and see which numbers come up, since none really has the pride of place over the other. Remember, we have two rounds of coin flipping to do and whatever coins we toss must square with the numbers and dates given elsewhere. The other side of my head says that this is the right way to go—and it has a headache over it!

Thirdly, we might allow the text to stand as it is and attempt to make sense of it. That is, we should explain the text rather than explain it away or amend it. That the text is at a juncture is argued by no one: before it is the reprise of the *mishpat ha-melech* ("the custom of the king") by Samuel—it is pure discourse. Following it is the account of Saul getting his core military set up—it is pure narrative. Verse one of the Hebrew begins with no conjunctions; it is a stand-alone verse clearly indicating the beginning to what follows. What follows is then logically in narrative sequence. Verse one describes the antecedent condition of what follows and the verse is the conditional statement for what follows—as we should expect.

Along with Bergen, I think we would do well to say that he legitimately reigned for a couple of years over Israel (following the larger text and Bergen's theological assessment of it) and within about a year of that total duration, he had himself set up about as well as he is going to (that from the text that follows immediately). Certainly, this is hardly anything but a provisional solution to the problem. In my opinion the problem with the first numeral ("son of a year") does not wash. However, it might go a long way to present the transition between the warning and self-fulfilling prophecy of Samuel in chapter 12 and the proof-positive of chapters 13–31. So, Saul, reigned for about a year, getting himself set up in the monarchy and with the military; within another year, the slide culminating in his rejection in chapter 15 and his subsequent de-legitimization, will have begun. Sorry, I cannot do better; but nobody else is doing much better either.

**Textual Applications and Anecdotes**

1 Samuel 13
vs.
1. Ambiguity reigns supreme when the text intends to becloud the monarch's reign.
   There should be a demarcation of the beginning.
2. The wise king establishes a core military unit that simultaneously acts as body-guard and core leadership for the conscripted soldiery.
   The wise king will not hoard the entirety of his military resources to himself.
   The wise king will maintain control of the majority of his military resources.
3. The conquest of a garrison will be considered an act of war to the overlord.
   There is considerable risk in the conquest of a garrison.
   At the conquest of a garrison is a good time to summon the conscripts.
4. High-risk position: becoming odious to the overload.
5. The home-field advantage causes the foreign army to over play the battle.
   Strategy is always in the favor of the home team: you can pick your place of battle.
6. Numbers can be intimidating, even with the home field advantage.
   Fear causes many defections.
   Some hide.
7. Some run.
   Some people are faithful even through fear.
8. The prophet may be late; but the prophet will keep his appointment.
   If the prophet is a no-show; the more timid will make a break for it.
9. In the ancient world, the prerogatives of the priesthood might be implemented by the monarch.
   In ancient Israel, the offices of the priesthood and the monarch are strictly separate.
   To some leaders, what ought to be done, ought to be done by them.
   Unless they are careful, they will overstep their bounds: cultural, legal, etc.

10.    A leader in God's sight will be caught if he or she does something wrong.
       A mistaken leader can cover with bravado.
       A mistaken leader can feign ignorance.
       A mistaken leader who knows what has been required of him should simply confess.
11.    A mistaken leader may blame circumstances (everybody defecting).
       A mistaken leader may blame shift (Samuel did not come on time).
       A mistaken leader may focus on external adversaries and miss details.
12.    A mistaken leader may pretend that he has been forced into a course of action.
       When in doubt, blame those pesky Philistines.
13.    Failure to keep a divine appointment is foolish.
       Failure to keep a divine appointment may have some serious ramifications.
14.    God is looking for a "a man after His own heart."
       God knows who that person is.
       God considers that person appointed already ("has appointed").
       Failure in leadership is an occasion, not a cause of replacement ("because").
15.    A prophetic rebuke uttered; a change of location noted—Samuel leaves.
       When leaders fail to win the hearts of their followers—no matter how noble the cause—the followers will be decimated.
16.    The wise and courageous son stays with the fearful, incompetent, sacrilegious father—the silence of the narrator regarding Jonathan's screams.
       In dire straights, pick your position carefully.
17.    The raiders split up and comb the land for resources.
18.    The raiders split up three ways to comb the land, the towns, and the roads for resources.
19.    When there are no weapon makers, the people's position is tenuous at best.
       When there are no weapon makers, a foreign despot makes the rules.
       When there are no weapon makers, slavery is the rule of the day.
20.    When there are no weapon makers, one must go across the border for tools and weapons.
21.    When there are no weapon makers, the charge across the border will be exorbitant.
22.    When there are no weapon makers on the day of battle, only the wealthy and empowered will have weapons.
23.    A big army in a narrow pass: Calamity!

## Conclusion

We have made the transition from the final words on the monarchy from the prophet Samuel to the narrative as to how his words will work themselves out in history. We have seen the new monarch's first fall in reference to his presumption regarding the priesthood. We have also seen the gravity of the situation both in the occasion of the presumption and in the aftermath of Saul's presumptive act. Saul, for the first transgression, has had the monarchy stripped from him—at least at the spiritual level. God is no longer with him as He was before and He is looking for a replacement for Saul. In the midst of desertion and defection, in the midst of failed leadership, in the midst of insurmountable odds—few against many and armed against defenseless—we see the need for a hero in the history of Israel. In the next chapter such a hero will arise. His appearance has been heralded: "And Jonathan smote the garrison of the Philistines that was in Geba" (1 Samuel 13:3). With his three formal introductions (13:3, 22; 14:1) in the proper literary format of the ancient Hebrews, let us move forward and see how this crisis will be resolved, in a sense, by Jonathan. There will be winners and there will be losers on that day—they will not all be whom you think they might.

# 1 Samuel 14
## Jonathan and His Victorious Servant
## Sometimes You Have to Go Against the Grain

—⁓—

## Introduction

One of the great epic texts on faith is this chapter about Jonathan raiding the garrison of the Philistines and winning against insurmountable odds. He went with a nameless companion he apparently trusted. He laid out something of a "fleece" in the situation of the attack: "and this shall be the sign to us" (1 Samuel 14:9). However, the events of that day turn deadly for Jonathan in that the rout of the garrison is the inception of a larger action involving Saul and what was left of his army (about six hundred according to 14:2), the priesthood and ark, the defected Hebrews, and the larger group of "the people" (14:24 and so on). Saul put the people under oath to fast until such time as he had avenged himself on his enemies (14:24).

That curse, uttered in ignorance by Saul-the-clueless, was one that would again put the heir apparent, Crown Prince Jonathan, in jeopardy that day. But in the offense, Jonathan shows himself to be a man who understood the times and, indeed, his own father. He said, "My father has troubled the land. See now how my eyes have brightened because I tasted a little of this honey. How much more, if only the people had eaten freely today of the spoil of their enemies which they found! Because now the slaughter among the Philistines has not been great" (vv. 29-30). In this religious oath, Saul commits what I feel is his second major error and in so doing, may not kill his son on the spot, but sentences him to death later. Perhaps that is too mystical an understanding; but, it does bring Jonathan into an unusually sharp focus for God's work. Others who will receive dishonorable mention later on are the priests (14:3, 18-19). They will have another near miss with using the ark as a talisman and that spells doom for all involved. They are still of Eli's family and will be swept away—Ahijah especially! Perhaps this is Ahimelech or his brother; but, it would, nevertheless, include any son of Ahitub in the travesty of 1 Samuel 22:9-19. Be that as it may, the chapter concludes with everybody receiving a temporary reprieve from the people (1 Samuel 14:45) and some notations about warfare and Saul's family.

**Reading from "Saul: A Life Suspended in Doubt"**

With attrition still pandemic, we approached Gibeah. We took a count of our military personnel and discovered that we had barely 600 core warriors. Then, suddenly somebody reported from our vantage point that there was a rout taking place among the Philistine garrison. I was later to discover that my son, Jonathan, and his armor bearer single handedly beat back the Philistine garrison 150 feet from the edge of the precipice. They had already killed about 20 crack troops from the Philistines when there was a bizarre killer earthquake. Even the fearless raiders were falling all over each other trying to get away. I guess when they saw Jonathan fight, the mercenaries among the Philistines from among the Hebrews suddenly changed sides and started fighting alongside my son. By the time all was said and done, the forces of the Philistines were heading back for the low country and my people were coming out of the caves and brush. It turned out to be a great day of victory for us. It was clouded by one thing though.

At one point, when things were clearly going our way, we were in hot pursuit of the Philistines. I had made the comment—which my generals picked up on—that we should not eat anything until the king had been avenged of his enemies. The people were tired: hand-to-hand combat is exhausting work. But we clearly had momentum and the hill slopes on our side! Unknown to me, Jonathan had tasted some honey that he found in the woods—because he had led his own offensive, he didn't even know of the "vow." I made the request that the priest divine for me whether I should consider pursuit of the Philistines. No answer! This was certainly a bad omen. So, I sought to ascertain why it was that God would not answer through normal means. As it turned out, I suspected that somebody had broached the ban. I assumed that it would not be either my son, Jonathan, or me, and yet our lot was drawn against the people. When the lot fell out to Jonathan, I was reluctantly prepared to follow through and put him to death. The people looked about to riot and would have nothing of it. I reluctantly conceded to the people's wish and so, we ended pursuit and everybody went home. I had never even thought about it before, but it seems that at that moment, Jonathan began to keep one eye firmly fixed on me.

Apparently, I had finally and ultimately betrayed the trust of my first-born son. Although he had never really done anything for me to question his loyalty, because he no longer trusted me implicitly, I never felt that I could trust him. It is funny the manner in which betrayed trust betrays trust. During my reign we were never to know peace again. I should have known that this was an evil portend. (1 Samuel 14)

**Textual Observations**

**Manage the Damage Jonathan, the Unlikely Hero**

Alright, who on earth is this "Jonathan the son of Saul" (1 Samuel 14:1)? Never mentioned before in the narrative, he is properly and therefore triply introduced into the narrative before he is given true voice in verse 6. First, we are told that Jonathan is to be recognized for the important relationship he bears being *the* son (perhaps the usage of the definite article indicates prominence) of Saul (v. 1). We are told that like much of the nobility described in these narratives, he has an armor bearer. In the first verse we are told that he said to the young man who was carrying his armor, "Come and let us cross over to the Philistines' garrison that is on the other side" (1 Samuel 14:1). Because the text backs up and restates nearly the same thing in verse 6, we are prepared for all the intervening material to be background to the ensuing conflict. That intervening material includes such things as the neglect in informing Saul about his intended action, where Saul was, how many of the troops remained loyal, the odd placement of material about the priesthood, and everybody's ignorance regarding Jonathan's plan (vv. 2-3). In that notice, is included the second usage of Jonathan's name. The second piece of backgrounded information includes something of the setting of the conflict: we are told that there are two ledges of rock and that they are named; we are also told the points of the compass to which they face, so as to grant us some orientation to the conflict (vv. 4-5). In this backgrounded information is included the third formal usage of Jonathan's name. With all the introductions complete, we are now ready for the story to begin. As stated earlier, it begins at verse 6 by resuming the words of verse 1 and expanding on them. This is the first time in the Samuel Narrative that the Philistines are given an anatomical epithet—"the uncircumcised" (v. 6). However, the nomenclature is current, having been recently used by Samson's father in respect to the relatives of Samson's prospective bride (Judges 14:3) and by Samson himself in a prayer to God to be delivered from the Philistines (Judges 15:18). The terminology will have a noble history and be canonized by David's epithets (1 Samuel 17: 26, 36)—his public declarations are, of course, much more noble. Finally, "these uncircumcised" become part of the speech reflecting Saul's final death wish (1 Samuel 31:4). The epithet may have been part of the speech of that perhaps more spurious of historical revisionists, the Amalekite, who informed David of Saul's death (2 Samuel 1: 1-16)—of course, resulting in the death of the messenger. But finally, the epithet is immortalized in the lament over Jonathan (well, Saul is named too, I suppose) in the hopes that the "daughters of the uncircumcised" might not gloat over his death. Jonathan starts it and Jonathan will end it. Never again will that epithet be used in the Samuel narrative (used once in Chronicles, once in Isaiah, thrice in Jeremiah, and sixteen times in Ezekiel).

Not only do Samson, Jonathan, and David collect and share epithets for the Philistines, they all seem to have another characteristic endearing them to militaristic literature—

they are berserkers! Samson's episodes of the berserk include at the least the antecedents mentioned above in Judges 15. Of course, you always go into battle armed to the teeth with the jawbone of a donkey, right? A formidable weapon, or so we are told—he killed a thousand Philistines with one, after all. If that is not an illustration of a berserker, I have no other, well, weapon to throw at you! In addition, the death wish side of Samson's berserk personality is shown at the end of his life when he pulls down the temple and kills thousands. In his view it was better to go down in flaming glory than to die like an animal caught in a snare.

Another berserker, in my view, is David. This will be developed later, but I will merely illustrate here. Armed with blind courage and a sling, he brings down the human killing machine, Goliath. Whenever the opportunity arises, he throws himself into the next fray with the Philistines. Marry into the royal family? David pays double the bride price in dead Philistines. David always seemed to find the thick of the battle and it got to the point that his men had to rescue him and finally forbid him to go into action lest he "extinguish the lamp of Israel" (2 Samuel 21: 15-17; cf. 2 Samuel 18:3).

How then is Jonathan a berserker? Consider the scene: two lightly armed men, fighting uphill against insurmountable odds nested in garrisoned fortifications, claiming only the aid of deity. I think I can rest my case there; but let me dig my pit a bit deeper: when they finally got the sign they were looking for, they advance and quickly dispatch twenty men in a "horse acre" (1 Samuel 14:14).[64] To do that, Bruce Lee movies notwithstanding, they would have to be very quick and not allow the opposition to form up and stand its ground. Possibly, they were already able to inspire some of those who had recently donned red jerseys to reverse them back to blue—double defections being what they were at the time (1 Samuel 14:21). It must have been some scene: killing on the way up (v. 13); killing on the flat (v. 14), and killing as the battle spread (vv. 20-46).

Perhaps Jonathan's fearlessness and his single devotion to God (vv. 6, 10, 12) are what inspired the relationship between David and Jonathan. In life, the relationship will very much appear in the narrative to be unilateral. We will know that Jonathan—indeed, all Israel—loves David; what David feels will be shielded from us. But as pertains to the story before us, perhaps word got back to the shepherd of how the battle went that day and who inspired the rout. When the berserker saw how the anointed-elect, David, would deal with impossible situations and insurmountable odds—a kindred berserker spirit—the soul of the crown prince of the deposed monarch would be knit to the one anointed to fill the place of his father, the one whom the crown prince would wish to serve (1 Samuel 16:12; 18:1; 23:17).

Why then is Jonathan an unlikely hero? Even at this point, Saul, having made his irretrievable error in respect to the usurpation of the priestly office, the crown prince will have no future. Any future he is to make for Israel is a future he makes for the real king of the narrative, David. He is introduced here properly and in proper form he demonstrates his valor; however, like the deposed king, his father, he too will proceed with the king and his kingdom to near oblivion and annihilation. David's song at the end of the narrative will keep Jonathan's memory alive. Beyond that and the deposition of his heir and his bones, Jonathan passes with the rest of Saul into the crypt of history (2 Samuel 9:21). Before his end though, Jonathan will teach us lessons on friendship and loyalty that David would have done well to have learned.

## Near Shipwreck on an "Ark-tic" Reef

At a strategic point in the events of the day, Saul calls for the priest and the ark of the covenant. After it has been ascertained that there has been a rout of the garrison of Philistines guarding the pass of Michmash and that Jonathan and his armor bearer are missing from the camp, Saul calls for this ancient artifact and its keeper. Ahijah has already been given a lengthy introduction along with his ancestors, occupation, and title (1 Samuel 14:3). However, he has not been given a triple introduction as we might expect by the time we see him reappear in verse 18. This suggests to me that this is not his main debut. If this man is the same as Ahimelech of chapter 22—and the family relations suggest that he is either the same man or his brother—then, his third introduction is when Saul calls him to account in 1 Samuel 22:11. At that point, then, he would be fully integrated into the story. Appropriately integrated, he offers one of the most stirring soliloquies in the Bible in defense of David (vv. 14-15). It is, in fact, his swan song and he will be executed for treason on the spot—well, after Saul can find somebody who will kill a priest. Conveniently, Doeg the Edomite is there. Regardless, 1 Samuel 14:3 reminds us that he is from the doomed family of Eli and so nothing ultimately of good can come of this event. Ironically, the call is abortive.

The real point here is that the ark of the covenant is called for. It is interesting that the narrator mentions Ichabod in the family of Ahijah the priest. That would then call to mind a former time when the ark of the covenant was called for and the result was disaster—both for Israel and the Philistines (1 Samuel 4-6). At that time, the two sons of Eli, Hophni and Phinehas, died. Upon the report back in Shiloh, Eli died and Phinehas' wife died in childbirth, but not before naming her son after the departure of the glory of God and the ark from Israel. She named him Ichabod ("No Glory"). Perhaps the reason that this scene is abortive is because Ahijah the priest reminded Saul of a previous time when Israel called for the ark and used it as a talisman. God will not be put in a box by His people or by foreigners; the results were the elimination of 30,000 Israelites, the decimation of three cities of the Philistine pentapolis, and the near annihilation of the people of Beth Shemesh. Saul's words to the priest, "Withdraw your hand" (1 Samuel 14:19), are then the words of either respect or superstition. The way Saul handles the holy, we will begin to suspect the latter more and more as the story progresses.

## On Forced Oaths and Other Despotic Tomfoolery

Beating up on Saul is great sport because nobody really minds. Anyone, however, that has ever done something stupid as a leader should feel a bit of a twinge when talking about or reading about Saul. His is one of the great negative examples of Scripture and some have unwittingly followed in his footsteps, only to have to recant, to retract, and retrace their steps. So what about Saul's oath? Saul the Clueless did not know that Jonathan and associate had gone and thumped the Philistine garrison and so he does several things, indicating both his ignorance and impotence. First, he counts noses so as to ascertain that the crown prince is missing. Right . . . the heir apparent is absent and nobody notices? Not only does the king have nothing between the ears, he also has a realm of the silent. Nobody says anything—they had to know. Then, as mentioned above, he consults the ark and then refrains from the shamanism of treating it as a talisman. Then when things are going his way—through no fault of his own—he puts the people under the oath of fasting to give them single-minded devotion to the task of executing his revenge upon the Philistines.

Saul words it this way, "Cursed be the man who eats food before evening, and until I have avenged myself on my enemies" (1 Samuel 14:24). Jonathan, who was out of earshot and apparently out of the monarch's mind, never got wind of this oath until it was too late. When things grind to a halt for Saul and the Lord will not speak with him—the story of his life, henceforth—he will cast lots to seize the culprit and find that Jonathan must die. Apart from a stay of execution imposed by the will of the people (v. 45), the heir apparent would have perished. In the meantime, Jonathan's prognosis of the situation bears repeating, "My father has troubled the land. See now, how my eyes have brightened because I tasted a little of this honey. How much more, if only the people had eaten freely today of the spoil of their enemies which they found! For now, the slaughter among the Philistines has not been great" (1 Samuel 14:29-30). His assessment is at once pathetic and profound: Saul's oath is one more bit of evidence that he really is not fit for command. But it is profound in that the crown prince, at this early stage in the monarchy, has observed that his father is trouble. He observed that the battle would have gone better if the people would have been permitted to take a lunch break. He also observed, against the forced opinion of the people in verse 45, that the battle went well but not as decisively as it should have. It has been a tactical victory but not a strategic victory. The Philistines would regroup to be a problem in the future. Jonathan also reveals his military strategy—the strategy of a true berserker—if someone's army is on your territory, take no prisoners! None of them may go home alive.

Perhaps, though, this is a portend of things to come. Jonathan would be David's lieutenant in the next administration (1 Samuel 23:17); but he will never live to see that happen. Perhaps the reprieve, the stay of execution granted him by the collective will of the people, is exactly that. As long as Saul and his family are alive, David will not be free to reign unencumbered. When Saul is brought down and the kingdom can be transferred materially as it has already been transferred spiritually, then Jonathan will have to have already exited the stage of history. Perhaps this scene with Jonathan falling victim to his father's own misplaced oath is a foreshadowing of things to come in the narrative. It would be easy to say so with the hindsight of knowing how things will end; but even from this point, it would appear that the shadow cast is long.

There is a valuable lesson to be learned in observing Saul's oath and its aftermath. People really are responsible for what they say and people in leadership are especially accountable. When people in leadership say something stupid and people act upon it, then there is a double culpability accrued to the leader. In Saul's case, they are only words. But they carry the force of pain of death. Saul could have potentially ended the life of his first-born son simply by forgetting that he was not around when the oath was uttered. What if the people did not rally to Jonathan's cause? What if the heir apparent was executed? What if the hero of the story was suddenly killed by those he so valiantly served? These are the worst cases of the scenario that can occur in the carelessness and recklessness of leaders who cavalierly ignore the power of their words.

### Seize the Culprit! Jonathan?!

We should have been ready for the "seize the culprit" motif. Jonathan has already given subtle mention of such a motif previously. In response to information about Saul's oath, he says, "My father has troubled the land." The word for trouble is, of course, *'achar* which harkens back to the naming of a valley of trouble (*'Achar*), after that troubler of Israel, Achan, was seized as the culprit and put to death.

> Then Joshua and all Israel with him, took Achan the son of Zerah, the silver, the mantle, the bar of gold, his sons, his daughters, his oxen, his donkeys, his sheep, his tent and all that belonged to him; and they brought them up to the valley of Achor. And Joshua said, "Why have you troubled us (*'achartanu*)? The LORD will trouble you (*ya'karka*) this day." And all Israel stoned them with stones; and they burned them with fire after they had stoned them with stones. And the raised over him a great heap of stones that stands to this day, and the LORD turned from the fierceness of His anger. Therefore the name of that place has been called the valley of Achor to this day.
>
> Joshua 7:24-26[65]

The point here is that Jonathan subtly indicates what is about to happen. He is about to be proven to be the culprit in the same manner as was Achan. He will be taken by lot. We should also remember that recently Saul has been taken by lot as the king of Israel (1 Samuel 10:17-27). We should also be reminded that this is not a positive motif—it is often the manner in which people are proven guilty and subsequently sentenced to death. In effect, it is not different here: Jonathan will be taken by lot with the impending death sentence and given a reprieve by the people of Israel. He will still die an ignominious death; he has merely received a temporary stay of execution. Ironically, the "great victory" inaugurated and partially effected by Jonathan would be the great reversal and tragedy of 1 Samuel 31.

We might also notice, while we are at it, the conflicting opinions of the players with respect to the events of the day. The narrator says, in words that echo Exodus 14:30, "And the LORD delivered Israel in that day" (1 Samuel 14:23). Jonathan says to the one who informs him of Saul's oath, "How much more . . . for now the slaughter among the Philistines has not been great" (v. 30). And the people's evaluation in attempting to save Jonathan from the consequences of Saul's oath is, "Must Jonathan die, who has worked this great deliverance in Israel?" (v. 45). And so we might assess the damage here: it would look like there was a very important tactical victory that day; but it would also appear that the end result was something short of a strategic victory. Israel now had the advantage of fighting downhill rather than in her own highlands.

But in this instance of the "seize the culprit motif," Jonathan's life has been threatened. It is the collective will of the people that he receive a stay of execution; but what of Jonathan? He is right, Saul has troubled the land and Jonathan is part of its people. Put yourself in his position: how much would you, as crown prince, trust a despotic father who had the power to have you executed for the sake of fulfilling his own reckless vow? Knowing what we know about political intrigue in the palaces of Israel and the kingdoms around, would it be so hard to envision yourself as the subject of discussion in regard to some conspiracy theory? It is a subtle reminder to those first in line for promotion to watch their back and check their information networks carefully. Jonathan is a good man; but he is a good man at risk. Now he is in a high risk position made even more precarious by a CEO who thinks of nothing but himself.

## A Brief Note on Saul's Family

Just as there are things that are harbingers of future events in biblical narrative, there are also things that come back to haunt us—besides Samuel himself! One of those has to do with a couple of notes referring to Saul's family. We are told "And the name of Saul's wife was Ahinoam the daughter of Ahimaaz" (1 Samuel 14:50). This is also the name of one of David's wives (1 Samuel 25:43). The spellings are identical and she is usually named before Abigail (e.g., 1 Samuel 30:5; 2 Samuel 3:2-3). We should not, most probably, suppose them to be the same woman because Saul was so much David's senior. However, two things might give us pause. After 1 Samuel 16, Saul will become increasingly unstable. For such a conspiracy-theory-laden king, it might be quite the temptation to peek more frequently into the royal harem and count noses. Saul had done what he could to divest David of any power in the family by taking away his first wife, Saul's daughter Michal. However, upon hearing that David had remarried a girl by the same name as his own wife, Saul might be tempted to wonder what kind of a coup was blooming. Taking the wives of the king was taking the kingdom (cf. 2 Samuel 16:20-23; 1 Kings 2:19-25). Ideological (nominal?) usurpation of the royal harem might be tantamount to ideological insurrection.

Another notation might give us pause. When Nathan confronts David with respect to the disastrous affair with Bathsheba, he acts as God's mouthpiece saying, "I also gave you your master's house and your master's wives into your care" (2 Samuel 12:8). Who were these of his "master's wives"? Are we merely referring to Saul's concubine, Rizpah? We know that David had some interaction with her after the Gibeonites exacted revenge for Saul's attempted decimation of their people (2 Samuel 21:8-14). Could there be some kind of a relationship between the two kings that is only hinted at in the narrative? Are these only coincidences? Is there more here than meets the eye? Although I am not willing to draw more inferences from these notations, I still think it must have driven Saul crazier than a March hare to know that he who would be king had a wife by the same name as his own wife. Ahinoam the daughter of Ahimaaz and Ahinoam the Jezreelitess—what's in a name?

## Textual Problems

Most of the problems with this text are referential. That is, how could all these things happen over the course of a day? It does seem that there is a bit too much coming and going and too much geography covered; but, we must always be reminded that it is a small country. If people defected or deserted, they walked away at about the same pace that they would have regathered. If they hid themselves, they could always crawl back out (1 Samuel 14:11, 21). The distance between Michmash and Aijalon appears to be about fifteen miles, as the crow flies—significantly longer if you follow the roads or are fighting a battle.[66] Nevertheless, with many events happening simultaneously (by contrast, a text has to follow in a line), it is possible that all the events of the day could have happened before sunset. However, it is easy to understand how the Israelite army might not have relished the idea of a subsequent night assault.

## Textual Applications and Anecdotes

1 Samuel 14

vs.

1. Recklessness and bravery look the same from the outside—only the results distinguish the two.
   Recklessness and bravery look the same from the outside—better not tell dad.
   Recklessness might require an accomplice.
   Recklessness is better if shared.
2. Saul the emblem of failed leadership: unable to gain or keep followers.
3. The introduction of a man from an accursed line: the beginning of the end.
4. Small operation? Look for the narrow pass.
5. Locations are important—if you live there.
6. "The LORD is not restrained to save by many or by few."
   Epithets prove knowledge of the enemy ("these uncircumcised").
   Observe the perfect obedience of the nameless servant.
7. The nameless armor bearer in Scripture is the other arm and the rear guard of the prince.
8. If God is going to work, a sneak attack may not be necessary.
9. The battle plan is the fleece.
   If they attack, we will defend.
10. If they invite attack, we will comply.
11. The enemy often takes a belittling attitude—their ignorance is exposed.
12. The sign observed: proceed!
13. Quick, powerful, efficient—neither survival nor victory depend upon ceremony.
14. Victory: the knowledge that God is on your side—or that you are on God's side!
15. The miracle of the "convenient" earthquake—an "act of God."
    Acts of God terrify His enemies.
16. The watchman is ever vigilant.
    The scattering of the people indicates the hopelessness of the situation.
17. Count, subtract two, find the heroes.
18. Call the doomed priest—find an occasion for his end.
    Beware of treating artifacts and symbols as talismans.
    Call for the ark—create another disaster.
19. Wisdom observes and reconsiders a course of action.
20. Observation of victory and others will join in the rout.
    There may be great confusion in victory.
21. Double defections may be convenient—depending upon which side you are on.

The clueless monarch and the valiant prince finally catch up with each other in the battle.

22. The word gets out and everybody joins in the fray.

23. Analysis of the battle indicates that nobody knew what they were doing and so obviously:
"The LORD delivered Israel that day."

24. When the king takes the battle less than objectively, the people suffer.
When the king takes an oath, everybody had better know about it.
Sunset and vengeance both bring darkness to a people.

25. A forced fast in the land of milk and honey—cruel and unusual punishment.

26. Double indemnity: empty stomach and royal oath.

27. Famished? Fatigued? The quick fix brightens the eyes.
Famished? Fatigued? Ignorance and the quick fix cause trouble.

28. Information on an oath often comes too late.
A royal oath is wearisome to the people.

29. Be careful how you refer to your father; it might come back to haunt you ("troubled").
A bad oath is trouble.

30. A bad oath is a hindrance.
A bad oath may have the opposite of the intended effect.

31. Double note: the people were weary (cf. verse 28); alarms should go off in the heads of leaders.
A partial victory: from the heartland to the slopes.

32. When the sun sets the repeal of the oath produces recklessness.

33. Drain the meat.

34. Superficial religiosity: letter over spirit.

35. From fear to false religion: Saul's first altar.

36. The danger of the night assault: ask God first.

37. God does not answer—something is wrong!

38. The king calls upon the leaders to ascertain culpability—there will be repercussions to infraction.

39. The clueless king witlessly indicts his own son.
The silence of the people screams at the leader.

40. The guilty choose the wrong side.
The compliance of the people indicates their innocence.

41. God answers the prayer to find the guilty.

42. The final lot cast, the truth known—the ancient divination.

43. Jonathan's confession is like that of Achan's, yet only one was delivered.
After the culprit is seized, only the highborn of valor may be acquitted.

44.     The king's willingness to keep his oath, even against the heir apparent, contains a silent message.
        No one is exempt from the wrath of the king.
45.     Out-voted, out-manned and out-gunned, the king accedes to the will of the people.
        The people's voice: the punishment wouldn't fit the crime.
        The people's voice: the punishment is counterbalanced by the victory.
46.     God silent, Jonathan acquitted: battle over.
47.     The life of the king of a small constitutional monarchy: constant warfare.
48.     The king battling enemies performs valiantly.
49.     The children of the king will be known and receive honorable or dishonorable mention as are the merits of the case.
50.     The wife of the king will be known; there might be some intrigue about her.
        The general of the king will be known; he may be the result of nepotism.
51.     The genealogy of the king will be known—such knowledge may be important later.
52.     When there is constant warfare, watch out for the draft.
        People with ability will be conscripted; either for leadership or for fodder.

## Conclusion

We should conclude with the ramification of this, the second strike against Saul. Jonathan has entered the story and has proven his valor. He will prove to be a key figure, especially in the exile of David. Saul has proven himself unfit for command due to his willingness to unnecessarily trouble the land and for his austerities toward the military. He has recklessly endangered the hero of the story and most probably betrayed his trust. He must yet be removed from office and that could be many years down the road; but Saul is going to fall and all the signs of the looming shadow are evident. Unfortunately, when kings go crazy, there are a lot of good people who go down with them. In my opinion, Jonathan is the greatest hero in the so-called "deuteronomistic writings." He will prove himself to be good in a fight. An unabashed, resolute, and passionate Yahwist (1 Samuel 14: 6, 10, 12), he will prove himself to be singly devoted to God. He will prove himself to be either shrewd enough to negotiate the intrigue of the palace or that he is able to rise above it. He will demonstrate his loyalty and friendship both to David and to Saul in such a way that will cost him his life. Jonathan is among the greats of biblical writ.

# 1 Samuel 15
## The Rout of the Amalekites
## Samuel Disowns Saul

—∿—

## Introduction

This chapter entails what I refer to as "strike three" in Saul's life. The first blunder had to do with assuming the priestly office. Saul was king and had been among the prophets, so perhaps he had thought of it as a natural consequence of his preeminent position. He was wrong and was already forewarned that there would be no dynasty. Saul's second mistake was to prove the effects of that warning in view of the fact that he cursed his own son. Although given a reprieve, Jonathan would never live to pass on a royal legacy. This third mistake has to do with much more shrill disobedience on the part of Saul. He is ordered to eradicate the Amalekites and he fails miserably. In the first place, the Amalekite king, Agag, is still alive. In the second place, the fact that they continue to harass Israel proves that he not only failed in the attempt but lied about it. Finally, all the livestock and valuables that were supposed to be devoted to destruction, "put under the ban," were not destroyed as directed by God.

Unlike David, when confronted, Saul gives several classic illustrations of blame shifting and blame sharing. He distorts the discussion and attempts to demonstrate piety by disobedience. This simply will not work for a God who wants obedience and truth along with devotion. The dissonance between prophet and monarch will become so shrill that they will separate from each other and "Samuel did not see Saul again until the day of his death" (1 Samuel 15:35). Let us follow the story and see how it will end for the disobedient and disenfranchised monarch.

## Reading from "Saul: A Life Suspended in Doubt"

Since military action was the rule of the day, I was not surprised when Samuel notified me that God had told him that we were to exterminate Amalek. We were to put them completely under the ban according to the prophet, killing men, women, and children and have nothing to do with the spoil. We followed through on that one valiantly. We even took some of the cattle and sheep from the Amalekites for a sacrifice to God. I brought along Agag, their deposed king, to prove to the prophet that we had done what he told us to. We searched for Samuel and when we found him you would have thought that he would have been pleased—no more Amalekites! On the contrary, he was livid! His words will forever ring in my ears, "What then is this bleating of the sheep in my ears, and the lowing of the oxen which I hear?" It was then that it dawned upon me, just like Achan, and just as Jonathan's words to his friend, "My father has troubled the land!" I was the problem. There was no immediate solution.

Samuel publicly rebuked and humiliated me. Samuel then loudly rehearsed the matters of my becoming king and then told all present that the kingdom had been stripped from me. He turned his back to leave me and I grabbed his shawl. When it tore, he used that as the occasion to dramatically grandstand the place and tell everyone that I was deposed. The people, of course, didn't immediately see it that way. Samuel went back with me and I felt better about the formalities of the ritual. Then Samuel called for the Amalekite king and then he killed Agag. Then, in what could be described as nothing other than rage, he hacked the remains of Agag into pieces with a sword. Watching such an old man do something like that is not something that quickly leaves the memory. Then Samuel walked away; as he left, I got the feeling that he had just hacked my carcass to pieces. I was never to see him again alive. (1 Samuel 15)

## Textual Observations

## The Mission

When God commissions Samuel to send Saul on the mission to annihilate the Amalekites, the words are simple enough: "Now, go and strike Amalek and utterly destroy all that he has, and do not spare him; but put to death both man and woman, child and infant, ox and sheep, camel and donkey" (1 Samuel 15:3). The killing of the people is clear: nobody; man, woman, or child is to be left alive. Because of the general nature of the ban on livestock, some wag of a prosecutor might say that you could keep a goat; but, the nature of the ban is clear. No people, no livestock, no possessions are to be taken; all of it is to be destroyed. But there is some textual mud that we have to sift through to find our lenses.

First, why is there the antecedent historical information about the anointing and its authority derived from God (1 Samuel 15:1)? Is it because that is at stake here and that this test of obedience will determine not the dynasty—that has been decided—but the viability of Saul's very reign? My theory is that we have some very sharp shadow-casting here and the shadow is over Saul the man.

Secondly, we are given the historical notice about Amalek's impolite treatment of Israel centuries earlier when in exodus from Egypt. The narrator has Samuel quoting God (discourse imbedded in discourse imbedded in narrative) as saying, "I will punish Amalek for what he did to Israel, how he set himself against him on the way while he was coming up from Egypt" (1 Samuel 15:2). This centuries-old grudge of God against Amalek is now to be settled once and for all. Saul looks for all the world as though he were in a position to redeem himself. It all hangs on his obedience. We are told of the offense and this grudge first in Exodus: "Then Amalek came and fought against Israel at Rephidim . . . So Joshua overwhelmed Amalek and his people with the edge of the sword. Then the LORD said to Moses, 'Write this in a book as a memorial, and recite it to Joshua, that I will utterly blot out the memory of Amalek from under heaven.' And Moses built an altar, and named it The LORD is My Banner; and he said 'The LORD has sworn; the LORD will have war against Amalek from generation to generation'" (Exodus 17:8-16).

Later notices include Numbers 24:20 and the oath revived and delivered to Israel on the verge of Jordan in Deuteronomy: "Remember what Amalek did to you along the way when you came out from Egypt, how he met you along the way and attacked among you all the stragglers at your rear when you were faint and weary; and he did not fear God. Therefore it shall come about when the LORD your God has given you rest from all your surrounding enemies, in the land which the LORD your God gives you as an inheritance to possess, you shall blot out the memory of Amalek from under heaven; you must not forget" (Deuteronomy 25:17-19).

Apparently, they had either temporarily "forgotten," ignored the mandate, or were finally in a position of "rest from all surrounding enemies" allowing them to take action. Now the matter falls to Saul. Amalek is a ripe plumb for picking and they are basically centralized in a "city." But even in this, the material looks like a test—and people often fail tests in the Bible. With what has gone before (usurping the priesthood and the cursing of Jonathan), Saul is not presented in the kind of light that bodes success.

## A Provision for Friends Living in Unfriendly Territory

After the summoning of a formidable fighting force, Saul advances. Perhaps parenthetically, it ought to be noted that Judah is rather poorly represented in the van and her absence is particularly conspicuous due to the proximity and sometimes encroachment of Amalek (usually) to her borders. Along the way, old friendships are remembered. Saul addressed the Kenites: "Go, depart, go down from among the Amalekites, lest I destroy you with them; for you showed kindness to all the sons of Israel when they came up from Egypt" (1 Samuel 15:6). Since part of the issue at stake is what certain peoples did to Israel at vulnerable times during the Exodus, it stands to reason that kindness at the same time should be recognized. Whether Saul is under the advice of the court historians at that point or is rehearsing from memory is unknown. What can be known is the use of the pronouns. Saul takes upon himself responsibility for the attack and the glory for the victory in a single word: "lest I destroy you with them." Apparently, the associations run something like this: Moses' father-in-law was the priest of Midian and was somehow related to the Kenites. Because of the kindness shown by him (Exodus 18), the same antipathy shown to the Midianites and received by them (Judges 6) is not shared by the Kenites. You can follow the trail yourself (Exodus 2:15–3:1; 18:9-10; Numbers 10:29-32; Judges 1:16; 4:11; 5:24), but the point here is that they are warned to flee the coming conflagration.

There are two things at issue here. First, in the warning, whether by himself or under the advice of counselors, Saul reciprocates in kindness to the Kenites for an ancient memory of kindness shown to Israel at the time of the Exodus. One should probably consider the ramifications of that with respect to foreign diplomacy. Ancient kindnesses can have desired paybacks at later dates. Secondly, if the Kenites were living among the Amalekites and warned to get away from ground zero, the information might have leaked to the Amalekites. If so, they would have had time to prepare for the "ambush" or to get out of town or some of both. In any case, a significant population of our neighbors simply gets up in the middle of the night and leaves, and nobody notices. . . . I think not and Saul probably announced his presence well enough. The size of the army would then have been necessary. Because of the usually nomadic state of the Amalekite culture, the "city" was probably more along the lines of a huge Bedouin village. If they were effectively surrounded, the Amalekites should have had grave difficulty in escaping. The fact that the king was captured is indicative of the fact that they decided to turn and fight. Be that as it may, it did not end well for them that day; but they were neither decimated nor unable to attack Israel in the future—and they would again one day (1 Samuel 30).

## The Mission as a Failure

"The sound of the words of the LORD" should have been easy enough to interpret for Saul: kill all the people and destroy all the property. However, Saul never did seem to have control of the situation—indeed, he appears as though he does not know what is going on from time to time. In this case, he seems more complicit in the crimes of the people. Be that as it may, it could be that he thought that he had complied in measure with the Lord's directive. He was probably elated over the results. Very much as had been the case in the rescue operation in Jabesh-Gilead, the battle had been very one-sided this day as well. Saul was victorious and none of the people of the "city of Amalek" were allowed to live. All well and good, but because they are resurrected by the end of the book, we might suspect that there should have been other operations yet to come. Because Saul was inefficient and incomplete in the task, he would never be re-commissioned to execute God's vengeance and wrath on the Amalekites.

Saul also kept Agag, the king of the Amalekites, alive. This makes me wonder how isolated an operation this must have been. Nevertheless and more to the point, "the people spared Agag and the best of the sheep, the oxen, the fatlings, the lambs, and all that was good, and were not willing to destroy them utterly; but everything despised and worthless, that they utterly destroyed" (1 Samuel 15:9). I am not really certain what kind of a trophy the Israelites thought they had taken in Agag; but the fact that the king of Israel allows him to live indicates that he is either complicit or fearful. We cannot know from the text. Saul has said that he was afraid (1 Samuel 15:24). However, this is only after a couple of rounds with the prophet and the king's inability to shake his tenacious pursuit of the truth. No doubt Saul was afraid of something; but was he afraid of the people, the prophet, the truth? We cannot tell from his words.

Because we are deep into Jerry's (My) Law of the First Offense here, it would seem that nothing Saul does or says from chapter 13 forward will prove of any avail. Here, no matter how he blame shifts, blame shares, or spreads the argument, he cannot escape a prophet skilled in all matters of jurisprudence. But even when he caves in, we have to ask ourselves: is his the confession of a broken heart or the admission of guilt so as to allay punishment? In short, is Saul sorry, or is Saul sorry he got caught? Ultimately, we cannot know; but because he couches his apology in the esteem of the elders and the desire for public worship, we suspect the worst. At this point the differences between Saul and David become stark: when confronted, Saul argues and then caves in for the sake of convenience and empowerment. However; when David is confronted he does not argue, he merely confesses and waits for his sentencing.

Humanly speaking, the mission is not really a failure. In wars of the time, a rout followed by a good hearty pillaging meant victory. But on the level of the spiritual, Saul's inability to follow orders to the letter proves to be his undoing. This is such a blinding failure as to cause the prophet to reject him "until the day of his death" and to be "grieved over Saul" (1 Samuel 15:35). There will be another solution, but we must wait a chapter for it. Saul will fight against that solution for the rest of his life.

### The Prophetic Confrontation of Failed Leadership

This dialog representing Samuel's tenacious dispute with the king will be his last—in the land of the living. He will take on the king for about three rounds and attempt to prove the truth to the king and then abandon the rejected monarch. Because the command was clear (1 Samuel 15:3), and the evidence bleating and lowing all about him (v. 14), it will be a matter of getting Saul to admit the truth. Saul first, apparently sees Samuel coming and goes out to meet him. He says, "Blessed are you of the LORD! I have carried out the command of the LORD" (v. 13). Because Saul's words are untrue, we begin the first round of Samuel, the king-maker's prosecution of the king.

He begins with a question regarding the self-evident. "What then is this bleating of sheep in my ears, and the lowing of the oxen which I hear?" (1 Samuel 15:14). Saul was supposed to destroy, and it is explicitly mentioned, the oxen and sheep (1 Samuel 15:3). That they are still around to tell their story proves that something is amiss. Saul admits no fault but immediately attempts to spread the argument. "They [pronouns scream at you!] have brought them from the Amalekites, for the people spared the best of the sheep and oxen, to sacrifice to the LORD your [!] God; but the rest we have utterly destroyed" (v. 15). Saul has really convicted himself of at least two crimes here: first, the cattle and sheep are in fact from the Amalekites, proving that he did not keep to the parameters of the mission. Secondly, he proves that he is unfit for leadership because, on his watch, his people disobeyed either flagrantly or ignorantly the clear directive of the prophet's commands. Perhaps Saul did not tell them—he is guilty. Perhaps they did not obey—he is guilty. Any way you lose, you lose. But observe the pronouns again, "They have brought them from the Amalekites." Saul is blaming the people rather than assuming responsibility for the crime. Secondly, in attempting to shift the discussion toward the prophet he says that the best of the livestock were brought "to sacrifice to the LORD your [Samuel, get this, it is you!] God. Samuel, of course, has no interest in phoniness with respect to the facts of the case, truth in general, or more especially, with respect to phony religiosity. Some of the lines following are the greatest in this regard in all of biblical literature.

Round two, though interrupted by the king, begins with Samuel telling him about what the Lord said the previous night. "Wait, and let me tell you what the LORD said to me last night" (v. 16). After being given permission to continue, Samuel rehearses the whole indictment, history, and all. He says: "Is it not true, though you were little in your own eyes, you were made the head of the tribes of Israel? And the LORD anointed you king over Israel, and the LORD sent you on a mission, and said, 'Go and utterly destroy the sinners, the Amalekites, and fight against them until they are exterminated.' Why then did you not obey the voice of the LORD, but rushed upon the spoil and did what was evil in the sight of the LORD?" (vv. 17-19).

The memorial of Saul's insignificance is something indicated by both the narrator in the story of his quest of the donkeys (1 Samuel 9) and admitted by Saul himself within that story (v. 21). Whether his statement is one of mock modesty cannot be ascertained from the text. That he came to have an inflated sense of self-importance and to oscillate between that and fear and doubt is the more evident reality to the reader of the Samuel Narratives. The account of Saul's elevation was a fact of national, indeed international, recognition. However, then comes the rub: Samuel indicts Saul for knowing the clear command to see that the Amalekites were "exterminated" and yet failed to do so. The crime is clear, the indictment is clear; prepare for equivocation from the king of denial. Saul responds: "I did obey the voice of the LORD, and went on the mission on which the LORD sent me, and have brought back Agag the king of Amalek, and have utterly destroyed the Amalekites. But the people took some of the spoil, sheep and oxen, the choicest of the things devoted to destruction, to sacrifice to the LORD your God at Gilgal" (1 Samuel 15:20-21).

Saul's understanding of things proves to be global upon inspection. He admits to going "on the mission on which the LORD sent" him. However, his words not only admit that he failed to carry out the mission but that he knew exactly what he was supposed to do. In claming to "have utterly destroyed the Amalekites" and bring back the "choicest of the things devoted to destruction," Saul uses both the verbal and the nominal forms of the word *haram*. It is the word from which the word "harem" comes from and has come to have the connotation of "forbidden" in our language. However, the technical usage in the Old Testament indicates that everything was to be completely devoted to destruction—on the spot! The historical case, we will remember, has to do with all the trouble Israel had when things at Jericho were put under the ban and Achan swiped some of them, apparently with the complicity of his family. When they lost the easy rout at Bethel and Ai, they started asking God questions, "seized the culprit," killed Achan and co-conspirators, and got on with the business of conquest (Joshua 7). Saul ought to have known better and, in fact, his usage of these two words (*heheramti* and *haherem*) proves that he did know better. Saul has admitted guilt and admitted that his crime was not one of ignorance. Samuel knows the gravity of things here; but first he deals with the heart of Saul's problem. That Saul will never get the point makes him one of the great tragic figures of biblical history.

Round three begins with Samuel uttering some of the most profound words in all of biblical narrative, words that are reiterated, shaped, and refined throughout the remainder of biblical literature. He says, "Has the LORD as much delight in burnt offerings and sacrifices as in obeying the voice of the LORD? Behold, to obey is better than sacrifice, to heed than the fat of rams. For rebellion is as the sin of divination, and insubordination is as iniquity and idolatry. Because you have rejected the word of the LORD, He has also rejected you from being king" (1 Samuel 15:22-23).

The initial question is, of course, intended to be rhetorical. This is rendered obvious by Samuel's answer to his own question: "to obey is better than sacrifice." Saul has attempted to win over the argument on the ban by appeal to religious ceremony. Samuel will have none of it. To him, religion apart from careful obedience is pure sham. Failure in obedience to a clear command is raw disobedience and Samuel calls it rebellion and insubordination.[67] He compares such a breach to defection in the areas of loyalty to God Himself. Divination is the appropriation of forbidden means for the purpose of ascertaining the future. God has not allowed us to use divination as indicated variously.[68] The knowledge of the future might lead to the presumptuous attempt to manipulate the future and God will reveal only that which He deems necessary for personal and general eschatology. In addition, the association of divination with other practices, such as human sacrifice or sorcery, in indicative of the fact that many of these evil birds fly in the same flock. God is trying to help His people avoid paganism of all stripes.

Samuel also compares such a breech to iniquity. Iniquity is the more general term "transgression." Sin always separates; but it appears to work in two directions. First, there is the missing of the mark or inaccuracy with respect to the efforts of life. We try to do something and we fail. The other side of the equation is more to Samuel's point: transgression means most simply, coloring outside the lines. That is, there are clearly demarcated commands and proscriptions that are given to the believing community and failure or transgression is going out of bounds in regard to them. That is what Saul has done. He was given a clear command, one he clearly understood, and he failed to comply.

Finally, Samuel also compares such a breech to idolatry. From the New Testament we understand that the root of idolatry is materialism and is expressed by greed (Colossians 3:5). Samuel has indicated that Saul's disobedience is little better than idolatry wherein one substitutes material and form for that which it represents. Saul, on the face of it, has said that he would bring in all this livestock to sacrifice to God and yet in the state of disobedience, he is no better than those pagan chieftains around him who include animal sacrifice to their worthless gods along with their victory celebrations.

We have concluded the three rounds of indictment and now we have a couple of rounds of aftermath. It will begin with Saul's admission of guilt and end with Samuel never speaking to him again. Along the way there are a couple of interesting things that never happen. The first is that Saul never becomes a responsible leader. In response to Samuel's great pronouncement, he says, "I have sinned; I have indeed transgressed the command of the LORD and your words, because I feared the people and listened to their voice. Now therefore, please pardon my sin and return with me, that I may worship the LORD" (1 Samuel 15:24-25). Saul blames the people, or his fear of them—if we can trust his tale—and so attempts to shirk responsibility for his failure. The second thing that does not happen is that Saul's admission is hardly repentance, according to the normal rules of engagement. Saul is sorry because it went against him and because he got caught. That he blames the people and requests forgiveness and reinstatement into fellowship is proof that he is more self-interested than concerned with either Samuel's or God's interests. The third thing that happens is that despite the request for forgiveness on the part of Saul, Samuel—and apparently God—never extends forgiveness to him. It could be, like Esau of old (remembered in Hebrews 12:16-17), despite having pleaded for it, Saul could not obtain it because his heart was never changed. Finally, the thing Saul never gets back is his old friend and mentor Samuel. That Samuel was a friend may be hard to ferret out; but that he is truly grieved over the man is proven by the text and God's words to Samuel (1 Samuel 15:35; 16:1). Samuel's response to Saul's words is at once alarming and not finally fulfilled. He says, "I will not return with you; for you have rejected the word of the LORD, and the LORD has rejected you from being king over Israel" (1 Samuel 15:26). That is, there is no forgiveness which Saul has requested and Samuel the prophet will no longer associate with this fallen monarch.

Upon turning to go, Saul grabs the fringe of Samuel's robe and tears it. One has to consider the positioning here: Saul was a tall man and the fringe was very low. Could it be that Saul was on his knees? Could it be that as the prophet and king-maker had turned to go, the deposed monarch literally dove for the prophet to slow his departure? Samuel used the torn robe as a teaching point: "The LORD has torn the kingdom of Israel from you today, and has given it to your neighbor who is better than you" (1 Samuel 15:28). This concludes this fourth round or the first round of the fallout of the indictment. In it, volumes are said. First, the kingdom is no longer Saul's and in holding it, his is an illegitimate government. Second, his government is publicly delegitimized that very day. Third, there has already been a transfer of the government in the mind of God and that is to someone Saul does not know but who is considered his neighbor (the Hebrew word often means "friend," a play on words that will extend throughout the narrative). The Samuel Narrative will thus become a treatise upon the deposed clueless monarch who has friends he never knew—or friends he thinks are enemies. Samuel concludes his words with words that ring of timeless prophetic authority. "And also the Glory [or Eternal One] of Israel will not lie or change His mind; for He is not a man that He should change His mind" (1 Samuel 15:29). We will have to deal with the decree to change the government and the change of God's mind, below. However, for now, we should be careful to note that this is the timeless truth the passage intends to convey. God is to be viewed as eternal, unchanging, and absolutely truthful. His subjects are, of course, less so, but they are to emulate Him in this communicable attribute of truthfulness as much as humanly possible.

The next round begins with Saul repeating what he said before with less of the excuses given in the other rounds. Saul says, "I have sinned; now honor me before the elders of my people and before Israel, and return with me, and I will worship the LORD your God" (1 Samuel 15:30; NASB has a purpose clause, "that I may worship"). Saul admits his guilt; he does not admit his regret over his guilt. He wants Samuel to legitimize him in the eyes of the nation. That Samuel does so might confuse the reader until we consider what might have happened otherwise. Perhaps Saul would have had Samuel killed. Perhaps there would have been insurrection and chaos after bloody coup after political disaster. Perhaps there was unfinished business! Samuel knows that there is at least one detail that must be attended to: the death of Agag. So Samuel went back with Saul and "he" (the apocopated form almost looks like a plural), Saul, worshiped the Lord. When they are finished with whatever formalities are entailed in the sacrifice, Samuel immediately tends to unfinished business. The thing that stands out after the sham is the prophet's rage. See "Settling Old Scores," below.

## The Important Yet Paradoxical Message of the Story

The paradoxical message is two-fold. First and because it is in the words of the prophet and king-maker, Samuel, there is the backgrounded message that God prefers good heart attitudes to material and formal worship. This theme will be rehearsed in the next chapter with respect to Samuel's attempt to view Eliab, David's oldest brother, as the next king (1 Samuel 16:7). But here, the words bear repeating. Beginning with the rhetorical question, Samuel says: "Has the LORD as much delight in burnt offerings and sacrifices as in obeying the voice of the LORD? Behold, to obey is better than sacrifice, to heed than the fat of rams. For rebellion is as the sin of divination, and insubordination is as iniquity and idolatry. Because you have rejected the word of the LORD, He has also rejected you from being king" (1 Samuel 15:22-23).

The message imbedded in a piece demonstrating the Law of First Offense is clear: The God of Israel, the God of the Bible, is One who is more concerned about obedience than He is with the functions of organized religion. In His view, as portrayed by the prophet Samuel, faith and obedience are paramount and upon them are based all aspects of true religion. The message has both a point and a counterpoint though. Disobedience, here called rebellion and insubordination, entails a payback as well. We are not Saul, neither were those who studied these texts in antiquity; however, this shows what God thinks about such things and what He would compare them to: divination, iniquity, and idolatry. When a member of the believing community is characterized by faithlessness and disobedience, he or she may expect not to be removed from the monarchy, but to be removed from a position of authority or responsibility nonetheless. It goes deeper: disobedience can be stupid or wanton or both. If someone completely rejects what they know to be true, as Saul did, they can expect to be rejected and de-legitimized in their position and eventually removed from their position. That is the message of the rest of the book: Saul, the de-legitimized monarch of Israel, gradually losing power and influence—indeed, his mind—and being removed forcefully from office to be replaced by his "neighbor who is better than" him.

One of the more paradoxical problems faced by the sincere interpreter of biblical narrative has to do with times when God apparently changes His mind. In the case of our text here, at the foregrounded level of discourse, the story will have God changing leadership and yet not changing His mind. The message is first backgrounded for us in the words of Samuel: "And also the Glory of Israel will not lie or change His mind; for He is not a man that He should change His mind" (1 Samuel 15:29). Reconciling this will be difficult until we step back and take a look at the big picture. The anointing of Saul as the king of Israel entailed nothing of the duration of the office. He was told that he would be "ruler over [the LORD's] inheritance" (1 Samuel 10:1; The pronouncement is actually a rhetorical question; but Saul the great question mark of 1 Samuel will prove that we are right to leave it an open question). But the story at the foregrounded level progresses to the point (1 Samuel 16:13-14) where we will begin to see Saul eclipsed by David. Chapter 13 shows the first stage of the answer to Samuel's rhetorical question: there will be no dynasty. Samuel says, "The LORD would have established your kingdom over Israel forever. But now your kingdom shall not endure" (1 Samuel 13:13-14). The second stage has to do with Saul the clueless monarch's unfitness for leadership in forcing the people to take an oath and unwittingly cursing his own son, the heir apparent (1 Samuel 14:24, 39, 44). Although the people give Jonathan a stay of execution, the die is cast. Saul's dynasty will not continue; the heir apparent will perish in the aftermath; and another will be found that meets God's qualifications. With the events of chapter 15, the monarch himself is de-legitimized and the kingdom is to be spiritually transferred. The remainder of the book and the first five chapters of the next indicate how the people of Israel finally caught up with God's plan.

In short, God's selection of Saul was conditional. Saul was, in fact, the legitimate theocratic ruler of Israel but lost his legitimacy due to repeated disobedience. If we believe anything of the omniscience of God, we have to include in that belief the knowledge that God understood the feebleness of the human condition. Humans grow old and die for one thing; kings do not necessarily leave a legacy to their legitimate heir. God will not establish a dynasty until He does so through that man singularly devoted to Him, David. The story is now about how that happens until 2 Samuel 7.

## Settling Old Scores: Samuel Swings the Sword of Justice

In one of the more grisly images in the Bible, we are invited to recreate in our minds what it must have looked like to have the antique prophet seize a sword, address his captive victim, and hack the king of the Amalekites to pieces. Either there is something of the ironic, perhaps comical, in this or Samuel was not as old as he let on and was merely trying to take out an early retirement (1 Samuel 12) or Samuel was in incredibly good shape for an old man. At the end of a day of battle—and we must remember that our hardened steel was not available to them—the sword of anybody engaged in the battle would have been bent, nicked, and dulled. This is not a good combination for dismembering captives. A couple of thoughts with respect to the blade: first, perhaps it belonged to Samuel himself. He had not been involved in the melee and could have brought one from home. It is an interesting image to consider the great prophet of Israel carrying the warrior's sword. Throughout history there has been the desire to blend theology and patriotism. The scene is reminiscent of the statue of Zwingli carrying both a Bible and a sword.

Secondly, however, the sword could have been that used by Saul. No doubt since the previous chapter there had been ample opportunity to scour the battlefield for abandoned weapons—or the weapons of those who no longer needed them—and I doubt that only Saul and Jonathan had swords any longer (1 Samuel 13:22). This might be indicative of Saul's place in the army. Whereas Jonathan and David were fighters—even berserkers, as I have indicated above—Saul was always hanging about behind things and conveniently arriving late to the fray. He was also relatively ignorant of the affairs of the day when he got there. Be that as it may, Saul is characterized by fear in the narrative and there is no indication that his stomach was not too squeamish to kill someone. Lots of orders, threats, and noise, but no action. That being the case and Samuel grabbing a clean blade, it would most likely have been sharp and oiled, ready for Agag. Samuel knows nothing of squeamishness.

Agag, demonstrating the typical cluelessness of the two monarchs in the story, is brought to the prophet for judgment. He says, whether out loud or to himself, we cannot tell, "Surely the bitterness of death is past." This little bit speaks volumes! Among other things it might mean that, as Jonathan had intimated in a previous context, "For now the slaughter . . . has not been great" (1 Samuel 14:30). Perhaps there were other settlements of the Amalekites and Agag knows that if he can broker a deal with his Israelite overlords, he can go back to business as usual. That they came back and sacked Ziklag in David's day (1 Samuel 30) says that either they replicate like rabbits, or there were quite a few of them left at the end of this day. Another possibility might be that Agag is hoping that bygones will be bygones and that he can in some way live to escape or even to fight another day. Although there might be more possibilities, the last one I offer is that perhaps Agag is hoping that the few Israelites killed in this action might be overlooked in view of their clearly aggressive attack on a peaceful settlement of the Amalekites. In this, he might be hoping that he can mollify his Israelite masters by indicating how many Amalekites were lost in relationship to the few Israelites and perhaps negotiate a cessation of hostilities and his own freedom. As you might guess, I opt for the first one: The Israelites "utterly destroyed all the people with the edge of the sword" (1 Samuel 15:8), but there were other settlements and Agag can recover quickly from the loss and plan a counterattack if he can negotiate his own release.

Samuel's judgment upon Agag should be of interest to us as well. He says, "As your sword has made women childless, so shall your mother be childless among women." Samuel's action as prosecution, judge, and executioner is important. Agag has to know why he, in particular, is dying. This has everything to do with vengeance; but it is the vengeance of God from times past. Agag could not have understood that, most likely, and so Samuel puts it into terms that he would understand and that would implicate him in the historical crime of the Amalekites.

Perhaps Samuel's ceremony may have been a bit overdone by our standards; but the symbolism is stark. When he indicted Agag and executed sentence, the narrator indicates that he implicated Agag in the murder of the rightful owners of the land and on behalf of all the mothers of Israel, Samuel is going to render retributive justice and blood atonement at once (see textual problem, below).

When Samuel is finished with his violent frenzy, he goes home. He leaves angry and he leaves grieved; but the one who will bear the brunt of that will be Saul. We are told by the narrator: "For Samuel grieved over Saul. And the LORD regretted that He had made Saul king over Israel" (1 Samuel 15:35). We have just been told that "the Glory of Israel will not lie or change His mind; for He is not a man that He should change His mind" (1 Samuel 15:29). What could this mean when it says that the Lord regretted something? It would appear that this is merely an attempt to express in an anthropopathic manner what

God feels about the situation. The situation has gone according to God's foreknowledge of it; but yet He feels bad about the choices that people make. He knows the limitations of the human condition and yet He feels bad about the bad decisions humans make. There will be a changing of the regime and Saul will have much longer to prove God's judgment true; but, God knows that neither Saul nor any dynasty inaugurated can long stand and so he begins moving Samuel in the direction of the next king—a king the king-maker prophet will never live to see enthroned.

## Textual Problems

Although we might talk about several things, I will only address two minor problems. The first is lexical. In verse 33, the word translated "hack to pieces" is apparently a *hapax legomenon* (used once). It is the *Pi'el* preterite *wayshasseph*.[69] The Septuagint has ἔσφαξεν (*esphaxen*<σφάζω [*sphazo*]) which means "to slaughter." The exact sense is unknown in Hebrew and there is no corresponding word in the ancient Near East.

". . . the exact sense of the vb. is uncertain; Vrss.: Sept. ἔσφαξεν; Vulg. *in frusta concidit*; Pesh. and Tg. *paššah* to cut up, divide up; the Pesh., the Tg., and most all of the Vulg., point to the traditional translation to cut to pieces . . . . For the problems of translating this word see also the note in TOB; NRSV and REB: he hewed him to pieces.[70]

At this it is best to follow the traditional approach and keep to what the ancient versions have offered. The approach of the Septuagint is an excellent ancient witness: "and he slaughtered." The parallel with the substitutionary atonement ideas where the Septuagint uses this verb is intriguing. It is retributive, yes; but it is also representative. Be that as it may, it would appear that Samuel got very physical at this point and went somewhat crazy in the execution of the Amalekite monarch.

The second problem has to do with the notation given to us by the Omniscient Narrator at the end of the chapter. We are told, "And Samuel did not see Saul again until the day of his death" (1 Samuel 15:35). And yet, it would appear that there was a meeting of the two when David began his odyssey in exile (1 Samuel 19:18-24). Samuel is reported to have died in 1 Samuel 25:1. This note will be rehearsed in 1 Samuel 28:3, immediately before the astounding report of Samuel's appearance from beyond the veil. In the meantime, what happens when David is on the run and Saul is in hot pursuit?

Then [Saul] himself went to Ramah, and came as far as the large well that is in Secu; and he asked and said, "Where are Samuel and David?" And someone said, "Behold, they are at Naioth in Ramah." And he went there to Naioth in Ramah; and the Spirit of God came upon him also, so that he went along prophesying continually until he came to Naioth in Ramah. And he also stripped off his clothes, and he too prophesied before Samuel and lay down naked all that day and all that night.

Therefore they say, "Is Saul also among the prophets?" (1 Samuel 19:22-24).

There are several ways we can reconcile these texts, one saying that Samuel did not see Saul until the day of his death and the other saying that Saul prophesied before Samuel.

1.  We can allow it to stand as a contradiction. However, I really doubt that the ancient writers were that stupid and I suspect that they really are trying to tell us something important. The story simply works too well to allow mindless Western considerations to poison our view of the text.

2.  We can fold the text some way and say that Samuel died that day. First Samuel 25:1 is, then, a recitation of less recent history. Although one might do that with the verb forms as they stand in the text, that would be an unusual usage of them.

3.  We can also allow the words to stand in a couple of ways: first, we might suggest that although Saul prophesied before Samuel, Samuel refused to look at him. Because of the deep emotion in Samuel and the abhorrence he has for Saul, I think this might be a viable option.

4.  We can, secondly, acknowledge what the text has said previously about matters when God changed him. We are told: "Then it happened when he turned his back to leave Samuel, God changed his heart; and all those signs came about on that day . . . and the Spirit of God came upon him mightily, so that he prophesied among them" (1 Samuel 10:9-10).

That is, when "the spirit from God came upon him, so that . . . he prophesied before Samuel" (1 Samuel 19:23-24), he was in fact not himself. That is, the narrator, without being inconsistent with either his belief system or what he has told us previously, is telling us that Saul was considered a different person when the spirit was upon him.

Obviously, none of these solutions will be perfectly compelling for the cynic. However, for those who are attempting to hear what the text is saying and do not believe that the authors were idiots, the last two of these solutions will resound in their consciences. Other solutions may be possible; but I prefer a combination of the last two in view of the fact that I think that they are fair with the text and the ideology it intends to project.

**Textual Applications And Anecdotes**

1 Samuel 15
vs.

1.  Reminder of ministry accomplished may be introduction to ministry future.

2.  To God, a centuries-old grudge is just as impending as it was on the day of offense.
    Opposition to God's program will eventually receive its recompense.

3.  The ramifications of God's command of annihilation are horrific.
    There was absolutely no redemptive value in Amalek.
    There was no value in their people or property.

4.  In a large army, a disproportionately poor showing from some sector makes them conspicuous by their absence.
    There is a reason why people are missing from the battle.

5.  An ambush can be the approach of a coward.
    An ambush can be the approach of one who would reduce his own losses.
    Guerilla warfare is older than the Bible.

6.  Even in war we can remember our friends.
    Proof of friendship is entailed in the friendly warning.
    Even a friendly act, centuries-old, can be remembered.

7.  Even a thorough rout can prove to be a defeat—if the Lord's will is not honored.

8.  Acknowledgement of a living king is proof of the violation of God's decree to put everyone and everything under the ban.
    A partial execution of a ban is a complete failure.

9.  Saving the best of the spoil and putting the useless under the ban is trading obedience for materialism.

10. Leadership in disobedience brings swift response from God.

11. Although we might expect it, the leader's disobedience results in God's regret.
    God's regret provokes the prophet's tears.
    Why is the prophet crying? God knows.

12. The seer, blinded by his tears, may not know where his next mission is.
    When the boss sets up a monument in honor of himself, he becomes his own god.
    When the CEO dedicates his own monument, a pride-induced, spectacular disaster is imminent, the aftermath of which includes the survival of only the cockroaches.

13. Bravado often masks the facts.
    Bravado is bluff needing to be called.

14. The prophet calls the king's bluff.
    The evidence literally screams against the offences of the king.

15. The king says, "That's my story and I'm sticking to it."

The king first spreads the blame—though he bears sole responsibility ("They").

The king admits only to that which puts him in the best light ("the best of the sheep").

The king offers religious reasons why he has done badly.

The king, in admitting partial success, admits complete failure.

16. The prophet tells the king God's word.

The king permits the prophet's words.

17. The king should be reminded of his humble beginnings.

The king should be reminded of where he is now.

The king should be reminded of how he got there—God's sovereign will.

18. When there is disobedience the prophet's job includes reminding the offender of the exact nature of his crime.

19. The prophet's question as to "Why," belies the fact that there is no cogent reason.

The substance of the prophet's indictment will usually include disobedience, materialism, and wickedness.

20. The culpable king may attempt to lie his way out of the situation (If Saul had killed all the Amalekites, where were there Amalekites to cause David problems later?).

The presence of counter evidence provides living proof of disobedience.

21. The culpable king may attempt to shift the blame to his subjects.

The culpable king may attempt to shift the discussion toward his own piety.

The culpable king may attempt to shift the discussion toward the prophet's orientation ("to sacrifice to the LORD your God").

Remember: "Religion is the last refuge of the scoundrel."

22. Obedience is more desired by God than sacrifice.

Obedience may be the foundation upon which sacrifice is offered.

23. To God, rebellion is like sorcery.

To God, insubordination is like wickedness and materialism.

Rejection of the word of the Lord proves His rejection of the rebel.

24. When there is no place to run or hide, the unrepentant leader admits some responsibility.

When the unrepentant leader confesses, he will still attempt to blame share.

When the unrepentant leader confesses, he will admit fear.

25. The unrepentant leader seeks pardon apart from true repentance.

The unrepentant leader will gladly substitute religiosity for repentance and faith.

26. Samuel did not offer forgiveness to Saul. This is a huge point.

The true prophet will most likely withdraw himself from those who wantonly disobey God's word.

The true prophet will most likely withdraw himself from association with rejected leaders.

27. Leaders used to power may resort to physical solutions to spiritual problems.
    The symbolism of the prophet's torn robe is grave.

28. The torn robe is a sign of a torn kingdom.
    The prophet should inform the fallen leader of replacement.
    The prophet should inform the fallen leader that the replacement will be more worthy.

29. In the matter of divinely replaced leadership, God does not lie and He will not change His mind.
    It is a human characteristic to change the mind, not a divine characteristic.

30. Admission of guilt along with exposed motives is honest enough—but does it entail a change of heart?
    A superficial person may only have a two-dimensional view of worship.
    Saul may have thought that by going through the motions he could get back on God's good side.

31. In "prostrating himself" (the real meaning of the verb) to the LORD, Saul was certainly going through the motions.
    When someone worships, are they going through the motions or is it sincere? It may look
    the same from the outside.

32. Old business: kill the Amalekite king!
    The killing of old cockroaches reminds us that there are probably still more.
    Old Agagites never die, they reappear in exile in Esther!
    If God has decreed the end of your people, the bitterness of death is never passed.

33. The Amalekite king is reminded of his crimes.
    What a spectacle! The ancient prophet hacking the warlord to pieces.

34. When it is all said and done, go home.
    When it is all said and done, slink off to the palace.

35. Disassociate yourselves from rejected leadership.
    The prophet grieves over failed leadership.
    The Lord "feels bad" about failed leadership.
    Failed leadership ruins the institution.
    Failed leadership may leave the successor with more difficulties—he will have to regain the people's trust, for one.

## Conclusion

We have observed several things in regard to this titan text of 1 Samuel 15. We have seen the third strike against Saul. He lost the right to dynastic succession in chapter 13; he lost the heir, himself, in chapter 14; and now he is the de-legitimized monarch of Israel. He is a ripe plum ready for picking; he has lost the backing of Almighty God and His prophet. He has been informed that there is one out there who is better than him who will take over the reins of government. Along the way, we have learned something about Israel's God: First, Israel's God is more interested in faith and obedience than He is in perfunctory religion. Second, infractions against what the community of the faithful knows to be true entail comparison to paganism and its attendant troubles. Third, we have several great truths revealed by the prophet and king-maker, Samuel. He says, as we have said above, "to obey is better than sacrifice." He has also said, "The Eternal will not lie or change His mind; for He is not a man that He should change His mind." Such things that touch the eternality of God, His immutability, and His veracity are great truths that the community of the faithful has taken with it throughout the centuries. God is weighed, measured, and never found wanting!

We have seen the rise and the fall of Saul. There were four chapters (9–12) where we were introduced to him and observed his threefold insertion into the story as well as his threefold introduction and presentation to Israel. Upon his meteoric rise to the ascendancy over Israel we saw him as an unlikely hero and then saw him successful and victorious. He seemed like a good man when we first met him and then unrighteousness was found in him. Then there were three chapters (13–15) where we saw him make consecutive mistakes and come crashing down about us. Along with those sons of Belial of old, we now ask, "How can this man deliver us" (1 Samuel 10:27) and with them we despise him and would not give him any presents. But, as it turns out, Saul can no longer deliver us and we were right to hang on to our gifts. Fear not! One is coming who will be judged by history to be more worthy of our attentions. It is to that one that we now look in chapter 16 of the Samuel Narratives.

# 1 Samuel 16
# Introduction to the Anointed Elect
# The Spiritual Tide Turns on Saul

—ɱ—

## Introduction

By way of overview, the section before us begins with Saul the king and Samuel the king-maker separated geographically and spiritually. The prophet, grieving as though his prodigy had died, is challenged by God to stop grieving and to go to an alternative plan. In so doing, the prophet will overcome his fear while being obedient in the dark. He will stumble and bumble his way through seven of Jesse's sons before being aware of an eighth. He will then fulfill his mission and hightail it back home to Ramah.

The second movement of this piece intimates to the reader the spiritual realities behind the transfer of the monarchy from Saul to David. Following that, we are shown the aftermath of a despot, tenaciously holding on to power despite God's disapproval. We will see that king gradually slip into darkness and finally, as the book concludes, he will die a violent and humiliating death at the hands of foreign enemies.

Conversely, in this second movement of chapter 16, we will be introduced to the boy-king. He will demonstrate himself first to be striking, if not particularly regal, and then to be omni-competent. This renaissance boy will be handsome, intelligent, athletic, and musical. He will prove to be the ultimate courtier long before he demonstrates competence as a monarch. Along the way, we will be introduced to his view of and love for God. But we must suspend all assessments of the boy-king, because in biblical narrative, things begun well often do not end that way. Let us see how the transfer goes.

## Reading from "Saul: A Life Suspended in Doubt"

Although I know nothing of the details, I was later to find out that Samuel had snuck off to Bethlehem to anoint another king. He was literally going to follow through with the last detail as kingmaker. I honestly believe that his whole goal in life was to see me deposed before he died. "Live long enough to survive your enemies," I always said. It is a matter of deep regret that I never knew who was an enemy and who was a friend.

As I was to find out, on the very day that my replacement had been anointed, something bizarre happened to me. It seems that there was this evil spirit that harassed me until it drove me insane. It seemed that the only thing that helped was music. So we attempted to find somebody that was a skilled musician to soothe me when the foul air was upon me. As it would turn out, it was none other than David ben-Jesse—the very one Samuel had appointed to replace me. If only I'd known! Perhaps I would have been a bit more persistent about dispatching with that boy. In any case, he really was quite an accomplished musician; and when he played the harp, it was as if there was a symphony. I would often become so distracted that I would forget what I was doing and, mesmerized, I would just drift off with the rhapsody. The description that I was given for the boy was apt: he was good looking, a skilled musician and a great fighter. That last was to play itself out soon. (1 Samuel 16)

## Textual Observations[71]

### Samuel's Grief, Fear, and Blindness—or Samuel's Resolute Faith in the Dark

In the conclusion to the last chapter (or the beginning of this one, see "Textual Problems," below), the narrator has told us that Samuel and Saul have parted company and that, "Samuel did not see Saul again until the day of his death; because Samuel grieved over Saul" (1 Samuel 15:35). Now we are told at the inauguration of God's new plan that He says to Samuel, "How long will you grieve over Saul, since I have rejected him from being king over Israel?" (1 Samuel 16:1). Like Moses of old when told to go to Pharaoh, questions follow that betray confusion and fear. Samuel replies—and hear his exasperation here—"How can I go? When Saul hears of it he will kill me" (v. 2). Then follows a carefully thought out plan to get him past Saul's watchdogs should they challenge him. But the statement about Saul killing him is more than a casual notice. Samuel is afraid. He has just had a very real encounter with the king of the land and gotten away alive. Perhaps he does not feel that he will be so lucky in the future. God has told him to go south, past Saul's homeland, and anoint someone from Bethlehem. He does not know how he can escape Saul's notice and he does not know who he is to anoint.

When he comes to Bethlehem, he is clearly recognized by the leaders of the community. Several nameless elders fearfully and respectfully greet him. At this point, we wonder if Samuel even knows who Jesse is. He simply tells the accepted leadership, "In peace; I have come to sacrifice to the LORD. Consecrate yourselves and come with me to the sacrifice." Then we are told that "he also consecrated Jesse and his sons, and invited them to the sacrifice" (v. 5). We wonder how it is that he becomes acquainted with Jesse and his sons. Are they introduced by the elders of the village? Did Samuel know Jesse and some of the older boys before? We cannot know the answer to these questions. The only thing we can know is that the one who was to be anointed was not among them initially. Indeed, it would be presumptuous to even think that he had been consecrated before he was summoned to the feast. The one to be anointed was merely forgotten, neglected, and left as one of the hired help to tend the sheep while everyone else was invited to the party.

As events unfold, Samuel thinks in the direction of the oldest brother, Eliab (1 Samuel 16:6). But God has rejected him (v. 7) and he must look elsewhere (vv. 8-10). None of these is chosen (v. 10) and so Samuel must blindly ask about the possibility of others (v. 11). Precluding the possibility of beginning the ceremonial meal, Samuel will have to wait to meet the anointed-elect until he can be brought in from the field (v. 12). As the meal grows cold, the boy is brought in. We are struck by his appearance — not necessarily regal — but striking nonetheless. Despite the admonition not to look at the eyes (v. 7), the narrator tells us of the handsome set of his eyes. His hair has the reddish tint of those who work out in the summer sun and the overall assessment is that he is handsome (v. 12). As we have seen before (Rachel, Joseph, Saul) and will see again (Absalom and Adonijah), when one is singled out by appearance, it is the harbinger of disastrous things.

Samuel, no longer in the dark, is now commanded to anoint this, the least of Jesse's sons. He does so, and as is his custom, he returns to Ramah straight away. However, this section does show something about the man Samuel. It does show us that he did not need to have everything spelled out in advance by God to be obedient. Even through potential opposition (death at Saul's hands) and in the face of not knowing all the details of Jesse's family or the human objective of the trip, Samuel is willing to stumble along until he blindly crashes into God's will. Unlike Moses, one question and one answer is enough for him. Despite the similar danger of a maniacal despot, Samuel goes blindly into the future. His obedience apparently was accompanied by an aura of confidence, because the old prophet was even an object of fear to the townspeople. There is probably a lesson here: the resolute determination to follow God even in the dark, may be enigmatic — even frightening — to people around us; but they will respect our confident respect for and obedience to God.

## Divine Deception or a Forgetful Prophet

That Samuel's fear is real is demonstrated by the fact that God was willing to sanction a cover operation for it — or remind the senescent prophet of the proper protocol! In the case of the introductory discussion between the prophet and his God, there is something helpful about the background notices. At the conclusion of the crash of Saul, we are told that Samuel went home to Ramah (1 Samuel 15:34a). We are also told that Saul went up to his house at Gebeah of Saul (v. 34b). This plays the stage north to south with Saul in the middle. Samuel is ordered, by God, to go from his home to Bethlehem, south of Jerusalem. Samuel says, "How can I go? When Saul hears of it, he will kill me" (1 Samuel 16:2).

Because the normal route between Ramah and Bethlehem would have been the highland road, Samuel would necessarily have had to walk nearly right by Saul's front door to get there. This is only a slight exaggeration; but the scene thus painted would be unnecessary had Samuel thought to go by a roundabout way—or would it? Because of the nature of the last several altercations between the king-maker and the deposed despot, it is entirely possible that Samuel's house was being watched for, shall we say, indications of disloyalty. Because Samuel was in the style of the old charismatic judgeships of the previous era, he was naturally an opinion leader. Any loose lips might possibly sink Saul's ship and any movement might be determined to be treasonous by the increasingly paranoid and conspiracy-theory-laden monarch.

So, God devises a plan—seemingly on the spur of the moment (we should probably not confuse the vivid descriptions of time-bound discourse imbedded in narrative for the abstractions of theology—especially in regard to the omniscience and eternality of God). God tells Samuel, "Take a heifer with you, and say, 'I have come to sacrifice to the LORD'" (1 Samuel 16:3). God might, at this point, be indicted for being disingenuous. That is, Samuel needs an excuse and this appears to be merely that, rather than a justifiable reason. However, we should probably remember that this is the way matters were done in ancient Israel. In chapter 9, the whole scene of the anointing of the monarch now deposed revolves around the context of the ceremonies and witnesses at a sacrificial meal (1 Samuel 9:12, 22-24; 10:1). Why should Samuel expect things to be any different? And that is, in fact, exactly what will happen. Jesse and his sons are consecrated for a sacrificial meal along with the elders of the city of Bethlehem and the anointing of David happens within that ceremonial context and with those witnesses (1 Samuel 16:5-13).

What would Samuel have said if confronted by Saul or his agents? "I have come (perspective counts: come if you are the elders of verse 5 and gone if you are an agent of Saul?) to sacrifice to the LORD" (1 Samuel 16:2). That is certainly the truth of the matter; but in the Omniscient Narrator's careful dance between the truth and the whole truth, something is strategically left out. The idea of Saul or his agents asking the aging prophet as to *why* he is going to Bethlehem (two tribes over) might give us pause. Saul simply cannot know that Samuel is going to anoint the next king. The fact that the text reports no such confrontation may be indicative of the fact that in portraying a God who has middle knowledge (knowledge of hypothetical situations that may never happen), we are also granted access to a God who knows how to get His frightened and somewhat nearsighted seer off dead center. This will be an interesting point when we talk about the aftermath of David's raid on the Philistine garrison at Keilah (1 Samuel 23).

## The Great Truth Given Voice By God Himself

In the previous chapter, the devoted reader exulted in the profound nature of biblical religion in ancient Israel as given voice by Samuel. In the heat of a forensic battle with Saul, the aging sage told us the timeless priority of obedience over sacrifice as well as vindications of the truthfulness and reliability of a changeless God. In this chapter, Samuel, the myopic seer, will be given a window into the mind and heart of an omniscient God. He will go blindly to anoint one of Jesse's sons and in so doing stumble upon one of the great truths of biblical writ as we shall see presently.

First Samuel 16:7 says, "God sees not as man sees, for man looks to his two eyes whereas God looks to the heart." It is said that the eyes of a man betray much about the man. However and with training and concentration, a man can be trained to give a message other than what he knows to be true. We have already been told that Eliab, Jesse's oldest son, was majestic in Samuel's estimation: "Then it came about when they entered, that he looked at Eliab and thought, 'Surely, the LORD's anointed is before Him'" (v. 6). That means to Samuel and to those who have read chapters 9 and 10, that Eliab looked every bit as potentially regal as did Saul; however, there is one problem—the heart. The temporarily sightless seer cannot look through Eliab's eyes and see his heart. If he could have done so, he would have recoiled in the horror of knowing of the man's rejection by Samuel's God.

In fact, that very rejection voiced in verse 7 is given voice by the same omniscient God who had rejected Saul in verse 1. Further, it is given in the same words and in nearly the same form. If anything, the language used to reject Eliab is stronger since the longer form of the pronoun is used (*me'astiw* for Saul in 16:1; *me'astihu* for Eliab in 16:7), in both cases translated "I have rejected him." Samuel probably recoiled inwardly when God told him of Eliab's rejection. As it will play out in the narrative, the same unjustifiable rage that characterized Saul for the rest of his life, will be briefly noted in respect to Eliab (1 Samuel 17:28).

## The Dramatic Multiplex Introduction to David

Because we know what and who the chapter is about, we are surprised—should we consider it—that David himself is not named initially. We know that Samuel is only told to go and anoint one of Jesse's sons (1 Samuel 16:1-3). We know that Samuel will sift through them without knowing who it is (vv. 4-10). But what comes next astounds him as much as it does us: There is no David in the group—no David has been "consecrated . . . and invited . . . to the sacrifice" (v. 5). And so, because "The LORD has not chosen these" (v. 10), Samuel has to ask, "Are these all the children?" And Jesse answers, "There remains yet *the youngest*" (v. 11).

With this introduction, we are told of what even Samuel was unaware: Jesse has a youngest *son who* is not present. We know that there is an individual referred to; but we know nothing about *him*. And so Jesse tells us why it is that *he* is not present: "behold, *he* is tending the sheep." And so we not only know why *he* is not here, but where *he* is and what *his* vocation in the family is. After that, Samuel refers to this unknown *son* by pronouns and verb affixes. He says, "Send and take *him* because we shall not go around [the table?] until *he* comes here" (v. 11). Then we are invited to get a look at *David* through cataphoric pronouns.

> And he [Jesse] sent and he brought *him*.
> Now *he* was ruddy, with handsome eyes and a good appearance (v. 12).
> And YHWH said, "Arise anoint *him*, because this is *he*" (v. 13).
> And Samuel took the horn of oil and anointed *him* in the midst of *his* brothers.
> And the Spirit of YHWH came mightily to *David* from that day forward (v. 14).

This, then, is the first mention of the name of the king-elect. We knew who it would be; but it took us at least fourteen verses to get from the separation of the king-rejected and the king-maker to the meeting of the king-elected and the king-maker. And finally we have the name of the man who will bring Israel into its glory—but not before many twists and turns.

## Spiritual Dynamics, Spiritual Transformation, and Spiritual Transfer

One of the most frightening texts in regard to the movements of the Holy Spirit in biblical literature has to be the one before us in 1 Samuel 16:13-14. Samuel has just anointed the nameless son of Jesse in the midst of Jesse's other sons; but the Spirit of YHWH came mightily upon David from that day forward (v. 13). That would be fine, but then we are told: "Now [or "But"] the Spirit of YHWH departed from Saul, and an evil spirit from YHWH terrified him." Because of the parallel syntax between 1 Samuel 15:34 and 1 Samuel 16:13-14, I am tempted to see that what Samuel did physically as the king-maker separated from the despot-deposed as mirrored in what the Spirit did in coming to the king-elect after anointing by the king-maker and subsequently (omnipresence?) leaving the despot-deposed. Observe:

> And Samuel went [preterite verb] to Ramah (1 Samuel 15:34a),
>> but Saul went up [perfect verb] to his house at Gibeah of Saul (1 Samuel 15:34b).

> And the Spirit of YHWH came mightily [preterite verb] upon David from that day on
>> (1 Samuel 16: 13c) . . . [13d is about Samuel going home to Ramah].
> But the Spirit of YHWH departed [perfect verb] from Saul (1 Samuel 16:14).

And so, all the spiritual dynamics are in place for the transfer of the monarchy from the house of Kish to the house of Jesse, from the tribe of Benjamin to the house of Judah. Saul has been at least twice rejected and now the Spirit has left him. David has been anointed among witnesses and the Spirit has come to him. David's rise will now be chronicled against Saul's fall. For several chapters of the Samuel Narratives, Saul will be the black velvet displaying the diamond that is David. Henceforth, we will observe an increasingly agitated Saul. He will become more violent, more insane, and more troubled (demonized), until such time as the situation in this life becomes irremediable.[72] It is not all blessings and light for the son of Jesse, however. We will have to see how he fares in the story.

Just a note: the words "from that day forward" (v. 13) are nearly the same collocation used in 1 Samuel 18:9. In the same sense that the Spirit of the Lord came upon David from that day on, so Saul was suspicious of David from that day on. As the Spirit had left Saul and transferred the anointing for the monarchy, Saul's spirit had a decided antipathy toward David from the time the woman sang the victory song: "Saul has slain his thousands, and David his ten thousands" (1 Samuel 18:7).

### The Description of David: Late Eleventh Century Renaissance Boy!

We have already been told by the Omniscient Narrator of David's appearance. We are told, "Now he was ruddy, with beautiful eyes and a handsome appearance" (1 Samuel 16:12). Certainly, he did not hurt to look at; although we are told nothing particularly regal—as with Saul's stature—about David. He must have qualifications other than looks and a shepherd's resumé. What kind of things were said about David, the son of Jesse?

We should be reminded of those inerrant servants who inform the protagonists of biblical literature as well as we, the readers of the truth. Remember, Saul's servant told him about the seer's location. The girls going out to draw water gave him so much detail as to nearly overwhelm him. Here, along with the rapscallions of the kingdom (1 Samuel 10:27), Saul is surrounded by those nameless servants with global knowledge of the lesser players in the realm. Like Joseph being brought out of prison into Pharaoh's court, some nameless servant of Saul will bring the least son of Jesse into the very court of the man whom he will one day replace. So what of the Renaissance Boy?

We are told by the nameless courtier (servant, young man) of Saul that the man to take away the king's ill humor is, in fact, a son of Jesse the Bethlehemite (1 Samuel 16:18). And since a skillful musician is required, we are told that he is "a skillful musician" (v. 18). I suppose we could not expect Saul to have him hanging around the palace if his appearance made babies cry. So this omniscient servant says that he is, "a mighty man of valor [or a virtuous man—all senses of that word: valuable asset], a warrior, one prudent in speech, and a handsome man" (v. 18). Perhaps now that the Lord is no longer with Saul, the one strike against David would have been that "the LORD is with him" (v. 18). Be that as it may, the yeas have it and David is summoned to the palace.

David's dad is no dummy and he knows that if you have to send away your kid to the palace, it is a good idea to send him with some kind of a gift. So Jesse sent along a donkey load of bread, wine, and a live goat (v. 20). There follows an interesting ambiguity. We are told, "And David came to Saul and he stood before him and he loved him greatly and he became his armor bearer" (v. 21). It is somewhat simple to get lost in the pronouns as to who did what and felt what for whom. The general read on this has been "and Saul loved him greatly." The problem has to do with the fact that Saul's name is not there and this would go against the law of the nearest antecedent. So, is it Saul who loves David? That would appear to be the case from the larger context. In fact, we will see that David loves no one in all of biblical literature; but everyone loves him (1 Samuel 18:16). If David can ever be said to love anybody, it is here. But because the Samuel Narratives go the other way, I have to go against the law of the nearest antecedent and say that it is Saul who loves David—then reversing again—and he [David] became his [Saul's] armor bearer.

When we pick up with proper names again, we see that Saul's estimation concurs with that of his nameless and omniscient servant, "Let David now stand before me; for he has found favor in my sight" (1 Samuel 16:22). And then, of course, the narrator tells us that David proves his competence in respect to his assigned responsibilities in the king's court: "So it came about whenever the evil spirit from God came to Saul, David would take the harp and play it by hand; and Saul would be refreshed and be well, and the evil spirit would depart from him" (v. 23). We are now ready to advance another virtue of David's character: his fearlessness. That will be demonstrated as the boy wonder meets the giant killing machine in the next chapter.

## Excursus: What Really Happened to Saul?

One of the more interesting studies that one can undertake as pertains to the scripture of the older testament is that of a character sketch of the life of Saul. I have been accused of being overly harsh on Saul and of being overly lenient on Saul—perhaps the middle ground is the best place for an instructor to be. We know that "the Spirit of the LORD departed from Saul." The question remains, then, did Saul retain or lose his salvation? In fact, we might even ask, did Saul ever have salvation? Millard Erickson describes one view as follows: "The Bible . . . also records concrete cases of specific persons who apostasized [*sic*] or fell away [noting Samuel Wakefield]. One of the most vivid is the case of King Saul in the Old Testament. He had been chosen and anointed king of Israel, but eventually proved so disobedient that God did not answer him when he prayed (1 Sam. 28:6). Rejected by God, Saul lost his position as king and came to a tragic death."[73]

The solution posited by the systematician is that, "It is a bit difficult, on the other hand, to know how to classify the situation of King Saul, since he lived under the old dispensation."[74] That is the end of the story with Erickson: When in doubt, if it is in the Old Testament, throw it out. This is called cavalier dismissal in the philosophical disciplines. I feel it is unnecessary in any case. There may be valid solutions to the problem. But first let us make the water more muddy!

1.     The problem is complicated by the fact that "an evil spirit from the LORD terrorized him." Often, theologians tell us that those specially possessed by God cannot be possessed by the demonic spirits.

2.     Depending upon the reports, we also know that Saul either committed suicide (1 Sam. 31:4 by the narrator) or commanded someone to finish him off (2 Sam. 1:10 as stated by an Amalekite — another fascinating backloop of the story). Regardless, church tradition says that anyone whose final act is sin should have no expectation of salvation (because, suicide is equated to the sin of self-murder or conspiracy to commit self-murder).

3.     We also are privy to the narrator's commentary that God would not even divulge any information to him through the "accepted" channels (1 Sam. 28:6; dreams, *urim*, or prophets).

Nevertheless, Scripture is silent in regard to exactly what became of Saul after his death. With the exception of precious few persons (Lazarus, Dives [the rich man], Jesus, Satan, the beast and the false prophet, Daniel, Moses, Samuel, and a couple of others) eternal destinies seem to be the exclusive domain of the mind of God. Even the fate of "the son of perdition" will be more clearly understood in that day. However, there are a couple of things that can be said in regard to the three problems related above:

1.     We do not know the level of the demonic involvement: we know that it made him crazy (1 Sam. 18:10-11, throwing a spear at the court musician; 20:30, challenging the legitimacy of Jonathan, his son; verse 33, throwing a spear at the heir apparent; chapter 28, visiting the witch at en-Dor and so on). Although I might concur that one cannot be demonically possessed, it becomes difficult at the point of "power encounter" in ascertaining the difference between obsession, oppression, and possession: only the latter is the point excluded. The phenomenological language of the text does not give you a window into the deepest levels of Saul's internal states.

2.     The issue of suicide as inherited from the Catholic Church seems a bit of a burden to bear. In the first place, salvation would be reduced to chance: vis. if a person were in a plane crash and the last word uttered by that person were an explicative, he would lose his salvation. If a person died in an "unspiritual" condition in incredible

agony as the result of a battle injury in a war not of his own doing, he would lose his salvation. If a person made a stupid blunder in traffic and got himself (and others!) killed, he would lose his salvation. If a person took a bit too much of the holiday brandy and fell down and hurt himself and bled to death, he would lose his salvation. Whether we would care to admit it or not, the differences are those of degree, not kind. This forces the question: why suicide and not any final sin? The church's answer? Because, it is one of the seven deadly sins and the church says so!

3.      Although Saul was not answered by the usual system of revelation during the time, it is interesting what happened at en-Dor. The fact that the medium screamed in terror and recognition indicates that there was something of a divine encounter about to happen. Samuel rebukes Saul for calling him up; but, God still permitted the two of them to get together. It cannot be as though it was merely the will of Saul and the will of the medium that brought Samuel up. It must be that God was giving Saul final notification of the rejection of himself and his line in the monarchy: "tomorrow you and your sons will be with me" (28:19).

This evokes another question: where was Samuel? Was he in hell? Was he in Hades? Was he awaiting final judgment and condemnation? Was he in paradise? Was he awaiting final distribution of rewards and glorification? When he says, "with me," what does he refer to?

Taking away Saul's kingship (as well as the right of heredity) is one thing; taking away his salvation may be more than the text permits. We may simply have to conclude: we do not know.

N.B.: It is not the opinion of the writer that David's words in Psalm 51:11 add any less heat than light: "Do not cast me away from Thy presence, and do not take Thy Holy Spirit from me."

1.      How are we to interpret this? Are we to say that the agent of regeneration is removed and a person loses his or her salvation? For many, that is the acceptable answer. It is, in my opinion again, based on a faulty hermeneutic: vis. confession is elevated to the point of doctrine.

2.      Secondly, the argument always assumes a reciprocal relationship between the historical narrative in 1 Samuel 16 and Psalm 51. That is, it is assumed that Saul lost his salvation and that David feared losing his. There is certainly sufficiency to such an argument—despite its patent circularity; however, its necessity is overthrown by the clear narrative of the text. The only thing we know for sure at the end of the day—or at the end of Saul's life, as the case may be—is that Saul and his descendents lost the monarchy whereas David and his gained it. It could be that David was very certain of his relationship with God, recognized that he had strained his fellowship with God to the breaking point, was genuinely repentant, and wanted

to ensure that he did not lose the monarchy for his descendents. Judging by the punishment, in the words of Nathan "the sword shall never depart from your house . . . The LORD also has taken away your sin; you shall not die" (2 Sam. 12:10-13), it would seem that the only issue left at stake would be that of the monarchy.

3.     We know by the wording in the text of 1 Samuel 16 that the historical flow includes "the Spirit of the LORD came mightily upon David from that day forward" (v. 13, preterit verb). We also know that the wording, "the Spirit of the LORD departed from Saul" (v. 14, perfect verb), is in a disjunctive context (possible pluperfect!) and could be an antecedent action of the Spirit as He disempowered one monarch and subsequently empowered the new rival monarch concomitantly with the anointing by Samuel.

## Textual Problems

Just a quick note: The text breaks better at 1 Samuel 15:34. In that verse the last preterite (simple past tense) takes Samuel home to Ramah—which was his custom after a draining ministry. In the text as we have it, there would be a discourse initial preterite. We have come to expect different clause structures for a change in scene (preterite of "to be" verb, perfect verb, *waw* + noun + perfect, or nominal sentence, etc.). It would be unusual to begin with a preterite. It would be easiest to break the text in one of two following places:

1.     In 1 Samuel 15:34b, we see a disjunction: "Now Saul went up to his house at Gibeah of Saul." This verse could simply be in contrast to the statement in 34a: "And Samuel went to Ramah."

2.     Better perhaps than the contrast indicated above is the disjunction providing back-grounded information to the matters that follow in 15:35: "Now Samuel did not again see Saul until the day of his death, because Samuel mourned Saul; Now YHWH regretted ["felt badly" at any rate] that He had made Saul king over Israel."

However, I wish I had as good an answer for the end of the text. If you held me at pistol point and tried to get me to obey my own rules, I would have to say that the best place to break the text for the military action of chapter 17 is at 16:21d, "Now, David became his armor bearer."

I should think that this would be hardly compelling, however, and that perhaps a provisional solution might be entertained in a different key, as it were. It is possible that the direction of the text is to show us Saul's progressive dementia (or demonization) and that several narratives are sandwiched in between to show us his advanced condition. At the front cover of it, we are told: "Now the Spirit of the LORD departed from Saul, and an evil spirit from the LORD terrorized him" (1 Samuel 16:14). Then we are told, "Now it would come to pass that whenever the spirit from God came to Saul that David would take the harp and play by hand; and Saul would be refreshed and be well, and the evil spirit would depart from him" (1 Samuel 16:23). Then we have the thrilling epic about David's conquest of the giant, Goliath. Because the story is epic—and is so long—we may have forgotten that this is about Saul's descent as much as it is about David's ascent. If we go deep into what we have as chapter 18, we find another scene of David playing virtuoso exorcist: "Now it came to pass on the next day [radical disjunction], that an evil spirit from God came mightily upon Saul, and he raved in the midst of the house, while David was playing by hand, as usual; and a spear was in Saul's hand. And Saul hurled the spear, because he thought, 'I will impale David to the wall'" (1 Samuel 18:10-11).

My conclusion is that despite the length of the piece, we should most probably allow the pericope to be from 16:21d to the end of 18:9. We might even go back as far as 18:8; but, there is an insoluble semantic problem here. I would like to see a viable solution to the semantic problem on the words "looked with suspicion" (written, *'oven*; but spoken, *'avin*) before I make a decision as to whether this is a concluding comment on the epic narrative folded into the larger Samuel Narrative, or part of the introductory material for story of Saul's treachery to follow.

## Textual Applications and Anecdotes

1 Samuel 16
vs.
1. There may be no point in grieving over that which God has rejected (v. 1).
2. Fear is not a good excuse for inaction; neither are excuses legitimate reasons (v. 2). God may provide a way to make His action look acceptable.
3. When God puts us in a position (sends us on a mission) we must be prepared to execute His commands in His way (vv. 2-4). This is righteousness: doing the right things for the right reasons because of a right relationship with God.
4. Our righteous actions in the name of God may not always be immediately transparent even to the established leadership (vv. 4-5).
5. Consecration is being prepared for a special engagement with God.
6. All things are not as they seem (vv. 6-7).
7. The spiritual one should not see only that which is external but should perceive the matters of the heart in those he or she meets. Also: Those the LORD has rejected (as Saul in verse 1) may reject us later on (17:28; Eliab and later on, Saul).
8. Finding the right one may be a process (vv. 6-13).
9. Finding the right one may be a tedious process (vv. 8-10).
10. Finding the right one may be a long, tedious process (vv. 11-12).

11.    What you are looking for is always in the last place you look for it. In the Bible there is the reversal of the rights of primogeniture—or the preeminence of the firstborn.

12.    Do not be surprised if God's choice looks a bit different (ruddy only used three times: Gen. 25:25, in regard to Esau; here in verse 12 and 17:42, a reason for which Goliath despised him).

13.    God will confirm the work of His true prophet; the Holy Spirit will become manifest (v. 13).

14.    The absence of God's Spirit will make one vulnerable to the progression of the demonic: obsession, oppression, and perhaps possession (v. 14).

15.    Music appears to be, at times, a language of psycho-emotional healing (vv. 16-18).

16.    If possible, obey the command of the king (v. 20).

17.    The logic may break down: play music, get better (v. 23, "whenever").

18.    Often, the real man of virtue will be so on many levels: integrity and talent (v. 18).

19.    Great things begin on insignificant days: "These are the days of small things" (v. 19; from sheepfold to palace).

20.    It is best to send your best to the king with a gift (v. 20).

21.    Even a demonized old fool may recognize real virtue when he sees it (vv. 21-22).

22.    It is too bad that leaders do not send more notes to parents (v. 22). We get the warnings; the kid gets the draft notice; but rarely do we get the congratulations.

23.    It would make sense that effective psychotherapy depends on the therapist and his method (vv. 21-23). David: Spirit-filled, theologian, composer and musician.

## Conclusion

Ministry is concluded: Samuel has anointed the least of the sons of Jesse and gone home to Ramah. He leaves the monarch-elect in the capable hands of the Holy Spirit. Young David will prove himself invaluable as a therapist to the crazed monarch bereft of the blessing and empowerment of God. David has been introduced, elevated, recognized, and witnessed as having been anointed by the king-maker, Samuel. Now, through a providential twist—and the help of a nameless omniscient servant—David has made his first successful appearance at court. He is the king's harpist and armor bearer. These are pretty good positions: at the back of the battle array, safely with the king. Here he can learn battle tactics and personnel from the leaders. In the palace, he would always be present—in case of a spiritual emergency—and he could learn politics and palace intrigue with light duty, on-the-job training. David is now well positioned to learn everything he will need to know to rule the country and to meet everybody he will need to become acquainted with to govern and administer the nation.

However, what we meet with next is many chapters of delay on David's way to the throne. History is replete with illustrations of despots whose time has long since passed and yet cling relentlessly to power. Saul will spend the rest of his miserable life trying to hunt down the son of Jesse and grasp power that evaporates before him. The country must entirely crash to ruins before the monarch-elect can bring it to the first stage of glory. But before we go through all that, let us see what the young man is made of.

# 1 Samuel 17
# David the Youthful Marvel Versus the Giant, Pagan Killing Machine

## The Story Is Now About How David Will Eclipse Saul

—ɯ—

## Introduction

Among the great epic pieces in biblical literature—indeed, world literature—this extended presentation of David's confrontation with Goliath stands toward the front of the pack. Embracing motifs that are at once Aegean and Semitic, occidental and oriental, the story moves in and out of compelling narrative and embracing dialog to give us one of the great stories of faith in the older testament. We are shocked by and impressed by David's action. He is as astonishing in this piece as he is disquieting. We know that he has been anointed king by Samuel; we know that he has received the Spirit's empowerment for the monarchy; we have seen him at court as a musical therapist for the deposed and now increasingly demented monarch; but what will all that gifting, talent, and skill look like in a life-and-death situation? What will it look like on the battlefield? This story answers that question. It will look very much like Jonathan and that will go a long way to explain the dynamics of chapter 18. Now, let us look as the boy wonder assails the monster and proves that he is the man for the job; all the jobs.

## Reading from "Saul: A Life Suspended in Doubt"

Oftentimes, when I seemed in a better frame of mind, I would send David back home. He seemed always to be distracted with the condition of his father's livestock. So I would frequently give him leave to go supervise those matters. Livestock is, after all, money; and I had three of David's older brothers as part of my standing army. If Jesse was doing well and could help with the war effort, it was good news. I was always in a better humor out in the field. I was born to fight, I guess. This case was to become something of an exception.

One time when I had sent David on leave, we had another altercation with the Philistines. This time, the field was a little closer to home—their home. I had hoped that we could make another rout of it and this time push them back to Ashdod.

What actually transpired was something of a standoff. They held the high ground on one side of the valley and we held the high ground on the other. Nobody seemed willing to engage battle. Timing was of the essence. The initial engagement had to be made while running downhill. This would shock them into a fallback maneuver that could abort and turn into a full retreat. Then all it was became a matter of chopping at their heels until there was no unified force to fight. Then we could kill the refugees and storm Eqron and Gath and push the whole mass of Philistia back to Ashdod, Ashkelon and Gath.

However, the problem had to do with a giant from Gath called Goliath. This man must have been about nine feet tall! He was huge and well armored and bristling with armament. He would come out and stand in the middle of the valley and hurl abuse at us and then invite some poor sap to come down and become scavenger scat. We had nobody of that size to pit against him. The "many or few" lesson taught to me by my son was to become one better: the scale of a battle can be tipped by one young man with one lucky shot.

Goliath's tactic was three pronged though: if nobody would come to fight him he had the psychological victory of humiliation. If one person came, he had the personal victory in single combat. If we attempted to take him with a force, he would see it coming and draw us back to the foot of the hill where the battle arrays of the Philistines would launch upon us downhill doing exactly what I had hoped to do to them—winning the first shock and setting us on our heels!

I had no expectation that could have prepared me for what came next: I saw this self-assured young man walk up to me with all the confidence of a general and speak to me—as if I was in a dream. He said that he would meet the challenge of the Philistine, Goliath. I tried to convince him that he was no match for the likes of that man-mountain. He assured me that he'd killed a bear that was bigger than Goliath—with his bare hands. I was so stunned that I offered him my armor. He was nearly as tall as me and the equipment almost fit. But he said that he felt awkward in it. So he took off the gear and ran forward. What was he carrying? A stick, a sling, a bag and he reached down and grabbed some rocks or something in the river bottom. I could hear his sling whistle as he wound up to throw. People from my tribe are famed as rock slingers—the sound is quite exhilarating. The silence of the valley was profound—and all the more so as he released. I was certain that he would hit Goliath's shield—it was the size of the side of a house! But, the giant insisted upon peering out over the top. How this young man did it I will never know; it was not a case of hit and miss—truly, he must have been a Benjamite! He fired once and his aim held true: he went right over the top of Goliath's shield and under the brim of his helmet! The armor bearer had had enough and ran away in terror. This young man didn't even carry a knife; he had to use the giant's sword for what came next.

He beheaded the giant and showed his grisly trophy to the Philistines. The chemistry was incredible: they ran away in full retreat and we followed. We pursued at their heels and also flanked their retreat to force them to the west, keeping as much as possible to the higher terrain. By the time we were done that day we had what survivors there were shut up tight in Eqron and Gath. This was good news. Our people were making an advance, reclaiming territory from the low hills and out onto the coastal plain—land that hadn't been ours since the days of Joshua.

I realized at the end of the day that I'd neglected to find out who the hero was—he was after all going to be my son-in-law. I had my general, Abner, go ascertain who he was. There was something hauntingly familiar about the boy; but, I could not put my finger on it. I felt the old torment coming on and I was sensing the need to hear some all-consuming harp music—maybe it was due to the fact that we hadn't taken back as much ground as I'd hoped for, I don't know. When Abner returned with the news, we were all astounded: the boy was David! My court musician had become a war hero! Had it been so many days since I had seen him? He seemed but a ruddy youth the last time he played at court. Now . . . he was full grown and a national hero. A good choice for a son-in-law, no? If only I'd have known. Now, he would have even more opportunity to learn about the workings of the military and the intrigues of the palace. When I spoke with him in person—still wearing that same confidence and yet carrying his grisly trophy and the huge blade of Goliath—the sword handle actually fit his hand— I realized that the boy was all grown up: his voice had changed; his beard was growing; he was as strong as a lion and sharp as a spear point (the lion of Judah. . .). I also noticed the special relationship that he had with Jonathan and my other generals. I would have to keep an eye on this one. (1 Samuel 17)

## Textual Observations

### The Setting of the Stage: Warfare Occident and Warfare Orient

The stage set with the taunt of a hero and a demand for single combat is, of course, current. One need only read the *Iliad*, *Odyssey*, and *Aeneid*—not to mention the *Tale of Sinuhe* from Egypt—to see similar scenes from the time purportedly portrayed by the Samuel Narratives. I will, however, defer: "The duel as a method of warfare was known in Canaan long before the arrival of the Philistines. The duel of Sinuhe the Egyptian with the mighty man of Retenu (Twelfth Dynasty) strikingly resembles the contest between David and Goliath. The fact that this type of combat seems to have lapsed and was reintroduced by the Philistines reflects their background in the Aegean world, where the duel was a recognized form of warfare that enabled commanders to secure military decisions without incurring the casualties of full-scale battles."[75]

"More pointedly: Furthermore, single combat, the mode of Goliath's battle with David, was an accepted, time-honored custom in the Aegean, as in the famous struggle between Hector and Achilles before the walls of Troy."[76]

And so it might appear that single combat was known in Coele-Syria during the twelfth dynasty of Egypt (1991–1786 BC),[77] but apparently fell into disuse during the lion's share of the late-bronze age. When the sea people landed en masse, they brought their material culture, yes, but they also brought their ideologies and strategies. Hence, a latter-day Achilles in the form of a Goliath, would then challenge and taunt the opposing army into giving him some grist for the mill. As to whether or not the terms of engagement were ever really kept without a more general mayhem, is questionable.

Goliath does, however, lay out the terms of the conflict. The narrator reports him as follows: "Why do you come out to draw up in battle array? Am I not the Philistine and you servants of Saul? Choose a man for yourselves and let him come down to me. If he is able to fight with me and strike me, then we will become your servants; but if I prevail against him and strike him, then you shall become our servants and serve us. . . . I defy the ranks of Israel this day; give me a man that we may fight together" (1 Samuel 17:8-10).

Because of the notation of his size, the descriptions of his armor, and his weaponry, the men of Israel "were dismayed and greatly afraid" (v. 11). After all, not everybody is that large and it would certainly take a lucky hit to fell the giant. In our vernacular, Goliath is very nearly "ten feet tall and bulletproof." Be that as it may, there is a lot that can be read into Goliath's words: he refers to himself as *the* Philistine (v. 8). This usage has bivalance: first, he uses the word to refer to himself as singular in nature. He is representative of his people, yes; but make no mistake, single combat is an individual sport, not a team sport. He is the one and the only Philistine who makes any difference in this story and he will be dust trodden under David's feet. Secondly, the narrator pulls these words forward to refer to the giant when "the head of *the* Philistine" goes up to Jerusalem at the end of the day and when "the head of *the* Philistine" meets the divinely deposed head of state, Saul. Yes, he is the Philistine; but only part of him will be of any consequence by the end of this battle and only part of him was necessary to prove that David will be supreme over any Philistine he selects.

A second keyword that will come back to hit Goliath in the face—literally—is "strike." Like the interpretation of a double dream in the Joseph story, Goliath predicts his own doom with the double usage of the word "strike" in two separate conditional sentences. Again, he says, "if he is able . . . to strike me . . . . but if I . . . strike him. . ." (1 Samuel 17:9). Indeed, when David slings a stone at the giant it "struck *the* Philistine on his forehead . . . and David prevailed over the Philistine with a sling and a stone and he struck *the* Philistine" (vv. 49-50). The message to Israel, foreigners, and would-be usurpers in all of this is clear. If you attempt to take the life of the king, your life is forfeit. If you threaten him, your threats will be fulfilled upon yourself. We will expand upon this notion throughout the following chapters.

## David on Stage

In chapter 16 at the climax of the scene where Samuel anoints the unknown son of Jesse, we are told, "and the Spirit of the LORD came mightily upon David from that day forward" (1 Samuel 16:13). This was our first introduction to David. The second is when an unnamed servant in Saul's court points out the skill of one of Jesse's sons in playing a musical instrument and we are told, "So Saul sent messengers to Jesse, and said, 'Send me your son David who is with the flock'" (v. 19). The third introduction is when Jesse sends David with gifts to Saul (v. 20). With David properly integrated into the story, he shows us that God really was with David and the boy wonder is able to live up to everybody's expectations. Saul loved him and evil spirits fled from him (vv. 21-23).

David exits the stage for a few verses now (1 Samuel 17:1-11) and is reintroduced through an extended piece on David's family (v. 12). Then we are told who of Jesse's sons have gone "after Saul" to the battle (v. 13). Finally, we are told why David was not a regular at the military pavilion (vv. 14-15). We are ready for David's reinsertion into the story proper.

The aging father, Jesse, wanted to send provisions to his sons at the front. David is the delivery boy and is responsible for that and for the additional matter of getting some savory gift to the commander of the unit in which Eliab, Abinadab, and Shammah were stationed. David proves that he can do more than expected of him because, without being told, "he left the flock with a keeper" (v. 20). That he does all things well is evident; that he will always do so questionable.

When David arrived on stage or at the scene of the battle, he properly disposed of the things he had brought and went to the encampment to greet his brothers (vv. 21-22). At that point we have a discourseless narrative indicating what we have had in greater detail before (cf. vs. 23 and 4-10). We should also note that the response was the same: fear (cf. vs. 11 and 24). David then entered into dialog with the men and ascertained several things: everybody is afraid of Goliath and the Philistines; whoever takes away the reproach of Israel will be made rich, tax-exempt, and a son-in-law to the king (v. 25). David checked his references again and ascertained two things: first, what the others said was, in fact, the nature of the case (vv. 26-27). Secondly, he stepped on a hornet's nest in respect to his own family. And so follows a series of:

## Questions: The Rejection of the First-Born — Phase Two

In my observations in the previous chapter, I noted how the language regarding the rejection of Saul and David's oldest brother, Eliab, were worded very nearly the same. As I will point out in a later observation, it would appear to me that all the brothers are tarred with the same brush. Be that as it may, it looks as though we have something of real time events and conversations that mirror what has already transpired at the spiritual level in chapter 16. In two ways Saul and Eliab's rejection was portrayed: rejection by the prophet and rejection by God. There will be a mirroring of that in this chapter with a further note on the rejection of Eliab.

First, in a series of two questions and an indictment, let us take a careful look at what Eliab says to David: "Now Eliab his oldest brother heard when he spoke to the men; and Eliab's anger burned against David and he said, 'Why have you come down? And with whom have you left those few sheep in the wilderness? I know your insolence and the wickedness of your heart; for you have come down in order to see the battle'" (1 Samuel 17:28). Of course, these are words uttered in the heat of rage. One has to ask as to why Eliab was so angry. Was there something at the spiritual level that accompanied his rejection in the same way as had been the case with Saul? Perhaps Saul's demons flew in flocks and exacerbated the pathos of any who supported Saul and the enmity of any who had been at enmity with David. Be that as it may, these are the questions that admit no answer. Eliab asked why David had come down and then assumes his conclusion in stating that he had come down to see the battle. Granted, battlefields in antiquity often became the theatrical spectacle we view them to be. They seemed to accumulate a motley crew of scavengers, sadists, and the otherwise curious that came to view the carnage and sift through the aftermath. The problem is not with the idea; the problem is with the indictment. Eliab says that he knows David's insolence and the wickedness of his heart. Right. How could Eliab know that? It is possible that he is still reeling under the jealousy of having the youngest brother chosen over himself in public for the attentions of the ancient prophet. Because of the thematic consideration of the reversal of the rights of primogeniture (first born), we are invited to examine this scenario through eyes that know the Joseph story in Genesis. Another theory is that Eliab, in his jealousy, is merely projecting his antipathy upon David. Allegedly, this is less ego-threatening than simply hating someone outright. In short, the insolence and wickedness of the heart are, in fact, Eliab's.

Eliab's diatribe includes a question — a challenge, really — about the care and welfare of the flocks of his father. As heir apparent in the house of Jesse, he would naturally be concerned with what would fall to his lot after the death of the reigning patriarch. Since, in large measure, that depended upon the care afforded them by David, Eliab might have some justification for concern. However, because we are told of his wrath, Eliab's tirade is simply over the top. Be that as it may, our Omniscient Narrator has already told us, "David arose early in the morning and left the flock with a keeper and took the supplies and went as Jesse had commanded him" (1 Samuel 17:20). At this point, David demonstrates that he is competent to carry out the orders of his father as well as take upon himself the responsibility for delegating the care of the sheep to another. But notice well that David does not answer this charge of Eliab. It is in this that David demonstrates both his ascendancy and the eclipse of the first born.

### Declarations: The Confrontation with the First-Born

David's response speaks volumes and the silence of what he left unspoken screams out at us as the multi-valance of Eliab's frustration spirals into oblivion. "And David said, 'What have I done now? Was it not just a word?'" (1 Samuel 17:29). Whereas we might be preprogrammed to see *'attah* ("now") as a text pointer, an emphatic word,[78] this usage seems to merely mean "now." Its position at the end of the clause is neither emphatic nor necessary in any case. Be that as it may, David's usage of the word "now" betrays some antecedent condition, events, or exchange of words. What I am attempting to get at is that in the usage of "now" David has tipped for public perusal a hand that includes him being browbeaten or even verbally abused by his oldest brother in a previous engagement— perhaps many previous engagements. Fearlessly, he deflects the words of his oldest brother by reducing the whole encounter to the level of conversation: "Was it not just a word?" (thing or question, implied) because, he knows that Eliab's diatribe appears irrational to any onlookers ("the men" in verse 26; "the people" in verse 27). David knows that there cannot be any immediate reprisals against him for asking about the giant and the matter of single combat. But what happens next screams at us.

As the narrator picks up the thread of his story from this explosion of dialogue, he tells us, "And he turned away from next to him to another and said the same thing; and the people replied to him the word as the former word" (approximately, "they answered him the same way" 1 Samuel 17:30). The point here is that David turned away from Eliab and addressed the issue to another. The verb is the same as that used in 1 Samuel 15:27. And so we may be invited to make the comparison that in the same manner that Samuel turned away from Saul to go, David also turned away from the oldest of Jesse's sons to address his questions to another. He could not receive any confirmation and support from his oldest brother and so he confirmed the results of his previous reconnaissance from another. Samuel turned away from one king to another and David turned away from one brother to another "brother" (kinsman, at the least).

Fine. Whether or not we agree to the mirroring as indicated above, what is the upshot for Eliab? Although included in the number of 1 Samuel 17:12, Eliab is only named twice: 1 Samuel 16:6 and in 1 Samuel 17:28. He will never be named again in the narrative. He passes into the oblivion of the rest of David's brothers. If he is still alive, he is one of "his brothers" that joined him as a refugee in the cave of Adullam (1 Samuel 22:1). He may have gone into exile in Moab with his parents (1 Samuel 22:3) and if he did, is never heard from again. Because I think the rest of David's brothers—perhaps including his cousins, the sons of Zeruiah (Asahel, Abishai, Joab)—are tarred with the same brush as Eliab, their further notations will be either negative or nonexistent. The only one who receives dishonorable mention further along will be Shammah (Shimeah?). In 2 Samuel 13, as David's family begins to unravel and with dysfunctional families being the order of the day for the Samuel Narratives, we are informed of one rapscallion sired by Shimeah named Jonadab. We are told that he is a "shrewd man" (v. 3). Indeed! He is able to conspire to fulfill Amnon's lustful desire (vv. 3-5), and report on Amnon's death (vv. 32-33) without any of the dirt sticking to his own tunic. We will have much more to discuss with respect to David's family. But this notice in our present location in 1 Samuel 17 does not bode well for the siblings of David.

### Decapitation: The Shadow of Things to Come . . . The "Head" Waters of the Stream

One of the more unnerving things about biblical narrative has to do with the bloodshed. That these were barbaric times will be contested by no one—that the barbarism was some-time shared by those we would call our heroes, is unsettling to say the least. David begins one aspect of this roughness by what he does to Goliath. Arguably, it is only the fulfillment of David's oath: "This day the LORD will deliver you up into my hands, and I will strike you down and remove your head from you. And I will give the dead bodies of the army of the Philistines this day to the birds of the sky and the wild beasts of the earth, that all the earth may know that there is a God in Israel" (1 Samuel 17:46). Of course, we know the story and David indeed fells the giant with a sling stone and removes the giant's head with the giant's own sword (v. 51).

What happens next indicates that disembodied heads have a life of their own in biblical narrative. "And David *took* the Philistine's *head* and brought it to Jerusalem, but he put his weapons in his tent" (v. 54). Because this is the first instance of decapitation in biblical literature, it may surprise us—even appall us—that heroes cause heads and bodies to come to separate resting places in the Bible. However, and as I will attempt to prove throughout the coming narrative, leaders, foreign or domestic, in opposition to David may suffer this fate (Goliath, Saul, Ish-Bosheth).

The purpose of taking the head may be a motif in biblical narrative,[79] but there are two real purposes for taking the head by real people in a real-time narrative in the Bible: portability and demonstration. In short, this was the tenth century BC equivalent of show and tell. Carrying around Goliath's body—or anyone else's, for that matter—would have been a formidable, indeed, lampoonable task. I sincerely doubt that Goliath's head was disproportionately small for his body and thus more easily portable, but for the one who had killed the lion and the bear (1 Samuel 17:36), it did make a portable and graphic display. Because the narrative concludes in Jerusalem and in David's tent (v. 54), we might be tempted to conclude that David offered this grisly display to all interested parties throughout the duration of the day.

In one particularly poignant backloop in the story, David makes an appearance before Saul at General Abner's behest, "with the Philistine's head in his hand" (1 Samuel 17:57). I would imagine that the king was unable to remove his eyes from the victorious warrior's grisly trophy. Perhaps that makes the questions of the demented despot a bit more realistic: "Abner, whose son is this young man?" "Whose son are you, young man?" (vv. 55, 58) In short, taken heads and their barbaric takers become a display case for importance in the narrative. Saul may not remember his court musician—indeed, he may not know much at all—but, he will certainly recall the taking of the head when the women come out to cheer on their champion in chapter 18. The larger problem looms: this begins a series of about a dozen "takings of the head" that spell the continuation of the dark ages for Israel.

## Textual Problems

The greatest problem has to do with Saul, the king of cluelessness, not knowing who the hero of our story is. Solutions are, of course, legion. There is one that I have tacitly suggested in my first-person narrative above. That is, that David had been periodically allowed to go home while he was occasional court musician and was no longer allowed to do so (1 Samuel 17:15; 18:5, 13). His responsibilities as a commander of a thousand, coupled with constant warfare, would have required his services fulltime. Before that, he might have gone back and forth by request or by contract to care for the sheep of his father. Boys grow up and perhaps on one of his extended furloughs David grew a couple of inches and sprouted some muscles and facial hair.

There is always the possibility that the narrative is folded. That is, the events as told us do not really happen in the order presented. We might ask, for instance, whether the two mentionings of the homecoming to Jerusalem are the same or different (1 Samuel 17:54; 18:6). If they are the same "from striking the Philistine," then the text is folded and we have to go back in time to arrive at the quest for David and the general's introduction of him to Saul the clueless (1 Samuel 17:55-58). Although this may be a possible solution for Saul's vacuous mind in respect to David, I think it is simplistic.

A solution I lean toward in view of Saul's progressive dementia is that Saul simply couldn't recognize anything or remember anything. Whatever was entailed in the evil spirit from God, there seems to be explosive rage and an inability to assess matters of reality. Saul will not know what is going on with the enemy, within his country, among his courtiers, or in his immediate family. The one thing that is certain is that "all Israel and Judah loved David" (1 Samuel 18:16) including at one point Saul (1 Samuel 16:21, pronoun problem?), but the kingdom is turning away from Saul. So, depending upon which of his demons happened to be looking through his eyes at the time, Saul could hardly recognize the members of his own family, much less David.

## Textual Applications and Anecdotes

1 Samuel 17
vs.
1. Valor can only be stated apart from conflict.
   Valor can only be demonstrated in conflict.
   When the enemy camps on foreign territory, they must be careful about where they camp.
   Geographical notations are important—who is on whose property and where.
2. Outmanned? Outgunned? Pick the place of battle carefully.
3. Neither side wants to attack uphill—if they can avoid it.
4. Giants make good cannon fodder.
   Cowardice surrounding a champion looks formidable.
   Notices about size and provenance are significant in literature—both forward and backward.
5. A big man can carry heavy armor. (Metaphor?)
6. A big man can move large weapons. (Metaphor?)
7. No matter how bulletproof, no matter how formidable the weaponry, another set of eyes and more equipment is helpful.
8. The taunt comes from a safe distance.
   Challenging, yes; stupid, no.
9. The dual as over against war, how civilized.
10. The monster was born for the ancient battle.
11. Fear from a safe distance is irrational.
    The dual delayed is a stalemate maintained.
12. Reintroduction indicates absence from the text for a while.
13. Three sons reintroduced—three sons rejected.
    Reversal of the rights of primogeniture, Eliab rejected a second time.
14. The youngest against the oldest; a story as old as time.
15. The shepherd, the youngest, is also the messenger and delivery boy.
16. The taunt grows no better with age.
    The long wait before battle gives time for fears to get out of hand.
17. The long wait before battle eats up time and provisions.
18. The father's mission: care for the troops; care for the commander; bring back information.

19. When the emissary knows what to do, knowing where to do it may keep him from being captured.
20. Execute any remaining responsibilities, leave early, arrive early, return early?
21. Evenly matched whether by power, position, or placement ensures a stalemate.
22. Check your baggage and then visit.
23. The narrator has told us; now the protagonist must hear it.
24. Size can be intimidating.
25. Victory leads to success in ancient Israel: wealth, marry the king's daughter, tax-free status.
26. Removal of the reproach of God's people is removal of the reproach of God.
27. Confirm the reports: You have heard of advancement, independently verify it.
28. The rage of the first born seems unquenchable.
    False accusation will be found out.
29. Repeated patterns of abuse cause defense mechanisms.
30. A triple confirmation increases certitude.
31. Ask the right questions, make the right replies; someone important will find out about it.
32. The fearless attempt to allay fear in others.
33. The worldly king observes the obvious.
    Contrast youth with warrior from youth.
34. In theory, contest with vicious, ravenous animals is good practice for battle.
35. Rescue the lamb and strike the lion if he objects.
36. The issue is not the warrior, it is the God.
37. The God of past deliverances is the God depended upon for the future.
    The dubious king can at least extend a well-wish.
38. The dubious king can at least lend some equipment.
39. Nice gear? Better go with that with which you have practiced.
40. Sometimes the least formidable-looking equipment is the most lethal.
41. Even the fighting monster throws his human fodder before him.
42. Even the fighting monster would like a challenge.
    Victory in battle should be glorious.
    Seasoned warriors usually despise youth and good looks.
43. The pagan proves his frustration and impotence by epithets and oaths.
44. When angry, threaten; prove yourself to be frustrated and impotent.
45. Weapons are powerless against righteous confidence and God.
46. Greater confidence? Greater threat.
    Knowing God is with you increases confidence.
47. God wins the victory—He should also get the glory.
48. Let the other move first and then move quickly.

49.     When the opponent is fast, even great power can be quickly undone.
50.     The ultimate humiliation—killed without a recognizable weapon.
        What happened to Goliath's armor bearer?! The silence displays his cowardice.
        The same thing as the army of the Philistines: they all ran for home.
51.     Keep your promise about the beheading; use his own sword.
52.     Victory in single combat can encourage the fainthearted army.
53.     Victory? Chase and plunder.
        The vanquished do not deserve their possessions. However, we could be generous, I suppose.
54.     Heads of the vanquished are for show and tell—the height of barbarism.
        Keep the weapons, you might need them later.
55.     The clueless king may not recognize his loyal subject.
        The other courtiers may not recognize a loyal subject.
        Do not assume that because you are there, people know you are there.
56.     Find out who the real hero is.
57.     Bring your trophy to the king.
58.     Answer the obvious question respectfully; your interrogator may be oblivious to reality.

## Conclusion

With the conclusion of this epic piece of classical proportions, what the story shows in literary categories is David's final presentation to Israel. Recall that he was first presented to Samuel, then to Saul's court, and finally to the army of Israel (Jonathan and the people of Jerusalem, too, but that is for the next chapter). Some motifs are begun here, such as the taking of the head and show-and-tell ancient near eastern style. We have met with the barbarism of the day and are convinced that the "class" with which the classics present warfare to us is only subterfuge for the real nature of the savage case. Whether we look at Achilles dragging Hector around behind his chariot or David placing Goliath's head on public display, we are aware that warfare has its rules—and the winner of single combat may have incredible say in the making of the rules. David will begin the display of heads—but Goliath's only begins the parade. There will be others and all will in some way have placed themselves in real or ideological opposition to David.

What the story shows in narrative technique is reversal. It shows, of course, a reversal in Goliath's taunt. No, in fact, it would be his carcass that would feed the beasts and birds and it would be those of the armies of Philistia that would join him. It would not be David. It would not be the underdog that day. It also shows the reversal of the rights of the first born (primogeniture). Eliab has any of his remaining dignity stripped from him and all glory and accolade given to the youngest of Jesse's boys. Eliab, rejected in the same terms as was the king after whom he had traipsed off to war, would be turned away from in the same terms as was the king anointed and rejected by Samuel the sometimes myopic seer.

What the story shows the eyes of faith is again reversal. The evil giant is undone by a stone hurled from the righteous boy's sling. Against overwhelming odds, David, as had Jonathan before him, conquered the giant, began the rout of the Philistines and took away the reproach of Israel. At the end of the day, a boy known for his musical abilities and his abilities to soothe a crazed monarch would become a man known by his faith and exploits against "this uncircumcised Philistine" (v. 26). To the eyes of faith, this epic story is about good versus evil. In this case, the evil Aegean giant, Goliath, lost and the good Israelite shepherd boy, David, won.

# 1 Samuel 18
## Saul, the Royal Disaster (Part One)
## David Wins the Girl

—⚶—

## Introduction

### Saul's Character and Personality: Multiplex

Polzin correctly indicates that the narrator of Samuel gives us more of a window into the soul of Saul than is the case with David.[80] However, that window is not a transparent picture window. It is a window more stained-glass in nature with textures, colorations, and opacities that darken our understanding as much as they illumine it; therefore, some inferences and deductions are necessary. As one of my colleagues, Dr. Mark Jacobson, has correctly surmised, one of Saul's problems was arrogance. Another—and here I believe they are different issues—is that of self-will. That is, whereas arrogance is an attitude, self-will deals more with intentionality or the direction that arrogance will take. Regardless, Saul, can be shown, yes, to be self-willed and/or arrogant; but he can also be shown to be faithless, inept, incompetent, jealous, careless, reckless, stupid, manic-depressive, passive-aggressive, victimized and victimizer; superficial and perhaps self-serving with respect to his religious sentiments, demonized—and more: marked by the heavy hand of God. As I suggested last time, if you sincerely believe that Saul is anything of the master of his own fortune, it may be justifiably questioned as to what text you are reading. Saul is a foil against which David, the real rising star, shines brightest—at least until the next book! Samuel will not be seen in too great a light—receiving even a rebuke from God—because of his pouring too much time and misspent emotional energy into Saul. As we saw with the 1998 embassy bombing in Nairobi, you want to be very careful which building you are close to—the embassy stood; others ceased to exist!

In 1 Samuel 18 and 19 (in case you had lost track), we will see Saul's malady become acute. Jealousy, hatred, and demonic influence work in synergy to produce one of the great monsters of Scripture. We see Saul grasping at straws—or spears, as the case may be—to both project his antipathy and to protect what is left of his power. The ship of state is sinking; the edifice of government is collapsing. What can be done? Let me tell the story from Saul's perspective, beginning with the last scene after the felling of Goliath.

### Reading from "Saul: A Life Suspended in Doubt"

My bad humor was back with a vengeance. It was acting in a way that I had not seen before. It was as though it had a will of its own. It would attack my most vulnerable senses and throw me into a rage. I never really understood what it was that was doing this. Some of my advisors suggested that it was demonic. I just dismissed them as superstitious. Why wouldn't Samuel answer my summons? Perhaps he could have diagnosed the problem. It was probably just bad diet—all my colleagues across the Jordan and all around have gout. I would have to be more careful about that in the future.

At that point, I made David a permanent fixture of my government. He was a strong man, both physically and mentally, and he looked the part of a general in my son's gear. He had donated Goliath's sword to the archives and it was in permanent custody of the national historians. That was part of the function of the priesthood in Israel—teachers of antiquity . . . things long-since dead. . . . One of the really unnerving things about David is that all the people loved him. He seemed to have a magical way with words and he could win the heart of the most crass, negative, and cynical people in the kingdom. And man, he was magic with a sword and a thousand men! He could hack apart a division of the enemy's forces faster than the other generals by twice. Oftentimes I've seen him cut through a division, divide his battalion, send them in opposite directions to flank two divisions and meet his fellow generals in the saddle—in a field strewn with dead enemies and live troops. His soldiers loved him because he suffered much fewer casualties than other generals. When he came back around, he could reduce the casualties in two other divisions as well. But there was one thing I hated: as a fighter myself and as king, I found it unnerving when the singers made songs that elevated David over me: "Saul has slain his thousands, and David his ten thousands." That was the way their celebration went—to me it became a dirge.

One day at court when I was in my bad humor, David was playing his harp. The young man was really good. Conversation lulled as people were transfixed by the music. I see it happening as though I were watching it from across the room: I picked up a spear and launched it at him with a full arm throw. He dodged it as though he'd expected the exact spot it would strike the wall. I threw another one at him and he evaded that one as well. He gave me a look somewhere between sorrow and disgust and quietly left the room. I decided then and there that I must make him a field commander and keep him away from the palace.

Because David had killed Goliath, he was the one who was to marry my first daughter. Merab was very phlegmatic and would have given me no control over him. Besides that, she worshiped the ground he walked on. She could talk about nothing else. David had something of an opinion on the matter however: it seems that he viewed being a son-in-law to the king as something for highborn families in the kingdom. So, I gave Merab to another man. It was, after all, time for her to marry. However, I was intrigued with the notion of having a set of ears and eyes within David's house—in case there was any *real* intrigue! So I orchestrated the marriage of David with my young daughter Michal. David gave some lame excuse about being a poor man and so on; but, I was only concerned with getting rid of him one way or another. Either the Philistines could have their day in battle, or I could use Michal to expose a plot. Finally, he agreed to the price of 100 dead Philistines "to avenge the enemies of the king." Amazing boy! He paid double. Unfortunately, my plot didn't work because Michal was smitten by David. Even that vixen was no match for the winsome young man. I lived ever in dread of him. What could I do? I had to protect my monarchy. All the people loved him and they seemed not to notice me. (1 Samuel 18)

## Textual Observations[81]

## The Dirge

The chorus of the little ditty that the women of Israel concocted would ring in Saul's ears for the remainder of his miserable life. "Saul has slain his thousands, and David his ten thousands." It would become an internationally famous bit of lyric poetry initially rehearsed but perhaps later ignored by the servants of Philistine King Achish. Later the dirge would even be sung by the Philistine warlords themselves.

## What Can Be Said on Behalf of Fear?

First, Saul and all Israel had hunkered down on the safety of a hillside. But now, after the comic relief of the boy wonder beheading the giant killing machine, Saul resumes his emotional roller coaster ride, by distrusting David (18:9). This escalates into full-blown terror (18:12, 15, 29), producing several attempts on David's life that are, of course, abortive—and ultimately politically crippling and self-destructive.

## Raving Lunatics and Other Prophets

The borderline twixt the evil spirits and the good seems drawn with difficulty. One of the several evidences of this is the fact that the same form of the verb is used for "rave" and "prophesy" in these two chapters. My suspicions are aroused! In verse 10 of chapter 18, we are clearly informed that an evil spirit *from God* came upon Saul "mightily." So of course, he raved like a lunatic and starts throwing stuff—a classic and somewhat pointed example would be spears—at people—a convenient example, of course, being any available Davids (v. 11). In chapter 19, we have the same song (still being played by David—poor kid ought to change his repertoire!), the second verse of which is that Saul has the evil spirit *from the LORD* (vv. 9-10, must be the J document!) and without either raving, prophesying, or any other expected notice, hucks a spear at him, attempting to unify David and the wall. Notice that in both cases this follows—textually at least, never confuse narrative distance and historical distance—hard upon the heels of a major rout of the Philistines. David's triumphs are thus shining brilliantly against Saul's failures and pathology.

The final act in three scenes is when Saul sends armed escorts to retrieve the state's number one fugitive. All of whom, "prophesy" using the same unusual form of the verb, including good old "among-the-prophets" Saul himself. In the case of the king it is said that the s/Spirit of/from God (the ambiguity is patent!) came upon him and he does his thing—to rave or not to rave, that is the question! To capitalize the S of Spirit or not, that is the crux. My suspicion is that, the village of the prophets not withstanding, Saul is immobilized by the evil spirit again as allowed by a sovereign God so that David can make his escape.

There's probably a good phenomenological lesson here: There are a lot of religious activities that look the same regardless of the impetus or motivation. Be wise as serpents and harmless as doves for we are all to some degree bum lambs amidst the wolf pack—and speaking of raving, personal experience indicates to me, the chief of all bum lambs, that some of the most ravenous wolves infest our Lord's church.

## Misspent Energies and Misplaced Javelins

A guy I went to school with made the mistake of running downrange on the javelin pitch—perhaps that is why there was a hiatus in spear chucking in high-school athletics in Oregon and Washington for a few years. In the same manner as Sarah, as some of the rabbis say, dying *immediately* after hearing about the near sacrifice of Isaac, her son (Gen. 22-23), I'm sure Bill's mom had kittens when she heard the news. Collateral damage? One ruined T-shirt. You see: after a flight of over 100 feet the javelin pierced the plane of Bill's body twixt his elbow and rib cage, effectively pinning him to the turf by one badly torn T-shirt.

Saul's throws had at once the same psychological and physical effect. That is, we are torn with David that the king would act in such a way against his most choice servant and yet we are relieved that there is no final physical damage to the one whom we already know as the king-elect. However, the king's reputation is now irreparably damaged not only by the fact that his spear was not like a weaver's beam with a point the weight of a bowling ball, but also by the fact that this head-and-shoulders-taller-than-all-Israelite-men wimp tried and thankfully failed to gun down Israel's number one hero. Remember, we are speaking in human terms; Saul couldn't have gunned him down point-blank with a hydrogen bomb because God has David in the palm of His hand. The sovereignty of God is a precious doctrine for the bullet-dodgers amongst our brethren. But when it comes to personality disintegration, loss of personal integrity will lead to loss of leadership integrity and finally to self-destructive behavior and ruin of the institution.

## Highly Placed Confidants

Palace intrigue—or misplaced javelins for that matter—does not happen a void. We're having dinner with all our high-ranking military personnel and other aficionados of state and the big guy throws a spear at the new kid. Of course, this completely escapes everyone's notice. Who is there? I've got a pretty good idea that the crown prince is there. It would not be much more of a reach to suggest that the supreme general was in attendance as well. And so on. When the boss makes a total blithering idiot out of himself—several times—the games of state are played. Blame-sharing, blame-shifting, fickle allegiances, convenient alliances, strategizing, positioning, posturing—and oh, the gossip! Nevertheless, and at the end of the day, David will find out that he has the allegiance of the crown prince and the general. Each will play out his various role and die an ignominious death in the effort. Jonathan's repeated role appears to be literally "to strengthen David's hand in God" (a.k.a. "encouragement"; e.g., 1 Sam. 23:16). Jonathan will die in Saul's last Philistine campaign. Abner's final role will be to finally turn the kingdom over to David. David may not even have known that Abner was really in his pocket until years after the death of Jonathan and moments before the general's assassination. David is called "the man after God's own heart." But to act in political friendship with this anointed king is the first step toward a body bag. Witness not only these but some of the executions following David's departure and the solidification of Solomon's empire.

## Textual Applications and Anecdotes

1 Samuel 18
vs.
1. Dopey, self-absorbed leaders may not notice heroism; but somebody important will.
2. To some leaders, people are merely ledgers—assets or liabilities.
3. It is a good thing to receive the love and respect of highly placed individuals—if they are individuals of integrity.
4. Marks of distinction, marks of honor, weapons, take them; they do not take away your reward in heaven.
5. A good point man may be hard to find—but will be recognized by all.
6. Victory celebrations are momentous occasions.

7. Victory celebrations may be bittersweet.
8. Victory celebrations may embitter the powerful and self-absorbed.
9. Embittered, powerful, and self-absorbed people will be suspicious.
10. Embittered, powerful, and self-absorbed person with a weapon: WARNING!
11. The best efforts outside the will of God result in complete failure.
12. The Lord has departed—the ultimate fear.
13. A fearful person removes the threat if possible.
14. The Lord is with one—the ultimate success.
15. The Lord is with someone other than oneself—dread.
16. The Lord is with someone—they may be victorious and receive the accolades of the people.
17. Political marriage—thinly veiled control.
18 Political marriage—beware.
19. Better to pass by the wrong one.
20. Love may look like a good idea initially.
21. Motivation may be multiplex.
22. Do not believe at first blush what the spin-doctor emissaries say to you.
23. A wise man recognizes his station.
24. The use of emissaries can be tedious.
25. The quest is a test and can veil a mortal hope.
26. Valor exceeds the demand in time.
27. Valor exceeds the demand in quantity.
28. Even the most conniving woman may be attracted to valor and winsomeness.
29. Protracted fear produces protracted enmity.
30. Someone on the rise by God's hand will rise high, rapidly, and continuously—the converse is also true.

## Conclusion

(See conclusion to chapter 19 below.)

# 1 Samuel 19
## Saul, the Royal Disaster (Part Two)
## The Girl Helps David Escape

—⁓—

## Introduction

(See Introduction to chapter 18 above.)

## Reading from "Saul: A Life Suspended in Doubt"

At that point, I had decided to have David assassinated. It simply was not going to be good enough to wait for the Philistines to finish him off—especially since he practically had the Philistines backed into the sea! In a private discussion with my son Jonathan, I disclosed my intentions. As heir apparent, he ought to understand the need to protect and pave the way for his ascendancy to the throne. What I got back from him was a defense attorney's rebuttal about David's innocence, valor, virtue, integrity, and value to the kingdom. In something other than a voice of my own, I vaguely recall making an oath that I would not do anything to harm the son of Jesse. The next thing I knew, my vice-regent had invited David back to court. Seeing him simply turned my stomach and I started to sense the rage rising. Again, as though I were watching from across the room, I saw myself fire a spear at David. Again, I watched him handily dodge it and walk, strident, regal, disgusted, and quickly from the palace, never to return during my lifetime.

Although he had left the palace rather hastily, he seemed fearless. He simply went to his apartment in Jerusalem not far away. I put sentries and spies in the vicinity to catalogue his movements and it looked as though he was merely going to go to bed. What I was later to find out is that my daughter had betrayed my confidence and helped David to escape through the window. When my men got there to take him into custody, she gave a bunch of excuses about him being sick or something—all designed to delay any pursuit of the most wanted fugitive in the realm! When my agents finally cleared away his bed, we found out that the whole thing was a ruse. Michal had actually hidden the teraphim in David's bed and made it look like he was there. Michal swore up and down that David had forced her to this deception upon pain of death. She loved him too much for her own good and so I doubt that a word of it was true. No way to prove anything though.

My intelligence determined that David had fled to Naioth to see Samuel. It was then that I was completely certain of the David/Samuel connection. So, I sent a detachment of soldiers to take David into custody. Three times they failed miserably. It seems that anytime they would get within the vicinity of Ramah they would go hysterical and fall down ranting and raving like maniacs. First rule of leadership: "If you want anything done right, do it yourself!" So, I brought some men with me to find out what the problem was. What happened next? I've no idea. When we got to Ramah, all of a sudden I had a feeling like I'd just been struck by lightning. I was literally beside myself! I watched myself for the better part of a day, ranting and raving among these religious fanatic Yahwists. It was as though I was either not entirely there or that I was completely divested of control of myself. I even took off my clothes. I'd had something like this happen to me before; but, it had never gotten this weird! That old saying was revived: "Is Saul also among the prophets?" I have no idea what was going on and I was powerless to regain control. Perhaps, I'd drunk poison or been drugged and this was all designed to give the son of Jesse time to escape, I have no idea. (1 Samuel 19)

## Textual Observations[82]

## Who Loves Ya, Baby!

Meanwhile back at transparency and opacity. Did you notice how everybody loves David, but nobody loves Saul? Of course you did. However, did you ever notice how everybody loves David—but David cannot be shown to love anybody (at least not until the death of Jonathan—and even there ambiguity abounds. In 1 Samuel 23 we read, "Saul and Jonathan, *beloved* " (v. 23, by whom?) and then, "Your love [Jonathan] *to me* was more wonderful than the love of women" (v. 26, what of David's for Jonathan?).

Back in our section we see that "the soul of Jonathan was knit to the soul of David, and Jonathan loved him as himself" (18:1). This is followed with several tangible evidences. Whatever he did, "was pleasing in the sight of all the people and also in the sight of Saul's servants" (5). Women sang for him (6-7). "The LORD was with him" (14). "All Israel and Judah loved David" (16). We assume this includes his prospective bride Merab (17-19). All bets are off with Michal, the next in line: "Now Michal, Saul's daughter, loved David" (20). Even the attempted deception hits upon an uncomfortable half-truth: "Speak to David secretly, saying 'Behold, the king delights in you [not by a long shot!], and all his servants love you [treasonously true!],'" so become the vixen's bridegroom and the king's son-in-law. And what is the final upshot? "Saul saw and knew that the LORD was with David, and that Michal, Saul's daughter, loved him, then Saul was even more afraid of David. Thus Saul was David's enemy continually" (28-30) effectively winning over each real player in Saul's family.

In chapter 19, all the above is proven by three confirming acts. First, Jonathan goes to bat for David against his father's vendetta (1-7) and gets him readmitted to palace life. Second, Michal saves the object of her infatuation by a ruse at the expense of her father (11-17). Third, and again at the expense of Saul, the prophets and God Himself make it absolutely certain that we know who is the object of the national and divine affection and approval (18-24). Again I ask, in all this, who does David love? What evidence will there be at the end of the day that he loved Saul? (The rhetoric in chapters 24 and 26 may be reduced to religious propriety, political expediency, or personal preservation.) How is he able to show his love for Jonathan? Jonathan shows his loyalty—but it is as lesser to greater! He is the scion of the king deposed speaking to the king anointed himself. "You will be king over Israel and I will be next to you" (23:17). What about Michal? One verbal misstep (maybe an illustration of the straw that broke the camel's back phenomenon?) and she is consigned to the status of widowhood and childlessness on house arrest (2 Sam. 6:20-23). Others? You be the judge.

There is probably a subtle lesson here: yes, "it is the LORD who chose me [David] above your [Michal's] father and above all his house, to appoint me ruler over the people of the LORD, over Israel" (2 Sam. 6:21). But let's not turn the song into a dirge, the party to a funeral, and the celebration into mourning by rubbing salt into festering wounds. A little grace, dignity, and gentle answers in the matters of church, state, and family—oh, how we blur the distinctions—might allay a lot of wrath in those same institutions.

Judging by some of the political moves David had Solomon make after his accession to the throne, maybe early on he viewed Michal (his first real wife, yes?) and any progeny she might produce as potential political rivals. Unfortunately the threat was really only to his hegemony and choice for successor—in matters of the hereditary rights of kings. Too bad he operated out of perceived fear rather than reality. It is too bad that the best planning and foresight could not protect him from the cancer that was to infect the palace in the not-too-distant future.

It is too bad that the home affects the other institutions: we know that Michal loved David once. We only know that all Israel and Judah loved David—probably including David's other wives—for a time! Their real sentiments, due to the unusually noisy silence of our Omniscient Narrator, remain unknown. When he began to multiply wives, in the genre of political marriages, we know that the other girls probably mixed their diluted affections rather liberally with a dose of political intrigue. Go through the list of rivals and examine the adventures and exploits of their sons.

Another not-so-subtle lesson: without picking favorites, leadership needs to do more than be a passive bystander to the divine utilization of persons accruing ultimately to His and our benefit. Is it possible for leadership to love? To genuinely care? Want a King James word? To demonstrate true biblical charity toward subordinates? My experience is that things are good while the apples are polished. Step out of line, voice your own opinion, and all the laws that Murphy could only wish to have written come into play—the *institution* exists to self-perpetuate (domestic, ecclesiastical, political, etc., *institution*); the good/need of the many exceed the good/need of the few—especially if the few rock the boat. Just because a part of the body doesn't want to be or want to act like part of the body doesn't mean that it is any less part of the body. So what do we do? We perform painful amputations that leave us finally debilitated. We do this in families, schools, churches, businesses, and governments. It is my opinion that such things of life run society into the ground. Be naïve if you wish, but America will be diminished by the Clinton years. She will demonstrate that lessened value and she will never recover from that era. Why should she recover? She certainly never recovered from the Nixon years. Think of all the physical and metaphysical graveyards you have seen in this life: schools that no longer orient toward the truth; churches that are no longer oriented toward Christ; governments that are no longer oriented toward their people; de facto parents who are no longer oriented toward their children and vice versa; and the deceased unheralded. Each disaster is merely the result and consequence of previously unresolved relationship issues and part of a process culminating in more and subsequent disasters. A disaster is art. A disaster is science. Disasters take time and careful planning. Love is an orientation. The love of or from leadership is its commitment to state and act in the best interest of its constituency—not a run-with-the-runners philosophy—its entire constituency, even at its own expense and to its own detriment. Can leadership demonstrate love? The jury is in recess.

### Skeletons in the Closet—Household Idols and Goat Hide Deceptions

Ever since the book of Genesis, we have known that where there is a goat, there is deception. We may be reminded that Rebekah had Jacob deceive Isaac with goat skins, Jacob deceived Laban with goats, his sons deceived him with goat blood, and Tamar held Judah for ransom with a goat and so on. Here also, Mical deceives the agents of her father the king with a goat hair— blanket—rolled up, I assume—covered with other clothes. Scapegoats are not the only place to look for trouble.

Why the extra household baggage of the teraphim, we may never know—but they come in handy from time to time. Rachel was able to pull off quite a ruse—with the attendant jeopardy of a high-risk oath from Jacob—to put her father completely off guard and require a ceasefire between the two of them. In our section of 1 Samuel, Mical is going to use the teraphim to make the bed look to be full of David. As was the case for the Nazghul however, the hobbits have escaped the ring-wraiths. Our favorite hobbit, David, has had the first of his near misses with sole ownership of pride of place as number one on the state fugitive list. But remember when things get wacky, loss of personal integrity leads to loss of leadership integrity and finally to self-destructive behavior and ruin of the institution.

## Textual Applications and Anecdotes

1 Samuel 19
vs.
1. A friend in high places can protect those who have not escaped notice.
2. If our agents in high places tell us to go underground for a while, it is best to comply.
3. If our agents in high places have private audience with a detrimental power, we should be able to know accurately what we need to know.
4. An agent in high places can tip his hand.
5. Logic means nothing when jealousy is in view (in the face of a political rivalry).
6. Public statements are not always what they seem—but sometimes they are positively prophetic.
7. A restoration to favor comes with a life lived under a microscope.
8. We do what we were designed to do well.
9. Music therapy is an ancient art.
10. If someone is firmly in God's grasp, they couldn't be dislodged with nuclear weapons.
11. The deathwatch may be circumvented by the princess.
12. There are unlikely accomplices.
13. Unlikely accomplices can be quite clever at times.
14. A lie buys time—success may require more than one.
15. The messenger's lot: a Ping-Pong ball on the great table of life.
16. A ruse discovered usually puts the perpetrator in an unenviable light.
17. A second lie? You might get lucky.
18. Plan ahead! Know to whom you would run.
19. Information travels fast.
20. God may use unusual means to defend His own.
21. He may use unusual means several times.
22. Be careful what information you request—unusual means may be used on you.
23. He may use unusual means on anybody.
24. He may use unusual means that are downright embarrassing.

## Conclusion

The ship of state is sinking; the edifice of government is collapsing. What can be done? The parallels between institutions and buildings are striking. Think of the buildings, metaphorically speaking, that you are in. Sometimes they stand strong, sometimes they fall. The institution does not matter. Even Christ said that He would build His church—but history is replete with examples of the fall of individual local churches as well as denominations. We must be very careful which building we build upon or build next to; we may find ourselves near an explosion or a collapse. But if the building is coming down, to beat up a dead metaphor, what do you do?

1.   You can *find* high ground and ride it down. That might take some stroke of good fortune.
2.   You can *fix* it.
     You must know yourself well
     a.      spiritual gifting
     b.      natural talents
     c.      learned skills
     Timing might be essential
     a.      before
     b.      during
     c.      after
     Requires
     a.      reflection
     b.      forethought
     c.      insight
     d.      positioning
     e.      snap-judgment
3.   You can *flee* it!

The answer lies within you. The ship is sinking. Find the lifeboat? Patch the hole? Jump over the side? Save yourself? Save others? Save others with you? These are all questions with respect to the various institutions you live in that you may answer. God bless you as you learn about yourselves, learn your assets, learn your limitations, learn your position.

# 1 Samuel 20
## The Pact of Friendship Learns a Hard Lesson

—⁓—

## Introduction

Jonathan, apparently thinking that all is well on the palatial front, does not seem to know that David has gotten himself into further trouble with Saul. In this episode, all the work that Jonathan had done to get David readmitted to court life will be undone. In what follows, Jonathan will reconfirm their allegiance to each other and attempt to sound out the sentiments of the king. They will set up an experiment to see whether David's understanding of Saul's hatred of him is justifiable. Upon ascertaining the demented despot's antipathy toward David, there is a brief display of emotion between the two that leaves us with more questions than answers. In this classic text on the continued friendship between David and Jonathan, we will find out that Jonathan is not omniscient about his father the king. He says, "My father does nothing either great or small without uncovering my ear. So why should my father hide this thing from me?" (1 Samuel 20:2). Apparently, new things are in the wind. We will also find out that David is a sometimes prophet as was Saul—though much more unwillfully and unwittingly. First, the reading and then the cryptic prophecy.

## Reading from "Saul: A Life Suspended in Doubt"

While all this was going on, David ran back to Jerusalem for some more consultation with the heir apparent. I do not know the details of these discussions; but, I have my suspicions. From that point on, Jonathan rarely talked to me privately. It was always within the safety of the larger group of courtesans, advisors, and officers that he met with me.

The next official time that the son of Jesse was to be at court was at a three-day new moon festival. When I saw that he'd missed the date the first time, I said nothing. If you were out in the field, a new moon appointment is pretty hard to ascertain—much less keep. However, I passed a casual question to my officers on the second day. Jonathan answered with some doublespeak about David going to Bethlehem to see his family for an annual festival. I had already told the family of Jesse that David was a permanent retainer in my forces and that they should not place very high family demands and expectations upon him. The fact that the

217

crown prince was present when such directives were given and that he, himself, should have given the son of Jesse leave to absent himself, simply made me livid! I called him a bunch of names (he never even flinched and his facial expression never changed), and then reproached him for jeopardizing his own future for the sake of a boy half his age. That voice again. . . . Then I ordered Jonathan to go arrest David himself and bring him to the city for execution for insubordination and conspiracy. When Jonathan equivocated, I fired a spear at him. It seems strange, I have always been an incredibly good shot with a javelin; but, in a rage, I could not even hit a grown man sitting in a chair. Jonathan left in a heated, seething rage—something I'd never seen in him before—he was always so even-tempered as to be unnerving at times. As though shocked back to my senses, I suddenly regained my composure and calmed down.

Nevertheless, some of my worst suspicions were confirmed when a little boy brought Jonathan's armament back to the palace. I asked him where he had gotten them and he said that Jonathan took a walk in a field and told him to return the equipment to the city. Jonathan? Unarmed? It could be nothing other than a signal, or so it seemed to me. . . . In any case, Jonathan never entered my presence again without someone accompanying him—always with a witness against his own father. (1 Samuel 20)

## Textual Observations

## Jonathan's Grief

Because of Samuel's words to Saul in 1 Samuel 13, because of Saul's curse on his son, Jonathan in 1 Samuel 14 and perhaps because of Jonathan's taking David's part in 1 Samuel 19, we know that Jonathan is in potential danger, theologically, dynastically, and mortally. There is a subtlety played out by our Omniscient Narrator as he carefully introduces this idea into the mouths of the two protagonists.

In 1 Samuel 20:3 David's words are somewhat prophetic. He says, putting words in Saul's mouth or mind, "Your father knows well that I have found favor in your sight, and he has said, 'Do not let Jonathan know this, lest he be grieved' [ye'atsev]. But truly as the LORD lives and as your soul lives, there is barely a step between me and death." Because we know the end of the story, David's words are a bit more pregnant with meaning than might appear at first blush. Jonathan will be grieved, as the narrator tells us in a few verses. We, the reader, will be grieved as well, because we know that Jonathan's life is forfeit in the transgressions of the king, his father. But David will also be grieved when he hears the report about Jonathan's death on Gilboa. David has next to no ability to display coherent emotions in the Samuel Narratives; but we know he is emotional—as will be seen at the end of this chapter.

In 1 Samuel 20:34, the narrator shows us how David's words are experienced by Jonathan. We are informed: "Then Jonathan arose from the table in fierce anger, and did not eat food on the second day of the new moon, because he was grieved [*ne'tsav*][83] over David because his father had dishonored him."

Was David's intent to be prophetic here? The conditional nature of the statement "lest he be grieved" indicates otherwise. However, the narrator may be intending to show, by the reuse of David's words, that the words are worth more than immediately strikes the eyes. It could be that the narrator in hinting at the pathos Jonathan will suffer in playing both ends against the middle for the rest of his life. Jonathan will have to dance tight choreography between palace life under the eye of his father Saul and the life of his fleeing friend David. Indeed, Jonathan's life will be one of grief as he watches his father slowly self-destruct. His life will be one of grief as he continues his service to his demented father apart from the company of his dear friend. His life will be one of grief as he surreptitiously leaves the palace, or the royal residence, to go out into the wilderness to meet with David and encourage him. His life will be one of grief as he dies an ignominious death in military service to his doomed father. His grief will live on in the broken heart of the emotionally enigmatic David. His grief will live on in the shattered family of Saul, left behind in the aftermath of the battle of Mt. Gilboa. His grief will find a provisional resting place when his son, Mephibosheth, obtains the favor of the new king. Finally, in the ambiguous judgment of David concerning Mephibosheth and Ziba, friends will be separated for the remainder of the reigning monarch's life. Jonathan's grief is truly our own as he cuts such a tragic figure in these Samuel Narratives.

## On the Deceiving of the King

Dredging up dirt on Jonathan will be dreadfully difficult to do. In my opinion, he is one of the truly great characters of biblical literature. However, after things shift from his father to his friend, things get a bit dicey. Jonathan will ever have to walk the tightrope between the palace and the hideout. The italicized text below shows the first instance where Jonathan slips into the grey area of deception. David tells him:

Behold, tomorrow is the new moon and I ought to sit down to eat with the king. But let me go, that I may hide myself in the field until the third evening. If your father misses me at all, then say, "*David earnestly asked leave of me to run to Bethlehem his city, because it is the yearly sacrifice there for the whole family.*" If he says, "it is good," your servant shall be safe; but if he is very angry, know that he has decided on evil. Therefore deal kindly with your servant, for you have brought your servant into a covenant of the LORD with you. But if there is iniquity in me, put me to death yourself; for why then should you bring me to your father? (1 Samuel 20: 5-8, emphasis mine).

Whatever we might say about David's motivations here—life and death, as he styles it—he is asking his friend to take part in a ruse. This is, of course, a ruse with a good precedent: it is very much like the one God told Samuel to use, if necessary, with the king in 1 Samuel 16 (see my notes there). There is a difference: it was apparently all right for God to suggest a sacrifice in Bethlehem with the elders. Since David merely waits in the field for a couple of days, there was no sacrifice in Bethlehem demanding his attendance. He has asked Jonathan to lie.

A second notice about the quote of David above is that he attempts to motivate Jonathan using the force of the covenant he had made with him. That is, David could hold Jonathan culpable of some kind of minor infraction should he not comply. The point is moot: Jonathan will not only comply, but go beyond the call of duty. Jonathan is such a true friend that he will compromise the king, his father, and the potential dynasty for his friend. Were the roles reversed, would David have done as much?

Jonathan demonstrates a bit of showmanship in the manner in which he addresses the king. We might say that he is trying to soften the force of David's conspicuous absence with a superfluity of words. However, for our conspiracy-theory-laden king, the ever neurotic, clueless, and sometimes demonized Saul, the proverb is true: in an abundance of words, transgression is unavoidable. Look at how Jonathan verbalizes David's absence: "David earnestly asked leave of me to go to Bethlehem, for he said, 'Please let me go, since our family has a sacrifice in the city, and my brother has commanded me to attend. And now, if I have found favor in your sight, please let me get away that I may see my brothers.' For this reason he has not come to the king's table" (1 Samuel 20:28-29).

The whole matter about his brother having commanded him to attend is a spurious embellishment. It is a dangerous one as well. In the first place, the matter could be easily researched. Saul could have called one of the brothers—most likely Eliab as the oldest— and inquired as to the necessity of the youngest son's attendance at some annual Bethlehem Mardi Gras. Upon finding the answer to this he could have either gone on the hunt for the least son of Jesse, or put the whole family to death one at a time until he surrendered himself to the king. Proof that David knows of this tactic and that the author is not making it up, is in the fact that David seeks asylum for all his father's household, first at the cave of Adullam; and then at the least, for his parents in Moab (1 Samuel 22:1-4). Hence, this is a dangerous ruse because of possible consequences to the whole family of David.

Secondly, it is dangerous because the whole thing, if discovered, could boomerang upon Jonathan himself. We have already noted that he is not safe from the king because of the oath in 1 Samuel 14. Saul, it would appear—though a bit theatrically—was perfectly willing to sacrifice his oldest son and the heir apparent, Crown Prince Jonathan, upon the altar of his mis-motivated oath and its attendant curse. This would have been strike three for Jonathan, most probably: first, the violation of the oath; second, bringing the least son of Jesse back to the palace; third, lying on his behalf to sound out the sentiments of the king.

Because the prophet had already told us that the dynasty will not continue and because the king has cursed his son in chapter 14, we know that the end of Jonathan is merely a matter of time. Anything that puts him in harm's way is merely suspense building for his final end on Mt. Gilboa. Each time, along the way, we ask ourselves, will Jonathan surely not escape his fate this time? At the end of this day, however, the only thing we know for sure is that David is a refugee and Jonathan is angered and grieved over David's dishonor by the king. Saul has thrown another spear—we are not even told that it stuck in the wall this time—and Jonathan has walked out of the room, not in fear for his life, but in anger for the humiliation of his friend. Whatever we do with Jonathan's falsehood at court that day, we will know the meaning of friendship. Jonathan's friendship was fearless, unwavering, and not without feeling.

## Textual Problems

Some have seen a conflation of stories between the telling of David and the shooting of the arrows as a sign to David. Because the story works, however awkward to occidental minds, I will not even dignify the theory with a response. I firmly believe that biblical literature is innocent until proven guilty and sufficiency is hardly necessity. We have here a coherent and cohesive narrative and we do it a dishonor by using supposition and innuendo in attempting to prove a disunity that does not exist.

## Textual Applications and Anecdotes

1 Samuel 20
vs.
1. An insider can help us in a desperate quest for understanding.
   When the sentence is death, know well the charges!
2. Denial and misinformation will not solve the problem.
   Intimate acquaintance and personal knowledge may solve the problem.
3. The suggesting of the undisclosed moves the discussion toward closure.
4. The true friend asks for suggestions and promises action.
5. Do you doubt your viability to the realm? Set up an experiment, a test.
6. The test must include a viable alternative.
   David follows his mentor Samuel here (1 Samuel 16:1).
7. The results of the test need to be clearly visible—up or down.

8. The wise man (David) knows when he has placed the life of a true friend (Jonathan) in jeopardy.

9. The true friend promises the release of vital information regarding his threatened friend.

10. The wise man wants to know how he will receive vital information.

11. Better an illustration in action than in ideas alone.

12. No matter the intentions, an answer in the form of a question still places responsibility for the answer upon the one who hears it.
    A question about action still implies the possibility of non-compliance.

13. A true friend may help his friend escape even if it is against the king, against the law, against his better interests, or even against reason.

14. Jonathan's question is the question of a friend, but it is also the question of a subordinate.

15. Jonathan hopes for his own life; but if not his, the life of his descendents.

16. Sometimes oaths do not make much sense.

17. Sometimes oaths do not make much sense until viewed through the lens of love.

18. The object of consternation is conspicuous by its absence.

19. Follow through on the whole plan—no matter how long.

20. The sign must be simple and recognizable to the one signaled.

21. One sign for safety here.

22. One sign for the Lord sending you away.

23. The "Lord between" is a stopgap against treachery.
    The "Lord between" is the assurance of loyalty.

24. The experiment laid out—players take their place.

25. The experiment laid out—one player is missing.

26. The first day, the tested one complies—perhaps appealing to religion.

27. The second day, the tested one queries—perhaps hoping to sniff out treason.

28. The answer baits the response.
    We might question the ethics of this staged ruse—does our hero Jonathan lie on behalf of his friend?

29. Embellishments on behalf of believability enhance the ruse.

30. Switch flipped, trap sprung—the king's wrath exposes his true sentiments.

31. Disestablishment of the dynasty may not be a bad thing.
    Disestablishment of the dynasty will hurt someone regardless.
    Denial of the prophecy of disestablishment makes the king's tirade doubly heinous.
    The true friend will not betray his friend in the face of the king's tirade.

32. The answer to the impossible question is obvious . . .

33. . . . kill the questioner.

34.     The true friend will be angered and grieved at the king's dishonor of his friend.
35.     The true friend will keep his appointments—for good or ill.
36.     The sign is put in place carefully.
37.     The sign is described carefully.
38.     The silent servant operates quickly.
39.     The silent servant operates without knowledge.
40.     The silent servant moves out of the way.
41.     The parting of the true friend is sorrowful.
        David crying more is enigmatic.
42.     The parting of the true friend is within the covenant.

## Conclusion

At the end of this dismal day, friends are parted; but they will not be parted forever. There is in the covenant made between them and their natural affections for each other, the power to maintain the friendship through the rough times ahead. There will come a time when, despite what it might mean to his father Saul, Jonathan will leave the palace and go to the stronghold to meet with David. David, at that point, will be at his wit's end and need his friend to "strengthen his hand in God." At that point, the depth of the relationship will be demonstrated in Jonathan's loyalty amidst hardships and in the dark. At that point, Jonathan will also prove that he is neither a prophet nor the son of a true prophet; but, he will prove himself to be the greatest of friends illustrated in this older testament. We could all use a few more Jonathans in this world. These are the guys who have to make the hard call and, depending upon your perspective, even the wrong call and live to prove their loyalty, if only for a short time to friends with whom they have covenanted. Jonathan was a good man and a man who understood the times and came to understand the transience of his own father the king. He supports David, the king-elect, and will die in that support and perhaps because of it.

# 1 Samuel 21
# Much to Worry about in Nob
# Nuts in the Winepress

—⁓—

## Introduction

Breathlessly, the text departs from the scene wherein Jonathan and David forge their pact of loyalty and moves on toward David's many months in exile. Indeed, the ancients could not agree upon where to break the text (see "Textual Problems" below) due to the nature of the change in scene. Be that as it may, at the same time, the text has Jonathan and David separate from one another. Jonathan returns to the city and David's first stop in exile is Nob, the community of the priests. His arrival provokes more discussion—indeed it would still be discussed in Jesus' day (Matthew 12:2-4; Mark 2:26; Luke 6:3-4). David is provisioned with both food and a weapon and sent off to stage two of his exile. Stage two is the abortive defection to the Philistines in Gath wherein insanity achieves its apex in David. It would seem that David only feigns insanity to save his life whereas Saul can barely feign sanity at all anymore. Let us follow David at the inauguration of his travels.

## Reading from "Saul: A Life Suspended in Doubt"

I had my agents well placed throughout the kingdom. One in particular proved to be most useful. A certain Edomite defector by the name of Doeg was hired by my officers to handle some personal financial matters: specifically my livestock. He was assigned a location close to Nob not merely to look after the flocks and herds of his king. He was a mercenary agent with the additional responsibility of acquiring information with regard to the effects of the priesthood. Religious leaders had often in history started grassroots movements and insurrections. I needed to be apprised of any such movements in advance of their gaining any momentum.

It was in this context that I was to learn that the kingdom's most wanted fugitive, the son of Jesse, had put in an appearance at Nob. He had come to visit Ahimelech the high priest. He only had a few retainers with him; but, what Ahimelech permitted really turned my stomach. He actually gave David and his men the bread of presentation from the tabernacle. This was strictly forbidden to anyone other than a consecrated priest. I am certain that Ahimelech must have done so under some kind of compulsion. But I am not sure why—and he wouldn't be around to ask in any case!

David was apparently not well armed when he left the palace. Doeg reported to me that Ahimelech had given him Goliath's sword. This was a clear violation of state law. That artifact of history was consigned to the safekeeping of the priests. They had given state property to a fugitive. In addition, they had given state property of strategic importance to a known violent man. Goliath's sword was the finest steel in the eastern Mediterranean. It would break a bronze blade on the first stroke and an iron one in only a couple. Our best steel was no match for it. In any case, this made the son of Jesse an armed insurrectionist and hence a project for the military.

After the son of Jesse had left Nob, we lost him for a while and had no clear report on where he went. There was a rumor that he had fled to Gath to Achish; but, that report seemed a bit farfetched. He had killed so many Philistines from that particular region of their territory that I doubted they would hand much of him back to us—except his head, perhaps. . . . Nevertheless the next clear report we had from him was from the south in Keilah. (1 Samuel 21)

## Textual Observations

### David Flees to Nob

With the separation of the two friends, each to his own destiny, the scene picks up David as he arrives in Nob to visit the priests. Formerly, he had visited Naioth in Rammah to visit Samuel and had barely escaped with his life due to repeated spiritual intervention (1 Samuel 19:18-24). Now on the run in earnest, David tries another approach and flees to Nob and the priestly community there.

In language reminiscent of that used earlier as the elders of Bethlehem met the approaching prophet, Samuel, and came "trembling to meet him" (1 Samuel 16:4), Ahimelech came "trembling to meet David." There was apparently quite some trepidation in view of the surprise of having such an important visitor unheralded. Whatever the reasons for Ahimelech's angst, David mollifies them with deception. Since David most probably recognized that everyone he came in contact with was at risk, he probably thought the proliferation of deception and hence ignorance would be Ahimelech's best protection. David's precautions are at once baseless and impotent: Ahimelech is doomed—as are many who act in friendship to the king-elect.

Ahimelech bends the rules a bit in respect to giving David the bread of the presence. In reality, no one but the priests were supposed to eat it (Leviticus 24:5-9). This is certainly the spin that Jesus puts on the text and He receives none of the usual flak from his Pharisaic antagonists about it (Matthew 12:2-4; Mark 2:26; Luke 6:3-4). Be that as it may, Ahimelech makes an exception under the condition of ritual purity. He says, "If only the young men have kept themselves from women" (1 Samuel 21:4). David makes the following sweeping generalization: "Surely women have been kept from us as previously when I set out and the vessels of the young men were holy, though it was an ordinary journey; how much more then today will it be holy in the vessel?" Ambiguities abound! One of these has to do with the meaning of "vessel" here. I will not go into that; suffice it to say it could intend an object, a member of the body or the whole body. The point is that David is trying to be ambiguous. He has begun this conversation with deceit (the king's mission, right!) and he will continue it that way. He wants provisions for himself and his men and he will get them in such a way as to make their acquisition certain and keep the priests out of the loop. As it turns out and unfortunately, it is but a quick fix—the boys get fed and the priests and their families get dead . . . as do many of David's friends.

## Where There Are Priests, There Are Sheep and Edomites and Such

A notice, important for the sequel, is that Doeg the Edomite was present when David showed up uninvited at Ahimelech's door. We are told that Doeg was "the chief of Saul's shepherds" (1 Samuel 21:7). We might assume that the king had a rather notable flock and hence the position of chief shepherd was a prominent position. Regardless, there are two things of importance in the literature as this man makes his appearance out of nowhere and seemingly is dismissed with the introduction. First, in the sequel, it will require that an outlander be present both to inform the king of the events recently transpired in Nob and to execute Saul's insane sentence against Ahimelech and company. We know that the Israelites will be reticent to inform on David and that some would be reticent to execute the priests and their families.

Secondly, what is in a name? As we hinted at back in chapters 9 and 10 in regard to Saul's worries, Doeg (*do'eg*) is the worrier (active sense). His name is from the root, in Hebrew, that means "to worry." He causes David to worry (1 Samuel 22:22). And he will be that to which the worrier himself, King Saul, turns to work a quick fix on the priesthood. This will then be one more cause of worry for Saul because he will have effectively alienated himself from the priesthood in Israel, and no one who is religious will trust him. Doeg is the multivalent worrier.

## David Takes a Sword to Gath

One of the things David will need in the coming days is an equalizer. He will need a weapon in his flight from the king and his officers bent upon his destruction. And so, continuing the ruse he began with he asks for "a spear or sword" (1 Samuel 21:8) because "the king's matter was urgent." Indeed! It was so urgent that David was made to run for his life. Technically—and I am under no compunction to "save" David here—this is not deception as much as it is ambiguous language predicated upon the initial deception of verse 2. Of course, there is no sword available other than the unparalleled blade formerly owned by the monster, Goliath.

Those familiar with the story in chapter 17 will recall that Goliath's hometown was Gath (1 Samuel 17:4, 23). In other places people from Gath are called Gittites (e.g., 2 Samuel 18:2); but the text in chapter 17 is unambiguous even to English readers. In chapter 21, the text is lightly ambiguated for the delight of discovery. The sword's former owner is merely called "Goliath the Philistine" (1 Samuel 21:9). And so, when David embarks upon the next stage of his exile, he takes Goliath's unique weapon back to Goliath's home town.

## Madness and David Feigning Madness

If the conversation between Achish and David is not enough to drive the reader deliriously dizzy, the course of David's adventures will drive the reader crazy. David is caught in the recognition that any high-profile person can rarely escape. The people surrounding Achish remind him that this guy is or at least looks like—they are smart enough to present their case before the king in question form—that infamous Israelite berserker, David. In doing so, they quote the text of the women's song and dance regarding the military prowess and comparison between Saul and David: "Saul has slain his thousands, and David his ten thousands" (1 Samuel 21:11). This is the second time (of three) that the lyrics of the ditty which would plague Saul all his life is rehearsed. Now, the song has crossed borders—it is an international hit—although not for the right reasons, if you happen to be from Philistia.

Be that as it may, perhaps another reason David had to feign madness before King Achish of Gath, was the insanity of taking a weapon that would have been the envy of any courtier and military man in all of Philistia and that it was recognized immediately for whose it had been. David's blunder became his insanity and he then must feign madness to escape with his life. As Goliath's sword slips from the text and from the reader's consciousness, one wonders what happened to it from that point on.

## Textual Problems

## No Good Place to Break the Text

Apparently, the ancients believed it was possible to hold more in mind with the telling and hearing of a story than we do. There is not a good place to break the text on either horizon. By the rules of engagement we have been handed from mediaeval times, we can break the text at any point there is a change in scene. That would seem more likely at verse 2 than verse 1 of the Hebrew text. This is the approach taken by many of our modern versions following, apparently again, the lead of the Septuagint. So far as the text is concerned, the only thing that changes is to whom David is talking. The notations about Jonathan and David going their separate ways are so incidental as to nearly escape the notice of all but the most tedious reader. By the same rules of engagement, one could have as easily broken the text at verse 10.

## No One and the Young Men: Conflict Between Verses One and Two

The only problem is that there is a difference in information between that given by Ahimelech and that given by David. Contradictions being what they are in the "progressive" mind, such claims are pretty difficult to sustain. This becomes more certain in view of the story's coherence and the fact that Ahimelech smoothly comes on line, acknowledging the numbers of associates in verse 4. This is not like crows that allegedly cannot tell the difference between one and many. This is simply that Ahimelech does not initially notice the others in the light of his distinguished and surprising guest as he comes "trembling to meet David" (1 Samuel 21:1). Notice that this is the same language used of the response of the elders to the approach of Samuel as they came "trembling to meet him" (1 Samuel 16:4). No doubt there is some association intended. Ancient art and the concealment and revelation of information do not usually subject themselves to the categories of post-Enlightenment, romance literary categories of the West.

## Textual Applications and Anecdotes

1 Samuel 21
vs.
1. Our arrival may not be understood by all.
2. Lying about our reason for being there accomplishes nothing.
3. No matter the urgency, food is required for the journey.
4. In Israel's economy, holy bread required holy recipients.
5. In Israel's economy, holiness included abstention.
6. David, not a priest, ate that holy bread.
   Exceptions may be made to some ceremonial rules.
   (Jesus made an issue of this in Matthew 12:2-4, etc.)
7. The introduction of a nobody in biblical narrative gains significance later.
   The introduction of a foreigner in biblical narrative may bode ill later.
8. No matter the urgency, weapons may be required in a barbaric world.
9. An artifact is good enough—depending upon the artifact.
10. Catch the irony: Goliath's sword went to Goliath's hometown of Gath—without him.

11.     Those who sing the song may know it well.
12.     Those who recognize us can cause us to fear greatly.
13.     Insanity hardly masks insanity.
14.     A plea of insanity may gain us a stay of execution.
15.     A plea of insanity may get us a hasty exit from the proximity of lethal trouble.

**Conclusion**

Achish's courtiers rightly present their case in the form of questions so as to make their indictment less forceful and to allow the king to make the discovery of David's guilt. David's guilt is forever hidden from the eyes of the Philistine king of Gath. However, the courtiers spark Achish's ire when David's stage antics prove entirely convincing. He fires back at them a barrage of questions: "Behold, you see the man behaving as a madman. Why do you bring him to me? Do I lack madmen, that you have brought this one to act the madman in my presence? Shall this one come into my house?" (1 Samuel 21:14-15). Good questions, all! But there is probably more of a barb in them than we might see immediately. Where are we in space and time? We are in an ancient throne room in Philistia. The present case is in the present tense. No, Achish, there have been plenty of madmen that have managed to attach themselves to royalty throughout the ages. No Achish, all you need to do is look around you—there is certainly no shortage of insanity in Philistia, Gath, your throne room, or even in your own house. In fact, history will prove that all you need to do is look in the mirror and you will see one of the biggest dupes and nut cases of history. He who feigned madness before you will one day become one of your closest allies and confidants (1 Samuel 27-29) and prove your own madness to you.

# 1 Samuel 22
## When an Edomite Shepherd Boy Is Sent to Do an Israelite Man's Job

—⟋⟍—

## Introduction

Although there is no break in the action, only a break in the barrage of Achish's questions, the scene is about to change and David will be forced to leave Gath. Fear not, he will return, not as an insane refugee, but as a very shrewd ally and confidant to the king of Gath, Achish. This will not make Achish look particularly bright; but Achish will go through some of his own transformations as well. In the sequel, the stage has already been set for the decimation of the priestly community and that will happen presently. However, in the interim, David must find safe harbor. He will find that in the cave of Adullam wherein he will be surrounded by family and friends and other like-precious misfits and malcontents.

Then will come the annihilation of the priests of Nob. When we come to the scene where Ahimelech addresses the king, we will see that David has many able advocates in high places. David has many friends, many of whom will lose their lives in the times of David's trials and elevation. But first, let us follow David into hiding at the cave of Adullam.

## Reading from "Saul: A Life Suspended in Doubt"

I decided that I was going to apply a little firm pressure to make the son of Jesse return to Jerusalem and face judgment. I sent to Bethlehem to bring his family to Jerusalem and hold them upon promise of release if David should appear. However, they had all departed to the wilderness to hide out with him. It would have been like trying to find a needle in a haystack. My eyes and ears in Judah said that David had made arrangements with the King of Moab to have his family stay there. Something about his great-great grandmother, I didn't feel the need to wage war on two opposite fronts to retrieve them, so I let them go. It seems that no matter how hard I pursued him, he was always just one step ahead of me.

I began to become very melancholy about the whole thing and asked my servants if there were anybody who could help me out of my dilemma. Doeg came through with the revelation that the priests at Nob had aided and abetted the fugitive. When

I summoned the priesthood to the palace, I found that they continued the national conspiracy and should therefore be sentenced to death. None of the Israelites under my command were willing to lift a hand against the priests. Doeg was more than willing and killed Ahimelech and 84 others of the priests.

Then we sent Doeg to Nob to kill everybody there. Only one refugee survived: Abiathar a young son of Ahimelech, escaped and fled, I assume to David, to declare the news to him about the priests. Somebody in my court told me that I had just fulfilled a prophecy given nearly a century earlier to Eli. I suddenly awoke to the realization of what I had done and felt very tormented by it. Because a state fugitive had unnerved me to the point that I would go to such lengths, I felt that I must pursue David and hunt him down in the badlands of Judah where it was rumored that he was hiding. (1 Samuel 22)

## Textual Observations

## David's Gathering of Misfits and Malcontents

Comparisons between the Joseph story and the Samuel Narratives are legion, and here a comparison between David and Judah (Genesis 38) is in order. We will recall that deception is the nature of the story in Genesis 38 and that appears at the surface level in the story as Tamar deceives Judah as well as subliminally in the name of places like Chezib (like Achzib, "deception") and in the goat motif—where there are goats or goats' blood, there is deception in Genesis. In like manner, coming out of a situation wherein David first deceives Ahimelech who proves to be his friend, and later deceives Achish by feigning insanity – a man who was his rightful enemy and yet proved to be his ally, confidant, and friend. What both stories share at the level of surface text is the word Adullam. From the Genesis reference we recall that Judah's friend is called *an* or *the* Adullamite (38:1, 12, 20), and here we see that the initial gathering of misfits and malcontents is at "the cave of Adullam" (1 Samuel 22:1). And so we can expect, following the Genesis themes, that there will be further deceptions, friends, and errands of fools.

And so they all gather at the cave of Adullam: "his brothers . . . his father's household . . . and everyone who was in distress, and everyone who was in debt, and everyone who was bitter of soul, gathered to him; and he became captain over them . . . about four hundred men" (1 Samuel 22:1-2). Imagine the logistics! Everywhere David goes, henceforth, he will have to figure out how to move and provision between four and six hundred men—many with families. But another thing to remember is that some of these are the worthless ones, the "sons of Belial" to be mentioned in 1 Samuel 30:22. This becomes excellent preparation for the monarchy as both Achish and Saul could attest: misfits and malcontents are exactly that—and they are ubiquitous!

**Home to Great-Grandma's House (Moab)** (Ruth 4:18-22)

One of the details that an aspiring monarch needs to attend to—beyond whether or not he really wants to be a ruler—is to see to the welfare of his family. Why do David's parents need to go into exile? There are a couple of reasons: first, they simply could not be safe in Saul's kingdom. Anyone who wanted to enter the good graces of the madman king might simply capture, torture, or kill members of David's family. Secondly, they might be held as collateral against David's not-so-safe conduct back to the palace. That is, they could be held, tortured, dismembered, or systematically executed until David should return to Saul's bar of injustice.

David then sends his parents into a safer and less mobile exile in Moab (1 Samuel 22:3-4). We might gather that the cave of Adullam is on the east side of Israel and that Moab was more easily accessed. However, there may be more reason than the mere facility in transferring his parents to Moab. As we see from the reference in the heading, there is a long tie that goes back to Moab and it is in the great grandparents. Because Jesse has Moabite blood flowing in his veins, it would be natural to seek temporary safekeeping in Moab. Because of Saul's constant problems with the Philistines and others, he might have been unwilling to open a war on another front for the sake of collateral against David. In my opinion, it is a wise move on David's part and one that will have some rather odd aftershocks (2 Samuel 8:1-2). After a couple more short hops, the prophet Gad told the fugitive, David, to move into the wilderness of Judah. And so we leave David for many verses while we cut back to the aftermath in Nob.

**Worry (*da'ag*) Revisited**

As we noted in reference to the previous chapter, Doeg, "the worrier," will become worrisome indeed. As we open the scene, we are told that Saul had received a report of David having successfully eluded his grasp yet again. At this point, Saul launches into a very convincing game of "poor, poor pitiful me." But nobody will speak up—telling Saul would be an admission of guilt and therefore complicity in David's escape. And so Doeg the Edomite makes his grand entrance from the environmental people in the background of Saul's stage. He was "standing by the servants of Saul" or in a position over them, depending upon how one reads the preposition (1 Samuel 22:9). Regardless, out of the backdrop and with the voice of all malice through all time of one who knows how to make people rise and fall, Doeg says, "I saw the son of Jesse coming to Nob, to Ahimelech the son of Ahitub. And he inquired of the LORD for him, gave him provisions, and gave him the sword of Goliath the Philistine" (1 Samuel 22:9-10). The king makes no response to Doeg that we have recorded in the story at this point. One cannot help but feel that the king is elated with this new information and the course of action he will now pursue. And so the king calls the priesthood on the carpet to give an account of its treasonous actions.

Because I will look at Ahimelech's speech in the following "excursus," I will not elaborate on his statements in defense of himself and David other than to say that he piles up epithets upon David such that any action taken by the king against him will be an act of both utter folly and consummate wickedness. As with any articulate and just speech before a deranged and demonized despot, it will be Ahimelech's swan song.

Be that as it may, Saul's henchmen are unwilling to execute the king's command to avenge him on the priesthood. We are told: "But servants of the king were not willing to put forth their hands to strike the priests of the LORD" (1 Samuel 22:17). The oscillations between sovereignty and impotence in the life of Saul are an interesting Ping-Pong match. What is he going to do if none of his courtiers is willing to execute, assassinate, kill—correct terms fail me here—the entirety of the established religious functionaries of the day? Find an outlander with enough antipathy toward Israel's religion, nothing to lose, and an opportunist with something to gain? Doeg presents himself as the logical choice and so the king tells the informant, the snitch-become-assassin, "You turn around and strike the priests" (v. 18). And then we are told with almost clinical detachment: "And Doeg the Edomite turned around and attacked the priests, and he killed that day eighty-five men who wore the linen ephod" (v. 18).

Moving on from there, Doeg apparently leads a detachment of assassins against the city of Nob itself. His becomes the name responsible for the decimation of its population. He killed "men and women, children and infants" (1 Samuel 22:19). Follow the word *sword* through the text beginning with "Goliath's sword" (v. 10), following with Saul's indictment to Ahimelech giving him a sword (v. 13), we might assume that he killed the eighty-five priests with whatever was at hand, for instance, a sword (v. 18), but then we are certain because he killed the inhabitants of Nob "with the edge of the sword" (v. 19). Not content with the killing of people, Doeg continues his insane killing spree by butchering oxen, donkeys, and sheep with the edge of the sword (v. 19). As I have suggested before (see notes on chapter 16 and 17), it would appear that Saul's demons flew in flocks and infested anyone around him. Thus is the contagion of despotic insanity.

Doeg "the worrier" will disappear from the stage of history and will live only in the mind of the reader as an emblem of all that is despicable, treacherous, violent, and perhaps demonic. However, he will not disappear before he lives for us in the memory of David. When a single refugee from the atrocities at Nob escapes to David in the wilderness, he informs him of what has transpired. That refugee, Abiathar, will live to have his own history explicated in the Samuel Narratives and in coming pages. However, the recounting of the events of the day inspire these words from David as scene changes and Doeg has exited: "I knew on that day, when Doeg the Edomite was there, that he would surely tell Saul. I have brought about the death of every person in your father's household" (1 Samuel 22:22).

Because of the ambiguity of the text, "I have gone around in every life of the house of your father," we cannot know that David is admitting fault, guilt, or merely occasion. It looks to me as though he is falling all over his words in an effort to hold himself together in the company of his men and in the face of his new friend. Whatever the case, David knows the gravity of the situation and the condition of the insane monarch and his servants and invites Abiathar to stay with him. "Stay with me, do not be afraid, for he who seeks my life seeks your life; for you are safe with me" (1 Samuel 22:23). Perhaps this is David's way of saying, "My enemy's enemy is my friend." Abiathar will prove to be David's friend. However, in the end, due to a mistaken loyalty, David will prove, through Solomon, to be Abiathar's enemy.

**Excursus: Falsehood and Deception—A Dangerous Pattern Developing in David's Life**

David neither begins nor ends his career in the Samuel Narratives (ending, of course, in 1 Kings 2) characterized by falsehood. If his response to Eliab, "What have I done now" (1 Samuel 17:29), is reflective of previous abuses as I have styled it in my notes on chapter 17, then perhaps the roots go back into his childhood. In short, he may have had to hedge his bet with regard to the truth to keep out of trouble. However he began, he does not seem to compromise the truth when he is in power. In fact, David will then show another oscillation by changing to political power moves when he gets old (cf. 1 Kings 1-2). After all, you should not require deception to the end of manipulation if you had the power of a sovereign despot. It is difficult to style David in such terms; yet examination of his methods will prove that he is pitifully passive at times and despotically aggressive at others. What can be known about David's brand of "truth" at the beginning of his story? David does not speak until chapter 17 and it is all about the asking and answering of questions. David has heard about the giant, heard what the giant has said, and has heard what will be done for the man who rolls away Israel's reproach (1 Samuel 17:23-25). But then things get really interesting: twice, after that, David checks his references and asks the same questions to others (vv. 26 and 30). Why? Does David doubt the truthfulness of the fellow soldiers of his brothers? Does he distrust them in the same way he distrusts his brothers? The turning away from Eliab says more than his words do (v. 30). Is part of the reason that David has to check his references so often, to paraphrase Isaiah, "he is a man of falsehood and he lives among a people of falsehood"? We will see. The problem surfaces early enough in his life. Suffice it to say at this point: what he tells Saul cannot otherwise be shown to be false (killing the lion and the bear, intent to kill Goliath, etc.). What he says to the giant is proven to be true (killed, head removed, carcass to feed the birds and beasts). So, what could David have known about the truth?

One of my students rightly objected when it was suggested that David was an out-and-out liar. In my humble opinion, it would be wrong to hold the ancients to the same standards to which the New Testament might hold them (e.g., Colossians 3:9, only in the community? First John 1:6; 2:21, 27 a bit more universal). Neither do I think that our modern juridical understanding of the matter, "swear to tell the truth, the whole truth, and nothing but the truth, so help you God," will be found to apply to individuals in the ancient world very well. Arguably, oaths of this nature mean nothing any longer in our society in any case as witnessed by the judges sworn to defend the Constitution who attempt to rewrite it during every hearing. Be that as it may, there are a couple of statements of David's that simply will not wash. So, what could David have known about the Law? Several places in the Law we are told about truth statements:

> You shall not answer against your neighbor as a lying witness (Exodus 20:16).
> You shall not answer against your neighbor as a vain witness (Deuteronomy 5:20).

I suppose that neither of these really apply to our case because, first, they are both in a judicial setting with the word "witness." Secondly, they both deal with neighbors and foreigners (Goliath, Achish, etc.) and reprobates (Ahimelech, condemned line of Eli) who are not really neighbors in the mind of the writer. However, I do not think this notion of neighbor works very well with Ahimelech, and David probably knew nothing of the curse on Eli's family when he out and out lied to Ahimelech (1 Samuel 21:2).

However, there are places where a more general approach to falsehood and deception are taken that would at least apply to Saul and Ahimelech: You shall not steal, nor deal falsely, nor lie to one another (Leviticus 19:11).

I suppose that we might argue that this is only within the community and so bears no weight in the case of Achish or among the disenfranchised lines of Eli or Saul. However, why should there be a covenant of truth between David and Jonathan or Abiathar were that the case? In this case, Israel is Israel and David is obligated, I believe. We might argue that this is just holiness code (Leviticus 17-25) and as such only applies to the priesthood specifically and not to Israel in general; but practically nobody takes it that way. Facts are facts though, if a statement someone makes is devoid of truth, it is false; or looked at another way, if a statement someone makes is vacuous regarding truth, it is false regardless of who makes the statement or who is addressed. Hence, if there is nothing of the truth in David's initial statement to Ahimelech, "The king has commissioned me with a matter," then it is false and David has lied to Ahimelech. Regardless of some possibility of David's good intentions in keeping Ahimelech out of the loop and thus ignorant of palace intrigue and perhaps out of trouble, David has lied to a countryman. The repercussions are disastrous.

Another of my class discussions suggests that David is not obligated to give the truth if his intentions are good. That is, if in lying David is trying to keep people out of trouble or trying to manipulate the circumstances to good ends, he is not culpable. And so, another way of looking at the truth and falsity of statements is through the lens of natural law. That is, there are things that work and things that do not work about statements made by individuals to other persons. When one takes upon oneself the responsibility for the fabrication of "truth" claims, one also assumes the responsibility for the results. In the case of David lying to Ahimelech, it did not work in any case and Ahimelech and a lot of other people got killed regardless of David's good intentions. I do not personally feel that David's falsehood got Ahimelech *et al.* killed. If David's intent was to keep Ahimelech in the blind about his "mission from the king" (1 Samuel 21:8), he succeeded according to Ahimelech's own statements (1 Samuel 22:15), however valuable a man's own admission of innocence might be. Be that as it may, I do not personally feel that David is responsible for their death. This is in opposition to his own words in 1 Samuel 22:22: "I have brought about the death of every person in your father's household." Although the translation of "brought about" is uncertain, the life and death context seems to indicate that David is claiming responsibility. Fine, David does not understand the difference between occasion and cause. He may have been there, but after acquitting himself well, Saul commissioned Doeg the Edomite to execute, apart from due process, Ahimelech. No, Saul is responsible as the efficient cause of Ahimelech's death and Doeg the instrumental cause of death for Ahimelech, his family, and community.

Be all that as it may, what is the net effect of a lie? When discovered it makes the liar doubly culpable: in the first place he has done something he felt needed to be covered by falsehood; in the second place he has covered it with the falsehood itself. There is also collateral damage that will accrue to a David or any other person accused and convicted of falsehood and deception. Statements made by him in the future will be regarded to be questionable. That person has lost his default position of believability. He does not automatically have the right to the unchallenged virtue of truthfulness. Third, since he has told a lie, he apparently believes that lies are all right in some circumstances. Because of that we can never regard anything he says as being true without collaboration from other sources. There are a couple of proverbs that David or others who do not believe the truth is critical in all situations fall to: the first: if you tell the truth you never have to remember what you said. This is, of course, less important in narrative literature, because lies do not always come home to roost. That is, we may never be told how it was that a person was caught or diminished by having lied. Secondly, there is the old adage, if I would not lie for you, I would not lie to you. Jonathan has been asked to lie to Saul on David's behalf in setting up the test for Saul's sentiments for or against David. What that might say about Jonathan is huge. If Jonathan would lie for David, he might then be in the position of lying to David. How could David ever finally trust his friend without reference checks and so on? In fact, David does not entrust himself to people at all. Since it is all situational, there can be a situation imagined in which Jonathan might justify the means of falsehood to David for some allegedly altruistic end. In the end, this will not wash. What you wind up with is a society characterized by liars and falsehood. Your whole life is one of sorting out statements as to truth claims and nothing progresses. But worst of all, one who cannot be trusted to tell the truth cannot be entrusted with the truth.

Where does this all begin? I have an idea, although we cannot know for sure, that it began in Jesse's house. It may be reflected in the recoil from abuse in the encounter with his brother Eliab (1 Samuel 17:28-29). Truthfulness seems to be the order of the day throughout much of chapters 18 and 19. When he is finally on the run, Michal is the one who engages in deception. We cannot know if she lies; that is, if David really threatened her (1 Samuel 19:17) although that might go a long way to explain their mutual hostility in 2 Samuel 6. My bet is on Michal's love being the cover for the lie to her father. As we will see, everybody lies to Saul.

The first and most obvious problem—lie or not—is in David's setting up the test of Saul's sentiments with Jonathan. David says: "Behold, tomorrow is the new moon, and I ought to sit down to eat with the king. But let me go, that I may hide myself in the field until the third evening. If your father misses me at all, then say, 'David earnestly asked leave of me to run to Bethlehem his city, because it is the yearly sacrifice there for the whole family.' If he says, 'It is good,' your servant shall be safe; but if he is very angry, know that he has decided on evil" (1 Samuel 20:5-7).

Jonathan has already said that he is willing to do whatever David requests of him (v. 4), and so we might expect compliance. Because Jonathan's life was already forfeit in Saul's recklessness (1 Samuel 13 and 14), perhaps he does not trust his father and expects none from him. Be that as it may, we should probably consider the gravity of the situation: David is asking his best friend the crown prince to lie to his father the king. There is no sacrifice in Bethlehem; there is no family gathering, and the whole thing is a ruse as proved by the fact that David stays in the field for a couple of days (1 Samuel 22:35). Indeed, if found out—and apparently it was—this ruse could be viewed as high treason (cf. 1 Samuel 22:30-31). The ramifications for such an act include the death penalty for David and/or Jonathan. (Because Jonathan had been rescued by the people from the insane oath of his father once before, perhaps Saul would not have been able to execute sentence this time. It seems odd to me that the father does not just merely commute the rights of the first born to whoever is next in line. But then Saul is an odd character. Saul seems to have some innate knowledge that the rest of his sons were losers as was he himself.)

As mentioned above, the second place where David might be accused of stretching the truth to the breaking point is in regard to his encounter with Ahimelech the (high) priest.[84] David said to him, "The king has commissioned me with a matter, and has said to me, 'Let no one know anything about the matter on which I am sending you and with which I have commissioned you; and I have directed the young men to a certain place.' Now therefore what do you have on hand? Give me five loaves of bread, or whatever can be found" (1

Samuel 21:2-3). In the first place the king had not commissioned on a matter. In the second place, the whole decree of commission is fabricated out of whole cloth. And since the entire statement is devoid of truth, David has lied.

David also assured Ahimelech of the young men's ritual purity—something about which he could only speculate. The escape was so hasty that he can only trust to happenstance that the young men have abstained from conjugal relations. This is ignorance proposed as truth. Again it is vacuous in content and intent and is deception at best and a lie at worst.

Continuing on, David tells Ahimelech, "Now is there not a spear or a sword on hand? For I brought neither my sword nor my weapons with me, because the king's matter was urgent." There is absolutely nothing false about this statement unless predicated upon the matters in verse 2. That is, David very well could very well have "gotten out of Dodge" with nothing but the clothes on his back and without any weapons. However, if this series of clauses is based upon the intended deception, disinformation, and lies of verse 2, then it merely continues the lie. The "king's matter was urgent" in point of fact; but, it is not the "matter" Ahimelech has been lead to believe. That is, David is a fugitive, not an emissary. As a footnote to all this, Ahimelech's words bear repeating here because he is a virtuous man and he is completely in the dark. It will not make anyone feel any better that he is in the condemned line of Eli and that he will die shortly after his brilliant swan song.

"And who among all your servants is as faithful as David, even the king's son-in-law, who is captain over your guard, and is honored in your house? Did I just begin to inquire of God for him today? Far be it from me! Do not let the king impute anything to his servant or to any of the household of my father, for your servant knows nothing at all of this whole affair" (1 Samuel 22:14-15).

Saul's only response to the truth is to kill it—which he cannot do himself, coward that he is—neither can he get any Israelites to butcher the religious leadership of the nation. Only an opportunistic outlander will do it. And so Doeg the Edomite, the "worrier," causes us to worry over the fate of Saul's and Eli's line. Are they both in the treacherous grasp of foreigners? Doeg first butchers the house of Ahimelech and then the inhabitants of the city of Nob. Only one escapes, Abiathar. He escapes to go through all of David's trials and live to be defrocked and go into oblivion in Solomon's reign (1 Kings 2:26-27). Again, I do not believe that it is David's fabrications that cause Ahimelech to die; it was the fact that his presence occasioned an opportunity for an opportunistic pagan to kill the priests of God— and that, according to prophecy. The culpability rests squarely upon Saul's shoulders as the efficient cause and Doeg as the instrumental cause.

Interestingly, David's power increases as his time in exile increases and so he is able to substitute manipulation, deception, and falsehood for power. This proves to be true in the four following episodes wherein David is a man of truth and a man of action. In Keilah he merely inquires of God and delivers the people of the town from the Philistines (1 Samuel 23). From there, he is constantly on the run. He meets Saul in the cave and demonstrates his integrity by not killing the king at an opportune moment in the cave (1 Samuel 24). With regard to the whole mess between David and the house of Nabal, only the wisdom of Abigail keeps the truth of his words from becoming the death of every male in Nabal's family (1 Samuel 25). Action and truth characterize all his dealings, including the sortie of Abishai and David into the camp by night and taking the spear and water jug. At the revelation, David's innocence is revealed—he did in fact keep Abishai from killing the king—and the items for show and tell are returned to Saul. But from there, things are on the slide badly.

In fear, David defects to Achich king of Gath (1 Samuel 27:1). Parenthetically, we must remember that nowhere in biblical writ do we find that the Philistines were to be eradicated in the same sense of the word that the Canaanitic peoples were to be. In fact, after the territorial notation given in Exodus 23:31, they are not mentioned in the three remaining books of Torah. This may be more reflective of the fact that Moses did not know much about them—they were newcomers to the land en masse long after the time Moses is reported to have lived. They do show up, not surprisingly in Joshua; but they show up in the same parenthetical parameters as they do in Genesis and Exodus. Because the Philistines as they existed in the late Bronze Age were not a factor, we simply cannot expect them to be worthy of the attention which they would demand when the books of Judges and Samuel roll around. In fact, the mention of land remaining to be conquered at the time of the writing of Joshua might be a historical—or cultural—throwback. It could be a notation from late in the life of Joshua signifying that the sea peoples were on the move and would soon infest their southwest flank. It could be a cultural throwback in that what had been little better than Canaanite city states governed by puppet kings of Egypt, became the warlords (*sarne-pelishtim*) more known from the Aegean region.

Now, they are a factor and David is going to live with them. However, his relationship with Achish is one that stirs our questions about David's virtue. As I noted before, David did this out of fear. His defection had the intended effect as we are told by the narrator: "Now it was told Saul that David had fled to Gath, so he no longer searched for him" (1 Samuel 27: 4). Then we are told of David's conversation with Achish wherein he acquires the right, with his six hundred men and, we must assume, their families, to take over Ziklag (vv. 5-6). Then we are told of David's raids upon several people groups that were perhaps allies of the Philistines, but more importantly, were enemies of Judah. I will address the specifics later when we discuss chapter 27 in more detail. For the moment, let us examine the text of David's words to Achish at such time as he is called to account. "'Where have you made a raid today?' And David said, 'Against the Negev of Judah and against the Negev of the Jerahmeelites and against the Negev of the Kenites'" (1 Samuel 27:10). We are then told of the savageness with which David prosecuted his *razias* against these peoples: "And David did not leave a man or a woman alive, to bring to Gath, saying 'Lest they should tell about us, saying "So has David done and so has been his practice all the time he has lived in the country of the Philistines"'" (v. 11). Because God has a frightened and perhaps disobedient (1 Samuel 22:5) David in the palm of His hand, David's ruse has the intended effect and we are told "Achish believed David, saying, 'He has surely made himself odious among his people Israel; therefore he will become my servant forever'" (1 Samuel 27:12).

Out of fear, David has chosen, perhaps in disobedience to the injunction of the prophet Gad, to go outside the place of blessing—land controlled by Judah—to the land of foreigners—land controlled by the Philistines. He deceived his friend and benefactor, Achish, into believing that he is engaged in practices contrary to those wealth-producing raids he has actually prosecuted. He has said that he has made his raids "against the Negev of Judah and against the Negev of the Jerahmeelites and against the Negev of the Kenites" (1 Samuel 27:10). Because he would never raid any of the three—Judah was his people and the other two were his allies, especially the Kenites through the family of Moses—there is absolutely no truth to David's words to Achish, including the geographical location of the three people groups. If the statement is emptied of any truth claims and if, in fact, the opposite of these claims is shown to pertain, then David has lied to Achish. Can we fault him for lying to an outlander while in exile? If truth has any value, I suppose we might. This point gets more interesting.

As we saw with the first ark narrative, the Philistines had an unusual tendency to read the handwriting on the carcasses of their deceased kinsman and add the God of Israel to their pantheon, claim that He was more powerful than any god in their pantheon, and distance themselves from their own pantheon (1 Samuel 5:6-6:9). Achish will fall heir to that legacy. In fact, Achish will prove himself to be a Yahwist and embarrass David's loyalty while in exile. In chapter 29, we see both what Achish thinks of David and what Achish thinks of David's God. "Is this not David, the servant of Saul the king of Israel, who has been with me these days, or rather these years, and I have found no fault in him from the day he deserted to me to this day" (1 Samuel 29:3). Of course, the warlords want nothing of it, perhaps remembering the day when the Israelites double-defected back to the side of Saul and Jonathan (1 Samuel 14:21). And they tell Achish to send David and the boys packing. This proves that David's ruse was complete and that he deceived his friend and benefactor completely. The deception will sting a bit though, for Achish is required to send David home and does so with these words, "As YHWH lives, you have been upright, and your going out and your coming in with me in the army are pleasing in my sight; for I have not found evil in you from the day of your coming to me to this day. Nevertheless, you are not pleasing in the sight of the warlords" (1 Samuel 29:6). Please notice that Achish takes his oath by YHWH. He does not say "YHWH your God." He claims Israel's God, by name, as his own.

Following this, David launches something of a tantrum with Achish (v. 8); but Achish mollifies the effect of it by deflecting David's comment. "I know that you are pleasing in my sight, like an angel of God; nevertheless the commanders of the Philistines have said, 'He must not go up with us to the battle'" (v. 9). In stating this in this manner, Achish has accomplished two things: first, he has deflected the blame away from himself. Achish wants David to know that he disagrees with the warlords and is not complicit in their scheme even at the level of theory (double defection). However, Achish also betrays another thing about himself. Achish has become something of a theologian. He compares David to an angel of God and so demonstrates that he has developed some theology over "these days or rather these years" that they have been together. He knows that the God of Israel, whom he has named, has emissaries called angels. Achish names no other god. Achish has no other god. And so, David has lied to a Yahwist, an outlander proselytized to his own faith. Too bad. I wonder how it will play out when Achish learns the truth of the matter. No doubt Achish will be among those who not only kill off the king and his sons but later those who make raids on Judah and who have to confront David. Torah makes no claims about the Philistines. They were people with whom Israel might have had diplomatic relation-ships—as senior partner, of course.

I would like to offer a provisional resolution and a point. I was not raised by Christians and I learned my understanding of truth from my parents and philosophers in the Western tradition. I am well aware of two things: first, in the Eastern tradition, truth is not owed to either an outlander or an infidel. Secondly, the way I was raised squares more with a New Testament understanding of the "truth, the whole truth, and nothing but the truth." However, David has effectively lied to countrymen (Saul and Jonathan); he has lied to his country-men's priest (Ahimelech and company); he has lied to an outlander apparently converted to his faith in the God of Israel who was his friend and benefactor (Achish). Again, if there is nothing of the truth in his recorded statements, they are lies. Their intent is deception and they are false. In view of several facts, I cannot excuse David: David makes his statements out of fear. He is afraid of his status with Saul and so tells Jonathan to lie to his father. He is afraid that he will be discovered by the priests loyal to Saul and Doeg the Edomite and he lies to Ahimelech. After the greatest spiritual victory recorded in David's life next to the revelation of the Davidic covenant, David is afraid and leaves the place of blessing, perhaps contrary to the prophetic edict of Gad and he lies to his friend and benefactor, the God-fearing king of Gath, Achish. David has not done well here, in my opinion.

But often we act as though there are only these two options: to tell the truth or to tell a lie. My dad, the philosopher, once told me that there is a third option; in fact, he suggested that to embrace the "tell the truth or tell a lie" is little better than a false disjunction—the fallacy of the excluded middle. Were David to remain in the land, he could have stayed on the run for a little longer and outlasted Saul. Historical hypotheticals being the absurdity that they are, there are other options. He could have told Achish the truth and let the chips fall where they may. If that seems to put the anointed at too high a risk for the sovereignty of God as depicted in biblical narrative, he might then have kept silent. He might simply have deflected Achish's concerns, changing the subject or otherwise and kept his benefactor in the dark. However, and as I will attempt to demonstrate when we get to chapters 27 and

29, this is all part of a package deal of David in the dark of exile. David does not mention God during these times—Achish does! Had David stayed in the wilderness of Judah as per Gad's instructions, there would have been no need for any deception on his part. He simply would have had to outlast Saul. What fear David showed at that point would have been his choice and would not have been compounded by the fear of being discovered and executed on foreign territory. David would have remained in the place of blessing instead of exile; David would have had less to fear and much less to cover up; David would not have had to lie to Achish to save his own life. David's choices require that he act deceptively. David's choices require that he act so barbarically to the people he vanquishes. David's choices require that he lie to his Yahwist benefactor, Achish. David's choices do not require the absence of the true God of Israel's name being mentioned in this time of his darkness. My point and the lesson for us respecting leadership? When we get outside of the place of blessing, when the name of God does not fall from our lips, we may have to live by other means. In David's life they were barbarity and deception. This is not a part of David's life I want to emulate.

## Textual Applications and Anecdotes

1 Samuel 22
vs.
1.    A refugee from lethal danger may well welcome his family knowing that they, too, are in mortal danger.
2.    A refugee from a tyrant may welcome other misfits and malcontents who defect to him for similar reasons.
3.    A refugee from a tyrant may seek asylum for his relatives in a foreign country until such time as the threat abates.
       The choice for political asylum will make some sense (ancestress from Moab).
4.    A refugee will find a place that is either secret (cave of Adullam) or defensible (stronghold, *matsadah/metsudah*—Masada).
5.    David is immediately obedient to the true prophet.
       We should be obedient to as much as we know of the prophetic word.
6.    A large group of refugees cannot escape notice forever.
       The clueless king sits in ignorance while his counselors surround him.
7.    The clueless king appeals to others based upon his power to provide—unfortunately for him, knowledge is the power he lacks.
8.    The clueless monarch will assume many conspiracy theories rather than embrace the truth.
       The clueless monarch will assume silence as treason.
9.    The foreign traitor reveals himself—he has nothing to lose.

10.　The foreign traitor reveals sentiments, provisioning, and arming.

11.　Beware when summoned to visit an insane king.

12.　Take care how you respond to an insane king.

13.　The king carefully lays out the charges.

14.　The righteous priest takes refuge in the truth—it will cost him his life.
The righteous man indicates the positive things about the alleged treasonous refugee.

15.　The righteous man affirms his customary manner of life.
The righteous man indicates his own ignorance truthfully.
(David did keep him in the dark a bit—although that will not protect him from Saul.)

16.　The only logical response to the truth is acceptance—unfortunately an insane man will not act logically.

17.　The king's men do not kill the priest.
The king's men are more righteous than the king.

18.　The foreign opportunist will act for the king against the king's own countrymen.

19.　The foreign opportunist will continue to act for the king against the king's perceived enemies.

20.　No matter how mad the king is, someone will escape to tell God's people.

21.　Refugees always seem to find each other.

22.　When a man's name means "worry" (Doeg the Edomite), we do well to worry.
The righteous refugee justly assumes his part in the culpability.
This may be a partial fulfillment of the prophecy to Eli in chapters 2 and 3.

23.　A sad refugee welcomes a frightened one.

## Conclusion

Although the events of this chapter may entail more than a single day's activities, this historical and theological day has seen several major shifts and movements. It is my suspicion that Nob was not the only community of priests in Israel—there were supposed to be several Levitical cities. Zadok will appear out of nowhere in the narrative in 2 Samuel but apparently only Abiathar is left of Eli's doomed line (see 1 Samuel 2 and 3 and 1 Kings 2:26-27). An Edomite has taken it upon himself to be the executioner of that condemned line. Saul had to commission an outlander to assuage his wrath against the perceived treachery of the priests at Nob. In doing so, Saul has further alienated himself from the heart of the people. Any leader responsible for execution of the clerics of a certain people will find that most of the people—of that parish at the least—will have no use for him. This will play to his disadvantage, no doubt, in the hunt for the refugee, David, as well as any attempts to plumb the depths of the divine good pleasure in the future. This will be seen especially as the king resorts to necromancy in chapter 28.

However, David has gained a new friend. Abiathar will now accompany the monarch-elect in his travels and become something of the court priest . . . for a while. In the story, friends of David do not usually do very well in the long run. In the time to come, we will see what Abiathar must go through with David and how he will meet his "forced retirement." To know a prophecy is to somehow be chained to it; and Abiathar may have known about the prophecy to Eli that effectively ended the life of all of his father's household that day. He may have wondered when grim destiny would appear at his own door.

Be that as it may, Eli's sins are one thing, the manner in which the prophecy is fulfilled entirely another. Saul is responsible for this ignominious killing spree of Doeg the Edomite. In addition, assassins bear a unique responsibility for the lives they take. Finally, one wonders where the men of Israel were who would not stretch out a hand against the priests and yet did nothing to protect them either. Has Saul surrounded himself with the effete of the kingdom? Passivity seems to be the order of the day as Saul oscillates between cogence and insanity, sovereignty and impotence.

# 1 Samuel 23
# Antagonists: Kings, Philistines, and Countrymen[85]
## (Four Pitfalls of Service and Leadership)

—ɱ—

**Introduction**

Imagine that it was you: like a mosquito in a nudist colony, you know what to do although you are not certain where to start—and everybody is swatting at you! You have been anointed by the prophet to be the next monarch of Israel. The job languishes presently under the burden of neglect. Of course, it would be a difficult job and at times a thankless one; but you are anointed, appointed, commissioned, and sent—and ready. It is your nation, and only the best is good enough for her. Be that as it may, times are dark and chaotic and you find yourself in the uncomfortable position of being regarded as an usurper. And so you find yourself on the run. You are an exile, a refugee; and you are not alone. You are in the company of many other misfits and malcontents and, as captain over them, you are responsible for their welfare. Some of these people, some with their families, are little better than the dregs of society and the rapscallions of society. You find at more upbeat times that everything around you is negative. If only you could just get a regular meal and a shower, it would all seem a little better. You know that if you survive this—literally—it could be worth it; but your whole life is out in the future. You can bank on no past capital and you have nothing to work with now. Again, you know what your job would have been had you landed in it in better times. You know that you could have brought a bit of order and light in to overwhelm these dark, chaotic times. Where are the beacons? Where are the points of reference? What do you know? How can that knowledge be used? How can you find your way in a dark labyrinth? There are several roadsigns along the way: sacred scripture, sacred history, and sacred community. We will see how these apply to David.

Thirty centuries ago, David was such a person. He was a young man with a heart for God. His words made sense in a dark world; his actions brought order from the cacophony around him. Nevertheless, he was a man with needs. He was a man on the run—a fugitive. The darkness and disorder around him had advanced to such a degree that he was reduced to running for his life. Focus is very simple when survival is all that is in view. However, it is very easy to lose sight of the big picture as a survivalist. Where we pick up David's story, we find him in the forest of Hereth (1 Sam. 22:5). In a sense, David literally cannot see the forest for the trees. In the next scene, Saul, by the proxy of a foreigner, kills all the living priesthood—but one. That one flees to David seeking asylum. Have things sunk as low as they can yet? No, God must bring Israel virtually to an end as a nation to re-institute His program. But along the way to the end, God's man, David, must have a look at the big picture or he will surely be swept away in the coming maelstrom.

David still knows his mission. Where we pick up his story, he asks God whether he should go about it in a certain way. He is not at his wit's end yet but he is slowly losing his bearing. Let us see how God deals with such a one; and let us see who He brings alongside to offer the needed encouragement.

**A note to the reader**

This narrative is so true-to-life that it is nearly impossible to divorce oneself from the tendency to moralize away the text. Suffice it to say at this point, that the transparency of the narrative and discourse is that which transcends the eons to today. It is as though we are right there trudging through the wilderness with David and his band of nasty-no-goods— and their families in some cases. It is as though we are looking over his shoulder when he inquires of God and when Jonathan comes to offer encouragement. And so it naturally provokes the question: how would it be for us in their place?

**Reading from "Saul: A Life Suspended in Doubt"**

The next thing I had heard about the son of Jesse was that he had engaged in some sort of unofficial military action against the Philistines in the south. It was beginning to look as though he was beginning to take territory that rightly belonged to the kingdom. I was told that the Philistine raiders were plundering the threshing floors of Keilah and that David had given a lightning strike attack and annihilated the Philistine forces. Then it seemed that the son of Jesse had claimed the town for his own and was going to set up residence there. It would have been a good place from which to engage in shock attacks and expeditions against us. I had determined that I would have to take him there—even if it meant laying siege against the city. However, my intelligence reported that the people in authority in Keilah would probably betray him and his men. Since some of his men were defectors from my army, there would probably be a number of executions.

For some reason, unknown to me, the son of Jesse instinctively divined that he would be betrayed. So after he had taken as much provisions as he could from Keilah—ostensively as partial payment for deliverance from a handful of Philistines, I'm sure—he and his men escaped to the badlands of Judah again. At that point, I was told that Jonathan had made a secret visit to the wilderness to talk with David. This time, I kept quiet about it.

At that point, the people of Ziph told me that they had a clear lead on the where-abouts of the son of Jesse. I had them ascertain the exact location of him along with his scouts and sentries, so that I could make a surprise raid and take as many alive as possible. Executions are better in an urban context. I had called together a large contingent of the standing army so that he would not elude the web or our grasp again. I am almost certain that we were within a few meters of him at one point, but we could not find him. At that point, a runner came to us telling us of more pressing matters—the Philistines were coming out of the sand dunes again and were harassing people in the uplands. I had to let the son of Jesse go, one more time—talk about a charmed life! (1 Samuel 23)

## Textual Observations

## David: A Case Study of Leadership by Example—Despite Reluctant Followers

The narrative text lays down the scenario and sets the stage in an almost parenthetical manner (1 Samuel 23:1-6). We are told that there is a confrontation between those of the southern Israelite frontier and the Philistines. We are then told, also by the insertion of discourse elements, that David is desirous of delivering the frontiersmen with the collateral damage of a few dead Philistines. And so David did what any faithful Yahwist should do, he inquired of the Lord. However, the answer he got was not satisfying to the band of fighters that had taken up with him, and so he asked again. Sufficiently assured, David and his men delivered the town of Keilah from the Philistine oppression.

Hopefully, without running the risk of overly moralizing, you can see from the text that the first pitfall of service—and by extension and application Christian service—is that one may be plagued by *reluctant followers*. We might be led to ask ourselves, why are they reluctant? There may be a multitude of reasons and we can never know for certain; but, they may break down into two categories: fear and perhaps masked fear. Reluctant followers may be afraid of the unknown. They may be afraid of change. But they will manifest symptoms of fear. If they do not manifest such symptoms, they may mask them. They may wallow in their laziness. They may bask in their ignorance. There may be neither the incentive nor the disincentive to move from a point of security into a stance of conflict. Whatever the case, any leader needs to be aware that not everybody will blindly, idealistically, and altruistically follow him or her into battle—of whatever kind.

With the narrative table properly set, we are ready for the real conflict. It would appear that in the course of the narratives, the Philistines give texture to David's life; but they are not the real challenges that face him. Things get downright bumpy when we have to deal with King Saul.

"When it was told Saul that David had come to Keilah, Saul said, 'God has delivered him into my hand, for he shut himself in by entering a city with double gates and bars.' So Saul summoned all the people for war, to go down to Keilah to besiege David and his men" (1 Samuel 23:7-8).

And so we might posit that the second pitfall of service and leadership is that you may have *adversaries*. It is bad enough that there are real projects to accomplish—even real dragons to slay; but there are also internal and external adversaries. External adversaries appear, as in the larger context of the Samuel Narratives, as the Philistines. These were supposed to be the real project of David—and by the way—Saul! But those adversaries may also be internal. They could be someone who should be on your side. Imagine David: he has demonstrated himself to be a man of integrity at court and in the field. He has done the various jobs for which he has been commissioned. Nevertheless, the king hates him and is seeking to kill him. It may prove to be that way in the life of the servants and leaders at any level. What does one do when one has sparked the ire of the person who is supposed to be his or her leader? As in the case of the writer, it may not end when you "flee the palace." Trouble may follow you for a while in life. As with David, we might do well to expect adversarial relationships from time to time. They are troubling, nonetheless, when they materialize and we would do well to speak to God about them.

Apparently, David did have certain expectations about Saul—or at least good reconnaissance about him because he knew that "Saul was plotting evil against him" (1 Samuel 23:9). And so Abiathar is enlisted to aid David in divining whether or not he is substantially at risk should he remain localized in Keilah. The ensuing set of discourses has sparked the imagination of the ages (see the item "Does God Have Middle Knowledge," below).

Then David said, "O LORD God of Israel, Thy servant has heard for certain that Saul is seeking to come to Keilah to destroy the city on my account. Will the men of Keilah surrender me into his hand? Will Saul come down just as Thy servant has heard? O LORD God of Israel, I pray, tell Thy servant." And the LORD said, "He will come down." Then David said, "Will the men of Keilah surrender me and my men into the hand of Saul?" And the LORD said, "They will surrender you" (1 Samuel 23:10-12).

As in the setting of the stage (1 Samuel 23:1-6), God does not seem too embarrassed when His people find themselves in the uncomfortable position of having to ask twice about the same situation. But another pitfall that David's life exemplifies and that is often a hydra with two remaining heads, is *ingratitude* in at least two aspects. Passively, the silence following a job well done—delivering the inhabitants of Keilah from the Philistines—is jarring. Actively, the silence may really betray the true motive: when people are essentially distrustful, when they are annoyed with how much the leadership costs to maintain, they may act against even the leader they might on another day view as a savior. The other side of ingratitude then is active betrayal. In our text the truth of the matter is carefully ferreted out by prophetic oracle. We may not have that luxury. We may have to read the handwriting on the wall to know when it is expedient to get out of town.

Any person in a position of leadership will tell you, in his or her more candid moments, that there are some very lonely times. Sometimes those times are when great victory is followed by great rejection. As in our text, sometimes these are times in our life story of great pathos. Notice how the text flows: "Then David and his men, about six hundred, arose and departed from Keilah, and *they went wherever they could go*" (1 Samuel 23:13, emphasis added). Having lived in the company of those who were recently refugees (from Somalia, Rwanda, Sudan, etc.), I feel the deep sense of abandonment of those with no home. And so, with David, at times of rejection, we go wherever we can.

David, therefore, went back to the strongholds (v. 14). We cannot know if this was in defiance of the prophetic proscription (1 Samuel 22:5) or merely subsequent to it with a new set of circumstances and conditions rendering the prophetic injunction invalid. However, we can know that it is a point of the pathetic to have to retrace one's steps after such a hopeful encounter with our own people and victory over the enemy. That was not to be David's lot. His was to continue to have to watch his own back for many months to come.

To that end, I would suggest that the fourth pitfall of service and leadership is that one may have to endure a time of *wilderness wanderings*. Certainly you caught the pathos of verse 13. As David and his people "went wherever they could go," they lived in the wilderness, in the mountain fortresses, in the desert. David lived in danger of pursuit by the king and his armies all the time. It is the life of the fugitive. It is the life of one on the run. It is not a life of rest. It is not a life when you can let down your guard—seemingly for even one moment. Our adversary is on the move all the time (1 Pet. 5:8) and should we drop our defenses for an instant, it seems we could be undone. So it may be for the Christian servant in a position of leadership. It could be that one will move about quite a bit at the inception of service. It could be that one might serve in very uncomfortable circumstances—perhaps with very difficult people. It appears at times that one should just give up and get a life and forget this idea of service and leadership. Nevertheless, there may be guidance along the way to help us get back on track (see the section, "Jonathan: A Case Study of Leadership by Example," below).

### The Question of the (Middle) Ages: Does God Have Middle Knowledge?[86]

We are often told by our theological systematicians that God only knows the things that have been, are, or will be. However, this passage seems to indicate that God knows some other things. The discussion is worth repeating:

Then David said, "O LORD God of Israel, Thy servant has heard for certain that Saul is seeking to come to Keilah to destroy the city on my account. Will the men of Keilah surrender me into his hand? Will Saul come down just as Thy servant has heard? O LORD

God of Israel, I pray, tell Thy servant." And the LORD said, "He will come down." Then David said, "Will the men of Keilah surrender me and my men into the hand of Saul?" And the LORD said, "They will surrender you" (1 Samuel 23:10-12).

Because of the nature of the prefix-conjugation verb in Hebrew, any suitable incompleted action form might do in English, given the proper contextual considerations. Be that as it may, there are several things worthy of note here. David asks two questions initially to which he receives a single answer and must re-ask. The final upshot is that God says that Saul will (or "would") come out, given the right set of circumstances and that, again in those circumstances, the magistrates of Keilah will (or "would") surrender David and his men to Saul. Elsewhere in biblical literature, we are led to believe that God has exhaustive knowledge of the future, whether by sight or by intuition.[87] However, here God claims to know things that will never exist. My wife, a disciple of the "endless duration" view of God and time and the first to my knowledge to discuss time as a created "thing" devolving naturally from God's existential attribute of orderedness, chooses to view this whole discussion as algorithmic. That is, beginning from a couple of X or Y beginning points, God reasons or intuits—apparently from deductive logic and also apparently instantaneously—to the conclusion that when certain sets of circumstances pertain, then certain courses of action would logically, perhaps necessarily, follow.[88] Fine. That is not exactly what I would address here: what I want to say is that God here claims to know things that will never exist. Saul, we are told, "ceased to go out" (1 Samuel 23:13). We know that that is not the end of the story because "Saul sought him every day" (v. 14). However, on that occasion Saul did not go out whereas God said that he would, should David remain at Keilah.[89]

If that case is a bit muddy, the sequel should be more clear: David asked God whether or not the magistrates of Keilah would surrender him to Saul should the proper circumstances pertain. God said: "They will surrender you" (1 Samuel 23:12; again, it is possible to modalize the verb: "would"). God effectively tells David that a set of actions would pertain (treachery), should a set of circumstances present themselves (Saul laying siege) that would never actually happen. Before we indict God for falsehood, we should remember that the verb can be either future or modal. If God is reasoning with David, then modality is a perfectly logical and ethical manner of communication for God. God seems to be willing to move His servants with the subtlety and art of language rather than merely to command, for instance, for David to "Get out of town, now!"

Because of the real-time nature of the conversation, I am led to wonder if my wife is not correct in her assessment of the relationship between God and time as one of endless duration. That is, because God is a being of order and because time is a reflection of that order, God is somehow here in His created order and here in time with us, so to speak—the "sempiternal" view of God and time.[90] Should we adopt the view that God is completely transcendent to time and space, we need only postulate that in the eternal "now," God eternally decrees the conversation that looks like real time to us in the narrative text. However, once you get into the sequencing of conversations between God and His sentient subjects, you may find yourselves victims of yet another level of confusion. Does sequencing entail timing and does God know what time it is to David and what time He will communicate with David? And we're off to the races.

## Jonathan: A Case Study of Leadership by Example—Encouragement Despite Circumstances

Meanwhile back at the mundane, we are informed of a surreptitious meeting in real time between two nobles. We are told, "And Jonathan, Saul's son, arose and went to David at Horesh, and encouraged him in God" (1 Samuel 23:16). Let us examine that little phrase: "encouraged him in God." It is, more literally, "he strengthened his hand in God." Certainly these words might lend themselves to a bit of ambiguity; but at this point the text gets quite explicit. In the next two verses we should be able to see at least four things that Jonathan did to "strengthen David's hand in God" and help us unpack the meaning of the text.

First, Jonathan says, "Do not be afraid, because the hand of Saul my father shall not find you" (1 Samuel 23:17a). And so we see that *Jonathan lays David's fears to rest.* In Jonathan's opinion, Saul would not get David. That is a powerful opinion when one considers that it is the crown prince who is speaking.

Secondly, Jonathan says, "and you will be king over Israel" (1 Samuel 23:17b). Here we see that *Jonathan reminds David of his future.* Jonathan knew about the anointing. He knew about the eventuality of the prophet's words coming true. There was not a single word of Samuel or deed that would fall to the ground unfulfilled (1 Sam. 3:19). Jonathan had faith for the future when David's faith was slipping away from him.

Thirdly, Jonathan makes the declaration, "and I will be next to you; and Saul my father knows that also" (1 Samuel 23:17c). In this brief section, *Jonathan promises David his allegiance.* It is interesting to note that he does so despite Saul's opposition. There is a certain necessity that the final clause covers all terms; but it is strategically placed after Jonathan's pledge. That is, it is as though he says, "In the face of my father's opposition I will deny my birthright and stand at your side, when the time comes, as faithfully as I have stood at the side of my father."

Fourthly, our Omniscient Narrator puts the capstone on it by saying, "So the two of them made a covenant before the LORD; and David stayed at Horesh while Jonathan went to his house" (1 Samuel 23:18). And so finally, *Jonathan makes this tangible by the custom of the covenant.* They had done this several times before; but, now, at perhaps David's lowest, can you imagine the encouragement of knowing that Crown Prince Jonathan has just pledged his allegiance and acknowledged faith in the prophet's words? What a blessing this must have been; perhaps only surpassed by the sorrow of his departure and this (perhaps) last time the two friends would see each other in the land of the living. That

Jonathan knows and believes the words of the prophet are nearly as certain as that he is no prophet himself! This is because the next mention of the crown prince is the narration of his death in 1 Samuel 31:2. He would not live to stand next to King David. Nevertheless, with such a friend, is it any wonder that David extols Jonathan so greatly? (2 Sam. 1:19-27). It is certain that David's friend gets more and better press in the text than does his king.

By way of application, how may we pursue creative ways to demonstrate our allegiance to our friends in need? There may be some culturally appropriate manner in which this is done. The closest thing in western society that we have to the custom of the covenant is the marriage ceremony. What is the level of friendship that one has with one's spouse? Is he or she merely that "significant other"? What about other friends? How can one demonstrate God's best in the lives of these others?

There are times in our lives when we walk into chaos, disorder, and darkness. These are our *wilderness wanderings*. Sometimes this is by choice, other times by necessity. We should not be so dismayed; it is my opinion that in chaos and darkness we can often find the will of God. Occasionally, He will call us into just such a situation so as to bring His light and order to this chaos and darkness. Nevertheless, it may still be easy to lose our way. Often in such times of *wilderness wanderings*, when the circumstances that surround us include *reluctant companions*, *formidable adversaries*, and the *ungrateful and treacherous*, we need a friend to come alongside of us—a friend who is confident of his relationship with God; a friend who has a handle on the great teachings of Scripture; a friend who better sees the big picture. Jonathan was such a friend to David; it is my opinion that so should we be to each other. At the risk of pedantry, I offer the following list:

A friend offers spiritual strength by
1.      quenching fears (silencing falsehood)
2.      rekindling hopes (reminding you of the truth)
3.      promising friendship (promising allegiance)
4.      sealing the agreement (being accountable)

## Textual Applications and Anecdotes

1 Samuel 23
vs.
  1.      News can be bad news.
          News can be an opportunity.
  2.      Before action, pray.
          Act upon what you know of God's will.
  3.      Fear may cancel or postpone an action—the leader's skill and relationship with
          God may turn the outcome.

4.  God is not too embarrassed to answer the prayers of His faithful twice.
5.  When we are certain of God's will, victory is assured.
    That victory will be sweet.
6.  The refugee should bring that which is useful.
7.  Always have an exit strategy for a tight place.
    If there is an opportunity for evil to overtake us, we should be ever vigilant.
8.  The cowardly enemy can only come against us with overwhelming odds.
9.  In a tight place? If you have time, check your references.
10. A vicious enemy will not care about collateral damage (people of Keilah).
11. The vicious enemy will take advantage of an opportunity.
12. A fickle friend will not care about an extended relationship with someone that might cost them dearly.
13. If possible, escape out into the open.
    You may not be able to hide; but you can run.
14. If you obey God's prophet (Gad; 1 Samuel 22:5), God will protect you.
15. Observe your enemy's approach from a safe distance and from a hidden location.
16. The true friend will encourage the fugitive in God.
17. The true friend will attempt to counteract fear.
    The true friend will attempt to remind us of God's promises.
    The true friend will promise loyalty.
18. The true friendship is sealed with a covenant (cultural).
19. No matter where we go, enemies will make themselves known.
    No matter where we go, enemies will make us known.
20. Enemies will do their part in allegiance to our other enemies.
    "My enemy's enemies are my friends."
    "My enemy's friends are my enemies."
21. Our enemies bless our other enemies.
22. Someone with a penchant for near misses should be researched carefully.
23. Careful research and reconnaissance should be reported; however, that will give time for escape.
24. Know your location well.
25. Know your escape route well.
26. The better you know the lay of the land, the more freedom and time you will have to make your escape.
    What looks like a near miss to us can be a mile to someone who knows geographical slight of hand.
27. When God has us in the palm of His hand, there may be a report from a third quarter that takes the heat off us.

28.     Near misses should be commemorated. Rename a geographical feature or build a monument.

29.     Find a wilderness fort and hide out there if you can.

**Conclusion**

It is dark out there. There is not a lot that makes much sense. Part of the job description includes speaking light into the darkness—bringing order out of the chaos. If biblical studies mean anything, God has given us His Word—part of which includes the examples of David and Jonathan. He has given us His Spirit to guide us. He has, by that same Spirit, given us His grace—His divine enablement,[91] so that we may actually and amazingly accomplish His will. He has given us brothers and sisters along the way to *allay fear, rekindle hope, promise friendship, and be accountable.* In the same way that David was not really alone, God has not left Himself without a witness, He has not left us alone—abandoned—or without direction. May God bless us and remind us of these things throughout the coming days as we seek to live for Him and encourage others so to live.

# 1 Samuel 24
## A Close Encounter of the Spelunker Kind
### "I will not stretch out my hand against my lord, for he is the Lord's anointed."

—∿∿—

## Introduction

Chapters 23 through 26 reflect the times when David was a fugitive in earnest. At these times, David is in the *place* of blessing, the Land, and is obedient to the prophet Gad's injunction to "go into the land of Judah" (1 Samuel 22:5). We will see him at his best: delivering the people of Keilah from the Philistine garrison (1 Samuel 23), potentially sparing Saul's life twice (1 Samuel 24, 26), and being diverted from a lethal course of action against the house of Nabal (1 Samuel 25). He will act with the Lord's counsel and he will act wisely. These are the places where we learn the most positively from David's life and leadership. Let us take a look at the second of these vignettes and watch as David attempts to demonstrate to his manic monarch that he holds no ill will toward him.

## Reading from "Saul: A Life Suspended in Doubt"

We chased off the Philistines quickly. It turned out to be either a raiding party or a reconnaissance party and didn't take much time away from this urgent task. I assembled a crack force of three thousand of the best troops from all of the country—not too many from Judah, of course, you couldn't depend upon their loyalty. Then we headed to the badlands again where we had left him. The son of Jesse had one problem: because he was leading about 600 men now, he always left a train behind him and people saw him coming. He was pretty easy to track—at least to a degree.

We followed him down into the Arabah and were certain that we were getting pretty close. At one point I had to relieve myself and I chose to use the privacy of a certain cave. I stood sentries outside and went inside. When I finished my business and got outside the cave I had just crossed a deep ravine with several bodyguards to rejoin my main forces. All of a sudden somebody yelled after me. It was the son of Jesse and he had had the nerve to cut off some of my robe in the cave. He had lifted his hand against his king. This was indeed proof of his conspiracy! For some reason, his apology struck me in an odd way. It seemed that the emotion of having such a near miss and hearing his voice again caused me to say some things that I really didn't mean at the time. Was it another voice again when I declared that he was more righteous than me? Who was saying that he would be king? It was as though I was taken over by something or someone that was foretelling the future! I decided that I must get something from him, so I asked him to swear that he would not hurt my family. David, after all, was the one who believed in oaths—maybe I could get him to live by one of his own. He did, and we separated. He went up into places where an army could lay siege for years and still not force him out. We returned to the palace and I to the royal residence until a more opportune moment. I knew I wasn't finished with the son of Jesse yet. (1 Samuel 24)

## Textual Observations

Robert Polzin introduces this section with the overarching continuity of chapters 24, 25 and 26.

Nothing excites a biblicist's historical impulses more than a series of parallel episodes strung out along the storyline like a string of pearls. If "these chapters (24, 25, 26) show David being saved from himself, or rather from the consequences of deeds potentially disastrous to his interests," and if in all three chapters "David refrains from violence against an enemy," then, indeed, such repetition inclines many interpreters to fond thoughts of redaction. . . . But what if I foolishly refuse to hand over the fruits of my interpretive labors to anonymous redactors who, as Nabal would say, "come from I do not know where"? And what if the story of David's sparing of Nabal's life, flanked by the twin stories of David sparing Saul's life comprise a narrative unit that, like Abigail herself, has discretion and good judgment quite apart from any literary-historical considerations one might entertain?[92]

My brief treatment of "textual problems" below will help clarify why I think Polzin is correct at the genetic level rather than the gut-feeling level. Be that as it may, in my opinion, Polzin shows what would happen if David gave in to his group of men (1 Samuel 24), his baser instincts (1 Samuel 25), and one of his best warriors and his cousin, Abishai (1 Samuel 26). So let us look at what happens—they are in the dark, yes—after all, they are holed up in the cave—but they are in a cave in Judah, the place of blessing, and they have the home court advantage.

## A Sensitive David as a New Refugee

The text is interesting in that it is either folded or there is a double demand of David's men to kill Saul. It does not matter which course we follow, the pressure upon David is incredible. Imagine for a moment what would have happened if David would have complied and Saul was dead. There would have been the uneasy wait of Saul's men outside the cave. David and his men would either have had to "come out shooting" or find another exit. There would have been the move to make Jonathan king, a charge probably lead by Abner as he would with Ish-Bosheth later. Then, David would have had to wait while God removed Jonathan, his friend, all the while knowing that the dynasty had been doomed since 1 Samuel 13.

But it did not happen that way and David only hacked himself a slice of royal robe. When he did this, the text tells us that "his heart struck him." We have that as a moving of his conscience in our modern translations. This is another unusual window into David's inner states. Because of the pressure, he perhaps thought that an act of single daring and stealth was just as good. His men still wanted more (v. 7). He had to restrain them, according to the narrator. What was it that bothered him about this first of three misadventures? Perhaps he viewed the robe as symbolic of the king's person. Perhaps he viewed the robe as symbolic of the king's power or both. I sincerely doubt that his conscience bothered him because he had ruined a perfectly good royal robe, although that is possible—what a waste! Whichever path we choose, it becomes a dead issue. The narrator tells us of David's crisis of conscience; but David never pursues the issue publicly. We simply do not know how David will expiate his guilt. We cannot even know if his guilt was justified. It could have been something that bothered him that was merely vapid.

Regardless, the robe is a motif that passes ghostlike through the narratives. Remember that it was Saul who first tore the robe *me'il* of the prophet Samuel (1 Samuel 15:27). We have hinted at how Saul's monarchy cut into Samuel's turf in the area of now being the supreme arbiter in legal matters. Now we have David taking a cutting of robe *me'il* from Saul the deposed despot (1 Samuel 24:4). But we have not seen the last of this phantom of the phonemes! Because, along with the shade of Samuel himself, the robe *me'il* is miraculously resurrected as an identifying characteristic of the deceased prophet. Regardless of the significance attached to this shred of regal robe by David, the narrator is subtly reminding us of how this plane is going to crash. The imagery is pregnant. In the words of Samuel himself: "The LORD has torn the kingdom of Israel from you today, and has given it to your neighbor [friend] who is better than you" (1 Samuel 15:28). Indeed, Saul not only never understood who his friends were, he never recognized the significance of the "robe as kingdom" that would be torn from him and given to the son of Jesse.

**David's Address to the King: Guilt Becomes Proof of Innocence**

Whatever we might infer from "David's heart striking him," the issue is apparently not made public. He simply claims that he did nothing wrong and uses the robe clipping as proof-positive. Then he spreads the blame among Saul's servants (1 Samuel 24:9) and among his own men (v. 10). His oratory is at once arresting and disquieting. I do not think that this is a place where David has falsified anything. However, were it not for the narrator's comment (v. 5), we would have no knowledge of David's internal state. David offers none to the king. Remember, this is another of David's public pronouncements. He can dance gracefully between the truth and the whole truth in such a way as to disarm the king and in such a way as to allow the narrator to disarm us.

The net effect of David's address is unknown. The king comes to pieces and makes promises that he has no intention of keeping. He gains oaths from the son of Jesse that he would never keep, but that David might. David has already covered for his family (1 Samuel 22:1-4) and the end of the story proves that he does not trust the manic monarch. "And David swore to Saul. And Saul went to his home, but David and his men went up to the stronghold" (1 Samuel 24:22). The fact that there will be a "threat on the life of the king" again in chapter 26, indicates that he did not get the message. At that adventure, the only thing we are sure of is that pressing matters in the form of a Philistine invasion will preclude the mentally incapacitated despot from causing there to be a third scene to this sad musical.

**From Which Side of His Badly Fractured Personality Is King Gollum Speaking This Time?**

Saul's question betrays his own status as the king of cluelessness. "Is this your voice, my son David?" (1 Samuel 24:16). Of course it is; who else would it be! But our musings are nothing in comparison to the narrator's comment: "Then Saul lifted up his voice and wept" (v. 16). One wonders what this looked like and how it was processed by the king's men. Remember, these were the three thousand crack troops of Israel (1 Samuel 24:2). The king admits to his guilt and David's righteousness (vv. 17-19). Then he acknowledges what Samuel had told him long before, that "your friend" would be king (v. 20). Then he attempts, from his ideologically disadvantaged position, to extricate himself from several predicaments—some real and some imagined—with an oath of safe conduct from David (v. 21). David has nothing to lose and so swears and gets out of there. The language of his exit from the scene might even be pluperfect: "Now David and his men had gone up to the stronghold" (v. 22). That would be indicative that they did not wait for fallout from the king—or an oscillation back to the more malevolent monarch.

## More on Oaths Between the House of Jesse and the House of Kish

There are several places where David and Saul and/or Jonathan swear oaths together. It is, of course, implicit in all the covenant scenes. The initial covenant between the house of Jesse and the house of Kish is when David and Jonathan make a covenant in 1 Samuel 18:3. It is accompanied with nearly a divestiture/investiture ceremony. A subsequent scene involves Jonathan more in the position of Saul in our current text. "So Jonathan made a covenant with the house of David. . . . And Jonathan made David vow again because of his love for him, because he loved him as he loved his own life" (1 Samuel 20:16-17). This is remembered by Jonathan—or Jonathan reminding David—later: "Go in safety, inasmuch as we have sworn to each other in the name of the LORD, saying, The LORD will be between me and you, and between my descendants and your descendants forever" (1 Samuel 20:42). Here it extends to the next generation. There is something of a covenant renewal at Horesh: "And Jonathan, Saul's son arose and went to David at Horesh and strengthened his hand in God . . . . So the two of them made a covenant before the LORD" (1 Samuel 23:16-18). In our text, Saul extracts an oath of safekeeping for his family from David (1 Samuel 24:21-22). Saul makes some revelatory statements in the reprise in chapter 26; but nothing at the level of an oath is shared between them (1 Samuel 26:17-25). The important new thing is that Saul, who once blessed David's enemies (1 Samuel 23:21), now blesses David—thus effectively and finally passing the torch (1 Samuel 26:25).

The net effect of these oaths and covenants is not great. The only one who truly reaps the benefit of the oath of safekeeping is Mephibosheth (2 Samuel 9). When the chips are down and the cards are called, David relinquished the sons of Rizpah, Saul's concubine and the sons of Merab and Adriel, to the Gibeonites for what could only be called the Gibeonites' vendetta. David asked God what was wrong; perhaps he should have asked God what to do about it rather than the Gibeonites. In all this, the only one who was safe was Mephibosheth, Jonathan's son—and that, arguably, because he was of no threat to the kingdom, being lame. However, because of a misunderstanding between David, Mephibosheth, and Ziba, the inheritance of Saul is split and both pass silently into oblivion. More later.

## Textual Problems

Because both texts are about the sparing of Saul, supposedly, 1 Samuel 24 and 26 form a doublet—both texts originally being the same story. Somewhere in the awkward, bungling mythology of form-critical theory, the stories forked and both were codified long afterward in the same compendium. Apparently this is due to their similarity. The differences so outweigh the similarities (Saul and David—that is!), that, again, it hardly deserves the dignity of a response. (If you happen to embrace the paradigm, I refuse to apologize to you since this is exactly the way your people treat us—they call us, and I quote: "funnydammentalists." Too bad, too, you could learn a lot from them.) The differences include accomplices (general versus specific), time, geography, and the crystallization of the oratory as David synthesized his thoughts on the matter of "the Lord's anointed." Chapter 26 shows progression in the fact that David received a blessing from the deranged despot—which textually shows a passing of the torch. When we arrive safely at chapter 26, we will see several more differences.

## Textual Applications and Anecdotes

1 Samuel 24

vs.
1. The mind of a madman: business aside, let's attend to the distractions.
2. When possible, overpower.
3. What a brilliant idea: use a cave for a latrine—certainly nobody else could be in there.
4. Be ever wary of epiphanies from your men.
   A clever idea can, in fact, be not so hot of an idea.
5. There is something that endears us to someone with a live conscience.
6. When you must restrain your men, your words must be clear, concise, and compelling.
7. The mindless monarch, oblivious to a near miss with mayhem.
8. When your life is forfeit, you might as well address his majesty properly ("My lord the king").
   When your life is forfeit, your body language, in this case Hebrew, speaks volumes ("David . . . prostrated himself").
9. David's question at once spreads the blame and deflects it from the deranged monarch.
10. David's statement blames his men and says nothing about his own crisis of conscience (v. 5).
    David's stumbling over the words here prove that the thoughts were not as well synthesized as time would prove them to be (1 Samuel 26).
11. David gives visual demonstration of his innocence and loyalty.
12. David rightly leaves judgment and vengeance with God and refuses to raise a hand against the king.
    This text may mean exactly nothing about the divine right of bishops.
13. Cap your argument with a culturally relevant proverb.
14. When in danger, it is a good idea to attempt to persuade your assailant of your own insignificance.

15. David rightly leaves judgment and decision as well as David's cause and deliverance to God.
16. Reality dawns hard on deranged despots.
17. Admission of guilt is the first step toward justice—however, it may take several admissions.
18. Life and death realities ultimately go back to opportunities provided by God.
19. The king's wish: may the Lord reward you for the good you did to me.
20. In moments of lucidity, the king knows his own transience.
21. In moments of lucidity, the king knows that his legacy is in the hand of the curators of history.
22. An oath to allow people to live and retain their memory should really cost us little.
    Crazy king? Don't trust him—go back to the stronghold.

## Conclusion

In what we might call today a daredevil stunt, David, goaded on by his men, refuses to cut off the king and rather, symbolically cuts off a piece of his robe. The prompting of his conscience promptly buried, David makes a claim of his own innocence. It is the symbolism of the cut robe that stands out. The kingdom is passing, as slowly as the hands of time, but passing nevertheless from the house of Kish to the house of Jesse. When all is said and done from this passage, oaths are shared which only David will be in a position to keep. When all is said and done, it will all have to be said and done over again in chapter 26. From that point, the oath will turn to blessing and the torch will be effectively passed and Saul will no longer be a threat to David.

In the second of these three stories of David's actions and words, he will be kept from risking the credibility of his monarchy by a high-handed act against one of its wealthy landowners. In that episode, he will win the prize because God will execute vengeance for him, seemingly, and he will run off with another bride. There will be several of those. But here, David has kept his honor intact and exculpated himself from the intended mayhem of his men against Saul. Real ethics happen in real situations and David has done better here than most of us would, simply by not raising his hand against the anointed of the Lord (1 Samuel 24:6).

# 1 Samuel 25
# David, Abigail, and Nabal: Love Triangle

—m—

## Introduction

As though the capstone upon the first volume of the Samuel Narratives, we are told that Samuel died and all Israel gathered together and mourned him. We might wonder if David and those with him were granted safe passage—or if they were the target of an intense hunt and as such stayed away. If that is the case, it gives an interesting meaning to "all Israel" being gathered when her anointed-elect monarch is conspicuously absent from the funeral. Whatever the case, there is a new style of writing apparent from the first words of verse 2. Whereas we have begun six of these episodes with, "And it came to pass that there was a man,"[93] now we have a new hand writing simply "Now a man."

Be all that as it may, Samuel is gone and David will have few that he can call upon to encourage him; Samuel is dead; the priests at Nob have been exterminated; Jonathan is apparently being watched too closely to break away from the palace, and David is alone in the world. These will break into the godless days of David so far as the narrative goes (from chapters 27–29), until that point when he "strengthens his own hand in God," in chapter 30. Let us follow David through a story and two sequels about David alone as a refugee in the wilderness. The stories are about real versus apparent power.

## Reading from "Saul: A Life Suspended in Doubt"

It was at about that time that the prophet Samuel died. That was a bittersweet affair. It was bitter in that I was never finally able to bring closure to matters between us. It never seemed that I was able to please the prophet, no matter how hard I tried. It always seemed that he would appear just as I'd accomplished something and then criticize it to the point of my public humiliation. Because of this it was sweet in that I would never again have my arch nemesis to stand in the way of what I tried to accomplish in the kingdom or criticize what I actually did accomplish. Because this was an event of national significance, I put in my appearance, performed my perfunctories, and eulogized Israel's prophet. It was becoming a regular matter that I often felt that I was being pulled in two diametrically opposed directions at the same time. It is incredibly difficult to eulogize someone who you know loathes your very existence. Nevertheless, I painted a good face on it and left the convincing impression that this was one of the great men in the history of the people of Israel.

In any case, I had to resume my role in the real affairs of state. It was always difficult to ascertain the loyalty of allies and agents in the south. Sometimes allegiance was as fickle as the wind. The Ziphites seemed to have particularly good and useful reconnaissance. However, people exclusively from Judah were problematical. Close to Ziph were those useful resources in Maon and Carmel. I had one ally by the name of Nabal, no account for the name, I suppose. He supplied a considerable amount of provisions to my military forces and civil servants—all at a price, of course. However, every now and again he would send a gift my way just to make certain that the cash flow kept its steady pace in his direction. Somehow, the son of Jesse and his group even made inroads into that avenue.

At one point I heard from the people in nearby Ziph that Nabal had died after an abortive maneuver against his holdings in Maon. For some reason, David never attacked. The next thing I knew was that Nabal's widow became David's wife. So, all of those resources then were to be channeled toward the son of Jesse. Because I still needed men from the tribe of Judah in my military—mostly as front lines fodder—I had to be careful about full-scale military operations in the south. My 3,000 elite were free to come and go at will, without threat of further defection. I was never really able to gain enough ground in finding the son of Jesse so as to make a raid on Maon for their treachery. So now, not only was the kingdom's number one fugitive armed, he was also provisioned. It was also indicated to me by my agents in Ziph that the son of Jesse was gaining in the numbers of his men. It seemed that any misfit and malcontent could join up with David's private militia and he could win them over and even exercise a measure of control. Nabal had never complained about the loss of anything—not even a goat—while David was in operation in the area. It seems odd, but, neither did anybody else.

In the meantime, things were not going well on the northern front. It looked like the Philistines were going to make an end run through the Jezreel valley. Because attrition was so problematical, I had to be very careful as to how I deployed my forces. It was as though I was fighting a full-scale war on three fronts: the Philistines on the west, their offensive on the north, and David on the south. Until it was nearly too late, I could never figure out how badly I needed the teamwork of Jonathan, David, and my General Abner. I had already managed to alienate the two and David would win the admiration of the last in a most amazing way, using the surprise of that magically charmed life of his. (1 Samuel 25)

## Textual Observations

## Samuel Is Finally Back Home in Ramah

Yogi Berra is reported to have said: "You can observe a lot by watching." Certainly that is the case with the prophet Samuel. Even though he sees with nothing of the clairvoyance given us by our Omniscient Narrator, one thing is certain: Samuel had a homing instinct to make pigeons or salmon jealous! It seems that often after Samuel engaged in some formal ministry—prophetic, judicial or didactic—we are informed that "Samuel [arose and] went to Ramah." Ramah, of course appears as the bookends of his life—his parents were from Ramah and he was buried in Ramah. But let us follow this man from the "tribe of the salmon people."

In 1 Samuel 1:19, we are informed that after Hannah gets her reputation cleared with Eli the priest, "Then they arose early in the morning and worshiped before the LORD, and returned again to their house in Ramah" after which she conceived and Samuel was born. Initially, we are told that Elkanah, was from "Ramathaim-Zophim" and we have wondered where this is. Now we know. It is the ancestral home of Samuel.

In 1 Samuel 2:11, we are subsequently informed that after Hannah has presented Samuel at the tabernacle and has sung her song, Hannah—we must assume—accompanied her husband back home. "Elkanah went to his home at Ramah. But the boy ministered to the LORD before Eli the priest." Like father, like son: we might notice that if the pattern is laid down by the father that after ministry or worship we return home, then we have a precedent for the son, Samuel. It might be a point of interest that for such a dislocated and transient society as ours, the idea of home is a difficult concept. Some people in our society have places that they gravitate to at holiday times, others do not. Some people have an ancestral (grandparents were homesteaders) land holding and gravitate toward that; but most do not. In Israel, no matter what, you had your land.

In 1 Samuel 7:17, we are told what the custom of Samuel was as a circuit court judge (and educator, I suppose): "And Samuel judged Israel all the days of his life. Now, he would go annually on circuit to Bethel and Gilgal and Mizpah, and he would judge Israel in all these places. And his return was to Ramah, for his house was there, and there he judged Israel; and he built there an altar to the LORD" (vv. 15-17).

The first verb is set up consecutively to the matters that precede with respect to the temporary subduing of the Philistines and Amorites. However, the rest is in procedural discourse and merely indicates what Samuel's manner of operation was. Whenever he was done with his circuit he went home to Ramah. We are also given the attendant note that he built a cult site there. To a degree, this could have been viewed as a rival site to that at Shiloh.

In 1 Samuel 8:4, we see that Samuel is not on circuit as was his custom and the elders had to come to him there to address several issues with him. "Then all the elders of Israel gathered together and came to Samuel at Ramah." We have already been told by our Omniscient Narrator that Samuel's sons were rapscallions and that they "turned aside after dishonest gain and took bribes and perverted justice" (v. 3). The elders are more diplomatic and merely tell Samuel that his sons do not walk in his ways and that they want a king. This simultaneously invests Samuel with the incredible power of appointing the king, humanly speaking, and divests him, potentially, of powers as the supreme judge of the land. As a note, the narrator does not explicitly state for us that Samuel went home; but we are told: "So Samuel said to the men of Israel, 'Go every man to his city'" (v. 22). It makes just as much sense to the story to have the events that transpired in chapter 9 (Saul chasing donkeys and finding a whole kingdom of them) in Ramah, as it does any place else. It is close enough to Benjamin as to be a place to look.

In 1 Samuel 15:34-35, after a very major and final rejection speech to Saul, we are told: "Then Samuel went to Ramah, but Saul went up to his house at Gibeah of Saul. And Samuel did not see Saul again until the day of his death; for Samuel grieved over Saul. And the LORD regretted that He had made Saul king over Israel." When Samuel is told to go anoint the next king, that puts Saul between Samuel and Jesse's house in Bethlehem. This give some grounds for Samuel's apprehension at going there. Again, whenever Samuel is finished with something, he goes home.

In 1 Samuel 16, and probably somewhat based on the fear of Saul indicated above, we are told the start-stop events concerning the anointing of Jesse's lesser son. After that "Samuel arose and went to Ramah" (v. 13). This is one of the most major events in Samuel's ministry; but being true to form, he goes home after anything major that he does.

The next six usages of the word Ramah in 1 Samuel 19:18-24 are in a tight configuration. In 19:18, we see that David has just escaped from Saul's emissaries with the help of Michal, Saul's infatuated daughter—the only woman ever said to have loved a man in biblical narrative. A point of interest: note that David must turn his back on Michal to run away to the safety of Samuel. She lies her way out of trouble; but this gives David, our protagonist, a nice head start. David, quite reasonably in the need of friends, goes directly to the ancient and sometimes myopic seer, Samuel. "Now David fled and escaped and came to Samuel at Ramah, and told him all that Saul had done to him. And he and Samuel went and stayed in Naioth." The piling on of the verbs of action is indicative of the intensity of the text: "fled, escaped, came, told, had done, went, stayed." Instead of viewing this as conflated manuscript tradition, it is just as reasonable to view Naioth as a district of Ramah.[94]

In 19:19, the report goes to that ever-frustrated monarch of a sandspit, Saul: "And it was told Saul, saying, 'Behold, David is at Naioth in Ramah.'" This would be the second introduction literarily of the place as though it were character. This is unusual, to say the least. But Saul sends "messengers" to take him and return him forcibly to the palace. Whenever the messengers get close to David in Naioth of Ramah—we must assume—they prophesy. The word here is in the *hithpa'el* form of the verb and often means "rave like a maniac." So what they actually do, is uncertain. However, the fact is that whatever they do, they do it on three different occasions and we should likely assume that there are different sets of emissaries who do the "prophesying."[95] Saul, being fed up with the failures of his underlings, undertakes to overtake the overstepped refugee, David and so. . .

. . . in 19:22 (twice), "Then he himself went to Ramah." Thus, Ramah is thrice introduced and is now the stage upon which the royal foil will act out his insanity. This will not be among Saul's best days for when, "he came as far as the large well that is in Secu; and he asked and said, 'Where are Samuel and David?' And someone said, 'Behold, they are at Naioth in Ramah.'" And in 19:23 (twice), "And he went there to Naioth in Ramah; and the Spirit of God [or mighty spirit, or spirit from God, or. . .] came upon him also, so that he went along prophesying continually until he came to Naioth in Ramah." So Saul concludes the day poorly dressed and raving like a maniac: "And he also stripped off his clothes, and he too prophesied before Samuel and lay down naked all that day and all that night. Therefore they say, 'Is Saul also among the prophets?'" Whatever the outcome of the word study on "prophesying," it is evident that Saul is temporarily mentally debilitated and thus prevented from his pursuit of David.

That it all happens in Ramah is intriguing because up to this point, when ministry is done, Samuel retires to Ramah. It is possible that Samuel viewed this as a final retirement after the rejection of Saul and the anointing of David. However, the text says that "Samuel went to Ramah . . . and Samuel did not see Saul again until the day of his death" (1 Samuel 15:34-5). One wonders at the reconciliation of the two texts. Could that day have been the death of Samuel? Could it be that Samuel would not even look at Saul that day despite being in such proximity to him? Or is it that the focus is on the clueless monarch and his not being cognizant of Samuel's presence? Difficult as these things are, the technique for the presentation of the progressive insanity of Saul is excellent. Everything is crazy: historically crazy, semantically crazy, crazy with respect to decorum. Three sets of messengers go crazy, Saul raves for about twenty-four hours after not having a clue where he is in space and time. Back to retirement in Ramah: the point is, that even when Samuel retires to Ramah, he still has a role with respect to the transition of the monarchy in Israel. The ministry will come to him.

There is really no break between chapters and so in 1 Samuel 20:1, we are told in a sequel that: "Then David fled from Naioth in Ramah, and came and said to Jonathan, 'What have I done? What is my iniquity? And what is my sin before your father, that he is seeking my life?'" The barrage of questions not withstanding, the sequential nature of the verb as used indicates that perhaps David was in hiding and saw the irrational behavior of the mentally unbalanced monarch before he left town. All we can claim for certain is consecution. Whether 20:1 follows immediately upon the heels of the events of chapter 19 or some time later is impossible to say. What can be said is that while Saul is indisposed, David hightails it back to have a consultation with Jonathan, the crown prince. As we will recall,

Jonathan is unable to assuage the anger of his father this time and so David will spend the remainder of Saul's life on the run.

In 1 Samuel 25:1, we have the formal account of Samuel's death. We are told: "And Samuel died; and all Israel gathered together and mourned for him, and buried him in his house in Ramah. And David arose and went down to the wilderness of Paran." Because this is in consecution to the matters addressed in chapter 24 rather than chapter 25, it could even be that David—incognito?—went up from the "stronghold" (24:22) to the "services." The real chapter break is after verse 1. This new pericope begins in verse 2, dealing with that agribusinessman of all fools, Nabal, himself. Nevertheless, did they actually bury people "in" their house? It could be; but the focus here is Ramah where Samuel finished ministry, retired, and finally died. Not much more is said "until the day of his death" (1 Samuel 15:35)—literally!

In 1 Samuel 28:3, we are reminded of the events of 25:1. We are told: "Now Samuel had died and all Israel mourned him and they buried him in Ramah and in his city. Now Saul had removed the mediums and the spiritists from the land." This is merely a paraphrastic reprise of what happened in chapter 25. But it is material that introduces the story of Saul and the witch of En-Dor. There are basically three conditional antecedents: The Philistines are gathered for war, Samuel is dead, and the necromancers are supposedly eradicated. Thus, everything is against Saul and the stage is set for his demise and David's accession to the throne. This verse adds the informative note that besides being buried in Ramah, in his house, he was buried in his own city. It is the final homecoming of the man with the pigeon-envied homing instincts. The point from all of this is, when ministry is finished, go home—it worked for Samuel. A further point is that we have ministry obligations to our families—no matter how badly Samuel failed as a father—he did go home. He itinerated, but he went home.

## David Takes a Dangerous Posture toward a Countryman

Because of where this falls in the text, between two opportunities to assassinate the sitting king, it might be said that this violent posture that David takes toward Nabal is representative of what he really felt about Saul. That is, were Saul in a weaker position so far as potential retaliation is concerned, David might have simply cut off more than the hem of his garment or stolen his waterjug and spear. However, because of the public nature of his comments (either to Abishai or to several of his men in the cave), we cannot know. David may be telling us how he really feels about Saul as the anointed and about Nabal as insubordinate, but we are still left to suspect that this is how David would wish to be treated by and will treat his subjects.

When it all comes down to wrath, David adopts the posture of mayhem. Because he is riding with four hundred of his men, we suspect that nothing will slake his fury other than the complete barbarian decimation of "everyone who urinates against the wall" (1 Samuel 25:22). David adopts not only an imperious posture toward a countryman, he adopts that posture with overwhelming force. No matter how prosperous the "family farm," we might suppose that four hundred armed men would shock any armed resistance such that the losses to David's forces would be infinitesimal by comparison.

That it was a real and terrifying threat is demonstrated by earnest words of the servant to Abigail and the haste with which she goes into action. The servant first notes the offense against the emissaries of David and then launches into a description of the virtue of David's men and their even treatment of Nabal's shepherds while in the field. Whether he knows or merely suspects impending disaster, as is the near inerrancy of all servants in biblical narrative, he proves to be correct: "evil is plotted against our master and against all his household" (1 Samuel 25:17). His final statement is one of abandon for he acknowledges that there is no benefit in trying to inform Nabal because, "he is such a son of Belial that no one can speak to him" (v. 17).

And so, Abigail goes into action: she packs up enough food to feed a small army — although not for much more than a single meal. Perhaps she was planning on taking some livestock in the field and having a barbeque. After all, "live" stock was, in the absence of irradiation and refrigeration, the original preservative. Then, when she intercepts the raiders, her oratory flowed until David's wrath is assuaged.

What she says is nearly as impressive as the fact that she is allowed to say it and the manner in which she says it. When met, David had to be a bit miffed that it was not a groveling Nabal who met him. However, the scene had to be arresting enough to get his attention. We are reminded of the time when Aragorn, Gimli, and Legolas are surrounded by the Riders of Rohan. Abigail would have been so surrounded and defenseless. She appeals to their mercy and at once their decency. What would it have been like to have been a woman in her time and be so exposed?

She speaks boldly and yet with all the deference and civility the language allowed. There are several strategic deployments of the particle of entreaty, *na*. There is the language of self-deprecation and the language of respect and elevation for David. And yet there is the confidence of a woman who is speaking words with the prophetic ring to them. She reminds us at once of Hannah declaring the king she had never met and the knowledge of Samuel's secret declaration and anointing in Bethlehem. And with this knowledge, it is certain that she will gain a hearing and so she invites the monarch-elect, more appealing to propriety than to him directly, to refrain from putting skeletons in his royal closet. She says: "And it shall come about when the LORD shall do for my lord according to all the good that He has spoken concerning you, and shall appoint you ruler over Israel, that this will not become staggering to you or a stumbling of the heart to my lord, both by having shed blood without cause and by my lord having avenged himself. When the LORD shall deal well with my lord then remember your maidservant" (1 Samuel 25:30-31).

The first question we might ask has to do with her astonishing knowledge. How did she know about "all the good that he has spoken concerning you"? Could it have been that all this was public knowledge and that Saul only held power by sheer force? Could it have been like the people under Islamic domination today that, as Winston Churchill might say, there are those in the vast majority who are so fearfully and fatalistically apathetic that they become a sea easily patrolled by the fanatical frenzied, extremist sharks?[96] Be that as it may, if Abigail's opinion is indeed the popular opinion, it is only a matter of time before the whole façade of government *à la* Saul collapses under his own weight. It is too bad that the Philistines would take so many men of Israel with him—or were they all smart enough to run as soon as the battle was joined?

## On Four Hundred Going and Two Hundred Staying with the Baggage

This is a prequel, and as such, a foreshadowing to the real issue that blows up in David's face in chapter 30. In 1 Samuel 25:13, we are told "and about four hundred men went up behind David while two hundred stayed with the baggage." This will become important when it comes to a real fight; but for now, there are no grounds for anybody's sensitivities to become inflamed. There is no one who bore the brunt of the battle and there is no one who will be potentially left out in the distribution of the plunder. When both cases pertain (1 Samuel 30:16-25), those men of Belial ("the worthless ones") will rise to the occasion and cause "The Development of Spurious Case Law" in Israel (see my development in that section below in 1 Samuel 30).

## Another of David's Wives; or, Save the Wives—Collect the Whole Set!

Since I really hammer on this theme throughout the coming pages, I will be brief here. Nothing seems as awkward in biblical literature as the proliferation of wives genetic to the institution of polygamy and the awkward and potentially hostile relationships that spring from it. (See, for instance, my discussion on polygamy at 1 Samuel 1). Be that as it may, David has been unlucky in love in several ways. First, he has been challenged with "ruggedly handsome, boyish good looks" (1 Samuel 16:12; 17:42). And one might well assume that when the narrator says, "all Israel and Judah loved David" (1 Samuel 18:16), that nothing is lost on the womenfolk of the land should be self-evident in such a potentially loaded statement.

Then again and secondly, it would seem that David has difficulty making a commitment and cannot decide to marry the king's oldest daughter, Merab—perhaps she was not as good looking as her younger sister, Michal (1 Samuel 18:17-28). We know that such problems in biblical literature can cause a certain selectivity (e.g., Genesis 29:16-18, 26). Perhaps David recalled the old bait-and-switch story from the patriarchs of old. Be that as it may, he finally formalizes the covenant and marries Michal (1 Samuel 18:27); really, his first real wife!

For whatever reason and thirdly, Michal elects not to go into David's fugitive status with him—someone had to hold the other end of the rope (1 Samuel 19:12) and cover for him with a covered bed of *teraphim* (artifacts of idolatrous religious practice; 1 Samuel 19:13-16), and then lie through her teeth to her father to save her own bacon. And then there are the others.

Because of the disjunctive syntax in 1 Samuel 25:43 and 44, we cannot know the exact timing of all the events; but the usage of the pluperfect (had taken, had given) is as good a guess as any. My theory is that upon hearing that Michal had been taken and given to Palti, David lost faith in monogamy and acquired (by whatever means) another wife, that being, Ahinoam. There is a lot in that name because it is the name of Saul's only named full wife (1 Samuel 14:50). Recall that Rizpah is called "the concubine of Saul" (2 Samuel 3:7; 21:11). Note also that Rizpah's first mention is related to the repossession of Michal from Palti by contiguity of textual material (2 Samuel 3:7-11, 12-16). This means that by the time of the repossession of Michal, David is philosophically a polygamist in earnest. Ah, but I'm getting ahead of myself. The nature of the syntax in 1 Samuel 25:43 leads me to believe that Ahinoam is acquired before Abigail. Abigail then becomes the second wife (favored status in some cultures) possessed simultaneously with Ahinoam.

If any of this pertains sequentially, it is of limited importance by the end of the story because David will proliferate wives and, by the time of Abishag, will have collected the whole set. One of the items in the collateral damage department has to do with the means of acquisition of these wives. We might assume, following the pattern of betrothal exemplified in David's marriage to Michal, that all David's marriages were of the "marriage-alliance" sort. Certainly, marrying the king's daughter can be so classified, as can marrying a wealthy widow (1 Samuel 25:42) and the princess of Geshur (2 Samuel 3:3). But the means of acquisition of at least three of them include violence. David exacts double indemnity of the Philistines and brings back a bag of grisly trophies to the king as the bride-price for Michal. That is fine; David is supposed to kill Philistines, is he not? Of course; but secondly, what about causing the locals to die of apoplexy? Following the ancient time-dishonored practice of *razia*, David has launched an attack on Château Nabal. One wonders, at this point, what David would have done after killing "everyone who urinates against the wall." Perhaps the womenfolk would have been "absorbed" into the traveling village of David, anachronistically perhaps, in Qur'anic fashion. It is possible that this is what is at stake with the trouble and the development of case law in 1 Samuel 30:18-25. (Please see my assessment below, "The Development of Spurious Case Law.") Third and finally, David's acquisition of Bathsheba, accompanied as it was with the plot to assassinate her husband, requires the manipulation of Joab, the general, and legal bungee jumping to avoid becoming a "son of death" and only being required to pay a four-fold restitution

(2 Samuel 12:5-6). As we will see in the future, this will not bode well for David, both in terms of wives and in terms of sons. (This is discussed in the forthcoming companion volume at 2 Samuel 3:1-5 and 5:13-16.)

## Textual Applications and Anecdotes

1 Samuel 25

vs.

1. Great individuals receive great mourning at their passing.
   The passing of great individuals receives the author's attention.
2. Rich people have to take care of their investments.
3. There is much we can learn in descriptions of people.
   Is Abigail tarred with Rachel's brush?
4. The actions of rich people cannot long escape notice.
5. As much as it depends upon us, we should attempt to maintain cordial relations with rich people.
6. As much as it depends upon us, we should be at peace with rich people.
7. We should be respectful of the possessions of rich people.
8. If we are respectful of the possessions of rich people, there is no reason we should not expect some token kindness from them.
9. Deliver your message and wait for a response.
10. We probably should not assume that everyone knows who we are—or cares, for that matter.
11. It might be illogical to assume beneficence from one who does not know us.
12. Return your response and see what happens.
13. Rash action follows a hot temper.
14. Wise servants will tell the real brains of the outfit what is about to happen.
15. Wise servants will know the true nature of the case where they work.
16. Wise servants will know if someone was truly protection for them or not.
17. Wise servants will know when calamity is about to fall.
18. The wise wife will know how to placate the wrathful avenger.
19. The wise wife may know when to hide things from her stupid husband.
    Note: she does not lie to him; she simply does not tell him what she is doing.
20. Chances are good that you will meet the avenger en route.
21. The avenger mutters to himself about a wrong suffered.
22. The avenger mutters oaths to himself.
23. The wise placator will posture herself properly before the avenger.
24. The wise placator will attempt to shift the blame to herself to mollify the avenger.
25. The wise suppliant may use humor in deflecting the avenger's anger.

26.    The wise suppliant may appeal to theological/ethical logic to deflect the avenger's anger.

27.    The wise suppliant may offer a gift to darken the vision of the avenger's anger.

28.    The wise suppliant will acknowledge the avenger's superior position.

29.    The wise suppliant will offer the best of well-wishes for the mollified avenger.

30.    The wise suppliant will offer a window in the future for the mollified avenger.

31.    The mollified avenger will not have to look back on dark days of vengeance.

32.    The mollified avenger will bless the suppliant.

33.    The mollified avenger will acknowledge that vengeance has been diverted.

34.    The mollified avenger will acknowledge the danger of the situation.

35.    The mollified avenger will accept the gift and should release the wise suppliant from further obligation.

36.    The successful suppliant may save the grisly details for when the old fool is sober.

37.    The successful suppliant may offer the old fool the grisly details when he can grasp their gravity.

38.    God will avenge an affront.

39.    God's avenging an affront should be remembered by His faithful.

40.    Recognize which way the wind is blowing? Go with the messengers.

41.    Recognize which way the wind is blowing? Go humbly.

42.    Go humbly and take some trusted folks with you.
       Promotion? Promote your corps.

43.    Be ever wary of those who would take more than one wife.

44.    Be ever wary of those who would take away the first wife.

## Conclusion

Nabal is dead and yet David has kept his hands relatively clean. We are reminded that Jesus, when He was here teaching, indicated that anger was murder at the ideational level (Matthew 5:21-24; cf. 1 John 3:15). Whereas David's heart may be in trouble—and that is a matter between him and God, I have no need to save David—his hands are kept clean by the woman who intercepted him along the path to a potentially ignominious deed. When Nabal later dies of fright, a coronary or a stroke, David absorbs Nabal's wife into what proves to be the beginnings of his harem. Abigail will henceforth rarely be named apart from the epithet "the wife of Nabal the Carmelite." Of course, our English translations will sanitize the matter by calling her "the widow of Nabal," but the truth is in the Hebrew text. The narrator recalls for us how it was this wise woman managed to dump one fool only, perhaps, to pick up another.

Potentially, Abigail saved many lives that day. But at what cost? She became one of David's several wives—perhaps his favorite as in the tradition of cultures wherein the second wife is the favorite. But what of the legacy of Nabal? What happened to the estate? What happened to her son sired by David in Hebron (2 Samuel 3:3). Why was he overlooked among those in the quest for the throne of their father (Amnon the first, Absalom the third, and Adonijah the fourth)? What is the legacy of this "wise woman" absorbed into the fold, as it were? She leaves her great oratory in the narrative in chapter 25 to become little better than a prop in David's harem and an acquisition repossessed from the Amalekites in chapter 30. From there she fades into the wallpaper of the harem. Has she been violated by the Amalekites? When we arrive at 2 Samuel 16:21-22, we hope that she has not descended to the rank of a concubine, left to keep the house. But we are left to wonder: is she yet another one who will die the death disgraced of women in Israel—childless oblivion?

# 1 Samuel 26
## A Close Encounter of the Bivouac Kind
## The Integrity of the Anointed

—ɷ—

## Introduction

It seems that often, bad things come in pairs. When misfortune repeats itself one frequently hears the old saying: "Same song, second verse; a little louder, and a whole lot worse." Would we not have to admit that a bad song sung twice is rarely better for the exposure? Nevertheless, in our text today, we will see many similarities with that of chapter 24 of 1 Samuel. When David was a fugitive from King Saul, it seemed that he had many near misses. Our text shows us a repetition of the treachery of the Ziphites (immortalized in song in Psalm 54). In both cases, the confession of King Saul sounds like a genuine repentance; but in neither case are we sure that the madman-king has genuinely changed his personal stance toward the anointed-elect, David. In both cases, however, David demonstrates himself to be a man of integrity. We have one anointed king rotting from within and another anointed being renewed by a righteousness external to himself. Both were anointed by the prophet Samuel; but, the first had had the kingdom stripped from him, concluding his years in jealousy, hatred, bitterness, and a murderous demonized insanity. The second proves himself to be clear headed, principled, self-controlled, and benevolent. The diamond sparkles most brilliantly against black velvet. The people of Ziph have sung their hideous song. Let us enter the scene and see what the integrity of the anointed looks like.[97]

## Reading from "Saul: A Life Suspended in Doubt"

Recon from Ziph told me that David was again on the prowl on the backside of Judah. So I took my three thousand man elite guard and headed to the southeast. One night when we were camped out and all sleeping peacefully—ALL, including the posted sentries—somebody snuck into camp and managed to steal a water jug and a spear. Anyway, we were all awakened by shouting from a ledge across the ravine. Somebody was yelling at Abner. As I came to, I caught the tone of the conversation. Whoever was safely across the ravine was upbraiding Abner for neglecting his duty to guard the life of the king and that that person, too distant to see clearly, had apparently arrested and disarmed the would-be assassin while in the very act!

He had as evidence my water jug and the royal javelin. I came to recognize that these were, in point of fact, missing and that the voice was very familiar. It was that wizard of stealth, the son of Jesse! It is interesting that he chose that javelin, the very one I had thrown at him a number of times. What a sorcerer! Not only could he elude it, he could swipe it and had complete control over it—about anytime he wanted.

The next scene was a repeat of what I'd experienced before. David feigned innocence and said that I was attempting to use superior force against an unworthy adversary. That voice again! I promised that I would leave him alone and this time necessity proved my words true. The Philistines were in fact gathering for a major offensive to attempt to cut the kingdom in half. It would take some time, but I would have to devote my entire efforts to raising, equipping, and training my standing army. I sincerely doubt that David believed anything I said anymore, anyway, since he slipped off into hiding again. We could have used a good fighter and strategist. As he disappeared, I assured him of his future prosperity and success—that voice! (1 Samuel 26)

## Textual Observations

### On Conflict and Preparation: When Integrity Is Rare in the Desert

Despite his words recorded for us in 1 Samuel 24:17-21, Saul has not really changed his stance toward David. His is yet a seek-and-destroy mission. After receiving the report from the people of Ziph, "Saul arose and went down to the wilderness of Ziph, having with him three thousand chosen men of Israel, to search for David in the wilderness of Ziph" (1 Samuel 26:2). Parenthetically, we might note that herein lies a principle: The madman acts according to impulse and often according to blind pattern (v. 2). At this point, we might determine that David's military intelligence was every bit as good as Saul's because David sent out spies, and he knew that Saul was definitely coming. At this point it might be good to point out a corollary to the principle indicated at verse 2: before setting out on a course of action, it is best to make certain of the facts (v. 4). And so David then observed the situation for himself and the layout of Saul's camp (v. 5).

In the tradition of berserkers everywhere, who go against insurmountable odds with an infinitesimal force and prevail, David asks two of his men as to who would be willing to accompany him. Abishai, the son of Zeruiah, Joab's brother says, at this point, "I will go down with you" (v. 6). We must note at this point that this is the first introduction to Abishai. He will have a long and uneven history in the text; but here, he is introduced in the context of his bravery—a theme that seems to continue along somewhat sporadically to the listing of David's mighty men in 2 Samuel 23:8-39. His willingness to accompany

David is a demonstration of his bravery; however, it will become clear that the mission was either misunderstood by Abishai or changed by David as we proceed through this episode. Because this is his first introduction, Abishai is given his full pedigree. However, only once will Abishai not be tarred by the brush that names him as brother to Joab (2 Samuel 19:21). Joab will meet an ignominious end (1 Kings 2:28-35); but Abishai will apparently begin to get a clue as to his fate should he continue on in the footsteps of his brother by about mid-flight through 2 Samuel.

## On Confrontation with Principle When in the Desert

"It was a strange thing, I was walking through the desert one night and smacked right into a principle." Those might have been the thoughts of Abishai as he accompanied David in a secret sortie to Saul's camp. The narrator tells us, "So David and Abishai came to the people by night, and behold, Saul lay sleeping inside the circle of the camp, with his spear stuck in the ground at his head; and Abner and the people were lying around him" (1 Samuel 26:7). To Abishai, the whole scenario is what we call a no-brainer. He says, "Today God has delivered your enemy into your hand; now therefore, please let me strike him with the spear to the ground with one stroke, and I will not strike him the second time" (v. 8). It is a cut-and-dried case, until you do some simple arithmetic. That is, Abishai, there are two of us and three thousand of them. It does not matter if anybody is awake now. Should we make any noise, somebody might wake up, sound the alarm, and our survival will depend upon how well we run in the dark. Of course, David does not pursue the issue from that angle. He stays a course he has laid back in chapter 24.

David attempted to explicate the principle of the case back in 1 Samuel 24:6, but appears to be a bit less coherent. He has time to crystallize his thinking and states his principle articulately: "Do not destroy him, for who can stretch out his hand against the LORD's anointed and be without guilt? . . . As the LORD lives, surely the LORD will strike him, or his day will come that he dies, or he will go down into battle and perish. The LORD forbid that I should stretch out my hand against the LORD's anointed" (1 Samuel 26:9-11). And so, apparently, an alternate plan develops. I have a couple of observations here. It would appear that the only answer to the utilitarian ethic—an end-justifies-the-means philosophy—is the appeal to a higher principle. From this text, there is also a corollary: it would be wrong to stretch out a violent hand against the Lord's anointed. We will have to wait a minute to see that to which this might apply. (See discourse on "the Lord's anointed" below.)

In the meantime, we have to ask the question: did David know what he was going to do when he and Abishai sallied out to the camp that night? Because of the way things are laid out for us by the narrator, I am led to believe that he had a plan and it changed when he looked at the layout of things or his conscience struck him as it did in the cave when he hacked off a piece of the royal robe (1 Samuel 24:5). Whatever the case, the narrator moves us away from our expectations and toward a new plan.

David concludes his discussion with Abishai with this directive: "But now please take the spear that is at his head and the jug of water, and let us go" (v. 11). That is, David commands Abishai to take the spear and jug, and yet the narrator tells us that there is some doubt as to who had control of what: "So David took the spear and the jug of water from beside Saul's head, and they went away" (v. 12). Perhaps it was that David wrested the spear from Abishai's hands after a menacing move or upon reflection of the gravity of Abishai's contention. Perhaps the narrator is merely informing us of who was in charge and although Abishai took and carried the items, David was responsible for the life of the sleeping monarch.

The whole scene is a bit surrealistic because of the nature of a heated exchange of words perhaps at the level of whispers while in the camp of Saul or right at its outskirts or within eyeshot of the spear and jug. It is surrealist until one considers the sleep of the camp. We are told, "but no one saw or knew it, nor did any awake, for they were all asleep, because a sound sleep from the LORD had fallen on them" (v. 12). The reader has to ask: were they inebriated, stoned, or anesthetized? How is it that they—even the sentries—could sleep while all this is going on within eyeshot of the king's spear? Part of the answer has to do with the understanding of the words often translated into English "deep sleep." (See "When God Casts a Deep Sleep [*tardēmāh*] upon Man" below.)

## Since We Are in the Desert, What on Earth Is "The Lord's Anointed"?

If it could ever be ascertained what or who the Lord's anointed was, it would certainly be wrong to stretch out a violent hand against one. In view of the termination of the theocracy of Israel, the concept of abiding validity is very difficult. What things really do cross the testaments and transcend time to our day? In short, what things from the Old Testament have an authoritative hold on us today? Perhaps if we look at the three major anointed-of-the-Lord groups, we might come to some provisional resolution in regard to this one question. The anointed of the Lord, in the Old Testament, were the prophets, the priests, and the kings in Israel. Of course, there were all sorts of phonies and pretenders to various of the offices; but, we will discount them. As we know, Jesus Christ is the final consummation of all three offices. But until the end of the ages, God has left provisional representatives of these in position here now.

The priesthood is that which acts on behalf of mankind before God. According to 1 Peter 2:9-10, we in the church should hold to the priesthood of all believers. According to 1 Timothy 2:5, each of us has direct access to God through the mediatorial work of Jesus Christ. We need no other priesthood. We should, therefore, not stretch out a violent hand against each other in that we are the anointed priesthood of the living God.

Kingship is a lateral concept that deals with the relationship between people here on this earth. Some countries have kings; some have prime ministers or presidents and so on. In any case, according to Romans 13, God has established human government to retain some semblance of order between the demise of the theocracy and its final consummation in the reign of King Jesus. Human governments, like those in power and those they govern, are fickle and subject to caprice. We should, therefore, remember that our citizenship is first in heaven; and secondly, not be too trusting of human governments—neither too disappointed when they fail us. It serves the place, in the present economy, of the anointed kingship of the theocracy. We should be very reticent to stretch out a violent hand against it. The bad news is that bad governments are oppressive; the good news is that they usually rot from within and are overthrown: but the *meek* shall inherit the earth.

The final category of the anointed of the Lord is the office of prophet. Generally, within Protestantism, this office is filled by the pastor of the church or teaching elder. The office itself is characterized by people who view truth and righteousness as more important than life itself. Often, the prophets of the Old Testament were martyred. Always, their life was one of austerity and conflict. In the ongoing struggle for separation of church and state: either the priesthood or the monarchy has always given the other the right to exist. It is only the ad hoc office, the office of prophet, which recklessly calls both to account. It is the prophet, often at the cost of his life, who reserves the sole right to call all before the throne of judgment and demand either repentance or justice.

N.B.: Perhaps a word is in order about the *concept* of stretching out a violent hand against the anointed—in whatever form they currently exist. It has been said that the pen is mightier than the sword. I doubt that the author at sword point ever asked for a pen refill though.

Nevertheless, words are mighty weapons, with which we do battle and commit mayhem. In the gospels, Jesus, the master teacher, masterfully pointed out the spirit and the intent of the law. For instance, in the matter of adultery: it is not only the act that is sin, but even the thought that is self-condemning. The tenth point of the Decalogue is the matter of coveting. This issue deals with the heart. One can covet, without notice. To act out is either theft or adultery, depending on the case. Interestingly, the case in point, covetousness, is what Paul uses in Romans 7 to get at the heart of the law. In Matthew we learn that one can be angry and guilty. James assures us that there is such a thing as righteous indignation. But the caution is to make certain that the indignation is righteous. From the above examples, we may see that the heart of a rule is the nearest point to the heart of God. In view of these things, I should think that we would guard our words carefully in speaking against the established leadership. Jesus' stinging words against the established religious and political hierarchy of His day were doubly devastating in view of the fact that no one could accuse Him of duplicity.

A third principle might be that if we perceive that God is bringing someone down, perhaps it would be a matter of expedience to get out of the way—lest we be taken away along with him (v. 10). In addition, it may be necessary to prove a point twice (v. 11; 1 Sam. 24:11). Also, it may be difficult to trust a person with a weapon who has just threatened mayhem. (Note the command to Abishai in verse 11, as over against the fact that David took the spear in verse 12.)

## When God Casts a Deep Sleep (*tardēmāh*) upon Man

This Hebrew word for deep sleep carries with it some ominous overtones. It is used seven times as a noun and six times as a verb. Let us examine some of the usages and draw some conclusions. The noun appears in the feminine singular absolute indefinite (or Lexical form). It is usually translated "deep sleep" or something similar. It usually appears with "to fall" (*nāphal*) + "upon" (*'al*). It usually pertains to a person and usually occurs by supernatural agency.

Genesis 2:21
So the LORD God caused a deep sleep to fall upon the man, and he slept; then He took one of his ribs, and closed up the flesh at that place.

Genesis 15:12
Now when the sun was going down, a deep sleep fell upon Abram; and behold, terror *and* great darkness fell upon him.

1 Samuel 26:12
So David took the spear and the jug of water from *beside* Saul's head, and they went away, but no one saw or knew *it*, nor did any awake, for they were all asleep, because a sound sleep from the LORD had fallen on them.

Isaiah 29:10
For the LORD has poured over you a spirit of deep sleep,
he has shut your eyes, the prophets;
and He has covered your heads, the seers.

Proverbs. 19:15
Laziness casts into a deep sleep,
and an idle man [soul] will suffer hunger.

Job 4:13
"Amid disquieting thoughts from the visions of the night,
when deep sleep falls on men" (quoting Eliphaz).

Job 33: 15

"In a dream, a vision of the night,

when sound sleep falls on men,

while they slumber in their beds" (quoting Elihu).

Evaluation: The agency may always be divine; however, God need not be the instrumental cause. This deep sleep, which God causes to fall upon men, need not always be positively viewed by its recipients. It can produce terror, imperception, spiritual blindness, and disquieting thoughts.

The verb (*rādam*) appears only in the *niph'al* (passive, also used of type verbs) and means "be in," or "fall into heavy sleep." It apparently has no relationship to the homonymic Arabic word. It also seems to have some ominous things associated with it such as the "sleep of death" and the "stunning effect of awe and dread."

Judges 4:21

But Jael, Heber's wife, took a tent peg and seized a hammer in her hand, and went secretly to him and drove the peg into his temple, and it went through into the ground; for he was sound asleep and exhausted. So he died.

Jonah 1:5

Then the sailors became afraid, and every man cried to his god, and they threw the cargo which was in the ship into the sea to lighten *it* for them. But Jonah had gone below into the hold of the ship, lain down, and fallen sound asleep.

Psalm 76:6 (Ps. 76:7, Hebrew).

At thy rebuke, O God of Jacob,

Both rider [chariot] and horse were cast into a dead sleep.

Proverbs 10:5

He who gathers in summer is a son who acts wisely,

*but* he who sleeps in harvest is a son who acts shamefully.

Daniel 8:18

Now while he was talking with me, I sank into a deep sleep with my face to the ground; but he touched me and made me stand upright [on my standing] (in conversation with Gabriel).

Daniel 10:9

But I heard the sound of his words; and as soon as I heard the sound of his words, I fell into a deep sleep on my face, with my face to the ground. (This pertained to Daniel's initial encounter with the angel that Michael needed to assist).

Evaluation: It would seem that in each of the six cases above, there is some moment—some important event—in the verse that uses such a word. In the Judges passage, Jael dispatches the general of the Canaanite forces. In the Jonah narrative, Jonah fiddles while Rome burns; but this is where his fraud is exposed by God and discovered by the sailors. The psalm appears to be recalling Exodus 15:1, 21. Like the proverb reference for the noun, the one for the verb has something ominous about it in that the repercussions for such sloth seem to be divinely retributed. The two Daniel references are rather self-explanatory in view of the angelic presences.

In the opinion of the writer, this word is appropriate to the context of 1 Samuel 26:12, due to the nature of the discussion between David and Abashai. It could be that they were some distance away from the camp when the discussion began. But, due to the pointing in the text, it seems just as likely that they were standing over Saul, and David had to physically remove the spear from Abishai's hand. In any case, the moment is dramatic—as it is with all other usages of both verb and noun. It is as though—Adam like—the whole of Saul's camp is anesthetized and unable to respond to the dangerous threat that Abishai poses. Only the integrity of the anointed-elect saves the life of the divinely deposed.

## On Confrontation with Adversaries When in the Desert

Eventually, the cat that swallowed the canary will cough up a couple of feathers. And so "Then David crossed over to the other side, and stood on top of the mountain at a distance with a large area between them. And David called to the people and to Abner the son of Ner" (1 Samuel 26:13-14). There might be something of a subliminal principle here: it is probably a good idea to place a healthy distance between oneself and a madman. And so David, at a safe distance, now adopts the role of prosecutor. In a series of virtually unanswered questions, David sets any verbal defense that might be offered back on its heels. He says: "Will you not answer, Abner? . . . Are you not a man? And who is like you in Israel? Why then have you not guarded your lord the king? For one of the people came to destroy the king your lord. This thing that you have done is not good. As the LORD lives, all of you must surely die, because you did not guard your lord, the LORD's anointed. And now, see where the king's spear is, and the jug of water that was at his head" (1 Samuel 26:14-16).

The evidence of the negligence of Abner and company and the innocence of David is at once demonstrated in his possession of the spear and the water jug. It is self-evident to the characters in the story as well as the readers that Saul could have been speared to the ground or his water poisoned due to their lax guardianship. And so David exclaims that they are all "surely sons of death" (v. 16), and he states the reasons why. David's words are pregnant with meaning because many of those hearing this diatribe at a distance will in fact die before the end of the volume (1 Samuel 31). Abner, will be a son of death; not for failing to defend the king, as much as for failing to defend himself from a more vicious and treacherous general, Joab (2 Samuel 3:26-30). There is a moral assessment to be made here: it would be a good idea to guard one's pronouncements carefully for we never know when someone else may have to eat them. Indeed, many would die on Mt. Gilboa in a short time. Ironies abound and Abner, who grew to be an ally and proved himself to be a friend to David, was killed by no less that Abishai's brother Joab.

While we are dealing with pregnant language, we might examine Abner's words when he said, "Who are you who calls to the king?" Unless there was some "line-loss" over the distance, we recall that our narrator has quoted David as giving direct address to the general, not the king. Time will pass and we will wonder who really wears the crown in Israel. At several points the generals of the odd clutter of monarchs are able to argue their monarchs into a corner (for instance, when Joab argumentatively corners David in 2 Samuel 19:5-7). David ruled for seven years during which time Ish-Bosheth ruled two years. Hmmm—I wonder who was really the king? Abner proves to be more than a capable military leader. He is, in effect, the power broker of the northern federation. No doubt he carried a lot of clout in King Saul's day as well. Be that as it may, there are five years of loose time in the northern kingdom where there is no official king. Abner put Ish-Bosheth up to the position (2 Samuel 2:8), but the lag time is foreshadowed in the narrative or prophetically predicted by David's words and Abner's reply: "Who are you who calls to the king?" I have an idea who was the real monarch in Saul's absence.

### On Recognition and Contrition When in the Desert

Finally, Saul intercepts Abner's inept role in the conversation and responds to David. True to fashion, David pelts Saul with a barrage of unanswerable questions. When David knows he has the attention of the king, he deals with the real issue—his innocence. His words bear repeating:

Why then is my lord pursuing his servant? For what have I done? Or what evil is in my hand? Now therefore, please let my lord the king listen to the words of his servant. If the LORD has stirred you up against me, let Him accept an offering; but if it is men, cursed are they before the LORD, for they have driven me out today that I should have no attachment with the inheritance of the LORD, saying, "Go, serve other gods." Now then, do not let my blood fall to the ground away from the presence of the LORD; for the king of Israel has come out to search for a single flea, just as one hunts a partridge in the mountains.

1 Samuel 26:18-20

David's argument distills to the fact that he has committed no capital offense. If God has a problem, let Him be propitiated; if there is some conspiracy to remove David from the country, then let them be accursed, is his assessment of matters. David seems to think that his only recourse will be to leave the country, at the risk of serving other gods. However, this is in fact what he will do in the next chapter—*sans* the "serving other gods" part apparently. David's concluding argument with the flea and partridge illustration is the pointlessness of the quest. David's appeal is to the king as monarch of a nation, not an assassin hired for the murder of one man. There is a reality check for us as well: a madman will have grave difficulty in weighing the real significance of a relationship. Insanity, no matter how grave or temporary, will tend to put reality and relationships out of proper perspectives—"obsession" is the keyword.

Be that as it may, Saul finally gets it. Not that the king of flip-flop is saying anything particularly new; but there will be one important addition. His words are the right and true words of someone who has, temporarily at least, come to his senses. He said, "I have sinned. Return, my son David, for I will not harm you again because my life was precious in your sight this day. Behold, I have played the fool and have committed a serious error" (1 Samuel 26:21).

Without overly moralizing away the text we might say that the first move in the direction of reality is always repentance. But wait a minute, Saul said many of these same words in the prequel. How are they an accurate reflection of his twisted inner state now? So far as the text is concerned, it is difficult to know. The narrator tells us that Saul stopped bothering David when he defected to the Philistines (1 Samuel 27:4). However, we may be able to reach a provisional resting place with respect to Saul's character vis-à-vis David.

## On Resolution and Closure When in the Desert—and Old Enemies Cease Hostilities

Saul has really admitted his crime in the matters above—in the company of thousands of witnesses! David's evidence is in his hands—full of spear and empty of blood. He said, "Behold the spear of the king! Now let one of the young men come over and take it. And the LORD will repay each man for his righteousness and his faithfulness; for the LORD delivered you into my hand today, but I refused to stretch out my hand against the LORD's anointed. Now behold, as your life was highly valued in my sight this day, so may my life be highly valued in the sight of the LORD, and may He deliver me from all distress" (1 Samuel 26:22-24). It would be a point of the tedious to ask about the water jug at this point. But this time, I am led to believe that Saul really got the point that David was not out to get him and that there was no point in being out to get David. He said, "Blessed are you, my son David, you will both accomplish much and surely prevail" (v. 25). What is different between this text and that of chapter 24 is the addition of the blessing. Oaths were sworn last time—which Saul had not kept! However, this time, he once again tells David that he will not attempt to harm him. We can believe it if we want; but he also philosophically passes on the torch by passing on the blessing to David. Saul will keep the palace and the army, but he knows that the country's heart has or will soon be passed to David. As episodes conclude in the Samuel narrative, each participant often goes home and so we are told, "So David went on his way, and Saul returned to his place" (v. 25).

There are a couple of summary principles that we might derive from the text. For whatever rests with us, really it is the Lord who is the only one responsible and objective enough to evaluate someone's ultimate righteousness and faithfulness. In addition, and although we wish it had been true finally and ultimately in Saul's case in chapter 24, it is still true that coming to one's senses will always mean seeing things from God's perspective. This last thought runs subliminally throughout the three chapters (24–26) in the conversations of the various protagonists and antagonists. Indeed, integrity is rare in the desert.

## Textual Applications and Anecdotes

1 Samuel 26
vs.
1. A bad song sung twice is rarely better for the exposure (the Ziphites; again, 1 Sam. 23:19).
2. The madman acts according to impulse and often according to blind patter.
3. The bivouac is vulnerable.
4. Before setting out on a course of action, it is best to make certain of the facts.
5. When things seem safest (Saul sleeping in the circle) they probably are not.
6. Our most courageous friends may not turn out to be our most faithful friends.
7. Surprising circumstances may invite surprising responses.
8. The man of war is not always the best counselor in a time of open hostilities.
9. Principle is the only answer to an end-justifies-the-means philosophy.
   It would be wrong to stretch out a violent hand against the LORD's anointed.
10. If we perceive that God is bringing someone down, perhaps it would be a matter of expedience to get out of the way—lest we be taken away along with him.
11. It may be necessary to prove a point twice (1 Samuel 24:11).
12. It may be difficult to trust a person who has just threatened mayhem. (Note the command to Abishai in verse 11, as over against the fact that David took the spear in verse 12.)
13. It is good to place a healthy distance between oneself and a madman.

14. Always attempt to go through channels (Abner was the commander of the king's forces including the guard).
15. A little embarrassment goes a long way.
16. Guard your words carefully, you never know when someone else may have to eat them.

    ("All of you are surely sons of death!" Abner, who grew to be an ally and proved himself to be a friend, was killed by no less than Abishai's brother Joab [2 Samuel 3:27].)
17. Recognition may often create an awkward moment.
18. A few pointed questions may open the door for further comment.
19. There has to be a better way to handle jealousy than bloodshed.
20. A madman will have grave difficulty in weighing the real significance of a relationship.
21. The first move in the direction of reality is always repentance.
22. It is always a good idea to return the evidence to its rightful owner.
23. The Lord is the only one responsible and objective enough to evaluate someone's ultimate righteousness and faithfulness.
24. An act of kindness may justifiably evoke a prayer for one's own preservation.
25. Coming to one's senses will always mean seeing things from God's perspective.

    If it is possible to resolve conflict apart from bloodshed, to do so is of the highest honor.

## Conclusion

The scene has concluded; the actors have left the stage, each to go to his own place; the story has attained a provisional resolution. We, who have read on, know that King Saul will never again see his old friend, court musician, general, and servant David in the land of the living. Saul will proceed from bad to worse—from occult practices, to destruction, and finally death. He will fail miserably. David, though still having some trials ahead of him, will, nevertheless, prevail. He will be king; his heirs for many generations will sit on the throne of Israel and Judah; ultimately, that descendant of David would come to the world to pay the penalty of its sins. Will many believe? In large measure, that depends upon us. Indeed, even this text lays out a choice for the chosen of God. Will we choose to live our lives based on jealousy and vindictiveness; or will we live our lives empowered by that divine Davidic son? Will our lives be such a testimony to His grace that, like children to candy, others will be drawn to it? Will we walk by the Spirit and so produce the fruit of the Spirit? Eternity begins now! By God's grace we can change; by God's grace we can grow; by God's grace we shall be perfected! God's blessing upon all who cherish such hopes!

# 1 Samuel 27
## Nuts to It, Let's Go Back to Gath
## When Bad Things Are Done by Good People
### (With apologies to Rabbi Kushner)[98]

—⟋⟍—

## Introduction

Harold Kushner's book, *When Bad Things Happen to Good People*, is a product of his odyssey from bitterness to an allegedly deeper understanding of God. Unfortunately, he arrives at the wrong answer and his understanding of God divests God of anything worthy of the title. But with endorsements from the likes of Norman Vincent Peale, *McCall's*, *Redbook*, *Publisher's Weekly*, *Library Journal*, *Washington Post*, Norman Cousins, Andrew Greeley, and, of course, no less than Art Linkletter, dessert will come before the main course, I suppose. To quote the back cover: "Through his family's shared ordeal, this distinguished clergyman came to see God as he never had before—a God who *does* weep with us, *won't* abandon us, and *can* fill the deepest needs of an anguished heart."[99] And in the final analysis, he had a loving God who would fix things if He could; but He cannot and so, He merely sympathizes with us in our weakness. Of course, for us, things are never so simple; and to divest God of His situational sovereignty is to create a monster of one's own imagination rather than a God according to biblical proportions. In fact, there are several reasons why bad things happen to people at all and the one that I want to address at this point is that there really are no good people—at least, I've never met any. The New Testament is less optimistic than the cynic you've probably already accused me of being.

> There is none righteous, not even one; there is none who understands, there is none who seeks for God; All have turned aside, together they have become useless; there is none who does good, there is not even one. Their throat is an open grave, with their tongues they keep deceiving, the poison of asps is under their lips; whose mouth is full of cursing and bitterness; their feet are swift to shed blood, destruction and misery are in their paths, and the path of peace have they not known. There is no fear of God before their eyes.
>
> Romans 3:10-18

With respect to strained interpersonal relationships between men and women and the battle of the sexes and women's rights and so on, I like to quote my wife who says: "Men are rotten; women are rotten; they deserve each other." There! That should set the tone for this section, no?

In 1 Samuel 27, we find ourselves in a Davidic parenthesis wherein there is no Saul. The major point of interest is that David is afraid of a Saul who is no longer present. The text says, "and Saul returned to his place" (1 Samuel 26:25). In any case, we should have been noticing along the way that the narrator's focus has been gradually shifting, especially since the spiritual transformations of chapter 16, verses 13-14, to show us more of the actions and words of David. We also see much more of the revealed inner states of a very unstable Saul. We do not get much of David's inner states until here in 27:1.

We have a story about David in exile in a foreign country. Where I used to live it was said that the last stop on the ascendancy to the presidency of some small sub-Saharan republic was either a jail cell or exile. Examples are, of course, legion: Kenyatta of Kenya, Mandela of the Republic of South Africa, Anwar Sadat of Egypt, Charles Taylor of Liberia, and so on. But back to our story in 1 Samuel 27; this chapter is really about David, but it still shows the demise of Saul. And so, I will be looking at my "Saul: A Life Suspended in Doubt"; but as you might guess, there had to be quite a bit of historical reconstructive surgery. So please bear with me while I "play the game"—the historical game, that is: correlation, causation, and analogy. And when we play the game by its rules, we will discover the obvious that Saul does not look so good, and what I consider far more profound: neither does David. In all this, I will be chasing a trail that says: *Godless leadership is but another sorry tale of money, power, and politics.*

### Reading from "Saul: A Life Suspended in Doubt"

Although it was no longer any concern of my own, intelligence on the west told me that the son of Jesse had defected to the Philistines. Again he went to the king of Gath. What a buffoon Achish was, he wouldn't recognize the devil if he looked him in the face. David would never be anything but a troublemaker to anybody he was around. Recon told me that he was making raids on the south and that there was troop movement nearly daily. However, there were never any complaints from the people of Judah that he was hurting anybody down there. He and his men seemed to be whacking the Amalekites, the Geshurites, and the Girzites. Although we had no open hostilities with the other two, up to that point, it seemed almost a service to the kingdom that he was continuing my unending vengeance against the Amalekites. I'd have to think about the Geshurites though. Regardless, the son of Jesse seemed to claim Ziklag for his own and use it as a base of operations. If he got out of line we could easily mount an assault against him there. He wouldn't hold out a month!

I really have no idea what Achish was doing though. It is as though he trusted the son of Jesse—a thing impossible for anybody who really knew him. Perhaps he hoped that the son of Jesse would provoke me to the point that I would attempt an incursion into Philistine held territory and then he could trap me and my forces there in the low country. I really have no idea. It was only a matter of time before the five warlords would move again. Perhaps Achish was thinking of levying them to his forces to please the warlords by having a few more seasoned veterans in his conscripted standing soldiery. Who knows? (1 Samuel 27)

## Textual Observations[100]

## Running Away from Fear with 600 Other Oxymorons

Notice that verse 1 follows hard upon the heels of chapter 26. In reality, there is no break and it should read: "And Saul said to David, 'Blessed are you my son David, you will both certainly perform and certainly prevail.' And David went on his way and Saul returned to his place. And David said to his heart, 'Now, I will perish one day by the hand of Saul.'" Verse one includes one of the very few candid moments in the thought life of the hero David. It is supremely fascinating to me that it does not show him in a very good light. Allow me to explain: This pericope follows hard on the heels of one of the most glorious victories of grace in the life of David. You will recall that David and Abishai came to the camp and Abishai was going to harpoon Saul with his own spear. David and Abishai have this rather odd word war after which they swipe the spear and water jug. The public words ring in our ears: "The LORD forbid that I should stretch out my hand against the LORD's anointed" (26:11). As a result of this and the dramatic matters that follow, David, for the second time, receives a promise from the king—but this time along with an oath and even a blessing! The king looks for all the world like he will really leave David alone. So why this flip-flop in the character of David? I have an idea; you knew I would.

In another place (1 Kings 19, if you're keeping score), I would have called it "The Elijah Syndrome." That is where the incredible drain from a great spiritual victory causes what nearly approximates bi-polar syndrome. That is: Elijah has become manic depressive. With respect to the events of 1 Samuel 26, there had to be a phenomenal adrenaline rush with having accomplished their little sortie. There were moments of high tension and probably high physical exertion. When the adventure turns out well for David and Abishai, one could imagine that our biblical hero, David, is both exhilarated and exhausted—textbook "Elijah Syndrome" antecedents! Whereas Elijah turns cowardly, goes into a self-appointed exile, and adopts a very nearly suicidal mental state (at least wishing to die with an unbroken tape recording to that effect blaring in his mind), David turns fearful and is content merely to become a refugee. Because we are given so little insight into his internal states—this being one of the few windows—we cannot know what his dread of Saul did to him, how much, how deep, or how long. That he was still able to function as the leader of his men is apparent—at least until chapter 29 when everything goes wrong. Nevertheless, from the foregoing observations, I deduce the following: *unchecked fear can lead to godless leadership.*

### Can Any Good Thing Go to Gath? Or, Gath, the Regional Nut Farm!

Having been born in the former great state of Kali-foreign-ya, I am no stranger to insanity. Having been born in the only hospital in Imola where my mother was a guest at the time, gives me a front row seat in the process. However, those who were there in my day would today suddenly be pronounced sane and given state government jobs with the coveted Riviera Chateau retirement package. Since most people in government are about my age, that must have been what happened. How was it for David, who once feigned madness and now feigns sanity?

Biographical considerations aside, the motto of our hero, David, at this point, seems to be, "If at first you try and fail, try and fail again." Let's review: the first time he attempted to defect to Gath, in a rather tight bit of irony, he grabs Goliath's sword—after all, Goliath shouldn't need it—from the reliquary of the priestly antiquarians (1 Samuel 21:9) and flees from Saul right straight to Goliath's home town, Gath (1 Samuel 21:10). Of course, nobody at court had ever seen either David or that immense blade before! David had just said, "There is none like it; give it to me." No doubt, he had examined a lot of them lying around the battlefield after each latest Philistine carnage. The upshot of the whole insane fiasco is that the courtiers of Achish, King of Gath, recite the Israelite women's victory ditty to their sovereign and David recognizes a near sighting of the Grim Reaper. So, insanity breeding insanity, David feigns madness and gets out of there with more of his life than his dignity.

So why does David go back there this time? Is this one more round of insanity—barring of course, the notion that an "Achish" is merely a dynastic title and these are different men.[101] Maoch's dad could have been "Achish," but the dates are a bit tight for that. Nevertheless, what form of insanity could drive David to Gath again? And further, what form of insanity could make Achish accept a David feigning sanity, at this point? Did Achish not recognize the one who has killed "his ten thousands" this time? Did his courtiers not recognize the one they had previously introduced as the subject of the victory song and "the king of the land" (21:11)? Has God rendered the eyes of all Philistia blind?![102]

The narrator merely brings us here. He does not answer those questions. Somehow, and to the eyes of faith, God is between every line and behind every word, David is accepted into Philistine society. Do the people not remember this general who butchered so many of their kinsmen? Perhaps it is a matter of more than perceived ethnocentrism that drives David to ask for a less urban location. One of the smaller towns would put him in a location where he could run for the wilderness, run to the palace, or run to his next round of murder, pillage, and burn.

Whatever the case, the apex of King Saul's insanity, as evidenced by his radical defection from biblical Yahwism and his escapades with the spirit medium at en-Dor in chapter 28, is mirrored by the narrative insanity of 27:1-28:2 on the front side and 29:1-2 on the trailer.[103] This is the case until a sudden bout with cogence strikes the warlords and they make Achish send David and the Saracens packing (29:3-11). Maybe they recognized Goliath's sword clanking along in the van! Again, the eyes of faith will see the providence of God in keeping David's cover, despite David's stepping outside the protection of His more perfect will. They will see providence in protecting David from battle against his own people and further jeopardizing His chances—humanly speaking—at the throne. Providence may be seen in the same way as it is seen in Esther: without even mentioning the name of God, in a godless society, surrounded by a very questionable lot, an Esther or a David for that matter may be protected in such a way as to move forward in the program of God. Do they even know that God is working through their practical agnosticism? I doubt it. I don't think the outcome is ever in doubt as to the final end of God's will. What I imagine that breaks His heart is that people do not, first, acknowledge Him in everything; and second, do not go about things in a manner consistent with His revealed will.

Perhaps one place where the silence of David's character and faith scream at us the loudest is in the fact that he was a killing machine. David has been a butcher of the Philistines and is known as "a man of war." In the final analysis, he won the wars but never won the peace. For that reason, God would deny David the right to build the temple and give it to the man whose name means peace, Solomon. David prosecuted his *razias* on the Amalekites in perhaps the fashion directed by God—they were to be eradicated, exterminated entirely—no trace, no memory. However with respect to these two other people groups, we have no directive in Scripture. Why did David kill the women (and we must assume, the children)? The text tells us why: "Lest [remember that "lest" is a word that betrays fear of consequences] they should tell about us, saying 'So has David done and so has been his practice all the time he has lived in the country of the Philistines'" (1 Sam 27:11). It had nothing to do with finishing what Joshua had begun centuries before; it was merely to continue the ruse of David against his Philistine benefactors. It had nothing to do with following a biblical plan for the prosecution of empirical expansionism prescribed in Deuteronomy 20:10-18; we are not even far enough from home for those laws to apply in the first place. The reason for David's deception was merely to protect himself from discovery in a foreign environment. Of course, accepted plunder would certainly have blinded the eyes of his benefactor, Achish, and it would offer David an entrance to the leadership of Judah when the time was right for his return. In short, he is surreptitiously making himself rich and preparing to buy votes. Where is the heart of the man after God? All we see played out upon the stage of history for this four to sixteen-month period of David's life is his fear of death at Saul's hand and his fear of being discovered a fraud by Achish. But see what this does to David, *et al.*: and so, I suggest that: godless places and godless people can mold us (either by default, design, or *de facto*?) into godless leaders.

**David and Other Saracens**

One time when I was speaking on 1 Samuel 28 (a very Saul-esque parenthesis in the life of David), I made the off-handed statement that "David was little better than a Muslim at this point." As you might guess, I kicked somebody's puppy and they confronted me at the door. Having just taught a course on Islamic thought and literature, I'm sure they got more than they bargained for; but, I did answer the question. What follows are some of the answers I used after recovering from the shock of a question that set me back on my heels.

Verse 9: David acquits himself in the eyes of his Philistine regent of several things of a questionable nature: first, he beats up on people who his benefactor might consider allies; second, he lies to his benefactor by saying that he is really prosecuting *razias* with a vengeance on Judah and other allies of Israel; third, he does not leave any living witness to his actions to betray his feigned loyalty to Achish; and finally, he probably sets himself up as a patron to the crown by giving considerable wealth to his Philistine overlord. As David's son would say, and as Moses had said long before: "you shall not take a bribe, for a bribe blinds the clear-sighted and subverts the cause of the just" (Ex. 23:8). Of course, a gift can become a bribe if there is a disclosure of indiscretion.[104] Living with a waitress (my wife) in a developing nation (Nairobi, Kenya in which the "developing" was a bit too much on the personal level), I've often said: "The only difference between a tip and a bribe is the side of the transaction on which it falls." Regardless, "A man's gift makes room for him, and brings him before great men" (Prov. 18:16). And that is precisely what David was doing—gaining access and paying his insurance premium. It will work until the warlords explore the possibilities.

But what does all this lying and deceit mean with respect to David's character? We know when the chapter began that his basic motivation was fear. When a theist embraces a psyche of fear, he becomes for all intents and purposes a Muslim. The Judeo-Christian theology is supposed to be one where God holds warm feelings toward His creatures—all His creatures—and wishes them to be in right relationship to Him. I have been through the Qur'an too many times now to believe that which the useful idiots in the universities and the deceptive clerics in the mosques use to try to anesthetize the West into ambivalence, apathy, and inaction. I do not believe that the Qur'an portrays a God worthy of the title but rather a capricious tyrant more diabolical in nature.

But a second point is exactly this point of Islamism against the West: because they are infidels, they are not owed the truth. This is what David is doing. He is lying to his Philistine benefactor, all the while undermining him. Worse yet, this deception will be used later to buy back the favor with the Israel—Judah in particular—that he has abandoned (see especially, 1 Sam. 30:26-31). Where is the faith David once had? Where is the memory of the anointing by Samuel? Where is the promise of Jonathan that David would surely be king? Where is anything other than man's means to God's ends? This is exactly the problem that so often entangled the patriarchs in Genesis: they frequently attempted to use man's means—sometimes in the guise of cultural convention—to the ends of accomplishing God's purposes. But in our text, where is the "man after God's own heart?" Where is any mention of God at all?

Often, our preconceived notions about who David was as "the sweet psalmist of Israel" and "the man after God's own heart" keep us from seeing him as a real human being, as other than larger than life. A question arose once in a group study I was attending as to how we are to take these great heroes of the faith. No real consensus arose until I suggested that there is one common denominator: "Jesus died for all of them the same as us. Yes, there might be a continuum and we might fall somewhere between a Samson and a Shadrach; but, the New Testament is clear: 'all have sinned and fall short of the glory of God' (Rom. 3:23). And the Old Testament leaves no doubt, 'There is no one who does good, not even one'" (Ps. 14:3). At times when fear dominates our psychological makeup; at times when the name of God is not mentioned;[105] at times when we find it easier to survive by subterfuge than by integrity; and at times when we wrongly sense the need to help God's program along: these are the times when we are living in practical agnosticism. These are the times we become like "David and other Saracens." And so, one of the more negative lessons we learn from David in this section is: *deception and violence are characteristics of godless leadership.*

## Textual Problems

I have quite a list of peeves here and so I will begin with two from verse 4. "Now": ("*Now* it was told Saul") is interpretive. The word is "and" and because of the verb to which the conjunction is affixed, it necessitates consecutive action, not disjunction as "now" assumes. Secondly, "so": ("it was told Saul that David had fled to Gath, *so* he no longer searched for him.") is interpretive. It is literally "and." It is a serious matter to substitute subordination for coordination and assume—with no further evidence—a result clause. Since Saul had already decided not to chase after David anymore, cause and effect in verse 4 packs a bit more freight than the grammar of the verse will bear, in my opinion.

In verse 6 we are reminded to always read the fine print: "therefore Ziklag has belonged to the kings of Judah to this day." There are a couple of important points here: first, as we have known since Joshua the town was claimed, as were others, by both the tribes of Simeon and Judah (Joshua 15:31 [to Judah]; 19:5 [to Simeon]. Secondly, this land then reverted either to the kings themselves or at least the people of Judah in finality.

But more importantly, there is another voice heard here. Unless we are hearing from the Philistines who called David "the king of the land" (1 Sam. 21:11), or their same spiritual counterparts in Israel, we are looking back over our historical shoulders and making an observation *ex post facto*. There would not have been "kings" (plural) of Judah until after the time of Rehoboam. Does this mean that our text is corrupt? Not by a long shot. It means that the prophetic office was superintending the process of inscripturation through the progress of time. Although Samuel would have been alive in the time represented by chapter 21, he would not have been so in this the twenty-seventh chapter. So, Nathan or Gad or someone else might have received the baton from Samuel to continue the work of writing biblical history.

Does the "to this day" clause require the assumption of a Deuteronomistic history written at the time of the final siege of Jerusalem in 586 BC? Certainly, the end of the book of 2 Kings does. But that does not mean that these sections do. It merely means that at some point during the divided monarchy (there is even an inference there!), it was recognized that Ziklag had always belonged to the kings of Judah and that fact was acknowledged at this locus in the text.

In verse 7 we do not really know how long David lived in the land of the Philistines. The Septuagint (early Greek translation of the Hebrew scriptures — about third to second centuries BC) has four months and the Hebrew has, literally: "days and four months." Tradition has passed it down to us that this means "a year and four months" and so most English Bibles will have something of that nature. Somewhere between four months (although I hardly think that to be enough time to hornswoggle Achish into unwatchful somnolence) and sixteen months, David was deceiving his Philistine host and wrecking havoc on the Amalekites, *et al.*

In verse 8 the written text of the Hebrew Bible has Girzites about whom nothing further is known. However, the marginal note, called the *qerê*, ("spoken" or "read"), has Gezerites which seems to be a bit too far to the north to escape the notice of the David's Philistine benefactor, Achish — or the other Philistine warlords and kings who were somewhat less than beneficent (cf. 29:3-5).

**Textual Applications and Anecdotes**

1 Samuel 27
vs.
1.   Bad ideas can still come on days of great personal victory.
     If at first you try and fail, try and fail again (twice to Gath: 1 Sam. 21:10-22:1).
     He with the anointing oil on his head often fears decapitation.
     Fear is not usually a positive motivator.
     Old Sicilian saying: "My enemy's enemy is my friend."

2. Bad ideas are always better when shared with six hundred misfits and malcontents. Kings should never have a shortage of madmen (cf. 21:15).

3. Go into exile as one big happy family.
Exiles and refugees glut the host to the point of bursting.
The life of David: yet another happy tale of polygamy!

4. Live a self-fulfilling prophecy (v. 1): go into exile and become a refugee.
David proves he is not a prophet (recon. told Saul that David was gone and needn't bother looking for him "in all the territory of Israel").

5. Distancing oneself from the benefactor: the first step of subterfuge.
An odd question disarms the benefactor.
Servants and royalty apparently shouldn't live in proximity, according to David.

6. Bad things and great and terrible things may come from out-of-the-way places.
Always watch those editorial notes—they give perspective (Ziklag to Judahite kings "to this day").

7. Time marches on: days in exile multiply.

8. The mention of sins redressed includes the mention of sins committed (David vs. Saul re: Amalekites).

9. Because of deception, brutality goes out of bounds (cf. Deut. 20:14, if that applies to a case this far to the southwest).
Civilized people do not kill women in battle.

10. David does not feel that he owes the truth to his benefactor.
David at this point functions as would a Muslim.

11. The old adage was old in Bible times: "Dead men (or women for that matter!) tell no tales." Thanks to modern forensics, the dead may yet speak.

12. Deception and murder and bribery are like a bluff well played, the benefactor will believe the gifts when there is no information to the contrary.

## Conclusion

And so we see that leadership without God is merely another in a series of sorry tales of money, power, and politics. Even someone of the caliber of a David is not immune to such a fall or to such charges. This chapter is not a place where David looks good to the reader of biblical narrative. There will be others we will encounter in 2 Samuel, especially after the affair with Bathsheba; but this lapse is striking because it is so early in the story of David. David is still able to function as the military leader of his men. But one has to wonder at David's relationship with God at this point. God will not be much of a factor in David's life until his life is threatened by those very men he has led for so many years and then he will strengthen "himself in the LORD his God" (1 Sam. 30:6). In the meantime, mentions of Israel's God will come from more unlikely places like Saul and Achish. Both of these men placed an unusual amount of trust in David, and both—for different reasons of course—were disappointed with him. One also has to wonder how David could make any claim to integrity with the treachery he dealt to his benefactor while in exile. And so I draw the conclusion that David is little better than a Muslim at this point. He probably would have acknowledged God if you were to ask him; but, that God would have been to him a very disinterested, cold, cruel, and distant reality, not the biblical God lovingly and intimately acquainted with all our ways. And so what can we learn from this? It is my opinion that when God gives a promise, He will keep it despite my intrusive attempts to help His program along. And so, I should probably be much less fearful than I am about what I know to be God's revealed will. And finally, it does not seem too much of a reach that if I avoid getting myself into desperate situations, I will probably not have to use desperate means—lies and deception—to get myself out of them. It also seems to me that periods of exile, and I've lived them in various ways, are times for reflection rather than lashing out against real and/or perceived enemies. These are the lessons learned negatively from the biblical hero David in 1 Samuel 27. David, along with you and me, will do better on another day; but let us not, with him, relive these four to sixteen months in exile living by lies and deceit and lashing out at everyone mercilessly.

## Epilogue

Am I saying that David is a ne'er-do-well at this point? No, he has had some rather unwitting influence over his Philistine benefactor. Despite the deceit, the false basis for their relationship, hear Achish's words: "As YHWH lives, you have been upright, and your going out and coming in with me in the army are pleasing in my sight; for I have not found evil in you from the day of your coming to me to this day. Nevertheless, you are not pleasing in the sight of the lords. Now therefore return, and go in peace, that you may not displease the lords of the Philistines" (1 Sam. 29:6-7). This shows a couple of things at the least: First, we see that David's ruse was complete—dead men (or women) told no tales. Secondly and of particular interest at this point, is that Achish has become something of a Yahwist . . . or, at least he is willing to add Israel's God to his own pantheon. Observe this as well: "I know that you are pleasing in my sight, like an angel of God" (v. 9). So we know that Achish has something of a theology—an angelology at least, none of which happens in a vacuum. It is something like Jonah's case who had more conversion by default than by design. David is still God's man and He will use him no matter what. But I wonder how it will go when Achish wakes up to the realization he has been duped? It is a backhanded argument for truth and ethics in evangelism, I think. If we make a claim to the truth, if we claim that the gospel is truth, we ought to be characterized as truthful people. Nobody appreciates a liar for a messenger. I suppose it would be an argument against the old adage: "Don't kill the messenger."

# 1 Samuel 28
## Saul and the Spirit Medium
## When God Refuses to Speak to the Anointed-Deposed

—⁓—

## Introduction

Life can be a barrage of questions at times. As pertains to our story, the whole thing is a question.[106] Saul's name, as a Hebrew passive participle itself, means "asked," "requested," or "questioned." As we draw textually toward the concluding chapters of 1 Samuel and eventually toward the concluding moments of the first and long-since delegitimized monarch's life, we see that the questions as well as the mysteries become more stark—more shrill. Saul will be driven to what I'm sure he felt were desperate measures and what we are more certain is insanity. What drives a man to desperate action? What drives one to defend himself, his family, his country? What is it that drives a person to use unconventional means to apprehend that rather conventional eventuality called the future? What is it about our mortality that makes us not merely open to the future but given to a morbid curiosity about it? Imagine if our Bibles had nothing of either a personal or general eschatology to them. How would you feel about the future? How would you feel about your assurance of salvation? Would you use your mind to machine means to the end of reasoning to or divining the future? Would you research as to how others have hit upon the future without that eventuality arriving first? If you can imagine any of this, you might have something of a window into the anxiety of Saul. In our text, the great question mark of 1 Samuel will now throw himself, with reckless self-abandonment—with perhaps a devil-may-care attitude—at the occultic. Why? That is on a "need to know" basis. The king needs to know. Let's follow him.

## Reading from "Saul: A Life Suspended in Doubt"

I really have no idea what Achish was doing though. It is as though he trusted the son of Jesse—a thing impossible for anybody who really knew him. Perhaps he hoped that the son of Jesse would provoke me to the point that I would attempt an incursion into Philistine-held territory and then he could trap me and my forces there in the low country. I really have no idea. It was only a matter of time before the five warlords would move again. Perhaps Achish was thinking of levying them to his forces to please the warlords by having a few more seasoned veterans in his conscripted standing soldiery. Who knows? (1 Samuel 27)

Samuel and Ahimelech were dead. The son of Jesse had been a fugitive for over five years. Recon indicated that the son of Jesse had even become a bodyguard to Achish. The king of Gath was a bigger fool than I'd thought! In any case, I was losing friends and associates; relatives distrusted me; advisors avoided me and there was nowhere to turn. The Philistines had amassed in huge numbers on Mt. Gilboa and in the Jezreel valley. I have no idea how they were able to put together such a huge army. Perhaps their caravan route and maritime trading contacts enabled them to raise mercenaries from elsewhere. Whatever, I had to know what to do. Although God had not spoken to me in quite some time, either directly or indirectly, I went through the accepted channels. The priesthood was unable to get the *urim* and *thummim* to generate any kind of coherent message by way of divination. We had several from the school of prophets as retainers to the court and they were all honest and confessed that they had absolutely no information about what to do in regard to the coming war. There were no dreams at all that could be interpreted favorably or otherwise. Nothing! In a move of utter desperation, I was able to ascertain that another of my efforts had proved to be a failure—the eradication of all the soothsayers. It just happened that there was one left that had gone into partial retirement right across the valley from where we were camped.

My naturally skeptical nature was the driving force out of which I removed all these spiritists. They were all a bunch of phonies and that was about to prove itself true. But a bizarre dynamic was working its way out in my normally skeptical habits—superstition! I just had to try one more thing. Another thing that bothered me was the fact that all these people were so dirty. Their penchant toward perversion made my skin crawl. Nevertheless, I was desperate and so I had to follow through. I disguised myself by changing into civilian clothes. I took along a couple of personal attendants in case things got awkward.

When we arrived, I found things not as I'd expected. I was expecting an old hag with a wart on her nose. What I found was something quite the opposite. I gave the monetary payment and promised confidentiality. I was ushered apart from my attendants into a secluded back room—why did these things always have to happen?! The act, it was alleged, was required in order to unify the emotions and will of the medium and the client. After these matters were concluded, she asked me who it was I wanted to talk to. I asked her to engage in necromancy and call up Samuel from the realm of the dead. What this woman really was was a prostitute! She had no natural or supernatural talent whatsoever. When she went through her hocus-pocus routine, what happened scared the beejeebers out of her as much as it did me. At that point she came to the revelation that I was in fact Saul. I asked her to describe what she saw as I kept my face buried in my hands. The description was convincing enough—but not nearly as convincing as when the apparition spoke. At that point I looked. Hoping that I would be addressing a friend, I once again realized that I was addressing my arch nemesis, Samuel. He looked kingly in this visage! I asked him what I should do. He assured me that if God was not revealing anything to me, I was nothing short of a fool to be asking anything of him. In not answering my questions, he did answer one thing though: he said, "Tomorrow you and your sons will be with me. Indeed the LORD will give over the army of Israel into the hands of the Philistines!" The finality of his words indicated to me that, in his opinion, there was nothing I could do about it: it was decreed, destiny, fate. . . . Never wanting to miss an opportunity to attack me, he told me that this was because I had not executed God's wrath against Amalek. God was going to tear the kingdom away from me and give it to the one I dreaded more than life itself: the son of Jesse.

I was in shock from fright. As Samuel vanished—was it only a dream?—I fell into a swoon. The woman and my attendants gathered around me and revived me. They finally persuaded me to eat something—the woman even made it smell good as she was preparing it. I ate, paid the lady a tip and then we went on our way back to the camp of Israel. Oddly, nobody even noticed we were gone. We had been gone the better part of six hours—and nobody, nobody had sought me out during that time—nobody even knew I was gone! In the hours before dawn, I did not sleep at all. I knew that something had happened. I suspected that I had had an encounter with the supernatural—with another dimension of reality; but, my natural tendency was denial—and so I attempted to rebuild my psyche for the coming battle. My people needed a king not a crazy, demonized (was that what they were whispering?) old fool to lead them into battle. (1 Samuel 28)

## Textual Observations[107]

### The Bedeviled King and the Dark Mistress:
### What Is This Witch-Medium *cum* Necromancer?

Saul was said to have removed all the mediums and spiritists—well, all but one.

What are mediums (*ha'oboth*) and spiritists (*hayyidd'oniym*)? "Necromancy" is not exactly romance with the dead although the parallels in obsession are intriguing. "-mancy" according to *Webster's Ninth Collegiate Dictionary*,[108] is "divination," as in *mantis*, a prophet or diviner. We modernize it by referring to the "mantic" arts. Anything *necros* is, of course, dead or relating to death, such as a "necropolis" or graveyard, "necrosis" or the death of tissue and so on. Hence, a witch who is a medium becomes a practitioner in the mantic arts for the channeling of the spirits of the deceased . . . supposedly. Remember, just because it happens here does not mean that it happens regularly—or truly happens at all. Trust me: the woman from en-Dor was more surprised by what happened than we are.

So then: necromancy is "conjuration of the spirits of the dead for purposes of magically revealing the future or influencing the course of events" or "magic, sorcery."[109] Finally, "Mediums . . . and spiritists . . . were individuals who claimed the ability to contact the dead, either serving as intermediaries through whom the dead would speak (cf. Isa. 8:19) or rousing the dead to speak for themselves."[110]

Torah says the following about mediums and spiritists: "Do not turn to mediums (ha'oboth) or spiritists (hayyidd'oniym); do not seek them out to be defiled by them. I am the LORD your God" (Lev. 19:31).

It is interesting that the notion of defilement, usually reserved for sexual misconduct, is mentioned here. Note the motive clause: "I am the LORD your God," not something else by which you would be likely misinformed but certainly defiled.

"As for the person who turns to mediums (ha'oboth) and to spiritists (hayyidd'oniym), to play the harlot after them, I will also set My face against that person and will cut him off from among his people. You shall consecrate yourselves therefore and be holy, for I am the LORD your God. And you shall keep My statutes and practice them; I am the LORD who sanctifies you" (Lev. 20: 6-8).

The repercussions are rather final and the motive clauses multiplied. How about some related ideas?

"There shall not be found among you anyone who makes his son or his daughter pass through the fire, one who uses divination, one who practices witchcraft, or one who interprets omens, or a sorcerer" (Deut. 18:10).

It is interesting also that this particular cluster of notions is found here: human sacrifice, divination, witchcraft, seers of, say, augury, etc., or sorcery and so on. But more as pertains to our story, look at what Samuel, himself, says to our giant question mark: "For rebellion is as the sin of divination, and insubordination is as iniquity and idolatry. Because you have rejected the word of the LORD, He has also rejected you from being king" (1 Sam. 15:23).

As we have seen, this is one of the key verses in the (rather long) turning point in the story of Saul's life. At least this aspect of the question mark becomes an exclamation point. Saul is going down; when and how unfold with the narrative.

Herein are a couple of principles: In narrative, the reminder of traps sprung, often foreshadows a trap that remains yet unsprung. Also, in life, when we leave traps un-sprung, we had best remember where they are or we will fall into them. If we decide to remove a particular kind of trap, we had better be certain that *all* that particular kind of trap is removed. There is also a corollary: There are such things as, for instance, truth traps; they are called lies. As pertains to the previous administration, the old saw was often rehearsed:

"If you always tell the truth, you never have to remember what you said." If you always tell the truth, you will never fall into a truth trap. Saul, if you really had gotten rid of all the mediums and spiritists, you would never have to worry about consultation fees.

## Samuel's Death *Redivivus*[111]

In case we had forgotten, we are reminded in verse 3 of the fact that Samuel had long since passed away. This point is brought to our attention, along with the review of Samuel's national mourning period in 25:1. Since you know the story, you also know that this intrusion into the narrative has a certain ominous feel to it. *It is the first part of the harbinger* of the final spiritual collapse of Saul.

## Mediums and Spiritists, Foreshadowing

As we have said above, Saul's failures include the removal of *all* these traps. "This note establishes Saul's clear understanding that it was forbidden for Israelites to consult these individuals, a fact necessary for understanding the severity and speed of the punishment meted out to him."[112] *It is the harbinger part "b."*

## Silence Is Hardly Golden

When Saul "asked" God about the future, the silence screamed the memorial of his failures.

His sleep was dreamless.

The *urim* was silent, since he had, himself, commissioned the decimation of the priesthood.

The true prophets were either dead (Samuel) or un-supportive. I see them as aloof lest their status approximate that of the priesthood. Being a religious person during the reign of a madman is risky business.

Merely ask yourself how it would be for you were the heavens as brass and there were no spiritual guidance. The answer is the silence of a leader alone.

## Which Witch Is Which?

She has been either in retirement or driven underground. She is suspicious and reminds the king-incognito what the king had done publicly. So she gets quite possibly the most incongruous oath she ever could have gotten: "By the life of YHWH, there will not occur for you a transgression in this matter" (28:10). If that doesn't turn God on Himself, nothing could! Hence, blasphemy is added to Saul's list of accomplishments. Ah, the new heights to which the king had fallen!

## What on Earth—or in the Netherworld—Happened Here?

Several possibilities present themselves in the history of interpretation:[113]

1.      an actual raising of Samuel by the wicked means of necromancy;
2.      a deception perpetrated by the necromancer;
3.      God causing either Samuel or a demon to appear;
4.      a demon acting apart from God to deceive Saul;
5.      a vision produced by hallucinatory drugs;
6.      a psychologically induced illusion; and
7.      a Satanic impersonation.

Whichever path we choose, our Omniscient Narrator seems to have Samuel speaking directly to Saul in this pericope. Whichever path we choose, the necromancer is more astonished than any of the other players on stage in the story and certainly more than we, the audience. Let me state this more strongly than has even Bergen:[114] it is my opinion that the level of communication between Saul and Samuel is indicative of past private conversations to which only the two of them, God, and the Omniscient Narrator, could possibly have been privy.

"Indeed, a straightforward reading of the biblical account suggests the possibility that mediums may possess the capacity to contact dead persons and establish lines of communication between the living and the dead. This view is not explicitly rejected elsewhere in Scripture; the Torah prohibits necromancy not because it is a hoax but because it promotes reliance on supernatural guidance from some source other than the Lord."[115]

Bergen balances this statement by saying: "Her strong reaction also suggests that Samuel's appearance was unexpected; perhaps this was the first time she had ever actually succeeded in contacting the dead."[116]

Perhaps a better view is that this was a unique event in history and that God brought Samuel up from the dead to put the final twist of the dagger in Saul's heart. Were I to know that within twenty-four hours I would be dead, I would probably get pretty hot on the trail of repentance. Perhaps this was God's design in either *allowing* such an unworldly event — such a netherworldly event — or *performing* it Himself.

## Suspicions Confirmed

The client is the king. She sees several things: the narrator quotes her as seeing first gods arising (plural) and then an old man arising (singular). Confirmation of such a nebulous sighting is easily accomplished. When Samuel speaks, and Saul answers in the same manner he would have were Samuel in the land of the living, all suspicions are confirmed. Saul and Samuel recognize each other and the woman knows that the king, who would otherwise have executed her, is her client. Old acquaintances are renewed as ironies abound.

## A Robe by any Other Name Should Bode Such Ill

Although there are other words for robes, the word used here for robe is the same as that of which was torn back in 15:27. Note the deferential posture of the king-to-be-doomed to the prophet-already-passed-on. Note also that Samuel uses the word "torn" in reference to the kingdom as he had done previously when Saul tore the prophet's robe.

## Don't Bother Me, I'm Dead! Or, Those Who Wake the Dead and Other Nuisances

Samuel does not answer directly to the king's satisfaction — indeed, did he ever really answer so? He merely rehashes what he has said before culminating in that eventuality we have long known that the kingdom will go to Saul's neighbor, David. The word "neighbor" or "friend" is chosen with care. Saul certainly never understood who his friends were.

## Where on Earth — or in the Netherworld — Is "Here"?

Now wait just one minute! Where is "here"? Samuel says that Saul and his sons would be with him wherever he was then. In the hall of shame of perdition, and right after Judas the veritable "son of perdition," himself, Saul often achieves dishonorable mention as one destined for hell in Arminian literature. Well then, where is Samuel? Is this the Greek idea of the Hades holding pen? Is this a window into the *Sheol* of Hebrew text and translator paranoia? Remember, when in doubt, transliterate! Why immerse when you can baptize? Why talk about the realm of the departed when you can talk about *Sheol*?

Be that as it may, here is certainly an enigma! It looks for all the world — or underworld, or netherworld — like the shade of the deceased Samuel is right there in the room with they who yet lived. We have a right to be confused. But we do not have a right to condemn Saul to hell; that is a right reserved for God alone. This might be a good lesson for us here now:

be dreadfully careful what you think about the eternal destiny of certain individuals—your thinking may be corrected at the Bema Seat of Christ with perhaps the commensurate withholding of rewards. Were we to condemn Saul to hell, we might justifiably question the salvation of Jonathan and Samuel. Saul and his sons were to be *with* Samuel on the morrow. There is another valuable textual lesson here: when there is considerable question as to verbal intentionality with respect to the events, be dreadfully careful of making dogmatic assertions with respect to—theology or to the spiritual conditions of those who speak and act in the text for that matter. We might be reminded at this point that, against all logic, some allies will become enemies—some of those enemies will be protected and that against all logic some allies will remain allies—some of those allies will not be protected.

## King Trumped

Commentaries seem overly careful to remind us of Saul's fasting on the eve of battle (1 Samuel 28:20). They seem to suggest that the reason Saul swooned was due to low blood-sugar. I have another suggestion: how is it for you when you have successfully conjured someone important and authoritative back from the dead who is just as surly in death as he was in life and who just prognosticated your death and that of your next of kin? I know little of such things—I have so much trouble with the past and present that I rarely meddle in the future—but my theory is that you or I would be rather undone by such knowledge of the future (as was Daniel, in chapter 10 verses 8-10). One little pet theory that I have nursed for the last three decades is that the reason the future is not open to us—perhaps rather along the analogy of the angelic/demonic realm—is that it would drive us mad. Maybe Saul has already gotten too much of a taste of both the demonic realm and the future. Those of us who have had an ominous sense of foreboding progressively eventualized, know that the process of watching it unfold is exhausting and, to say the least, unsettling. Believe in free will? Stop a train wreck. To know the future is, in some sense, to be shackled by it.

## More Rules of Engagement

Meanwhile, back at Samuel, David, and so forth. It is about as good a place as any for Jerry's three-point law on biographical narrative interpretation from the Old Testament.
Rule 1: Most of the characters of the Old Testament were schmucks. (That is a technical term drawn from Yiddish which, according to *Webster's Ninth Collegiate Dictionary*, means "jerk," definition number four. I shall risk the assumption that you know what a jerk is.)
Rule 2: God uses them anyway.
Rule 3: Along the way and from time to time they get a clue.
Illustrations are, of course, legion. Exceptions seem to be exhausted with Enoch. There is simply not enough text or holes we can punch in his character so as to dredge up the dirt

on him. Do you think Abraham was a great guy? Ask Pharaoh, Abimelech, and Sarah. Isaac? Ask Abimelech, Rebecca, Jacob, and Esau. Jacob? Ask Esau, Laban, and ten or eleven of Jacob's sons. Joseph? Ask his brothers who had to tolerate his flaunted favoritism, who had to listen to his repeated dreams, especially the second one that did not exactly come true, and who probably never really trusted him. Ask especially Simeon who had to cool off in the tank for a couple of months as collateral against Joseph helping God's program along. Ask all the others of Potiphar's household servants who would not go to bat for him. Ask his servant who had to lie for him to set up his ruse and so on.

The judges are a bit more transparent. Samson was such a paragon of virtue that I will forgo a close examination of his character. How about Jephthah? Ask his daughter. What about David? Ask Uriah. Ask Bathsheba's first son. Solomon? Ask all those officials and others he had executed.

What about kind Hezekiah? Sort of a crybaby I think—we will see when I get to my deathbed. What about Josiah? Certainly there was a paragon, right? Well, not bad; but, at the end of his life he has a "stupid attack" and he and his puppet kingdom declare war on one of the world superpowers of the day. He goes down looking like a pincushion. The list goes on. The point I am making should be obvious and hence to Jerry's three-point law on the *application* of biographical narrative interpretation from the Old Testament.

Rule 1: *I'm* a schmuck (you are entirely too agreeable).

Rule 2: God uses *me* anyway.

Rule 3: Along the way and from time to time *I* get a clue (pronouns are mere conventions).

## Textual Problems

## The Apparent Discrepancy Between 1 Samuel 28:6 and 1 Chronicles 10:14

Ronald J. Youngblood indicates that the collocation: "'Saul asked" *wayyish'al sha'ul beYHWH* thus provide[s] at the least an excellent pun on Saul's name = "requested."[117] The word in Chronicles is from *darash—welo' darash beYHWH*. Hence, it might be legitimate to question the depth of the inquiry. So despite the overlap in semantic field ("ask" being a more general world than "inquire"), commentators seem content to overlook the discrepancy. One thing we may state with absolute certainty is that there is no contradiction at the formal level—we would have to affirm and deny exactly the same words for that. We not only have dissimilar wording, we have nothing of the same syntax (*wayyiqtol + X* vs. *wX + qatal*). As a note respecting analytical philosophy, historical propositions don't contradict well in any case. Philosophers generally prefer to posit their propositions in the universal present tense.

Robert Bergen adds that, "The comment in 1 Chr 10:14 that Saul died because he 'did not inquire of the LORD' does not contradict this passage. Instead, it affirms the contention of 1 Sam 28 that Saul's final source of guidance was not Yahweh."[118] So there is no real textual problem.

If, however, Saul's life to this point is any indication, we might be suspicious as to the sincerity, the motivation, the real desire of his inquiry. Was this inquiry a normal part of his life? Was this last desperate measure an indication of the depths to which he had finally descended? Does he just want to know if he will die? Why is there no answer to the story's principal and now very mortal "question" — Saul, himself?

## Textual Applications and Anecdotes

1 Samuel 28
vs.
1.  Valiant men in strategic positions will be called upon to perform paradoxical tasks (David potentially waging war against the Israel he was anointed to rule).
2.  Good performance plus good answers equals good position (promotion).
3.  The strategic reminder of a momentous event is an ominous harbinger of the future.
    In narrative, the reminder of traps sprung, reminds us that an un-sprung trap yet remains.
4.  Bivouac on high ground.
5.  The "enemy" kindles blazing fear in the heart of the natural man.
6.  Isolation: The LORD's silence.
7.  The unnamed servant knows the unsprung trap.
8.  Forgetting his appointment with death, the demonized may manifest an obsession with death.
9.  In narrative, a tense moment builds drama, suspense.
    The traps know who they are and they have their suspicions as to who we are.
10. People living a lie are liars; liars lie about lies.
11. Obsession with death attempts to join death and life.
12. Imagine the charlatan's amazement when sleight-of-hand becomes sorcery — ruse becomes necromancy.
13. *Carpe diem!* Forget that what you are doing is against the law and as Martin Luther once said — probably in one of his rather tipsy "Table Talks" — "Sin Boldly."
14. See how far we have fallen: homage to the dead!
15. The question is only as absurd as the reason.
16. The prophet's answer belies the absurdity.

17.  You did not pay attention the last time I spoke to you in the name of the Lord, why ask me now?
18.  Sins, like old ghosts, may come back to haunt us.
19.  Lightning may never strike twice; but bad news always does and twice as hard.
20.  Impending failure, loss, and death leaves the natural man without strength.
21.  In the midst of a capital crime, deferential language before rulership is wise.
22.  Oh, how the mighty are fallen—usually with their last meals in them.
23.  Last meal? Eat!
24.  Royal last meal? Make it worth his or her while; you may yet save your own life.
25.  In narrative, a barrage of action verbs may betray the fact that much time passes.

**Conclusion**

(See the conclusion to chapter 29 below.)

# 1 Samuel 29
## David and Company Sent Packing

—m—

**Introduction**

(See the introductions to chapters 27 and 28 above.)

**Reading from "Saul: A Life Suspended in Doubt"**

A runner came to us with the news that several hundred riders had split off the main force at Apheq. It seemed that these were different from those of the main vanguard of the Philistine army. These raiders had turned back south and then there was the report that they had gone back into the low hill country in the southwest of Judah. We never heard any more about them. My suspicion was that either the Philistines had sent raiders to cause trouble from the rear, or the warlords had had enough of Achish's stupidity. The son of Jesse was always an X factor in a battle— if he had wanted to regain my favor, the warlords probably suspected that a quick shock attack on themselves and the elite officer corps of the Philistines was the best manner in which to do that. David would not be the X factor in this war.

As the Philistines moved up the main western road, we had trouble quickly deploying forces. It seemed that our entire military was marching in tar. We had less distance to cover than they did and yet we were unable to mount the obvious assault in the pass southeast of Megiddo. The best we could do was to skirt the ridge to the south of the Jezreel valley. When they formed up, they had amassed an unprecedented battle array. We had been outnumbered before and beaten them; but, not with these kinds of odds. It appeared that my worst suspicions were confirmed: they had managed to purchase Aegean mercenaries as archers. (1 Samuel 29)

**Textual Observations**[119]

**Those Troublesome Hebrews**

The last time the Philistines had relied upon Hebrew defectors (chapter 14:20-21), there had been trouble. Those Hebrew defectors double-defected back to Jonathan and his valiant, but nameless, armor bearer's side. Why would the warlords be willing to risk such nonsense again? It makes about as much sense as bringing several enemy officers—with cell phones—to the Pentagon and giving them a private, soundproof, and bug proof office.

## David and Satan, Round One

David is discussed by the warlords as a potential *satan* or an adversary. One would be raised up against him one day (1 Chron. 21:1; which is all you will get today of "Round Two"—by the way, translations that actually say "Satan" at that point are wrong. If it really means "Satan" it is the only place in Hebrew Bible where it is used as such without the definite article).

There is probably a valid principle here as well: no matter which side you are on and no matter which battle you are fighting, it is best to get rid of as many self-evident or possible X factors as you can ferret out. If you are an enemy of righteousness, you really don't want any Davids hanging around; they really tend to make a mess of things overtly, or in Achish's case, covertly. Conversely, if you are an enemy of evil, you want to expose as many Sauls and Philistines as possible, but timing and ability to extricate oneself strike a delicate balance.

## Heads of State and Other Artistic Decapitations

In what could only be indicative of the most *bald* imagery imaginable, the warlords remind Achish that David could do nothing greater to gain the favor of his former master than to turn over their heads in the same manner he had turned over Goliath's head. Achish and Goliath share the dubious fortune of both being Gittites (i.e., from Gath)! In narrative, you always want to read the fine print.

## The Final Chorus of the Song

The song goes as follows: "Saul has struck his thousands but David his ten thousands." It is first used in 1 Samuel 18:7 by the women who come out from the cities of Israel in the dance of celebration. It is remembered by the servants of Achish, King of Gath (1 Samuel 21:11) at which time David feigns insanity and escapes with more of his life than his dignity. Now here we have it immortalized by the warlords themselves.

## Of Kings and Warlords

One thing that may not be immediately clear is the relationship between the five lords of the Philistines and the kings. I have called them warlords—the *seranim*—following the idea of the tyrannical from the Aegean region and Greek mythology and history. We must remember that there was a warlord from each of the five cities of the Philistine pentapolis. That means a warlord from Gath as well as Achish the king. This may illustrate the principle that when war is engaged, it is best for the politicians to turn over diplomacy to the generals. That is, we do not wage war on the floor of Congress or the United Nations for that matter. It used to be said, "If they're talking, they're not shooting." Thanks to the wonderful invention of the United Nations, we can now talk and shoot at the same time. What blessings I've been able to share firsthand with the UN in sub-Saharan Africa.

## Homogenized Good and Evil

Achish says that he has found no "evil" (*ra'a*) in David, whereas the warlords had not found David "good" (*tobh*) in their eyes. This perpetuates, by way of litotes or meiosis,[120] a theme frequent throughout narrative Bible—the opposition of good and evil. Please notice that depending on who is talking, good and evil get all crossed up in the mix. You see, to us David is *good* in our eyes (until the next book); whereas to Achish, were he to know the truth, David would be found to be *evil*.

## Saul and Achish as Simultaneously Type and Foil

I can do no better than to defer to Bergen at the point:

Ironies abound in Achish's relationship with David. . . . Both [Achish and Saul] made David their personal bodyguard (cf. 22:14; 28:2); both were impressed with David, particularly his fighting abilities, yet both ended up removing him from the ranks of their armies; both were responsible for David's making his abode in southern Judah; and both badly misjudged David. Saul considered David his mortal enemy, yet he was in fact his most loyal subject; Achish considered David his most trusted subject, yet he was in fact his most dangerous enemy. Both kings also made inappropriate use of oaths taken in the Lord's name (cf. 14:39; 29:6). The parallels between Saul and Achish suggest that Saul was indeed a king "such as all the nations have" (cf. 8:5).[121]

## "My Lord the King" and Other Like-Precious Ambiguities

If David wanted to fight against the enemies of "my lord the king," who is he talking about? Could be those of Achish; could be those of Saul; could be those of God. When David says, "Then you shall see what your servant can do," what is he talking about? Is he predicting defeat for the Israelites and his siding with the Philistines; or is he predicting defeat for the Philistines and his defecting to the Israelites? It is a difficult call, but Achish reads it the first way and makes him his bodyguard for life. We wonder if it might not go the other way—Hebrew defections being what they have been. Thanks to the warlords, we can never know because he is sent home to wreck havoc on the Amelekites—again, a real sore spot in the relationship between the eternal exclamation point (God) and the transitory question mark (Saul).

### Deception for the Infidel—How Islamic!

David completes his ruse by completely bamboozling his Philistine sponsor. He is viewed as an angel of God. Oaths are taken by YHWH—from Philistine lips! How he escapes discovery can only be an act of a sovereign God defending and concealing His anointed. And so he rises early in the morning and returns in peace to the land of the Philistines—a mouse in a cheese factory. Ethics being what they are in the Old Testament, we see that a hazy line is drawn between truth and falsehood, between truth and the whole truth. Deception for an outlander is not even given a second thought. And yet truth and falsehood are serious issues, as are the truth and whole truth within the covenant community.

It seems to be more of an effect of Christianity that the truth and the whole truth apply to everyone whether inside the community or not. Too bad we often dance so carefully between truth, the whole truth, and deception even within the community. After all, with skeletons in our closets, truth is on a need-to-know basis, right? I wonder how many Sauls "need to know"?

### Textual Applications and Anecdotes

1 Samuel 29
vs.

1. Keep a safe distance between armies until the fateful moment.
2. Generals lead the war party; trouble follows.
3. The best defense may be the death of our argument.
4. A double agent certainly could make a mess of things.
5. The third round of a dirge is both a charm and a bore.
6. David's ruse proves that dead men tell no tales—the previous chapter notwithstanding.
7. In an impending battle it is best to comply with the wishes of the field marshals.
8. David's public statements may not always betray the whole truth of the matter.
9. A deception complete; oh, how satisfying!
10. Rest and then travel; it is the ancient way.

11.     One verse: Never confuse temporal distance, spatial distance, and narrative distance.

    ". . . and miles to go before we sleep."

## Conclusion

Desperation! Only obsessive-compulsive winners can understand the abyss of desperation into which Saul has plummeted. What would, on the eve of your departure, drive you to such desperation that you would engage in occultic practices to divine the future? When faced with a no-win situation, what do you do? Reprogram the *Kobiachi Maru*? Cut your losses and run? Obsessive-compulsive winners don't do that; they battle their way through to a spectacular and total loss. And not merely a great personal defeat, they engage the problem in such a way as to create total humiliation and misery for every person and institution they influence. What can we learn from the life of Saul as it winds down to its miserable demise? We can learn to get out of the way, accelerate the eventual calamity, save the women and children and so on. Times of institutional train wreck are times when supreme wisdom is required. The train wreck may occur right around the corner or over the hill. But there will be signs of its immanence: we can be certain that the engineer will see it before we do. He will begin to use some rather bizarre means to ascertain the eventuality of the wreck. If the destination is more important than the safety of the expedition, the notion of hitting the brakes will have completely escaped him. In the church and her para-organizations, the judicious application of biblical brakes should not be thought of as a last resort—or overlooked altogether.

Another thing that happens before the ship of state strikes the proverbial reef is that assets either become liabilities or disappear altogether. What do we do when we see the disappearance of assets in the church? Do we merely say, "Good riddance to bad rubbish"? Do we impugn their spirituality because "they were not really part of us"—not part of the old guard, "were not willing to preserve the unity at all cost"—they were factious in any case, "were not willing to persevere through trials"—the quitters. Remember, it is always easier to lampoon than to engage. What do we do when assets shift the balance and become liabilities? Are they merely argumentative, divisive, or implacable? Are they staging a coup? Are they trying to increase their own influence—to enhance their own agenda? Are they the spirit of the antichrist merely trying to bring the whole place down around our ears?

How we deal with these people, questions, and problems will in large manner be determined by the biblical wisdom and timing of our attitudes, words, and actions. Let it not be said of us that we did something in an unbiblical manner to help God along. Let us remember to speak the truth in love and recall that we must be shrewd as serpents and harmless as doves—as very bright and gifted lambs among the wolves. Remember, for you, your friends, your associates, toward the end, things get strange. Let us be the kind of people who turn the chaos and darkness of our institutions and our larger world into the order and light that our God would wish us to bring to it. And so it might bear repeating at this point: when the institution finally crashes to the ground, there will be some bizarre side effects. First, leadership, grasping at straws, will entertain bizarre methods to gain information and results. Second, against all logic, some allies will become enemies—some of those enemies will be protected. And third, also against all logic, some allies will remain allies—some of those allies will not be protected.

# 1 Samuel 30
## David and His Men Return to Disaster
## David Returns to God
## David Returns to Leadership

—ᴍ—

## Introduction

It has not been mentioned by name since it was given in 27:6, but Ziklag which "has belonged to the kings of Judah until this day" has ever been in the background. It is the place from which David stages his *razias* against the enemies of Judah. It is the place to which David returns after reporting in with Achish and after being decommissioned by the lords of the Philistines. It is the place to which David returns after this episode and from which he will launch his bid for the monarchy over all Israel beginning with Judah. It must, therefore, be reintroduced after so long an absence from the text. In verse 1 of this chapter, it is therefore triply re-introduced. We are told that he returned three days after leaving Achish in Jezreel to Ziklag. We are then told that, in the absence of David and his men, Ziklag had been raided by the Amalekites. This reminder of one of Saul's major failures on the eve of Saul's death is timely. It will not be added to the list of failures of the king-elect. Then we are assured of the details that Ziklag was overthrown and burned.

It does not seem that there was a great loss of life. Perhaps Ziklag was more of an open town and the capture and plunder of the city were easily effected by the raiders. After plundering anything they could move, livestock and other more portable precious commodities, they also gathered up all the people, the wives, the sons, and the daughters and herded everyone away to disappear in the wilderness. As they left town, it succumbed to the final denigration, it and anything of too little value or too heavy to carry off was burned.

We know that David will be victorious over this band of raiders. We must see what turns of events, what breaks, what bounces, go his way. We will also see him weather a few storms: the desire to kill him because of the anger of his men, the actual deployment of his forces, and the desire to withhold returned material to those who did not engage in the nocturnal raid. When he is victorious, they even call the returned goods, "David's plunder." From verse 6, where they wanted to kill him, until verse 20 where they want to reward him, we will see David again oscillate from pit to pinnacle in the estimation of his men. What jewels were dropped along the way?

**Reading from "Saul: A Life Suspended in Doubt"**

Last night, a runner had come with the news that Ziklag had been burned to the ground and that all the people and property that could be abducted and stolen had been taken away by a residual group of Amalekites. Deep down, I hoped that the son of Jesse had been stung deeply by that one. I imagine that this is a misplaced antipathy. I suppose that sorcerer would manage to survive even a setback like that. With such a charmed life, I suppose he would even manage to turn such an event to advantage. (1 Samuel 30)

**Textual Observations**

**On Wives and Sons and Daughters; When Someone Is Missing**

The text tells us, "and they took captive the women who were in it, from small to great they did not put a person to death and they led them away and they went on their way" (1 Samuel 30:2). In the fiery aftermath, we are told that "their wives and their sons and their daughters had been taken captive" (v. 3). We are told that the entire returning band cried until the emotional storm blew itself out. Then it is parenthetically noted for us that David's two wives are taken captive. However, the cause of the anticipated insurrection and stoning of David is what is the most intriguing. We are told that it was "because all the people were bitter in soul, each one concerning his sons and his daughters" (v. 6). Reading reticence teaches us to look for what is not there. Again, we must be careful because something that is not there—well, it is not there! To make an assertion from an argument from silence is bad enough; but, to make an assertion from a textual silence broaches on tomfoolery. However, we have been programmed since the beginning of this section to look for "wives and sons and daughters" in the text (vv. 2-3) and so when one does not appear, we should ask why. An argument from silence is only as strong as the set of expectations surrounding it. Carson says, "Scholars usually recognize that arguments from silence are weak; but they are stronger if a case can be made that in any particular context we might have expected further comment from the speaker or narrator. . . . various fallacies can attach themselves either to arguments from silence or to the construction of contexts used to give arguments from silence some force."[122]

What I am suggesting here and in the following scenes, is that there is some ground for surprise regarding the estimation of wives and daughters. Notice that "sons" will never fall from the groupings. My conclusion is that the men are mad at David for taking them on this abortive military campaign and upon returning home they are emotionally shocked to see the destruction of their homes, the pirating of their possessions, and the captivity of their families.

However, they are embittered against David due to the loss of their sons and daughters and not necessarily their wives. Why this omission? It is difficult to say; but, my theory is that it is either an oversight by the narrator—screaming at us the lower estimation in his eyes of women in monarchical times, or it might be genuinely lower estimation and importance of women in the minds of the men. It could be that we have a chorus of voices here—the narrator and the men in the story—that indicate to us that over the length and breadth of Israelite society, grown women were valued only for childbearing. Sons and daughters, on the other hand, represent future and posterity. Sons, of course, pass on the family name and could potentially take care of us when we get old. Daughters, if well cared for—read: "sheltered" or "cloistered"—might bring us a fine bride price. Wives, unless young, were probably already through some of their child-producing years. Wives, if young, would probably be raped and there would be all that to sort through. Calloused? Not much different from our society, no? The difference was that women tended to be a bit less vocal and active about the difficult relationships they got themselves into—or their fathers got them into.

After the twists and turns of finding the emaciated Egyptian slave, reviving him, and being guided to the camp of the Amalekites (remember, servants never miss in biblical narrative), we are told of what we knew would come to pass, that David engages in yet another successful campaign against outlanders. We are told that "David recovered all that the Amalekites had taken, and rescued his two wives. But nothing of theirs was missing, whether small or great, sons or daughters, spoil or anything that they had taken for themselves; David brought it all back" (vv. 18-19). Again the great omission: nothing was missing, small or great, sons or daughters, spoil or anything. Where are the wives? They are in the "nothing missing." They are in the "small or great" (as in verse 2). They are in the "anything," but they are not accorded the importance of "spoil," or "sons or daughters" for the reasons mentioned above. However, things will get a bit more tangled.

Remember those sons of Belial who always attached themselves to military units, governments, and societies? They reappear at this most inopportune moment and demand that David withhold possessions from the men who stayed behind from exhaustion (v. 10) and guarded the baggage (v. 24). The list of possessions to be withheld is instructive as well. They say, "We will not give them any of the spoil that we have recovered, except to every man his wife and his sons that they may lead them away and depart." Translations that use the word "children" (e.g., NASB) here, could quite possibly be doing us a disservice. The word is sons and may on occasion indicate female children as well; however, a bit more circumspection needs to apply than the political co-rectitude or the day. The text seems to be making a distinction based on the relative worth of various members of a society. Why then the omission of the daughters? These are "men of Belial" after all and they would want what was of value to them.

Sons of Belial are usually wanting and expecting immediate gratification. *Spoil* in terms of portable, precious commodities and livestock has intrinsic value: it can be eaten or sold for money which can be spent upon that which may be consumed. Sons were a part of the heritage of *bene-belial* as well. Perhaps they viewed it as something they themselves would fight for and decided against the risk. Perhaps they viewed sons enslaved as an insurrection looking for a family in which to happen. "Wives" is a quick fix: they were already part of someone else's family and perhaps had been ravished by the Amalekites. When taking additional wives into one's home, one must be selective and make absolutely certain that no more problems than necessary are coming along with them. Why would they, along with the spoil, refuse to return the daughters? It was a cheap source of servants, concubines, or wives. They would have gotten the pleasure out of the girls and perhaps the production (of sons) without having had to pay bride-price for them.

Regardless of whether or not this is merely another "oversight" by either the men or the narrator. It shows something about the times. Women were second-class citizens and were of value only to the degree that they brought pleasure and posterity to the men. The text also shows the potential of what might have been the case, if David had not made his declaration and had not "made it a statute and a custom for Israel to this day" (v. 25). That is, recovered daughters, along with other spoil, might have gone to the captor rather than the original owner. More later.

Since the aftermath of chapter 25 we have known of the fact of David's two or so wives. Because Michal was taken away by her father and given to somebody else (25:44), David returned the favor by taking a wife of the same name as the psychotic conspiracy theory-laden king, Ahinoam. Her name means something on the order of "my brother is pleasant." Whenever brothers are mentioned, there is trouble brewing. In this case it is in the harem. Be that as it may, she is accompanied in derivative wifehood by Abigail, who being "the joy of her father" now becomes part of the obliviously ignored residents of the future monarch's harem. She is part of what is referred to by David's men as "This is David's spoil." Okay, I wonder how they were treated by the Amalekites. They are reported to have had one son apiece—was that before or after their recent abduction by the Amalekite raiders? In view of what would transpire when Absalom raped David's concubines, I have an idea as to their place in the harem. They do not have much worth. Ahinoam's only voice is that of her son the rapacious fool, and firstborn of David, Amnon. At least Abigail gets a voice in chapter 25. She proves her wisdom by raising a son who keeps his head.

We are told in the story in 1 Samuel 30 parenthetically that, "David's two wives had been taken captive, Ahinoam the Jezreelitess and Abigail the wife of Nabal the Carmelite" (v. 5). We are later informed of their recovery after the raid on the drunken Amalekite revelry: "and David rescued his two wives." Again, it is a backgrounded comment and could be pluperfect "had rescued," stated as an afterthought. Just part of the repossessed spoil—how was it when they returned "home." We know that David thought more of the love of Jonathan—which he never really requited—than he did the love of women. He himself says, "I am distressed for you, my brother Jonathan. You have been very pleasant to me. Your love to me was more wonderful than the love of women" (2 Sam. 1:26). It was more wonderful to him than the love of the three he had known to that point, I suppose. Unfortunately, this tends to be the case with polygamists—at least those of whom I have heard. They tend to be more interested in their friends than their wives. Probably no mystery there. When they go to Hebron, the two will go with him: "So David went up there, and his two wives also, Ahinoam the Jezreelitess and Abigail the wife of Nabal the Carmelite" (2 Samuel. 2:2). In the course of the next seven Hebron years, there will be more added; but they will be listed first: Ahinoam, Abigail, Maacah, Haggith, Abital, and Eglah (2 Samuel 3:2-5). And when David moves to Jerusalem, these six will only be indicated as the back-reference of the additional nameless "concubines and wives from Jerusalem after he came from Hebron" (2 Samuel 5:13-16). In short, they get lost in the harem of the military and monarchical quests of David.

Abigail has an unfortunate epithet that follows her through life and in the text. After the intriguing events of 1 Samuel 25, wherein David threatens Nabal and the males of his household with mayhem, Nabal mysteriously leaves this life (stroke, heart attack, bad wine) and his wife becomes the latest acquisition of David, the future monarch of Israel. Nevertheless, Nabal does not leave the text and his testimony to folly lives on. Abigail is usually sanitized in our English Bibles by the words, "widow of Nabal." The word is really "wife." There is a perfectly good word for widow, if that is what they really had wanted to say: *'almanah*.[123] Although used throughout biblical literature, it is even used in the Samuel Narratives to describe the woman sent to David by Joab in a ruse to return Absalom to the capital (2 Samuel 14:5). Another is used, *'almenuth*, which means "widowhood."[124] It is used in 2 Samuel 20:3 to refer to the status of the ten concubines that Absalom had raped. "So they were shut up until the day of their death, living *as widows*" (NASB, emphasis added). And so we must ask ourselves, why, in the presence of two perfectly good words, does the writer prefer to refer to Abigail with the epithet, "the wife of Nabal the Carmelite"? It would be fine, if it were just here. We could use the simple narrative approach of reintroducing people who had been absent from the text for a while. But following Abigail through the text reveals something that the narrator does not want to keep hidden. "Abigail is the wife of Nabal the Carmelite" You will want to look at the references in 1 Samuel 27:3, where she is referred to as "the Carmelitess, the wife of Nabal:" our text, 1 Samuel 30:5, 2 Samuel 2:2, 2 Samuel 3:3 (other "Abigails" appear to be relatives [a sister?] to David, 2 Samuel 17:25, and 1 Chronicles 2:16-17). Only in 1 Chronicles 3:1 is she referred to as being merely "Abigail the Carmelitess." However, even here they have her son by a different name as well. In the Samuel Narratives he is called Chileab and the Chronicler has it as Daniel. These are hardly irreconcilable "contradictions": either the same boy went by two names—I know which of the two I would choose—or Chileab died and Abigail bore a second son by the name of Daniel. If this latter be the case, then it would paint Abigail in a different light from the rest—that is, like Bathsheba, Abigail would have been "comforted" after the death of her son and given another son to take his place. Because several of the wives only appear to bear a single child (only sons counted or named?), it would appear that like Bathsheba, Abigail had a more privileged station in the harem. I personally think it was just two names for the same boy because the rest of the Chronicler's list parallels the Samuel Narratives so closely for the other six wives and their sons.

What is it that the narrator is trying to keep in our minds and in our eyes? What with the repetition of the words "Abigail the wife of Nabal the Carmelite," we become anesthetized to their importance. The importance is that as Abigail has already informed us (1 Samuel 25:24-31), David would have sinned had he continued on without her intercession. David had mayhem in his heart and mind. His intention was to destroy every "male" of Nabal's household—one might presume that that included any children already borne by Abigail should there have been any. Be that as it may, intentionality was already locked in place and it literally scared Nabal to death. This is an odd way to acquire a wife—scare her former husband to death! The narrator wants to remind us of the notion that David gets wives on occasion by some rather unusual methods. Michal is acquired by killing a double portion of Philistines. Abigail is acquired by the convenient death of her husband. Others here and others there; but Bathsheba will be acquired by the treacherous betrayal of her husband and then put out of favor by that beauty contest winner, Abishag. Wow! What a womanizer! David is not the kind you want your daughter to date. Neither is he the kind that you would want to thwart in his quest for your daughter. Nabal? Abigail is ever called the "wife" of Nabal. Even though dead, he lives on, as perpetual testimony to a questionable and sour set of relationships, as a perpetual reminder of the tale of two fools.

## The Development of Spurious Case Law

When we read with New Testament eyes, we see that the law was added because of transgression (Galatians 3:19). Regardless of the New Testament understanding of Torah, we know that in our own days in the multiplied madness of juris-imprudence, case law seemingly expands exponentially annually. As in our day, ancient Israel was beset with "men of Belial" who would have us expand case law. Case law expands because statute law does not deal with all the variables. For those who would engineer a perfect society, omniscience is required to handle all the loopholes and peculiarities and infinite variations in the human condition as it pertains to society. Perhaps that is why Goethe, I believe it was, said approximately: the best government is that one which teaches its members to govern themselves. I can hear the exasperation in the voice of one who, upon studying the various forms of human government exhibited across the centuries and the cultures, throws up his hands at the likelihood of any of it working.

What we have is the formation of a "statute and a judgment" in the van of David. The ruffians amongst the pack return and act stingily toward those who guarded the baggage. David comes in and makes a pronouncement that the shares should be alike for those who bear the brunt of conflict as well as those who stay by the supplies. As I have noted in the section above, there was the potential that some of the men would not get back their daughters. Part of what makes Nathan's parable so electric to us is that the poor man really loved his "daughter," the ewe lamb (2 Samuel 12:3). Perhaps some of the baggage tenders really cared for their daughters the way I would for mine. However, for those more of the line we have grown accustomed to, it would seem that they would lose a valuable investment in terms of house help and potential bride price. And so when, after some conditional antecedents, David makes his pronouncement: "As his share is who goes down to the battle, so shall his share be who stays by the baggage; they shall share alike" (1 Samuel 30:24), we see that it becomes an item of case law. We are told that it becomes a *khoq* and a *mishpat*. Regardless of whether or not we reduce *mishpat* to the level of custom as is often done,[125] we do not have the freedom to do that with *khoq*. This word means statute. In effect, case law has become apodictic law before our eyes. We have seen the facts of the case (narrative history), we have witnessed the pronouncements (*mishpat*), and now we have it effectively codified "for Israel to this day" (v. 25).

Henceforth, this is the way things would be done. In a way, it makes sense: if your fellows are exhausted, you might waste more time trying to keep them alive as opposed to sticking to the business before you in battle. If they are there resting by the baggage, those opportunistic scavengers who inevitably follow the van, will feel less likely to misappropriate some of the goodies left in anticipation of their owners' safe return. If the baggage people are rewarded by leavings of the plunder, perhaps they will sense the incentive to keep a watchful eye on the belongings of their fellows on the one hand, and not to join the scavengers and misappropriate the belongings of their fellows, on the other.

## On Gifts Going to Hebron and Miscellaneous Other Places

One of the most important parting shots of the chapter is the last verse: "and to those who were in Hebron, and to all the places where David himself and his men were accustomed to go" (1 Samuel 30:31). That is, in the list of places where David sent gifts (vv. 27-31), Hebron is named last. That will be of significance when we come to 2 Samuel 2. Why? Because, it is to Hebron that the Lord will have him make his initial access to the public back in Israel. Recall that he will inquire twice, as he does repeatedly, and God will tell him to go up to Judah and then more specifically to Hebron. This city, then, will become the seat of his power when he is crowned king of Judah (2 Samuel 2:4). From here, David, will wage his half of the civil war against Abner mostly but also Ish-Bosheth. From here, David will wage his disinformation campaign in an effort to clear his name from any dirt that Saul and his ilk might have attached to it (2 Samuel 2:5-7; 3:13). From the safety of Hebron, David will negotiate with Abner for the transfer of the northern federation to David's reign (2 Samuel 3:20-21). To Hebron, the elders of Israel will come to anoint David king after the assassination of Ish-Bosheth. While in Hebron, David will expand his harem from two to six wives and a similar number of sons will be born to him (2 Samuel 3:3-5). And from Hebron, David will move to create the royal city of Jerusalem (2 Samuel 5:9, 13). Hebron and the seven-and-a-half years David spent there figure in a most important way in his life. It was reintroduction to the life of Israel. It was the first player in his bid for the monarchy. It was the seat of his power and his power struggle. It was the place of four more, most likely political marriages—certainly wife number three, Maacah, from Geshur was of that genre. It was the birthplace of six of his sons. It was the place from which the monarchy over all Israel would be resumed and solidified. Hebron was paramount in David's life.

## When There Is No One to Strengthen David's Hand in God

One of the more heartening notices in the text of 1 Samuel 30 is that "David strengthened himself in the LORD his God" (v. 6). One of the things we will observe as time and text go on is that David, though surrounded by people, is increasingly alone. These words are memorial that his friend Jonathan is no longer around. Jonathan is the one who came to Horesh and "strengthened his hand in God" (1 Samuel 23:16). The change of themes (intensive to reflexive) is not the only thing that indicates that David is alone. "The people spoke of stoning him, for all the people were embittered" (1 Samuel 30:6). Everyone has turned on David because the abortive mercenary adventure with the Philistines proved to be disastrous on the home front. David has no allies and must quickly think of something to do. He strengthens himself in the LORD his God and then immediately calls to the priest to divine what God would have him do. (Everything at this point is breakneck action. There are no backgrounded clauses—the text moves only forward.) A man of action will do something, even if it is wrong—and here David is dead-on right. God tells him to pursue and promises that he will overtake the Amalekite raiders.

With the exception of a minor dip in the story in respect to the emaciated Egyptian servant, the story will move through to the glorious conclusion of his men after the recovery of everything. The narrator tells us, "Now nothing of theirs was missing." And his men say, "This is David's spoil." This is a major coup for David. He has gone from being the guest of dishonor at his own stoning to being the guest of honor at the distribution of the spoils. This is excellent work in only a few days. Even though the text moves rapidly through fifteen verses, we must remember that David's neck is on the block for the entire period of time—several days—represented by those few verses. Here the fact that David is able to "strengthen himself in the LORD his God" is what not only allows him to live on, but it ensures that he will move on and finally arrive at victory.

## Textual Applications and Anecdotes

1 Samuel 30
vs.

1. Triple mention, triple reintroduction, triple problem: destruction, theft, and kidnapping.
2. Women, young and old, are the plunder of the warrior.
3. Return, recognition, and regret: they all accompany the abortive expedition.
4. Emotional shock leads to exhaustion.
5. Two wives—both gone! So it goes for the polygamist.
6. Sometimes what is missing from the text is indicative of what should have been mentioned.
   When raiders are embittered, heads may be lost.
   In the absence of a friend, the godly leader must encourage himself in the Lord his God.
7. Whether in pretense or in truth, dealing with the religious will give the threatened leader time.
8. The godly leader receives his marching orders directly from the Lord.
   The godly leader with a track record will be followed when he receives his marching orders.
9. Some follow all the way; some follow part way. Neither should be disparaged apart from examination.
10. Exhaustion is a good reason to follow no further; continuation jeopardizes the campaign.
11. Raiders leave a trail behind them. Sometimes that trail left behind can talk.
12. A resuscitated informant could become a loyal one.
13. Let the victim tell his story.
14. Dead men revived need not fear the truth.
15. A bargain may only include the preservation of life.
16. Raiders are indiscriminate in who they plunder; they are also sloppy about security.
17. Defeat and recapture might be necessary; but annihilation?
   The Lord's old grudge against the Amalekites in action: David wages war.
18. Victory brings recovery. Not much is said about David's wives in the narrative.
19. Victory brings recovery of the children.
20. Victory bring recovery of the livestock and accolades for the leader.
21. The victorious leader can afford pleasantries and kindness.
22. Wicked and worthless people are greedy and may use propriety as a smokescreen for it.
23. The wise and godly leader will acknowledge that the Lord has brought the victory.

24. To David, equitable distribution of restored possessions as well as newly acquired plunder is in order for both warriors and rear-guards.
25. An idea brought about by a momentous occasion—whether good or bad—can become both custom and law.
26. There is nothing wrong with sending a gift to old acquaintances and associates.
    A well-placed gift will pave the road ahead.
27. Gifts far and wide are not wasted.
28. Gifts here and there are not wasted.
29. Gifts to kinsmen and foreigners are not wasted.
30. Gifts to people we do not know well are not wasted.
31. Gifts to those closest to us are not wasted.
    Gifts to those who have borne the burden of our sojourn and troubles are never wasted.

## Conclusion

The darkest period of David's early life is now over. Recall that these are the "agnostic times" of David. Apart from the commemorative psalms, David does not use the name of God, neither is he referred to as having done so between 26:24 and 30:6. In the meantime, the Lord's name and title will be referred to by some rather unusual persons: Saul, King Achish the Philistine, and a resuscitated Samuel as well as the narrator's reference to their usage. David is out of his dark ages and will begin to move in military victory and in ascending the hill to political conquest. These are places where David looks particularly good. However, his treatment of women and his seesaw battle to control his men make him appear to oscillate between weakness and cruelty, between apathy and overreaction. Soon he will receive the report from the battle on Mt. Gilboa. In the meantime, we will be told how events really transpired by the Omniscient Narrator. David butchers Amalekites—yet another Amalekite is on his way from the battlefield to the grave.

# 1 Samuel 31
## The Battle on Mt. Gilboa
## The End of Saul's Life

—⁊⁊—

## Introduction

We have arrived at the battle of Mt. Gilboa. The armies of Israel will lose today. God will reset the stage for a new cast after Saul and three of his sons perish in the battle. Saul will battle through to a glorious and complete defeat. One wonders if it might have been different.

## Reading from "Saul: A Life Suspended in Doubt"

The battle today went badly. We could not even hold the high ground. We were out-manned and out-equipped. As though reading the handwriting on the wall, many men from the northern areas of Israel simply took positions on hills to watch the outcome. Warriors from Judah hardly answered the summons. My elite guard was cut down like harvest wheat. I never saw what became of Abner. He oversaw the whole fiasco from up the hill further. He was probably able to escape to the forest or the badlands strongholds. The attack came so quickly and from so many directions simultaneously that we never knew what hit us. I tried to run and was badly wounded by archery fire. Three of my sons died before my eyes. There will be no dynasty. My armor bearer would not finish me off and so I am still alive. Of all the things to do badly, I could not even deal the death stroke efficiently to myself. My armor bearer did a much better job of it with himself.

Suspended between two worlds, agonizing over my life, I wonder how it all came to be this way. Here on Mt. Gilboa, bleeding to death, suspended between the land of the living and the path of the departed, I reflect back over my rapidly ebbing life and wonder, how did it all come to be this way? Everything I tried to do ended up a reversal of failure. I got rid of the Amalekites, except their king—well, most of them. I removed all the mediums spiritists, necromancers, and sorcerers—well, except one. I got rid of those pesky Gibeonites—history—something about a treaty they had made with Joshua. We had the Philistines backed up to the sea and now they've divided the country in half. I tried to preserve the kingdom for Jonathan and today I have seen three of my sons—including Jonathan—die before me.

What happened?! It seems that my pride got in the way. Despite the best of intentions, I felt that once I had control, I had to maintain control using man's means to man's ends—all the resources at hand to maintain the dynasty. I know I don't have it to do over again, but if I did, I think I would not have taken so much into my own hands. I think I would have been a bit more careful about discriminating between the sacred and the mundane. I know that I would act more wisely. I know that there was an important place for Jonathan, Abner, and even perhaps David. I know that I should have paid closer attention to those religious leaders with integrity like Samuel and Ahimelech. I know that I would not have misunderstood when things changed and my understudy, David, was anointed king. Probably the best I could have done was to step quietly into retirement and hope that he would have dealt with me and mine graciously. Oh, the pain! I know that I would not have ended my life with so much regret and guilt. May God be gracious and merciful to me. Today my sons and I are to join Samuel—my last hope—and I am the last to die. (1 Samuel 31)

## Textual Observations

## Defeat and Defilement upon Mt. Gilboa

Robert Polzin has already made much of the issue of "Death and Pollution upon the High Places" with regard to this battle.[126] We must be reminded that there are two given accounts. Our Omniscient Narrator has given us this one where Saul ends his life effectively by suicide. However, and seemingly the next day, one Amalekite will run to David and tell how, as was the case with Abimelech of old (Judges 9:54), he finished off Saul (2 Samuel 1:10). This is the story told by the narrator, but in the words of the Amelekite. There is, therefore, no contradiction: the Amalekite is simply a lying opportunist. Since this messenger is a foreigner, David senses no restraint and commissions an executioner to terminate the life of the one who might have been merciful to Saul. This sets up a pattern that will be revisited in David's life. It also appears to be the only account that David knows about. The manner in which he relays the information to the assassins of Ish-Bosheth years later, indicates that he does not know exactly how it was that Saul met his fate. David says to the sons of Rimmon: "When one told me, saying, 'Behold, Saul is dead,' and thought he was bringing good news, I seized him and killed him in Ziklag, which was the reward I gave him for his news" (2 Samuel 4:10). David then "commanded the young men, and they killed them beside the pool in Hebron" (v. 12). But David leaves himself an out with respect to the actual events of Saul's death: "when one ["he," (pronoun implicit in the verb form) the Amalekite] declared to me." Does he ever really know how Saul died? Or is he suspicious that the story he has received is spurious? Has David received other reports? We cannot know. We can only know that this is the occasion for the killing of an Amalekite liar and two Benjamite assassins.

Back to the idea of death and defilement: "The root, *hll*, occurs in the Bible in two rather separate semantic fields: it may mean to *pierce* or *wound* and just as frequently may mean to *pollute*, *profane*, or *defile*. As we would expect the context of the first meaning is often military, that of the second mostly cultic."[127] As we might expect, the differences might be outweighed by the similarities. Here the environments are so greatly separated contextually as they are when comparing a battle scene with a text from Ezekiel. So let us follow the trail of verbs that have crossover military-cultic significance.

v. 1. "Now the Philistines fought *nilhamim* . . . and [the men of Israel] **fell slain** *halalim* on Mt. Gilboa."
v. 3. "And the battle was **severe** *wattikebbad* to Saul. "And the archers, men of the bow, found him and he was severely **wounded** *wayyahel* by the archers."
v. 4. "And Saul took a sword and he **fell** upon it."
v. 5. "And his armor bearers saw . . . and he **fell** . . . upon his sword."
v. 8. "And it came to pass on the next day and the Philistines came to strip **the slain** *hahalalim*. And they found Saul and three of his sons **fallen** upon Mt Gilboa."
v. 9. "And they **cut off** his head and stripped off his equipment and they sent it . . . for ***good news*** to the **house of their images** *'atsab* and the people."
v. 10. "And they placed his equipment in **the house of Ashtaroth** and they exposed his corpse upon the wall of Beth Shan."
v. 12. "And all the men of **valor** *hayil* arose and went all night *hallaylah* and they took the body of Saul and the bodies of his sons from the wall of Beth Shan. And they came to Jabesh and they **burned** them there."
v. 13. "And they took their **bones** *'atsm* and they **buried** them under the tamarisk in Jabesh. And they **fasted seven days**."

The battle on the heights of Gilboa has gone poorly: many have fallen (vv. 1, 4, 5, 8), the few have fallen, the mighty have fallen as will be immortalized in David's song in the next chapter. In the heights, there is to be sanctity and victory and yet there is falling from the heights and wounding, slaying and defilement (vv. 1, 3, 8). In addition, the words that sound similar, although etymologically unrelated, give their voice to those "slain" (*chalalim*): "fought against" (*nilchamim*) (v. 1), "valor" (*chayil*) and "the night" (*hallaylah*) (v. 12). The voice of futility mocks the monarchy of Saul in the comparison of images and bones (vv. 9, 13). The comparison of rituals, the burning of the victim (often, unfortunately at a high place by a green tree), and the disposal of the ashes outside the camp/city versus the burning of the corpses of Saul and his sons and the burial of their bones (by a tamarisk tree) along with fasting, is not lost on the reader either. The placement of the offerings, the artifacts of conquest in the house of the Philistine god, may also be compared with the burning, burial, and mourning rites with respect to Saul and his sons. And many are fallen: the men of Israel *fell* slain; Saul and his armor bearer *both fell* upon their swords slain; and Saul and all the major players of his house are found *fallen* by the Philistines, stripped, mutilated, desecrated, and exposed.

## The Death of Saul's Sons

The first reported dead in this engagement with the Philistines are the "men of Israel who fled from before the Philistines" (v. 1). It is the many who fall first; but that is followed by the few. "And the Philistines overtook Saul and his sons; and the Philistines killed Jonathan and Abinadab and Malchi-Shua the sons of Saul." So, the crown prince, the heir apparent, has been killed along with others who might potentially survive to the monarchy. The table is nearly set for David's feast. There will be only one more fly to swat and that will be the protracted and somewhat tedious and delicate process of dealing with Ish-Bosheth and Abner. But what of Saul? He is left alive briefly by our narrator.

## The Death of King Saul: How the Mighty Are Fallen!

The words "How the mighty are fallen!" are from David's song of memorial in 2 Samuel 1:25. It is somewhat of an opaque phrase, as we shall see, because of how little the song really says about Saul, himself. In any case, the detail of how Saul leaves this worldly existence is given by our Omniscient Narrator. Saul was wounded by the archers and apparently realized that his flight was not a viability. So he asked his armor bearer to finish him off. Interesting position taken by Saul's armor bearers! David had held that office at one time and he refused to raise his hand against the Lord's anointed (1 Sam. 24:6, 10, 12; 26:11, 23). This armor bearer also refuses to dispatch Saul. Saul must serve the full sentence—no easy exit! Saul then commits suicide by falling on his sword. Rather than have to answer to anybody, as would the Amalekite messenger in the next chapter, the armor bearer follows suit and kills himself in the same manner as his sovereign. We have the concluding summary notice: "Thus Saul died with his three sons, his armor bearer, and all his men on that day together" (1 Sam. 31:6). But what of this account?

That this does not seem to be a story known by David is indicated by how he handles the assassins of Ish-Bosheth later on (2 Sam. 4:9-12). He seems to only admit to knowing the story as told by the Amalekite emissary (2 Sam. 1:2-16). The ramifications are intriguing: if David found out the story of 1 Samuel 31, he also found out that he had killed a man for being a liar and not a murderer. As in the case of the *Arabian Nights*, when the Sworder (captain of the bodyguard) of the Caliph is commanded to execute someone who is not guilty and later proved to be innocent, the Caliph merely says words to the effect that, "The truth of the matter could not have been known at the time," and everybody gets free of their guilt. David would not have cared either way, because he still had his bloodlust for the Amalekites (2 Sam. 1:1). Executing an assassin carries greater weight than executing a liar. Regardless, there were rules of due process—even for aliens and sojourners (Ex. 22:21; 23:9; Lev. 19:33-34; Deut. 1:16-17; esp. Deut. 24:17 and 27:19). The end of David's life indicates that he was more interested in control than justice.

## Disgrace and Honor: The Aftermath of the Battle of Mt. Gilboa

God has said, "Those who honor me, I will honor, and those who despise Me will be lightly esteemed" (1 Samuel 2:30). The two words for honor are from the *kbd* word group; despise is from *bzh* and lightly esteemed is from *qll*—frequently translated, "curse." Honor being what it is in biblical literature, the double meaning of *kabad* plays well here. Saul did not honor God in all that he did or in his several major failures and so he winds up having the battle go severely, heavily *kabad* against him (*wattikbad hammilhamah*). This serves as a reminder to the reader that he or she must honor God; but also, it serves to remind us that the monarchy of Saul was early doomed. This is not the only time Israel has lost a war. There was a great slaughter among the people as indicated by the narrator in 1 Samuel 4 and reported by the refugee from Benjamin in chapter 5. However, God proving both that He cannot be put in a box (or "ark," as the case may be) and that he needs nothing of the armies of Israel (allowing thirty thousand of them to fall in battle), takes His toll on the north and eastern cities of the Philistine pentapolis. It is said, "Now the hand of the LORD was heavy on the Ashdodites (1 Sam. 5:6). The syntactical arrangement of the words being identical: Preterite verb (identical), subject, preposition *'el*, and object. When one does not treat God in the manner of His choosing, He chooses to have things go with severity against them.

To rehash the ugly details: on the next day, Saul and his sons are found. They are stripped of their armor. Saul is decapitated and his head and other artifacts are sent to the land of the Philistines for display in the temple as museum pieces. Oddly, they put these national treasures in the temple of Ashtaroth instead of Dagon. Perhaps they remembered a time when Dagon did not fare so well when his temple was used as the antiquary for the public display of Israelite artifacts (1 Samuel 5:1-6). Meanwhile, back in the north, Saul and his sons have their corpses dishonored further by being displayed upon the wall of Beth-Shan. The trans-Jordanian peoples hear about this and revive that old relationship from the occasion when Saul bailed them out against their Ammonite assailants (1 Samuel 11:1-13). The men of Jabesh-Gilead come across and retrieve the remains of the deposed and decapitated monarch along with the corpses of his three sons. They burn the bodies and in ceremony bury them and mourn and fast for seven days. That ends the monarchy of the Saulides, yes? Well, not yet. There is still Ish-Bosheth and like a leaky balloon, Abner, the general, is going to attempt to blow a little life into the Saulide dynasty—until such a position is no longer tenable.

## Textual Applications and Anecdotes

1 Samuel 31
vs.
1.  When God is not in the war along with His people, they lose.
    When God's people lose, they tend to lose ugly.
    When God's people lose, they cannot even hold the high ground.
2.  Bad leadership of any kind tends to bring down anybody in the vicinity—even family.
    Bad leadership tends to bring down anybody in the vicinity—even before they fall themselves.
3.  The fall of bad leadership: a protracted, tedious discussion of the details of the inevitable.
4.  Poor choice for a lieutenant: one who allows us to bring it all, all the way down.
5.  Poor choice for a lieutenant: one who is just as self-destructive as the leader, himself.
6.  A bad day in the life of the leader: when it all ends together.
    A glorious ruin: we all participate together!
7.  When leadership is bad, unrelated institutions may even falter.
8.  When leadership is fallen, parasites and scavengers abound and flourish.
9.  Parasites and scavengers do not have a lot of class or scruples.
    Parasites and scavengers care nothing for what would have been appropriate to the fallen.
10. Parasites and scavengers tend to serve other gods.
11. Even in the demise of the fallen, there may yet be an act of friendship.
12. Even in the demise of the fallen, there may yet be acts of propriety and decorum.
13. Even in the demise of the fallen, there may yet be hope for a point of final equilibrium (2 Sam. 21:11-14).

## Conclusion

Thus we have the end of Saul and very nearly all the Saulides. Our Omniscient Narrator has given us a window into events that perhaps even David will never know. It is doubtful that anybody was around to hear the conversation between Saul and his armor bearer at the least. The rest of the Samuel Narratives will include notices from time to time about how the family of Saul will fare after his demise. Ish-Bosheth will be assassinated by two of Saul's captains (2 Samuel 4:6-7). Because of a domestic dispute regarding proper regal decorum, Michal (who really ought to know—or to know better—after all, her father was a king) dies the death of women in Israel: childless oblivion (2 Samuel 6:16-23). Mephi-Bosheth, because of the agreement between David and Jonathan will be treated in a royal fashion (2 Samuel 9:6-8, 13), but does not have a life in the text beyond this notice in 2 Sam. 6:13—perhaps his line ends as well. Saul's concubine, Rizpah, will be bereft of her two sons in the Gibeonite purge. Saul's daughter Merab and her husband Adriel, the son of Barzillai, will lose relinquish their five sons to the same purge.

But David is now in position—almost—to receive the kingdom as was indicated in the prophetic anointing by Samuel. We shall see what adventures unfold with respect to the biblical hero, David, in the coming chapters of the Samuel Narratives. David is in position to take his first step toward the throne: he will first demonstrate that he was not complicit in the fall of Saul. He will, in my opinion, genuinely mourn his friend Jonathan—although all friends are not equal. He will then make ovations toward Judah and be advanced by them. After a series of intriguing twists and turns, David will find himself the king of the land as anointed by Samuel and predicted by the Philistines (1 Samuel 21:11).

# Appendix

# The Longer Introduction to "The Darker Side of Samuel, Saul and David."

—⚏—

## A.    How to Proceed

The following study proposes to be expositional in nature, yes; but it intends to be something more of a literary study. We will be looking for plot and character development, foreshadowing, repetition, props and setting, nuancing, etc. We will observe what is said as compared and sometimes contrasted with what is done. We will observe what is said and done from the standpoint of the speaker or performer. Is it the narrator? Is it one of the characters? Is it God who says and/or does things? Following Shimon Bar-Efrat, we will examine compositional strategy by observing parallels at the verbal level, the level of narrative technique, the narrative world, and conceptual content.[128] Finally, recourse will be made to the matters of clause analysis at the micro level and text-linguistics at the more macro level.

The Joseph story (Genesis 37–50) has long been a point of interest to expositors of Scripture as have the books of Samuel. New discoveries from the times of the patriarchs has excited the mind of the orientalist as have those discoveries from Iron Age 1 and 2. Such a high art form has inspired the literarily oriented; and for the devotionally minded, such applications to character and wisdom are here as have accrued to the benefit of mankind for millennia. As one might expect, the volume and variety of the literature on such an intriguing portion of the Bible is incredible. With respect to Joseph, one may quickly ascertain this by examining, for instance, the bibliographies of Hans-Christoph Schmitt, George W. Coats, Claus Westermann, and Donald B. Redford.[129] With respect to Samuel, one need only peruse the notes and/or bibliography of Robert D. Bergen, Robert Polzin, Walter Bruggemann, and Ronald F. Youngblood.[130]

But, as one begins the task of sorting through what others have written on these texts, one quickly becomes convinced that each writer only sees that to which his or her presuppositions and method are oriented. As well, each writer has his or her own particular foci and interests and so may fall prey to problems created by selective interpretation resulting from selective observation of the researchers' accumulated data. The present treatment makes no claim to objectivity in evaluation of the textual data any more than those exegetes who have gone before.[131] What is sought is to attempt to judiciously synthesize three textual approaches to the material at hand and offer a description, analysis, and application from these approaches.

The purpose of this discussion is to discuss the methodologies of three modern approaches to the Samuel Narratives. These methods include recent applications of narrative interpretation, modern text-linguistic theory, and modern compositional analysis. The first of these categories will be represented by a work on narrative art regarding Scripture. The second category is an approach based on text-linguistic and communication theory. The third category has been variously classified as redaction criticism and/or compositional analysis. In the present study, the approaches to the text listed above will be analyzed with a view to their internal consistency as well as the advantages and disadvantages of each approach.

## In Defense of the Approach

The question might be asked at the outset as to why this type of project has been chosen as over against an exegesis or an evaluation of some other types of methodologies. First, although other methods are working with a textual datum, they do not necessarily work with textual categories as their primary focus. Secondly, although form critical methodologies seem to be gaining ground in popularity lately,[132] it will be argued below that these are not necessarily textual in their initial orientation.[133] It is the goal of this discussion, above all, to develop and describe an omnibus textual approach.

Also, though it is within the writer's capability to do an exegesis of the Joseph Narrative or the Samuel Narratives, exegesis is not part of his more recent training. Much of the last two decades has been spent in language acquisition, linguistics, comparative literature, and hermeneutics. Therefore, it seems much more logical to use this recent learning to attempt to advance scholarship in the direction of method. That exegesis must be done along the way should be self-evident.

The third and final area of research that this discussion proposes to handle is that of composition criticism or compositional analysis. This is a method that seeks to establish meaningful, authorial relationships within recognizable units of texts. Such materials are analyzed to discover the overall intent of the author in arranging and shaping the final form of the text. Often, critical applications of this method are called redaction criticism. However, there is a fundamental difference between redaction criticism and compositional analysis.[134] Georg Fohrer notes how compositional analysis differs from redaction criticism. The former is concerned with exploring the "art and manner" of the connection (*Zusammenfügung*) of various passages. The latter seeks to explain "the extent and art and manner" of editorial revisions (*der redaktionellen Bearbeitung*). The focus of compositional analysis is, therefore, synchronic. It emphasizes the way an author's work is organized into a unified whole. The focus of redaction criticism, then, is diachronic. It emphasizes the changes various editors have made in the process of combining materials into larger units.[135] Let's look at these in some greater detail.

## 1.    Narrative Interpretation

What is narrative interpretation? What are narrative art, poetics, and so on? Let us be led briefly through the maze by Robert Alter.[136] As we peruse and digest his chapters, we will be given a rather exhaustive yet unsystematic view of the field. This should not trouble us much: it seems that the Bible was not given to us in much of what we Westerners would liken to a system.

## a.    Biblical Type-Type Scenes and the Uses of Convention

After two chapters of introductory matters wherein the author head-butts his way into the literature by minimizing the effects of critical scholarship, all the while denying any reality to the narratives themselves, Robert Alter then begins to tip his hand with respect to his categories. Chapter 3 is entitled "Biblical Type-Scenes and the Uses of Convention." Alter believes that for coherent reading, some detailed understanding of the accepted interconnected conventions of the day are required. Sometimes they are codified; sometimes they are not. "Through our awareness of convention we can recognize significant or simply pleasing patterns of repetition, symmetry, contrast; we can discriminate between the verisimilar and the fabulous, pick up directional clues in a narrative work, see what is innovative and what is deliberately traditional at each nexus of the artistic creation."[137]

For classically trained scholars, Alter indicates that the closest thing we usually have to anything approximating literature or poetics is form criticism. Unfortunately, that has taken a rather negative in the literature. Alter then describes the difficulty in establishing conventions within such a small corpus of literature as that of biblical literature. Without a dozen or so illustrations of a "convention" it becomes difficult to establish the fact. He notes repeated stories with different protagonists and antagonists that often result in different explanations. If stories go different directions, can they be said to be the same story as criticism would have it? Or can they be shown to be conventional as narrative interpretations would have it? From a paucity of data come a paucity of applications. One of the more striking conventions is thus repetition. Alter then lists the repeated biblical type-scenes that he has been able to identify: "The annunciation . . . of the birth of the hero to his barren mother; the encounter with the future betrothed at a well; the epiphany in the field; the initiatory trial; danger in the desert and the discovery of a well or other source of sustenance; the testament of the dying hero.[138]

Alter then details the betrothal scene:

The betrothal type-scene, then, must take place with the future bridegroom, or his surrogate, having journeyed to a foreign land. There he encounters a girl—the term *"na'arah"* invariably occurs unless the maiden is identified as so-and-so's daughter—or girls at a well. Someone, either the man or the girl, then draws water from the well; afterward, the girl or girls rush to bring home the news of the stranger's arrival (the verbs "hurry" and "run" are given recurrent emphasis at this junction of the type-scene); finally a betrothal is concluded between the stranger and the girl, in the majority of instances, only after he has been invited to a meal.[139]

As pertains to our literature, it would appear that this particular type-scene has been aborted in 1 Samuel 9.

Having set out with this servant in search of his lost asses, he decides to consult the local seer, who turns out to be Samuel, the man who will anoint him king. "They were ascending the mountain slope when they met some maidens [*ne'arot*] going out to draw water, and they said, 'Is there a seer here?'" What we have in this verse, I would suggest, is the makings of a betrothal scene: a hero at the outset of his career in a foreign region (Saul has wandered out of his own tribal territory) meeting girls who have come to draw water from a well. As an audience familiar with the convention, we might properly expect that he will draw water for the girls, that they will then run home with the news of the stranger's arrival, and so forth. Instead, this is what ensues: "They answered them saying, 'There is. Straight ahead of you. Hurry [*maher*] now, for he has come to town today, for today the people is [*sic.*] offering a sacrifice on the ritual platform.'" The type-scene has been aborted. The hero swings away from the girls at the well to hurry after the man of God who will launch him on his destiny of disaster. This is probably a deliberate strategy of foreshadowing. The sense of completion implicit in the betrothal of the hero is withheld from this protagonist; the deflection of the anticipated type-scene somehow isolates Saul, sounds a faintly ominous note that begins to prepare us for the story of the king who loses his kingship, who will not be a conduit for the future rulers of Israel, and who ends skewered on his own sword.[140]

In my opinion, it could be a variation of the woman-at-the-well theme so often seen in Scripture. There are a couple of universals: where there is a woman and a well, there is water and information that drives the story forward. Regardless, Alter's point is well taken: from the outset there is something wrong with Saul and we will find it everywhere. It could also be a case of the unnamed servant (*na'aroth*'s other definition) having omniscience. In Hebrew narrative, the unnamed player, especially servants, never get the wrong answer, their information is usually heeded and productive when so followed. Their information also blasts the narrative forward.

This abrogation of the betrothal motif may also be pertinent with respect to David. It seems that with respect to three of his wives the woman-at-the-well theme is replaced with one of ascending questionable violence. Altar again:

> Finally, the total suppression of a type-scene may be a deliberate ploy of characterization and thematic argument. The case of David, who has rather complicated relations with at least three of his wives, may be an ambiguous one, for perhaps the author, working closely with observed historical data about David, did not feel free to impose the stylization of a betrothal type-scene when he knew the circumstances of David's marriages to have been otherwise . . . the two hundred Philistines he slaughters in battle as the bride-price for Michal; his threat to kill Nabal, Abigail's husband, who then conveniently dies of shock; and his murder of the innocent Uriah after having committed adultery with Bathsheba. Are the betrothals by violence a deliberate counterpoint of the pastoral motif of betrothal after the drawing of water?[141]

If any of this may be ascertained regarding the biblical hero David, we might seriously question whether or not the authors of First and Second Samuel really intend to paint David in all that positive of a light. Like Saul before him and Solomon after him, the narrator has the protagonist undone by women and the quest for power. We may perhaps be justified in asking the question, "Has the narrator come to praise David or—like his predecessors and progeny—to bury him?"[142] Unlike the others, though, there are the narrator's comments about him being the man after God's own heart. As we proceed we may explore the relationship between the two images presented in Samuel.

## b.      Between Narration and Dialogue

One of the characteristics developed by Bar-Efrat, below, is the relationship between narration and dialogue. This, then, becomes the subject of Alter's chapter 4. After first distinguishing between a report and a narrative event in which things slow down enough to get some perspective on the words and events intended, Alter then illustrates the relationship between narration and dialogue. This will have a life beyond these pages when we get to text-linguistics and the relationship between narrative and discourse, so stay with me. Alter illustrates this with recourse to 1 Samuel 21:2-11. Astonishingly, the lion's share of the story is told by dialogue. This has the simultaneous effect of slowing the events down to a near standstill while blasting us with huge quantities of informational content—of various levels of opacity. Verses 2, 7-8 and 11 are narrative—verse 2 and 11 may even be mere report.

"The episode is framed by an introductory half-verse that tersely reports David's flight to Nob and Ahimelech's reception of him, and by a brief concluding verse that tells how David, now armed and provisioned, continues his flight to the Philistine city of Gath. The ancient Hebrew audience would have immediately recognized this last verse as the end of the episode because it invokes the formula of rising up and going off to a different place which is one of the prevalent biblical conventions for marking the end of a narrative segment."[143]

Meanwhile, the largest number of verses and quantity of material are handled by dialogue. This has the effect of minimizing the importance of the narrative and even making it nearly redundant.

> It should be noted that the first of these two verses [7 & 8] repeats almost verbatim Ahimelech's statement in verse 5 about the absence in the sanctuary of any bread except the consecrated loaves. . . . In any case, verse 7 illustrates a general trait of biblical narrative: the primacy of dialogue is so pronounced that many pieces of third-person narration prove on inspection to be dialogue-bound, verbally mirroring elements of dialogue which precede them or which they introduce. Narration is thus often relegated to the role of confirming assertions made in dialogue.[144]

And so we might be led to infer that biblical writers were more concerned with the responses given by the biblical characters than to the actions and events themselves. One might additionally infer from this that this is all a part of the message: the writer wants the reader/hearer to emulate or conversely take warning from the actors on the stage of biblical narrative. That is, we are to learn from what is said and done by the characters as well as from the consequences of their actions, God's responses, and the narrator's comments. There may be instances where the reverse is true. That is, there is more art put into the narrative than into the dialog and hence the dialog appears to merely reinforce the narrative—redundantly.

We are also reminded to be wary of word-play: For instance, *d'g* for Do'eg the Edomite means "worry." These little details add much to the joy of reading the story. They also portend the ominous with respect to the folks at Nob.[145]

There is an apparent issue with respect to direct and indirect speech. It would appear that direct speech as opposed to reported speech is a stronger vehicle through which to convey the thoughts and intentions of the characters. "The rule of thumb is that when speech is involved in a narrative event, it is presented as direct speech."[146] This even extends to the realm of thought: "The biblical preference for direct discourse is so pronounced that thought is almost invariably rendered as actual speech, that is, as quoted monologue . . . when an actual process of contemplating specific possibilities, sorting out feelings, weighing alternatives, making resolutions, is a moment in the narrative event, it is reported as direct discourse."[147]

We are then led to the question as to why dialog is more important than narration. It is my opinion that it is not; but the question is intriguing in any case. Let's follow Alter's trail:

> The answer, I think, must be sought in what I have called the bias of stylization in the Bible's narration-through-dialogue. The mechanical agency of consulting the oracle is in the eyes of the writer a trivial matter and not worthy of narrative representation. What is important to him is human will confronted with alternatives which it may choose on its own or submit to divine determination . . . political or historical alternatives, question and response, creaturely uncertainty over against the Creator's intermittently revealed design, because in the biblical view words underlie reality. With words God called the world into being; the capacity for using language from the start set man apart from the other creatures; in words each person reveals his distinctive nature, his willingness to enter into biding compacts with men and God, his ability to control others, to deceive them, to feel for them, and to respond to them. Spoken language is the substratum of everything human and divine that transpires in the Bible, and the Hebrew tendency to transpose what is preverbal or nonverbal into speech is finally a technique for getting at the essence of things, for obtruding their substratum.[148]

There is a certain truth to this, of course; but, I would also compare it to a "figure-ground error." That is, how the characters respond to words, acts, and situations is important—at the least interesting; but, what the narrator says is "true," perfect, and beyond question. If there is a narrator comment ("for this reason shall a man leave his father and mother") it is accorded the status of law. Whereas if a player says something ("I will not harm you, my son, David.") the actors may or may not believe it; but we the readers are placed in so exalted a position by the Omniscient Narrator as to know well the truth or falsity of such a statement.

To get back to what the chapter is all about, Alter is trying to walk a tightrope between formal stylization and dramatic memesis. That is, what is the set of expectations with respect to the stylized forms as over against the unexpected, the surprising drama of the story. Another way of contrast is that of differentiating character in dialogue. We can tell something about the portrayal (at the least) of the character by the length of his or her oratory. Joseph speaks much longer than does Mrs. Potiphar. David's soliloquy stands in stark contrast to the question of Saul and the few syllables of response to it. Tamar says much; Amnon acts much. Hushai's counsel is three and a half times as long as that of Ahithophel and oh so much more colorful than that of Ahithophel's few jussive verbs. There is what could be an important side note given by Alter at this point: "In biblical narrative it is almost always the characters, not the narrator, who introduce figurative language. . . ."[149]

This leads us to a few rules about dialogue in narrative. First: "In any given narrative event, and especially, at the beginning of any new story, the point at which dialogue first emerges will be worthy of special attention, and in most instances, the initial words spoken by a personage will be revelatory, perhaps more in manner than in matter, constituting an important moment in the exposition of character."[150]

Secondly, we might observe that "in a narrative tradition where dialogue is preponderant, it may often prove instructive to ask why the writer has decided to use narration instead of dialogue for a particular block of material or even for a particular brief moment in a scene."[151]

Now, switching to the other side of the equation, Alter discusses three general functions served by the narration. These are: "the conveying of actions essential to the unfolding of the plot . . . the communication of data ancillary to the plot . . . (expository in nature) . . . the verbatim mirroring, confirming, subverting, or focusing in narration of statements made in direct discourse by the characters"[152] Often the story is propelled forward by verbs in the historical tense. "Verbs tend to dominate this biblical narration of the essential, and at intervals we encounter sudden dense concentrations or unbroken chains of verbs, usually attached to a single subject, which indicate some particular intensity, rapidity, or single-minded purposefulness of activity."[153]

## c. The Techniques of Repetition

Chapter 5 of Alter deals with "The Techniques of Repetition." Why is biblical narrative so repetitious? Alter makes several hesitating suggestions as to the why, such as the people's primitive nature or an inherently pleasing esthetic to the oriental.[154] He dismisses reasoning from classical criticism: "The last of these three explanations is the least interesting and finally accounts for the smallest number of cases. There are occasional verses repeated out of scribal error, but under scrutiny most instances of repetition prove to be quite purposeful, and this would include the repetition not only of relatively brief statements but . . . of whole episodes presumably compiled from parallel traditions."[155]

The argument that proposes a "folkloristic reason" is really not compelling but may account for data of competing etiological tales and current folk sayings. Although I will suggest another possible reason below, Alter seems to think that this accounts for the repetition of the question/exclamation: "Is Saul also among the prophets ?"

Thus, to account for a current folk-saying (*mashal*) . . . two different stories are
reported of his meeting a company of prophets and joining them in manic ecstasy.
Samuel presides, in rather different ways, over both encounters, but the first (1

Samuel 19) deflects him from his pursuit of David and stresses the fact of his rolling naked in his prophetic frenzy. One can of course, argue for a certain purposeful pattern even in such a repetition: the same divine power that makes Saul different from himself and enables him for the kingship later strips and reduces him as diving election shifts from Saul to David. There is however, at least a suspicion of narrative improbability in this identical bizarre action recurring in such different contexts, and one may reasonably conclude that the pressure of competing etiologies for the enigmatic folk-saying determined the repetition more than any artful treatment of character and theme.[156]

Alter also discusses the cumulative effect of repetition. There is a delaying of the conclusion and the building of suspense. But we need not assume the need for some mnemonic device as requisite of some protracted oral tradition. It seems clear from biblical cues given that the narratives were written to be read orally. That is, if we presuppose a largely illiterate society—which I'm not certain is justifiable—then there would be a class of people (the Levitical priesthood?) who would have circulated to read the stories to the people of the land. Alter helps us visualize this: "The unrolling scroll, then, was in one respect like the unrolling spool of a film projector, for time and the sequence of events presented in it could not ordinarily be halted or altered, and the only convenient way of fixing a particular action or statement for special inspection was by repeating it."[157]

As in our time, repetition contains the latent power of memory.

And speaking of power: in repetition, it is wise to look for subtlety in repetition as in subtlety for all of narrative in general—witness the note above on Danny Hays' article. Alter views command and fulfillment as a window into an ancient view of historical causality—what I will refer to as paradox determinism or compatiblism when accompanied by choices humans make.

"The constantly reiterated pattern, then, of command or prophecy closely followed by its verbatim fulfillment confirms an underlying view of historical causality; it translates into a central narrative device the unswerving authority of a monotheistic God manifesting Himself in language."[158]

As so we have confirmed, at the least, the power of narrative: "If the requirement of oral delivery and a time-honored tradition of storytelling may have prescribed a mode of narration in which frequent verbatim repetition was expected, the authors of the biblical narratives astutely discovered how the slightest strategic variations in the pattern of repetitions could serve the purpose of commentary, analysis, foreshadowing, thematic assertion, with a wonderful combination of subtle understatement and dramatic force."[159]

Alter then moves on to word-motif which is rather frequently discussed in the literature. What this means is that keywords will pop up from time to time to the degree that they may even become code words or thematic in the text. Because of the nature of the language of biblical Hebrew (three letter "roots" and small vocabulary), the text is given to a rather higher degree of repetitiveness than in other mediums. Because of homonyms, we may even have subtleties that convey meaning without directly expressing it.[160] I was reminded of such a subtlety while quietly following the Sunday school teacher through his rendering of Exodus 18. As you will recall, it is the place where Jethro tells Moses that he is working hard but not working smart. In verse 18, he says, "You will most certainly exhaust (*nābōl tibbōl*) both yourself and these people who are with you." Because I am drawn toward puns, the first thing I thought was that Moses' father-in-law was calling him a fool (*nābāl*)—the same *nābāl* as the Nabal of 1 Samuel 25:3ff. Then I also thought of the silently screaming message Moses projects: "If you want anything done right, you have to do it yourself . . . I am the only one competent to judge . . . Nobody but me is capable of handling even the most minor responsibilities." This might be just a bit patronizing and confusing to the people. Hence, I thought of the folk etymology given for the name of Babylon in Genesis 11. "Come, let us go down there now and let us confuse (*wᵉnābᵉlāh*) their language" (v. 7). Although it is from a different root (*bll*) in Genesis, the sound of it (*blh*) in Exodus 18 is still that of "you are a fool, Moses, if you continue to do this." In addition, it could pass mixed messages to the people, confuse them and, in a sense, dehumanize them.

Alter then goes back into text and discusses 1 Samuel 15 by way of illustration. He cites the usage of three words generally translated *listen, voice,* and *word*. I do not have time to develop this in great detail now, and so I will let it pass. Alter notes the usage of the approximately homonymic pun on blessing and birthright from the Jacob cycle (*berakhah, bekhorah,* respectively) and the Joseph Narrative where the so-called *Leitwörter* are *recognize, man, master, slave,* and *house.* Samson's cycle is given in *fire* where its repetition signals the destruction of whatever gets in its way or his eventual fizzling out.[161]

The idea of repetition is relatively simple; but, there are several kinds that affect how we read the story. Alter lists and defines five of them and I will quote them for our instruction:[162]

a.    *Leitwort.* Through abundant repetition, the semantic range of the word-root is explored . . . by virtue of its verbal status, the *Leitwort* refers immediately to meaning and thus to theme as well. *The word.*

b.    *Motif.* A concrete image, sensory qualtiy, action, or object recurs through a particular narrative . . . it has no meaning in itself without the defining content of the narrative; it may be incipiently symbolic or instead primarily a means of giving formal coherence to a narrative (e.g., dreams, prisons and pits, and silver in the Joseph story). *Concrete image.*

c.    *Theme.* An idea which is part of the value-system of the narrative—it may be moral, moral-psychological, legal, political, historiosophical, theological—is made evident in some recurring pattern (e.g., rejection and election of the monarch in Samuel and Kings). *Abstract image.*

d.     *Sequence of actions.* This pattern appears most commonly and most clearly in the folktale form of three consecutive repetitions, or three plus one, with some intensification or increment from one occurrence to the next, usually concluding either in a climax or a reversal (e.g., the three captains and their companies threatened with fiery destruction in 2 Kings 1). *Narrative sequence.*

e.     *Type-scene.* This is an episode occurring at a portentous moment in the career of the hero which is composed of a fixed sequence of motifs. We discussed this one above (e.g., the annunciation of the birth of the hero, the betrothal by the well (woman/ female servant at a well, the trial in the wilderness). *Expected drama.*

Alter looks for the conceptual matrix of repetition in the parallelism of biblical poetry. By seeming to repeat a poetic direction, by intensifying, specifying, complementing, qualifying, contrasting, and expanding the semantic material of each stitch, the poetic discussion is advanced.[163] Parallelism is generally expressed as synonymous, antithetical, climactic, emblematic, or synthetic (not really parallelism at all—except, perhaps, metrically). One might readily see how this might pertain to narrative except that the repetitions will be more of the word-for-word restatement rather than creative restatement.

By way of illustration, Nathan tells Bathsheba what to say and that he will fill in the blanks. "My lord king, did you not swear to your handmaid in these words: 'Solomon your son will reign after me and he will sit on my throne?' Then why has Adonijah become king" (1 Kings 1:13). There is, of course, a vacuum of information here. Narrative is silent about the truth of the king's alleged oath.[164] The restatement is profound. In the first place, Nathan tells her to give the message as an open-ended question; Bathsheba expands on Nathan's directive beginning with the same words—non-interrogative (v. 17)! Her expansions include the feast, the invitations (the exclusions!), and the national politics of the situation. Nathan, unaware of what has passed between David and Bathsheba, enters at the point of expectation and picks up with where he had left off, and follows her description of the events and implications and expands upon them.

"The effect of this whole process of repeating and adding is to overwhelm David with a crescendo of arguments. Incremental repetition, which in its more schematic usages simply provides a progressive intensification or elaboration of an initial statement, here has the fullest dramatic and psychological justification."[165]

Alter goes on to discuss variation in repetition and to demonstrate its effects on the task of reading. To illustrate, he uses 2 Samuel 3:21-24 where there are three "and he went in peace" (*wayelekh beshalom*) phrases in rapid succession followed by "and he went indeed"?! (*wayelekh halokh*). I think exasperation is called for here in Joab's quote. Alter says that this "falls like the clatter of a dagger after the ringing of bells."[166] It certainly strikes me as the ring of an unsheathed sword.

Illustrating finer, more minutely interrelated movements, Alter uses a short section of Genesis 39 with Joseph's success in Potiphar's house. At one point, I counted eight ways the narrator says that God was with Joseph in chapter 39; Alter sees more than that in only verses 1 through 6.

> Joseph is successful ... God makes him succeed .... God repeatedly "is with" Joseph ... a condition that ... manifests itself as *blessing*. ... The word "all" ... is insisted upon five times, clearly exceeding the norm of biblical repetition. ... the scope of blessing or success this man realizes is virtually unlimited; everything prospers, everything is entrusted to him ... confirmation of his own grandiose dreams and an adumbration of his future glory as vizier of Egypt. The seemingly incongruous last clause of the frame, which appears in the Hebrew parataxis as an equal member of the sequence of parallel statements that it concludes, is a signal of warning in the midst of blessing that Joseph may suffer from one endowment too many. We are now prepared for the entrance of Potiphar's wife.[167]

In short, Joseph is cursed with the death-knell endowments of his mother Rachel (good looks and favored status) and is therefore in some way doomed in the narrative. Alter continues by discussing Mrs. Potiphar's twisting of words and events to finally see to Joseph's second step to the vizierate. The final three verses assure us of what the first five or six have already: that God is with Joseph, that he had God's everlasting lovingkindness, that he was favored by his keeper, and entrusted by him with all the prisoners and events, and that whatever he did was successful. As to whether or not Joseph really believed he was in God's grip, we have no idea until chapter 42 at the earliest and chapter 45 certainly. Success—as God's blessing and providence—is confirmed by the three notes: Joseph was successful in Potiphar's house, in the prison house, and in the great house (from the Egyptian word, "Pharaoh"). Three concluding thoughts on repetition from Alter:

> Again and again, we become aware of the power of words to make things happen. God or one of His intermediaries or a purely human authority speaks: man may repeat and fulfill the words of revelation, repeat and delete, repeat and transform; but always there is the original urgent message to contend with, a message which in the potency of its concrete verbal formulation does not allow itself to be forgotten or ignored.[168]

Beyond this constant interplay through repetition between speech and narration, biblical personages and events are caught in a finer web of reiteration in the design of thematic words and phrases constantly recurring. No act or gesture is incidental and the sequence of events is never fortuitous.[169]

The human figures in the large biblical landscape act as free agents out of the impulses of a memorable and often fiercely assertive individuality, but the actions they perform all ultimately fall into the symmetries and recurrences of God's comprehensive design. Finally, it is the inescapable tension between human freedom and divine historical plan that is brought forth so luminously through the pervasive repetitions of the Bible's narrative art.[170]

## d.    Characterization and the Art of Reticence

Chapter 6 of Alter's book deals with the "Characterization and the Art of Reticence." Alter begins with the question as to how, with such an economy of words and without much verbal plumbing of the depth of the characters, the Bible is able to present such rich characterizations. He suggests that this is possible through the vehicle of reticence.

It is true enough to say . . . that the sparely [sic] sketched foreground of biblical narrative somehow implies a large background dense with possibilities of interpretation, but the critical issue here is the specific means through which that "somehow" is achieved. Though biblical narrative is often silent where later modes of fiction will choose to be loquacious, it is selectively silent in a purposeful way: about different personages, or about the same personages at different junctures of the narration, or about different aspects of their thought, feeling behavior. I should suggest, in fact, that the biblical writers . . . actually worked out a set of new and surprisingly supple techniques for the imaginative representation of human individuality.[171]

Whereas Alter follows this by his cosmogony and view of human freedom, it would seem that this is more of a statement of the compatiblism mentioned above. That is, there is a dynamic tension in the narrative portrayal itself between a sovereign God and an apparently volitionally free humanity. And so he illustrates this selectivity, this narrator's reticence using the biblical story about David. In doing so, Alter will explore the relationship with his (first?) wife Michal and thus relationships with Saul, David's other wives, and David's men. The Spirit of the Lord has turned away from Saul and Saul has turned David away—all the while David is remarkably successful.

In a discussion of scale of explicitness and certainty for conveying information, Alter begins with the lower end of the scale.

The lower end of this scale—character revealed through actions or appearances—leaves us substantially in the realm of inference. The middle categories, involving direct speech either by a character himself or by others about him, lead us from inference to the weighing of claims. Although a character's own statements might seem a straightforward enough revelation of who he is and what he makes of things, in fact the biblical writers are quite as aware . . . that speech may reflect the occasion more than the speaker, may be more a drawn shutter than an open window. With the report of inward speech, we enter the realm of relative certainty about character . . . intentions, though we may still feel free to question the motive behind the intentions. Finally, at the top of the ascending scale, we have the reliable narrator's explicit statement of what the characters feel, intend, desire; here we are accorded certainty.[172]

To this I might add that when God is said to speak or act, there is as much relative certainty as with the Omniscient Narrator. Indeed, it is the narrator's characterization of God that is immediately transparent at the literary level of the discussion. By way of disclaimer, I am making no statements about inerrency or authority at this point. Tacit in everything I do is the presupposition that the texts of Scripture were inerrent in their autographs and that reclaiming the original, while a titan task, is neither as fruitless nor as impossible an endeavor as the cynical obscurantist might have us believe.

Alter compares this text (1 Samuel 18:14-30, in case you'd lost track) with Genesis 39 to which he presumes an allusion. David is greatly successful, marked by God's hand of blessing and immensely popular—as was Joseph in a much smaller narrative world—and the text is framed with [bracketed by] such notices as was Genesis 39. And so, we are told by narrative art about God's election of David.

In any case, the frame-verses here tell us something about David's divine election to the newly created throne of Israel, but nothing about his moral character, and one of the most probing general perceptions of the biblical writers is that there is often a tension, sometimes perhaps even an absolute contradiction, between election and moral character. But it is important for the writer to leave this tension under a shadow of ambiguity in order to suggest a complex sense of David the private person and public man. David, then, remains a complete opacity in this episode, while Saul is a total transparency and Michal a sliver of transparency surrounded by darkness.[173]

Saul's character is presented from the top of the scale—the narrator tells us exactly what Saul thinks and feels. Parenthetically, Alter notes the elegant subtlety the narrator deploys in describing the speech acts of Saul from outward to inward by using the same Hebrew verb ['amr] (vv. 17 and 21 respectively where Saul's flowery speech is replaced by his mental scheme for David's demise). We ask ourselves as to why David plays along with the king on the second time around. Does he see through Saul's scheme? Does he recognize the cost-to-benefit ration and decide to follow through—with the help of his men? Why are David's excuses for Merab not sufficient for Michal? Is this another case of where the gentlemanly narrator does not call any of the women of the Bible ugly? Possibilities are legion; resolutions are difficult. Michal, nevertheless is transparent: "Michal leaps out of the void as a name, a significant relation (Saul's daughter), and an emotion (her love for David). This love, twice stated here, is bound to have special salience because it is the only instance in all biblical narrative in which we are explicitly told that a woman loves a man."[174]

What her motivation for such explicitly depicted love is, we are left to conjecture. However, in David's family and with specific reference to Amnon and Tamar, "love" means little more than infatuation in some instances. David is a hero and he is attractive—what more do we need to know than that?

Alter tells us that the means used to depict David's character are from the middle and lower echelon on the scale of certitude. We know about his exploits on the field and about the fact that everybody (but Saul) loves him; but, we do not yet know him. David is a public person with public speeches that may hardly be read as anything other than politically motivated. We do not begin to get much of a window into the soul of David until the death of Bathsheba's first son. The narrator perpetuates such ambiguity through the vehicle of uncommented upon public speech. In my opinion, the biblical narrator never really gives us the authentic David. We are shown a man with many useful talents and as many or more liabilities. In theory, it is only in the Psalms that we truly see the "man after God's own heart."

David is difficult to characterize and hence comes off often as a politico. In 1 Samuel 19, several things in Michal, David's first wife, remind us of Rachel, Jacob's favorite and Joseph's (another of Jacob's favorites) mother. Since the idea of the teraphim is not bandied about much in Bible, the allusion, the memory at least, is stark. Like Rachel before her, Michal is doomed. I will develop—with Polzin's help—the notion of David's loveless opacity below; but for now, Alter is lucid on the opaque!

> . . . the only words purportedly spoken by David to Mical are merely her invention to protect herself. So far, their relationship has been literally and figuratively a one-sided dialogue. First we were told twice that she loved him while all that could be safely inferred about his attitude toward her was that the marriage was politically useful. Now she vigorously demonstrates her love, and the practical intelligence behind it, by her words and actions at a moment of crisis, while the text, faithful to its principle of blocking access to the private David, envelops him in silence, representing him only as a man in mortal danger who goes off, flees, and escapes.[175]

And thus, she slips into the background. Close association with this king-elect is a body bag for a man and oblivion for a woman. The proliferation of wives and the proffering of the ex- [?] wife of David to another politico is given no emotion by our narrator—to anybody: Michal, David, Palti. We have no idea what David feels until he decides (as an afterthought?) to bring her back. Even there, the statement is public, political, and passionless. It is merely a matter of his right of bride price (2 Sam. 3:14).

During the Amalekite captivity of Abigail and Ahinoam, the narrator is strategically reticent with respect to David's emotions. We know that those with him are upset about the loss of their families; but the positioning of the causal clause is more indicative of David's distress over their wanting to stone him to death than over the loss of his two remaining wives. Alter shows the eclipse of David the opaque by David the public:

> Where we thought we had a spontaneous expression of David's grief over the loss of his wives, we are again confronted with David the political leader in a tight corner, struggling to save both himself and the situation—which he promptly does by a devastating counterattack on the Amalekites in which the captives are rescued. It is not that we are led to infer any clear absence of personal feeling in David, but that again the private person has been displaced through the strategy of presentation by the public man, and the intimate David remains opaque.[176]

In the reunion between Michal and David, all emotions are suppressed except for those of Palti. He is said to weep for the loss of his wife and to follow until driven back by the demi-god—yet doomed—general, Abner. Between David and Michal there is no dialog until that final, ominous exchange. At that point, there is a rapid exchange of sarcastic commentary and consequence that leaves the head spinning. He takes her words, opposes them, and throws them back in her face with the narrator's comment that she remained childless.

"The writer is careful to conceal his own precise sympathies. He does not question the historically crucial fact of David's divine election, so prominently stressed by the king himself at the beginning of his speech; but theological rights do not necessarily justify domestic wrongs, and the anointed monarch of Israel may still be a harsh and unfeeling husband to the woman who has loved him and saved his life."[177]

Although we know that all Israel (including Merab and the rest of Israel's women) loved David, and although Michal is said at least twice to have loved David, we know of none of the others of David's wives who are so transparently (level one, above) depicted as loving David. Perhaps, expediency outweighed devotion in the palace harem. Regardless, the narrator has allowed David to have the final say in this pericope; 2 Samuel 6:23 then serves as an epilogue to the event, to the text, and as an epitaph to the life of Michal. There are at least three, non-competing ways to look at these events—theologically, it is part of the end of the family of Saul and his potential dynasty; dramatically, it is the end of the romance between the king-elect and the daughter of the king-deposed; the parataxis of verse 23 indicates that this is the final twist of fate in the wronged woman's life. It is as bad as it can be: Palti gave her no children either.

> ... causation in human affairs is itself brought into a paradoxical double focus by the narrative techniques of the Bible. The biblical writers obviously exhibit, on the one hand, a profound belief in a strong, clearly demarcated pattern of causation in history and individual lives, and many of the framing devices, the motif-structures, the symmetries and recurrences in their narratives reflect this belief. God directs, history complies; a person sins, a person suffers; Israel backslides, Israel falls. The very perception, on the other hand, of godlike depths, unsoundable capacities for good and evil, in human nature, also leads these writers to render their protagonists in ways that destabilize any monolithic system of causation, set off a fluid movement among different orders of causation, some of them complementary or mutually reinforcing, other even mutually contradictory.[178]

So the intricacies of divine causality are worked out upon the less-than-perfect canvas of human actions, attitudes, and words. This is done in such a way as to elude blind apostles of unilinear causality. Again, I call it paradox determinism or compatiblism. That is, both worlds, divine causality and human volition, work themselves out in thoughts, feelings, words, and actions of the players on the stage of biblical narrative history. "Every biblical narrator is of course omniscient, but ... the ancient Hebrew narrator displays his omniscience with a drastic selectivity."[179] And because of this selectivity, certain aspects of the characters of biblical narrative may be alternatively displayed or withdrawn. This is certainly the case respectively with Saul and David as will be examined below.

Characters develop and change and this is shown in the sense of character as a center of surprise. Biblical characters do not have Homeric epithets attached to themselves (e.g., clear sighted Thrasymachus) but relational markers: Saul's daughter or David's wife. Homeric characters undergo violent fluctuations,[180] but David evolves: "David ... is first a provincial *ingénu* [sic] and public charmer, then a shrewd political manipulator and a tough guerrilla leader, later a helpless father floundering in the entanglements of his sons' intrigues and rebellion, a refugee suddenly and astoundingly abasing himself before the scathing curses of Shimei, then a doddering old man bamboozled or at least directed by Bathsheba and Nathan, and, in still another surprise on his very deathbed, an implacable seeker of vengeance against the same Shimei whom he had forgiven after the defeat of Absolom's insurrection."[181]

And finally, with respect to the unknowable and unforeseeable in human nature, Alter examines the difference (really a double extreme) between Homeric grief and that of biblical narrative. In Homer, the oscillations are stark but not surprising but in the Bible,

David's character is surprisingly chilly and in my opinion, public and political again. This is seen in the death of Bathsheba's first son. At the point of perception, the protagonist rises from his fast and prayer and the text proceeds at a breakneck pace through a chain of nine uninterrupted verbs embracing a relatively corresponding space of time. Alter's take on this is as follows:

> All men may indeed grieve over the loss of their loved ones, but this universal fact does not produce a universal response because the expression of feeling, the very experience of the feeling, takes place through the whorled and deeply grained medium of each person's stubborn individuality. As readers, we are quite as surprised as the servants by David's actions, then his words, for there is very little in the narrative before this point that could have prepared us for this sudden, yet utterly convincing, revelation of the sorrowing David, so bleakly aware of his own inevitable mortality as he mourns his dead son.[182]

And yet, even here, it would appear that David is opaque: first, this is a somewhat public declaration to officials of the court—chamberlains and officials of state; second, we are unaware as to what David is referring to here. Is he talking about following the child in death or following the child to glory or following the child to oblivion or . . . . This still has the air of a political statement of the public David. It is at once intriguing and ambiguous.

Later, there will be a barrage of seven verbs encompassing no less than nine months. At this point the narrator puts the epilogue upon the affair concerning David, Bathsheba, and Uriah. Or does he? Perhaps the four-fold retribution detailed by David to Nathan before the trap is sprung is to be worked out on the stage of the narrative for the rest of David's life. The sword—four-fold sword—will not depart from David's house. We will again let Alter have the last word:

> The Greek tendency to narrative specification . . . seems to be one that modern literary practice has by and large adopted and developed. Precisely for that reason, we have to readjust our habits as readers in order to bring an adequate attentiveness to the rather different narrative maneuvers that are characteristic of the Hebrew Bible. . . . The monotheistic revolution in consciousness profoundly altered the ways in which man as well as God was imagined, and the effects of that revolution probably still determine certain aspects of our conceptual world more than we suspect. This altered consciousness was of course expressed ideologically in the legislative and prophetic impulses of the Bible, but in biblical narrative it was also realized through the bold and subtle articulation of an innovative literary form. The narrative art of the Bible, then, is more than an aesthetic enterprise, and learning to read its fine calibrations may bring us closer than the broad-gauge concepts

of intellectual history and comparative religion to a structure of imagination in whose shadow we still stand.[183]

### e.  Composite Artistry

Looking back at some of the introductory matters in this section, Alter examines the charges that the biblical text as we have it is a mindless bit of stitchery with no coherence. And as Wellhausen would have, this redaction of the various texts has made the final form "unreadable."[184] Having lost count of the number of times I have "read" the text, Wellhausen and his philosophical progeny seem to be guilty of nothing less than cynical obscurantism. In any case, "the intricacies of the argument need not concern us here, only the basic proposition, which seems convincing enough, that the text as we have it was not the work of a single hand, or of a single moment in time.[185]

Alter presumes at least some focus in a coherent structure of the final form of the text. It is in fact readable; it does have design; it does have intentionality; it does have purpose.

> The biblical text may not be the whole cloth imagined by pre-modern Judeo-Christian tradition, but the confused textual patchwork that scholarship has often found to displace such earlier views may prove upon further scrutiny to be purposeful pattern.[186]

> There are passages of biblical narrative that seem to resist any harmonizing interpretation, leading one to conclude either that there were certain circumstances in the transmission and editing of ancient Hebrew texts which would on occasion lead to intrinsic incoherence, or that the biblical notion of what constituted a meaningful and unified narrative continuum might at times be unfathomable from the enormous distance of intellectual and historical evolution that stands between us and these creations of the early Iron Age. My own experience as a reader makes me suspect that such insoluble cruxes deriving from the composite nature of the text are a good deal rarer than scholars tend to assume. . . .[187]

Alter uses the accordion-like structure of the dual rebellions of Korah and Dathan and Abiram to illustrate. By the end of the day, we are never really certain if Korah got swallowed up by the earth or burned to death by God (Numbers 16). Alter quotes Abraham Ibn Ezra who is lucid with respect to the difficulty: "Some say that Korah was among those swallowed up, and the proof is 'The earth swallowed them up, and Korah.' Others say he was incinerated, and their evidence is 'And Korah, when the congregation perished, when the fire consumed.' And our sages . . . say that he was both incinerated and swallowed up. But in my opinion, only in the place of Dathan and Abiram did the earth split open, for

Korah is not mentioned there; in fact, Korah was standing with the chieftains who were offering the incense."[188]

So, we have the right to ask the question, "Why did the narrator seem to blur these two disasters together?" Alter compares the artistry of the passage and concludes: "I don't think the confusion can be facilely attributed to mere editorial sloppiness, for there is evidence of some careful aesthetic and thematic structuring in the story."[189] He observes such collocations as: *It's too much for you*; *Isn't it enough for you? Isn't it enough? to go up*; *go down*; *to take*; *to come* [or *bring*] *close* and so on. He says that these are "terms of horizontal movement toward the center of the cult instead of vertical movement toward or away from dominion."[190] He makes several suggestions to avoid the fact that some of our notions of how history-like narrative ought to go "are all flagrantly violated."[191]

1.    compelling political reasons for fusing the two rebellions
2.    they comprised one archetypal rebellion against divine authority
3.    they [it?] echo[es?] the first act of sibling violence [Gen. 4] that prefigures all later struggles for power
4.    they echo the story of a society destroyed because it was utterly pervaded by corruption [Gen. 19]
5.    hence they are the two paradigmatic images of divine retribution

The illustration given next in the Joseph Narrative will not be entertained here,[192] since I don't think the problem (reappearance of the money) is anything other than a brothers versus Jacob problem. The false display of fear is probably different objects. The first time there was an ambiguous problem. The second time, they were afraid specifically of Jacob's reaction to the problem. Alter rightly debunks any solution to the problem based on the documentary hypothesis. The problem is just a little too obvious to blame on sloppy editing.

The next illustration is with respect to the Creation Narratives. He says that these are "two parallel accounts."[193] However, like classical conservative exegetical approaches he says, "It is obvious enough that the two accounts are complementary rather than overlapping, each giving a different *kind* of information about how the world came into being."[194] He indicates that, using documentary nomenclature, P is more cosmic in scope and J is more interested in humanity and his immediate surroundings. At which point he, in my opinion, creates a problem that wouldn't exist were it not for three centuries of critical scholarship—and subsequent building of windmills upon clouds: "The most glaring contradiction between the two versions is the separation of the creation of woman from the creation of man in *J*'s account. P states simply, 'male and female He created them,' suggesting that the two sexes came into the world simultaneously and equally. *J*, on the other hand, imagines woman as a kind of divine afterthought, made to fill a need of man, and made, besides, out of one of man's spare parts."[195]

While trying not to get too far afield from narrative criticism, we must here engage in some expository criticism—which I shall call "rhetoric criticism." Were it not for the way the section was worded, we might be inclined to let him have his say; however, in the twentieth century, egalitarianism is patent. There is no "suggesting that the two sexes came into the world simultaneously"; there is merely the statement that the two sexes came into the world—period! Alter has made an unnecessary inference and then trumped it with egalitarian nomenclature. I suppose we should expect that from his era at Berkeley. If it deals with equality (however defined) it must be right. Secondly, and since he has already indicated that a different kind of information is related in chapter 2, the question arises: "How is it contradictory to indicate the specific manner in which the woman happened upon the scene after only cataloging the fact in chapter 1?" It seems a fitting follow-through to chapter 1 to detail the fact in chapter 2.

Alter goes on to indicate the symmetry of chapter 1 and the linearity of chapter 2. Discounting the two canonical source theory, he suggests that the symmetry is indicative of the author's concept of coherence ("very goodness," I think) of the universe. However, difference in the accounts does not prove contradiction in the accounts. In my opinion, formal contradiction only exists in propositions. To have a contradiction we must affirm and deny the same words. We have nothing of that in the first two chapters of Genesis. As Alter affirms, we have the coherence of the cosmic dance in chapter 1 and the creation of moral agents in chapter 2: "In this version of cosmogony, God, as Einstein was to put it in his own argument against randomness, decidedly does not play dice with the universe, though from a moral or historical point of view that is exactly what He does in *J*'s story by creating man and woman with their dangerous freedom of choice while imposing upon them the responsibility of a solemn prohibition."[196]

Neither of these perspectives run contradictory to the intentions of "either author" or to the "editorial unity" or to theology, history, or science for that matter. It is more of that compatibilistic worldview that I have hinted at above. That is, a God of this quality and character is such that He can create a universe of such vast proportions, intricate complexity, and extraordinary beauty and still allow the appearance, at least, of human freedom—all the while accomplishing His purposes undaunted.

Another alleged contradiction that Alter follows has to do with little more than confusion between the "earth" and the "garden." It would seem to me that all issues can be resolved by change in location as indicated clearly in the text. Nevertheless, Alter proceeds from the mantra:

> The differences between our two versions [*J* and *P*] are so pronounced that by now some readers may be inclined to conclude that what I have proposed as a complementary relationship is in fact a contradictory one. If, however, we can escape the modern provincialism of assuming that ancient writers must be simple because

they are ancient, it may be possible to see that the Genesis author chose to combine these two versions of creation precisely because he understood that his subject was essentially contradictory, essentially resistant to consistent linear formulation, and that this was his way of giving it the most adequate literary expression.[197]

Whereas I might be persuaded to agree that the writer of Genesis is neither simplistic nor necessarily linear in his formulation, I have no need to follow Alter's conclusion that this is the only way to arrive at "the most adequate literary expression." Neither do I see the need to read the Bible with a dualistic, polarized view of women and thus trump the argument in typical egalitarian fashion.

"Analogously, the Hebrew writer takes advantage of the composite nature of his art to give us a tension of views that will govern most of the biblical stories—first, woman as man's equal sharer in dominion, standing exactly in the same relation to God as he; then, woman as man's subservient helpmate, whose weakness and blandishments will bring such woe into the world."[198]

The discussion is so rhetorically prejudiced as to hardly merit discussion; however, for the sake of argument let us grant him his premise. The dynamic tension in the subsequent narratives is patent, as we shall see with respect to the male/female tensions in the Samuel Narratives. However, to say that in Genesis these are different perceptions and drive the wedge further in them by rhetoric such as "subservient," "weakness," "blandishments" and "bring such woe into the world," show only that Alter is heir to a certain ossified exegetical tradition and a certain period in American philosophical history. Equality before God and equality in relationships among humans are totally different spheres and are hence not contradictory. We can continue the hypothetical discussion: Alter was a full professor in a prestigious American university. Does that mean that he views himself as equal in every aspect to the high school dropout? I doubt it. Does this mean he feels that there should be equal pay and that the royalties for his books should go to the high school dropout? Does this mean that he is positionally equal to the female graduate student who must (some way or another) pay him tuition for courses, exams, and papers? Is this just a temporary set of circumstances which produces in his mind a fiction of positional equality? Even were we to grant that Alter is a true Marxist according to the axiomatic, "from each according to his ability; to each according to his need," who is that positionally exalted individual or oligarchy that determines that distributive "from" and "to"? "Comes the revolution" equality is a myth! To demand equality is an insult and affront both to our fellow human beings and to the omni-creative God. We are all different. Difference completely bedevils any egalitarian discussion.

Perhaps the biblical author is grappling with all of these issues in an attempt to portray humankind as of equally infinite worth before its creator God, all the while indicating an economic relationship that provides the greatest onus of responsibility upon the male of the species. His statement that the woman "will bring such woe into the world" is only an error in the history of interpretation that fails to acknowledge the original sin against knowledge committed by the first male and is hence hardly worth a second look.

Nevertheless, and as pertains to our literature, Alter uses the introduction of David as the illustration for purposefulness in composite narrative artistry. Criticism has said that there are two (perhaps three) mutually contradictory introductions of David in 1 Samuel 16 and 17: shepherd, musician and warrior. Although I find nothing particularly contradictory about these—any more than I do about the alleged three succession narratives concerning Saul—let us follow Alter's trail, for we shall learn something!

First, Alter notes the progression: Anointing by Samuel, wherein we again see the thematic reversal of the rights of primogeniture; then the court musical therapist appointment wherein he also gains the title of armor bearer; then the introduction after the beheading of Goliath wherein he becomes son-in-law material. The contradiction, according to Alter, is in the matter of "his total unfamiliarity with armor."[199] Unfortunately, this has almost nothing to do with either the text or its referent. Time could have passed, boys grow up, voices change, and so on. It might not have been as much familiarity as size and weight: perhaps David's statement is transparent—he had not tried them (1 Samuel 17:39). Maybe he still wasn't as big as Saul the head-and-shoulders-taller-than-any-other-Israelite man. Awkwardness in armor is hardly equivalent to "his total unfamiliarity with armor." So we've made a mountain out of a molehill. But it does reflect something about the relationship between David and Saul. "The two introductions of David correspond to two different aspects of the future king which are reflected in his relationship with Saul and which will remain in tension throughout his story—the private person and the public figure."[200]

Alter then chases the trail of the thematic keywords (*Leitwörter*) as he has in the past. Such things as choice ("to see in") and rejection (*ra'oh be; ma'os be, lo' bakhor be*) really point to the fact that the story is about seeing rightly.[201] And by the end of the day, we will see that the Samuel Narratives do not even paint Samuel himself in that fine a light. Samuel, in fact, does not see well. He does not see as God sees.

The comparison between Joseph and David is valuable. As with Joseph, David and Saul have brushes with the Spirit; there is choice (roots *bhr*, and *r'h* "to see") and there is success as seen in the pun on "spirit."

Because . . . the spirit of the Lord has descended on him, his personal allure, his gift for succeeding, have begun to make themselves felt, and people already sense, as with Joseph, that "the Lord is with him." Having been graced with the spirit, David is then seen exerting mastery, through song, over the realm of spirits, a point underscored by a pun in the last verse of the chapter (1 Sam. 16:23): "And whenever the [evil] spirit [*ruah*] of God was upon Saul, David would take up his lyre and play, and Saul would be eased [*ravah*] and feel well, and the evil spirit [*ruah*] would depart from him."[202]

In what Alter calls "the second version of David's debut"[203] we see the closest thing to epic that the Bible offers. One is reminded of scenes in the "Iliad" and "Aeneid" wherein there is a series of challenges and contests between individual heroes, the outcomes of which in some way or another affect the story. Alter makes much of the action sequences in which David is seen as victorious. We see, from 17:49-51, the breakneck pace of the narrative as David is the subject of the following verbs: he stretched out his hand; he took a stone; he slung it and he struck; he prevailed; he struck; he put him to death; he ran and he stood and he took the sword; he drew it out; he put him to death and he cut off his head.

So what is the net effect of juxtaposing these two narratives? Alter makes the comparison between the creation narratives and these two:

> It might be noted that there is an approximate analogy to the interaction of the two sources for the creation story in Genesis (though I am by no means suggesting that one derives from *P* and the other from *J*): a human-centered, richly detailed "horizontal" view following a more concise, more symmetrically stylized, "vertical" view which moves from God above to the world below. These two views correspond in part, but only in part, to the public and private David, the David Saul envies, then hates as his rival, and the one whom he loves as his comforter.[204]

In the first account, God's election, though private, is without ambiguity and absolute. In the second account, David publicly seizes the limelight by military action, thus beginning his slow arduous climb to the top of the political ladder. There is the sense of ratification rather than initiation.[205] Or perhaps we could say public confirmation of the private anointing.

Let us allow Alter three final comments: First, upon composite artistry: "The characteristic biblical method for incorporating multiple perspectives appears to have been not a fusion of views in a single utterance but a montage of viewpoints arranged in sequence. Such a formula, of course, cannot smooth away all the perplexities of scribal and editorial work with which the biblical text confronts us; but we are well advised to keep in mind as readers that these ancient writers, like later ones, wanted to fashion a literary form that might embrace the abiding complexity of their subjects."[206]

Second and with respect to the compatibilistic worldview of the Bible: "The monotheistic revolution of biblical Israel was a continuing and disquieting one. It left little margin for neat and confident views about God, the created world, history, and man as political animal or moral agent, for it repeatedly had to make sense of the intersection of incompatibles—the relative and the absolute, human imperfection and divine perfection, the brawling chaos of historical experience and God's promise to fulfill a design in history."[207]

Third and with respect to joining worldview with narrative art: "The biblical outlook is informed, I think, by a sense of stubborn contradiction, of a profound and ineradicable untidiness in the nature of things, and it is toward the expression of such a sense of moral and historical reality that the composite artistry of the Bible is directed."[208]

In conclusion, we should ever be wary of critical theory—from whichever quarter. Nevertheless, we cannot help but learn from these narrative theorists that reading well and reading carefully pays certain dividends. Often, as conservatives, we are so afraid of falling headlong into problems and alleged contradictions that we avoid looking at the text carefully. This says something about our view of God: we really do not believe that He is big enough to stick up for His Word! We are practical agnostics when it comes to canonicity and bibliology. We should never be afraid to give the Bible itself—apart from historical studies—a very close reading. Because of the way it is written and who is responsible for the writing, it certainly can defend itself—indeed, generations of scrutiny have left it only the most read, translated, and studied subject in history.

## f.    Narration and Knowledge

Alter reverts to the big picture and notes for us that the text as we have it was motivated by "a sense of high theological purpose."[209] That is, in a vast sea of pagan enticements, there was a small and somewhat volcanic island of moralistic monotheism. The text attempts to answer the question as to how the Mosaic system that had been set up worked its way out on the stage of history. The answer, of course, is: not so well. Regardless, it does so, in dissimilar manner to the prophets' second person soliloquies and dialogues, in the manner of indirect discourse. It tells you a story within which is a subliminal message. This raises problems and dissonance that can become, at times, quite shrill:

> The degree of *mediation* involved in talking about what the Lord requires by making characters talk and by reporting their actions and entanglements opens up what may seem to the moralistic theist a Pandora's box. For would it not be frivolous on the part of an anonymous Hebrew writer charged with the task of formulating sacred traditions for posterity to indulge in the writerly [sic] pleasures of sound-play and word-play, of inventing vivid characters with their own quirks and speech habits, of limning with all the resources of stylistic ingenuity the comic frustration of a failed seduction, the slow diplomatic progress of bargaining over a burial site, the wrangling of brothers, the foolishness of kings?[210]

The point that Alter is making here is something that we evangelicals often miss—and that I am just naïve enough to think is critical: our biblical narrator is so skilled (under that superintending hand of a sovereign God) that he can do both tasks—the theological and the artistic! In addition, Alter is correct, in my opinion, to suggest that there is more correspondence—and it will require a reorientation of our thinking, I'm certain—between novels and plays, and biblical narrative than between them and other theological writings. In point of fact, you read biblical narrative the same way you read a novel. The difference between the two is the stance you take at the end of the reading task—that stance deals with the truth or falsity of what has been encountered in the reading task. It may even go so far as what kind of novel or play you read and compare or contrast. I remember being thoroughly annoyed when one professor told me to compare "The Tale of Two Brothers" to the Joseph Narrative while another told me to contrast that one and compare "The Tale of Sinue." There is more crossover of narrative world in the latter.

Alter makes a few good points about his fictional approach that also transcend to the approach of historical fiction, historical novel, or narrative history. He suggests that fiction might probe characterization on the backdrop of circumstance in a way that we might not imagine. However, this can also be true at any new reading of history or biography. I will remove the "fiction" from the following:

> What I should like to stress . . . is a mode of knowledge not only because it is a certain way of imagining characters and events in their shifting, elusive, revelatory interconnections but also because it possesses a certain repertoire of techniques for telling a story. The writer . . . has the technical flexibility, for example, to invent for each character in dialogue a language that reflects, as recorded speech in ordinary discourse would not necessarily reflect, the absolute individuality of the character, his precise location at a given intersection with other characters in a particular chain of events.[211]

Alter claims for the biblical writers complete freedom to switch between the narrator and the characters as to how the story is told and characterization developed. And to a degree we must concur that the narrator has a certain sovereignty over his craft and his audience.

One of the more important pioneering efforts Alter claims for the writer of biblical narrative and one that you will see me use repeatedly has to do with what I will call "the Omniscient Narrator." Alter says that this is an incredibly powerful tool in narrative art.

> The narrators of the biblical stories are of course "omniscient," and that theological term transferred to narrative technique has special justification in their case, for the biblical narrator is presumed to know, quite literally, what God knows, as on occasion he may remind us by reporting God's assessments and intentions, or even what He says to Himself. . . .[212] The biblical narrator, quite unlike the Prophet, divests himself of a personal history and the marks of individual identity in order to assume

for the scope of his narrative a godlike comprehensiveness of knowledge that can encompass even God Himself.[213]

Certainly, this is indicative of incredible power. For the Christian, this poses little dissonance in view of the fact that we view Christ as the Lord of the Word.

"It is a dizzying epistemological trick done with narrative mirrors: despite anthropomorphism, the whole spectrum of biblical thought presupposes an absolute cleavage between man and God; man cannot become God and God . . . does not become man; and yet the self-effacing figures who narrate the biblical tales, by a tacit convention in which no attention is paid to their limited human status, can adopt the all-knowing, unfailing perspective of God."[214]

I recall reading of a comment made by Meir Sternberg denigrating the same effect in the gospel of Luke. I also remember commenting that Sternberg might meet his "Omniscient Narrator" someday and find out that his and ours were the same. At that juncture, it might be too late to be of much consequence.

The biblical tale might usefully be regarded as a narrative experiment in the possibilities of moral, spiritual, and historical knowledge,[215] undertaken through a process of studied contrasts between the variously limited knowledge of the human characters and the divine omniscience quietly but firmly represented by the narrator. From time to time, a human figure is granted special knowledge or foreknowledge, but only through God's discretionary help. . . . Various of the biblical protagonists are vouchsafed promises, enigmatic predictions, but the future, like the moral reality of their contemporaries, remains for the most part veiled from them, even from an Abraham or a Moses who has been privileged with the most direct personal revelation of God's presence and will.[216]

By way of illustration and that pertaining to our literature in Samuel, Alter discusses the myopia of Samuel the seer. This will be expanded upon below: "Dedication to a divinely certified career of visionary leadership is itself no escape from the limitations of human knowledge: Samuel the seer . . . mistakes physical for regal stature in the case of both Saul and Eliab, and has to undergo an object lesson in the way God sees, which is not with the eyes but with the heart—the heart in biblical physiology being the seat of understanding rather than of feeling."[217]

With respect to Jacob: "Human reality, perhaps most memorably illustrated in the cycle of stories from Jacob's birth to his death in Egypt with Joseph at his bedside, is a labyrinth of antagonisms, reversals, deceptions, shady deals, outright lies, disguise, misleading appearances, and ambiguous portents. While the narrator sees the labyrinth deployed before him in its exact intricate design, the characters generally have only token threads to grasp as they seek their way."[218]

And so we see, in conclusion, that the narrator's omniscience overshadows that of the characters and even runs parallel with that of God. We are invited to participate in the narrator's omniscience; but we are only allowed brief glimpses into the motives and feelings of the characters—the moral nature and spiritual conditions of the characters. Often, the view conceals more than it reveals. We see into the characters' inner workings through their speech acts, their overt actions, gestures, and the props they choose.

There is a horizon of perfect knowledge in biblical narrative, but it is a horizon we are permitted to glimpse only in the most momentary and fragmentary ways. The narrator intimates a meaningful pattern in the events through a variety of technical procedures, most of them modes of indirection. In the purposeful reticence of this kind of narration, the characters retain their aura of enigma, their ultimate impenetrability at least to the human eyes with which perforce we view them.[219]

This will prove to be especially true with respect to the opacity with which the narrator paints the character of David. See problems and observations: "At the same time, however, the Omniscient Narrator conveys a sense that personages and events produce a certain stable significance, one which in part can be measured by the varying distances of the characters from divine knowledge, by the course through which some of them are made to pass from dangerous ignorance to necessary knowledge of self and other, and of God's ways."[220]

And with this in mind, we will see that the author paints a picture of David that is consonant with our understanding of "the man after God's own heart," and yet an enigmatic picture that reminds us that David is one who is of like-nature with us—inconsistencies abound as well as flagrant deviations from Mosaic norm. Alter then stages the Joseph story as a paragon in the reticence and disclosure of knowledge. Although I share his sentiments, I do not feel that the Joseph story reaches much more than a provisional resolution. I always have to ask, "Do Joseph's brothers ever really get it?" (See especially, Genesis 50:20.) Nevertheless, Alter is right to point out that things hang upon the words "recognize" and "know."[221]

Alter feels that the Joseph story is one of the most compelling stories ever written—and yet he dismisses the possibility of it being a faithful recording of the facts and words of real people in real life. Nevertheless, and for the last time in this introduction, we will allow Alter to have the last word. The Joseph story "unforgettably illustrates how the pleasurable play of fiction in the Bible brings us into an inner zone of complex knowledge about human nature, divine intentions, and the strong but sometimes confusing threads that find the two."[222]

And this would also be true of the Samuel Narratives.

The consummate artistry of the story involves an elaborate and inventive use of most of the major techniques of biblical narrative that we have considered in the course of this study: the deployment of thematic key-words; the reiteration of motifs; the subtle definition of character, relations, and motives mainly through dialogue; the exploitation, especially in dialogue, of verbatim repetition with minute but significant changes introduced; the narrator's discriminating shifts from strategic and suggestive withholding of comment to the occasional flaunting of an omniscient overview; the use at points of a montage of sources to catch the multifaceted nature of the fictional subject.[223]

Attempting to give us a window into the characters in the Joseph Narrative we might make the comparison with the characters in the Samuel Narratives.

"What is it like, the biblical writers seek to know through their art, to be a human being with a divided consciousness—intermittently loving your brother but hating him even more;[224] resentful or perhaps contemptuous of your father but also capable of the deepest filial regard;[225] stumbling between disastrous ignorance and imperfect knowledge; fiercely asserting your own independence but caught in a tissue of events divinely contrived; outwardly a definite character and inwardly an unstable vortex of greed, ambition, jealousy, lust, piety, courage, compassion, and much more?"[226]

The biblical artist's craft "fundamentally serves the biblical writers as an instrument of fine insight into these abiding perplexities of man's creaturely condition. That may help explain why these ancient Hebrew stories still seem so intensely alive today, and why it is worth the effort of learning to read them attentively as artful stories."[227]

This is a point well taken.

"It was not an easy thing to make sense of human reality in the radically new light of the monotheistic revelation. The fictional imagination, marshalling a broad array of complicating and integrating narrative means, provided a precious medium for making this sort of difficult sense. By using fiction in this fashion, the biblical writers have bequeathed to our cultural tradition an enduring resource in the Hebrew Bible, and we shall be able to possess their vision more fully by better understanding the distinctive conditions of art through which it works."[228]

And so I would concur apart from the disclaimer about truth claims: that is, fictional writing and good historical narrative and biography do not differ in form as much as content. At the end of the day the contrast between the two would be the truth claims that each is prepared to make. In the case of our biblical narratives, real events can really be portrayed to really have happened in that way without making a mockery of truth. The Bible is, in effect, and even as it dances down the tightrope of the characters' lies, the truth, and the whole truth, true truth. And with this we leave Alter until he should happen to reappear *ad loc.*

## How Can You Go Wrong?

I should think that there are only a few ways: First, because of the flexible nature of language itself, there are practically an infinite number of ways to tell a story. Really, if you think about it, you can gather up the necessary words for any sentence, any complete thought, and rearrange it or substitute parts, words or clauses, and virtually be assured of communicating approximately the same cognitive content. However, because of the nature of our task, we really have to make absolutely certain that we are telling the right story. We have to tell the biblical story in the biblical way. In most instances (I'm trying to be careful here), there is only one way to read a text. In the case of narrative Bible, we must find that way and tell only that story.

Secondly, this storytelling business becomes especially critical with respect to reticence. Why? Because you have to ask yourself, "What is reticence?" Isn't it silence? So then, and I don't think it is a huge inference, any argument you might make with respect to "what's in the gap" would necessarily be an argument from, in fact, silence. Arguments from silence have some weight based upon expectations of something's presence—but you can never really achieve certainty. von Rad has suggested, and no, I do not have the reference, that we must resist every temptation to fill the gaps in the narrative. Certainly, in his mind, the redactor left them there for a reason. Nevertheless and convenient ghost writers aside, it can be safely stated that reticence does exist based upon repetitions where presence is observed. However, just like making dogmatic statements from the character's words (except, of course, when God verbally breaks into our narrative world), we must resist the temptation to fill the gaps and then infer theology or ethics from it. Hence, although I do not want to be as dogmatic as von Rad, I would be a bit more cautious than Alter, *et al.* I wouldn't want to base something as a principle on an inference from silence.

Thirdly, because of the nature of narrative biblical texts, and how they proceed along a chain of past tense verbs (see below), it is possible to emphasize something that the author might not want highlighted. That is, we might be so busy looking for puns, *Leitwörter*, and motifs that we lose track of the story itself. What the story is and what the story is about are two different things and the material below may help us to keep this straight.

## 2. Narrative Interpretation with Text-Linguistics and Clause Analysis[229]

Because I have already written extensively on this topic, I will only shape the following to fit from my study on the Joseph Narrative. Quite frankly, most of the analogies pertain due to the dual facts that we share the same textual tradition along with parallels at the verbal level, the level of narrative technique, narrative world, and conceptual content. It would seem the height of the arcane to reinvent the narrative wheel, so to speak. One who handles well the Joseph Narrative will handle well the Samuel Narratives.

Though many of the following matters have been cursorily handled in the general intro-duction to this book, it is still necessary to expand upon those matters only alluded to above. An attempt will be made first to explain what text-linguistics is. According to Teun van Dijk text-linguistics "Cannot in fact be a designation for a single theory or method. Instead, it designates any work in language science devoted to the text as the primary object of inquiry."[230]

This will be important as some of the comments and criticisms of Longacre's work are examined in the forthcoming pages.

## Textuality

According to de Beaugrande and Dressler, as well as Bergen, a text requires greater length than a mere sentence.[231] If "the primary object of inquiry" is the text, then it is required that a view of textuality be established. In this context, I will enumerate the following seven essential elements:

1. Cohesion: grammatical dependencies of the surface text hold together.
2. Coherence: the concepts and relations that underlie the surface text are consistent.
3. Intentionality: this involves the text producer's attitude to the text: goal, plan, strategy.
4. Acceptability: this is the receiver's attitude toward the text.
5. Situationality: these are factors that make the text relevant to a situation of its occurrence.
6. Intertextuality: this is dependency on previous texts.
7. Informativity: a measure of the rate of information being processed in the text; this includes expected versus unexpected occurrences in the text.[232]

It is now profitable to look at these categories in slightly greater detail.

## Cohesion

Cohesion is the concept that deals with the text as it immediately strikes the eyes; it is words in grammatical dependencies. That is, cohesion is how the component parts of the text—words in configurations of sentences and paragraphs—hold together. As Beaugrande and Dressler word the matter: "The first standard will be called COHESION and concerns the ways in which the components of the SURFACE TEXT, i.e. the actual words we hear or see, are *mutually connected within a sequence*. The surface components **depend** upon each other according to grammatical forms and conventions, such that cohesion rests upon GRAMMATICAL DEPENDENCIES. As linguists have often pointed out, surface sequences of English cannot be radically rearranged without causing disturbances."[233]

Often, grammatical inquiry is as far as the exegete goes in his pursuit of textuality. Beyond this, the exegete often pursues argumentation for the plausibility of his or her own historical contextualization, application, theology, and/or interpretation. Nevertheless, there are several more steps to be evaluated in the process.

## Coherence

It is easily possible to have grammatical dependencies that work that are meaningless. For example: "The stone slept audaciously." The sentence has all the necessary attributes of syntactical arrangement. But—unless there were some bizarre context to which such a thing might apply metaphorically—it lacks the ability to generate meaning in the mind of the interpreter. This is explained by de Beaugrande and Dressler as follows: "The second standard will be called COHERENCE and concerns the ways in which the components of the TEXTUAL WORLD, i.e. the configurations of CONCEPTS and RELATIONS which *underlie* the surface text, are *mutually accessible* and *relevant*."[234]

This means that in general, the cognitive content conveyed by the grammatical relationships of the textual world will predictably produce the same results of understanding in a broad cross section of the intended target audience. These results seem to presuppose principles of causality, sufficient, and/or necessary conditions, reason, time, and proximity.[235] If these conditions are realized in the mind, all things being equal, communication will have occurred. Generally speaking, the above two attributes of textuality are more likely to be referred to as text-centered notions. It remains for us to examine some other non-text-resident notions of textuality.

## Intentionality

The first of these user-centered notions is the producer's attitude toward the text production. This is explained by Beaugrande and Dressler as follows: "The third standard of textuality could then be called INTENTIONALITY, concerning the text **producer**'s attitude that the set of occurrences should constitute a cohesive and coherent text instrumental in fulfilling the producer's intentions, e.g. to distribute knowledge or to attain a GOAL specified in a PLAN."[236]

It is possible to subordinate the goals of intentionality under the goals of text production: cohesion and coherence. In fact, it may be argued that the goal or intended result will provide the impetus for text generation. However, it is possible to achieve an intended result without successfully accomplishing cohesion in a text. Ellipse is an example of this. Words have fallen out of a text or conversation that would have completed the syntactical arrangement and observed the conceptual coherence, but that nevertheless accomplish their intended effect due to closure efforts of the recipient.

## Acceptability

If it can be demonstrated that the speaker/writer had a purpose in the composition of his "text," then it may be demonstrated that the recipient will have a certain attitude toward that text—whether or not it is the intended attitude. This is explained by de Beaugrande and Dressler as follows: "The fourth standard of textuality would be ACCEPTABILITY, concerning the text **receiver**'s attitude that the set of occurrences should constitute a cohesive and coherent text having some use or relevance for the receiver, e.g. to acquire knowledge or provide co-operation in a plan."[237]

Factors involved include text type, social or cultural setting, and the desirability of the intended goals. Via a process of inference, a text receiver may supply information that is required to make sense of the text. It may often be the case that the hoped-for intent of the text producer is that the receiver will supply some exact piece of information. This seems to produce greater credibility due to the fact that people generally prefer their own rationale to that imposed by others. It is possible that much of the silence in biblical narrative regarding things considered abhorrent (as indicated by the Law and Prophets) is due to such a process imposed by the writer.

## Informativity

This standard of textuality deals with the rate of information being processed in a given text. This is explained by Beaugrande and Dressler in the following manner: "The fifth standard of textuality is called INFORMATIVITY and concerns the extent to which the occurrences of the presented text are expected vs. unexpected or known vs. unknown/certain."[238]

For example, given the two separate statements quoted by Beaugrande and Dressler, it may be assumed that roughly the same amount of information is being processed; yet note how much more efficiently the second one does so: "Call us before you dig. There might be an underground cable. If you break the cable, you won't have phone service, and you may get a severe shock. Then you won't be able to call us. Call us before you dig. You may not be able to afterwards.[239]

If it is presupposed that there is a normal rate of information processing in a text, then portions with the type of surprise illustrated in the second example above produce interest. Long prosaic sections, where content is largely predictable, reduce interest and may produce boredom. This can finally result in a fulfillment of the law of diminishing returns. Communication can be stifled. The reverse is also true; that is, if there is too much that is unexpected, too much surprise, then the receiver's processing functions can be over-loaded and communication stifled as well.

## Situationality

The word of wisdom in Proverbs is "A man has joy in an apt answer, and how delightful is a timely word!" That is, there will be times when a text fits a particular situation to which it is addressed. It may be true that this situation is not particularly the one to which it was originally addressed. Situationality is explained by de Beaugrande and Dressler in this manner: "The sixth standard of textuality can be designated SITUATIONALITY and concerns the factors which make a text RELEVANT to a SITUATION of occurrence."[240]

The authors use the illustration of the traffic sign: "Slow Children at Play." As the motorist approaches a playground, the sign's ambiguity (what kind of slow children are at play?) is immediately cleared up. The motorist perceives playing children and—having read the driver's manual, we hope—reduces his vehicle's velocity to such a speed at which it could be stopped easily in the event of a child chasing a ball or whatever. The pedestrian realizes that the sign is not meant for him, since his speed will not likely place these "children at play" in any jeopardy. The text in the latter case is not relevant to a situation of occurrence.

## Intertextuality

As was indicated in the example above, the sign presupposes some involvement with a manual. Though a picture may be worth a thousand words, often the diagrams and outlines on road signs merit little more than a paragraph in the driver's manual. Nevertheless, it is crucial that such signs have this antecedent textual condition or else they would defy meaning. Intertextuality is explained by de Beaugrande and Dressler as follows: "The seventh standard of textuality is to be called INTERTEXTUALITY and concerns the factors which make the utilization of one text dependent upon knowledge of one or more previously encountered texts."[241]

One way to explain this might be to imagine the approach of a motor vehicle to a "Resume Speed" sign along the road. The notion of "resuming" presupposes the idea of "reducing." Somewhere in the line of appropriate "situations of occurrence" there had to be a sign that said "Speed Zone" or "Reduce Speed Ahead." Subsequently, when the position is achieved where such reduced velocity is no longer needed, the traffic safety commission has authorized placement of a sign which allows the increase of speed. Again, as regards our topic in biblical studies, it becomes crucial to realize that often the writer is glancing back over his shoulder, as it were, and drawing our attention to those words which he (or another) has written previously. In many cases the text at hand may approach meaninglessness without an antecedent text. In fact, it may be argued that much of the materials in the prophets and writings are of reduced intelligibility without the priority of the Pentateuchal writings. In regard to the Joseph Narrative, more could be said, but as it affects matters at the compositional level, suffice it to say at this point, that without the promises to the patriarchs, (the land), the Joseph Narrative's epilogue loses its impact and gropes for closure as a conclusion to the Patriarchal narratives and a bridge to the Exodus narrative.[242]

## Text-Linguistics

Authors de Beaugrande and Dressler trace the study of text-linguistics from the classical studies of rhetoric.[243] However, some more recent applications appear to have come through anthropologically based studies on primitive tribes and applications to their languages to expedite translation and literacy among these peoples. Kenneth Pike has been instrumental in pioneering this technique as well as has Robert E. Longacre.[244] This technique, largely developed in the mid-nineteen sixties through the nineteen seventies, is called tagmemics. The method is described as follows by de Beaugrande and Dressler:

> The method called for gathering and analyzing data in terms of "slots" and "fillers", i.e. according to the positions open within a stretch of text and to the units that can occupy those positions. Tagmemics looks beyond the boundaries of both sentences and texts toward such large complexes of human interaction as a football game or a church service. The slot-and-filler method, a basic technique of code-breaking, is eminently useful for describing languages about which the investigator knows nothing in advance. The investigator uses means of *language elicitation* which impel native speakers to produce utterances of particular types.[245]

This is the foundation of the method that Pike and Longacre use in all areas of literature. However, as was noted in the general introduction to this book, Longacre qualifies his method in a very careful way so as not to generalize the procedures of tagmemics in regard to a living language with the resources of living informants, onto his study of text-linguistics, where not only is there no living informant but the language has long since ceased to be spoken.

Robert D. Bergen attempts to take the area of study noted above, also called discourse analysis, and bring it across to the evangelical audience less fluent in anthropological terminology.[246] He calls his method "discourse criticism," which appears, by the name, to desire a wider readership than the merely evangelical audience to which it is addressed. Bergen notes five major elements of inquiry in regard to analysis of the paragraph—his minimum element of textuality.

First, since language is a code, it is necessary for both the writer and the reader to share a set of symbols that are understood by all parties to possess certain agreed-upon meanings. That is to say that language is simply a societal convention. All the members of such a community agree upon the symbols that are used to gain a mental hold on their world for the purpose of discussion.

Second, most of the communication process occurs at the subliminal level of human consciousness. So far as texts are concerned, this subliminal level includes the notions of size of information units, the order of information presentation, and the kind of information being presented. The difficulty with this criterion has to do with the designation of the word "most." Indeed, if intonation and inflection are important in living languages, then perhaps these so-called subliminal cues are all the more important. Nonetheless, they are all the more difficult to ferret out. It may be argued that in a language that survives only in a text, truly subliminal cues cannot exist. They are either part of the textual data that survive or they are not. Such cues may be somewhat extraneous to raw grammatical considerations, but they are part of the overall textual picture nevertheless. As compositional considerations are examined, this will become more evident.

Third, these subliminal factors contain data essential for making judgments about authorial intention. That is, when the interpreter investigates these three so-called subliminal factors—order, quantity, and kind of information presented—he or she is in a better position to understand the author's intended meaning. Notice, another reason why the present writer tends to distance himself from the notion of subliminal elements in the text. It is necessary, to avoid the intentional fallacy, that the interpreter examine data resident in the text itself. Such notions as sub-strata meanings must be avoided if an interpretation is to be textual.

Fourth, language is genre specific; that is, each genre will be characterized by particular verb tenses. Longacre develops this category further than does Bergen. Longacre produces a (nearly) complete discourse grammar for the Joseph Narrative. This will be handled shortly.

Finally, a common set of principles governs the structuring and application of the language code in all languages. These are as follows: language texts are composed of successively smaller organization units of language. Each successively higher level of textual organization influences all of the lower levels of which it is composed. Language texts are grammatically and semantically contoured. That is, not every part of a text is intended by the author to be equally significant. The code itself contains the capacity to indicate the level of significance for each organizational unit of language. The significance level of an organizational unit within a text is designated by the writer through the employment of the language code.

In application of Bergen's method, then, generally what is required is simply to read the text. The mind naturally makes all the necessary adjustments to the textually created world. However when there is a problem in interpretation, it requires that the interpreter look more carefully into the three critical factors: order of information presented, quantity of information presented, and the type of information presented. These factors enable the interpreter more readily to gain access to the author's intention.

There is a critical difference between what Bergen is attempting to do and what Longacre accomplishes in his work. It appears that Bergen generalizes his work in discourse analysis onto text-linguistics by presupposing criteria that are germane only to living languages with available informants. It may simply not be possible to check all reference points in the interpretation of a section in a text written in a dead language if the textual datum represents an example where there is no other available point of comparison. In a living language there is always the possibility of an informant to tell us when we have made a mistake. There are times in biblical interpretation when the interpreter is not so fortunate. In short, the processing and monitoring efforts of the speaker/writer and interpreter are not available.

Longacre is careful not to generalize his training in discourse analysis onto his work in text-linguistics. Observe how he qualifies his method:

> In applying this model to a written text where the text transmitter and receiver are not in a face-to-face relationship when the text is given, our scheme is necessarily fissioned into two halves . . . . The writer is presumably writing for a given audience but the audience is not immediately present. A written work may even prove to be of not [sic] great interest to the audience to which the (hopeful) writer addressed it and may prove instead to be of interest to a rather different sort of audience (especially when a work is ahead of its time). The reader likewise has no immediate access to the writer, whose intentions he must judge wholly from the written work itself. Indeed, as so eloquently put by Ricoeur, the text is alienated from its author and must be appropriated by its reader in spite of distanciation.[247]

This has several ramifications. If the speaker/writer and hearer/reader are not in proximity (either spatially or temporally) to each other, then monitoring efforts of the speaker/writer and the processing efforts of the hearer/reader are made impossible. If communication is to occur at all, the data in the text is all that transmits the message. This means that the writer will tend to write in the terms of his language most suited to the type of communication he intends. He will purposely avoid ambiguity for the sake of clarity and efficiency in the communication process.

By way of illustration, the present writer was in Kenya in 1984 studying, among other things, Swahili. One of the many cultural phenomena that strike the visitor is the multi-lingual nature of the populace. Generally, at least three languages are known by the indigenous population of coastal Kenya: their own tribal language, Swahili, English, and often Arabic. In English conversation with an American, fluent in Digo, Swahili, and English, in the presence of an indigenous Kenyan fluent also in all three languages, a difficulty arose. When conversation was made with the Americans, the Kenyan could not understand the conversation. When either American spoke directly to the Kenyan, the communication process was unhindered. Why was this? When Americans speak, they speak in jargon. That is, for the pleasure of the communication process, Americans will allow for more ambiguity and innuendo in conversation. When a problem arises, the phoneme "huh?" or a quizzical facial expression signals a breakdown in the communication process. Those in the conversation simply back up a step, clear up the fog, and proceed. The Kenyan, who never had the slightest problem in communicating with Americans, was completely befuddled by highly idiomatic American English. This shows two things: First, English as spoken in East Africa is generally designed for maximum efficiency in information-packing content. Secondly, without processing and monitoring efforts of those in the conversation, communication breaks down rapidly for the non-native speaker, and potentially for the native speaker as well.

So, as when speaking in Kenya, one must carefully choose one's words if one desires his communication to transcend cultural and temporal barriers. It is this that largely characterizes biblical narrative in the opinion of the present writer. Generally speaking, the text of the Bible was intended for longevity — to transcend such barriers as time and space. It looks forward to a time when its writers (or the subjects of its texts) no longer live upon the earth. For example, though no documentation is needed here, several biblical texts (as does the Joseph Narrative) make mention of a time when the promises made to the patriarchs would be fulfilled.[248] The biblical text was intended to transcend temporal barriers, and, it may be argued, cultural barriers as well. Any text may be translated into the linguistic and cultural conventions of another. Such a process may be more or less efficiently expedited depending upon the expertise of the translator in both contexts. Nevertheless, it is possible; and that is one of the goals to which this work aspires.

In an unpublished work, John H. Sailhamer has indicated how some monitoring/processing problems may be overcome in the process of textual transmission.[249] As the author composes his text, he anticipates the "ideal reader."[250] As he develops the strategy of his textual communication, he plans for various types of questions. What the author does is to anticipate ambiguity and attempt its resolution. The text is not complete as it is begun; rather, it is completed through successive progressive stages. The text is composed with audience in view. "The concept of the READER is a way of focusing on the dynamic aspect of a TEXT'S capacity to generate meaning."[251] Sailhamer goes on further to elucidate this stair-step concept of ambiguity resolution as he describes the concept of the "reader" as a text-resident notion.

The notions of levels of "information states" and "communication based" TEXT-formation only make sense in conjunction with the notions of a TEXT STRATEGY that affects in the READER a series of changes in "information states". The form of the TEXT itself represents a series of distinct levels of READER "information states". Thus, the form of the TEXT is a realization of the AUTHOR'S planned READER-idea as the normative figure for every "actual reader" of the TEXT. The TEXT itself gives the measure for its own correct reading by the "actual reader".[252]

So, as the composer of the text fashions his communication instrument he idealizes the reader and plans into his text progressive increases in information states. That is, as the document advances, more information will be communicated due to the fact that the writer has purposely composed his text anticipating questions, ambiguity, and their subsequent resolution.

Longacre assumes some other dissimilarities between discourse in a living language and an ancient text. He indicates that with a contemporary work we often inquire as to the circumstances under which the piece was written. However, he is quick to acknowledge that once a piece has left the writer's hand his "composition has a life of its own."[253] He qualifies this even further with regard to an ancient literary work: "With a truly ancient text, however, most of the above information is either nonexistent or highly speculative—the text is "on its own." But, precisely because the text has stood the test of time it is a literary work that has something to say to another time, place, and set of circumstances other than that in which it was originally composed. It *is* a literary work because it has something to say to us, as well as to its original audience."[254]

The notion Longacre advances here fits well into the idea that a text has creative powers of its own. The text generates worldview when it lives beyond the time in which it was originally written. The text, then, becomes less reflective of its own cultural milieu and becomes potentially a force more creative of a future cultural milieu. Longacre however softens the force of some of the more radical ramifications of the above with the following qualification: "Even though here and there a word, an expression, a turn of argumentation is somewhat opaque to us as contemporary readers until it is clarified by reference to the original milieu of the composition."[255]

It seems that Longacre feels little need in the Joseph Narrative to use recourse to "reference" in discovering the meaning of the text as it stands. It would also seem logical that if these texts truly have a life of their own, then that which requires reference to "information [that is] either nonexistent or highly speculative" would be information of lesser significance to that which is most central to "the overall meaning and plan" of the textual message. In short, neither the foregrounded macrostructure nor the backgrounded macrostructure would be affected by any supposed attempts at "precision" in regard to the cultural milieu in which the piece was originally written.[256] As shall be seen shortly, these macrostructures are both the key to the meaning of the story as well as resilient to problems created by questions of reference in the text.

## Longacre's Text-Linguistics

Longacre's purpose is to develop a discourse grammar using Joseph to illustrate the categories he derives from ordinary experience in discourse analysis.[257] Frequently, he will attempt to make correlations between living languages with which he is familiar and the categories of clausal usage in the biblical text.[258] He seeks to analyze nine components as applied in discourse grammar to a living language.[259]

The first of these is the "speaker." That is, there is one who transmits the message. In a text it is more common to refer to the text generator as the writer; nevertheless, Longacre's nomenclature is valid. This is the person who composes the text. The writer develops his strategy as he proceeds and systematically removes ambiguity and progressively increases the information states of his idealized perfect reader.

The second category is the "hearer." This is the recipient of the message. He may be called the reader or the interpreter as well. In a living language, the hearer or interpreter may frequently be somewhat less than the perfect reader idealized in the first category. However, in a text where processing/monitoring efforts (eight and nine, below) are less possible, we are not afforded the luxury of anything less than a reader capable of making a nearly perfect interpretation of the text.

The third is the text itself. Longacre is careful to qualify this category as a linear progression of words: word-for-word. Textuality involves the seven categories elucidated by Beaugrande and Dressler above: cohesion, coherence, intentionality, acceptability, situationality, intertextuality, and informativity. In a text written in a language where we have no living informants, it must be concluded that all categories are derived from the text. However the text itself may be looked at in particular from the seven angles listed above.

The fourth category is called "the situation." That is, there is a commonality of experience shared between the writer and his reader. Longacre says that this situation "like a cartouch encompasses the whole process; no communication can take place without at least a minimum of commonality."[260] At the very least, they must have the same shared set of symbols as indicated above in the first of Bergen's five categories.

The fifth category is the dual elements of the macrostructure. By the term "macrostructure" Longacre (following van Dijk) means "an overall meaning and plan."[261] Longacre sees both a foregrounded macrostructure and a backgrounded macrostructure into which five sub-thematic elements feed. These notions will be expanded upon immediately below in the subsection under macrostructure.

The sixth category that Longacre addresses is the idea of "texture." This involves the first two categories elucidated by Beaugrande and Dressler above: cohesion and coherence.

Again, this is how the text holds together on both the grammatical level and the ideational level. When the same set of symbols are shared between writer and reader, breakdowns in communication will most frequently occur at this level. That is, either—via ellipse or some other problem—grammatical dependencies are not clear, or the ideas, semantics, that undergird the communication are not adequately communicated.

The seventh category is the "constituent structure." This relates more closely to Bergen's category 5a and b above.[262] That is, how is the text interrelated via words, phrases, clauses, sentences, paragraphs, and imbedded discourses. The analysis at this level attempts to show relationships between the constituents in the text at all levels.

The eighth category is the monitoring efforts of the speaker. That is, in normal discourse analysis of a living language, the investigator examines how the generator of the message checks for audience response. Such things as non-verbal cues—gestures, body language, etc.—are also included in these examinations. Since this involves a text—and an ancient text at that—the only monitoring efforts would have to be text resident. That is, in his compositional strategy, the writer plans as though he were monitoring a living audience.

The final category that Longacre analyzes is the processing efforts of the hearer. That is, the hearer/reader/interpreter will make efforts to understand his text. In a living language this will involve the asking of questions. In a text where the author is not present, the reader still asks questions of his text; however, he will be unable to predict if or when his question will be answered. If our reader is the ideal reader postulated by Sailhamer above, and our text generator is a competent writer, such questions as would naturally occur in the course of a dialog with the reader (a conversation) will be progressively (systematically) answered by the writer.

## Macrostructure

As has been briefly stated above, Longacre defines macrostructure as "an overall meaning and plan." He explains this as follows:

> The story itself contains its own interpretive summary as we shall see in a moment. The macrostructure, however, need [*sic*] to be considered on two levels. One is overtly *given* within the story itself, is perhaps the more didactic, and lends itself to personal applications, while the other must be *deduced* from the story and has to do with the national origins of Israel. In that the former is explicitly given, I shall refer to it as the foregrounded macrostructure while the broader concerns that can be deduced belong rather to what one might term the backgrounded macrostructure.[263]

Longacre sees, then, both a foregrounded macrostructure and a backgrounded macrostructure. For instance, he sees the foregrounded macrostructure in Joseph as: "Joseph's brothers, meaning to harm him, sold him into Egypt, but in reality God sent him there so that he could save Jacob's family and many others from death by starvation."[264] In essence then, Longacre has elevated Genesis 45:5-8 and 50:20 to the status of theme in the Joseph Narrative.[265]

Longacre notes five elements that feed into the foregrounded macrostructure. The first is the intent of Joseph's brothers to harm him. The second is his being sold into Egypt. The third is the divine intent to make Joseph the one who in effect saves the world from starvation, as well as the implied providence of God involved in Joseph's elevation to power. The fourth is the specific salvation of Jacob's family as well as many others. The fifth is the oft-repeated notion of the severity of the famine.[266]

By backgrounded macrostructure, again, Longacre means that which is deduced from the story and pertains to the national origins of Israel. It appears that the backgrounded macrostructure, as Longacre defines it, is not to be derived from the immediate surface text but rather from the principle ideas at the compositional level. Regarding the backgrounded macrostructure Longacre says: "Furthermore, the latter macrostructure, while pervading the *Joseph* story, probably belongs rather to the entire *toledôt ya`aqob* of which the *Joseph* is a part."[267]

Longacre sees the backgrounded macrostructure as: "Among the descendants of Jacob, Joseph and Judah are to be preeminent both as individuals and as tribes."[268] That is, as he examines the flow of the story he observes that one of the purposes of the narrative as a whole is to show that these two are to be elevated to preeminence both within the family of Jacob and among the tribes of Israel. This will be of further interest because it may be argued that compositionally, the whole of Genesis is designed to promote the preeminence of Judah. It seems that Longacre has captured the correct notion regarding the Joseph Narrative. However, more may be said regarding Genesis—and indeed the whole of Pentateuch.

## Discourse Grammar

In the introduction to part two of *Joseph*, Longacre takes exception to the classical modes of grammatical presentation and presents the matter in terms of textlinguistic and sociolinguistic analysis.[269] He states the terms of his grammatical presuppositions in terms of six theories of language. The first is that "every language has a system of discourse types (e.g., narrative, predictive, hortatory, procedural, expository, and others)."[270] The second is that "each discourse type has its own characteristic constellation of verb forms that figure in that type."[271] The third is that "the uses of given tense/aspect/mood form are most surely and concretely described in relation to a given discourse type."[272] The fourth is that "the verb forms that characterize a given discourse type are plotted according to the mainline of that type and progressive degrees of departure from the mainline, then local spans of text that are identifiable as that discourse type can be analyzed by the rank of its main verb."[273] That is, he attempts to established a taxonomy by which "relative height in the rank scheme determines relative salience in the local span."[274] The fifth is that "a structural unit, the paragraph . . . is posited as intermediary between sentence and discourse, and a system of paragraph types . . . is used to facilitate the description."[275] The sixth and final category is that "a system of logical relations or notional categories is assumed to underline the paragraph."[276]

Out of these rules and the resulting taxonomy, Longacre develops hierarchies of verb usage for four basic types of texts and paragraphs: narrative, predictive/procedural, hortatory, and expository which will be explained and described below.[277] The diagnostic Longacre uses to describe the narrative text "is the sequence of preterite clauses."[278] The most typical cue for identifying the predictive paragraph is the principle usage of the *w + qatal*.[279] Longacre feels that it is not possible as yet to offer a secure taxonomy of expository discourse and paragraphs. However, he feels that "expository discourse can be defined as discourse in which the most static verb forms of a language predominate and have the highest ranking."[280] He suspects that nominal sentences fill the top and therefore identifying rank. Hortatory discourse is chiefly identified by the preponderance of cohortatives, imperatives, and jussives (all of equal ranking).[281]

## Ranking

Longacre offers the following statement on the taxonomies he constructs as a verbal ranking scheme to help him characterize the types of paragraphs and texts within which he is operating: "The constellation of verb forms that figure in a given discourse type are structured so that one or more privileged forms constitute the mainline or backbone of each type, while other forms can be shown to encode progressive degrees of departure from the mainline."[282]

Since we will be dealing primarily with narrative discourse and various kinds of discourse imbedded within narrative, we will examine only Longacre's taxonomy for what he calls "narrative discourse." For narrative discourse Longacre's (*Joseph*) hierarchy is as follows:

Storyline          1. Preterite: primary.

Backgrounded       2.1. Perfect
Actions            2.2. Noun + perfect (with noun in focus).

| Backgrounded | 3.1. *hinnēh* + participle |
| Activities | 3.2. Participle |
| | 3.3. Noun + participle. |

| Setting | 4.1. Preterite of *hāyâ*, `be' |
| | 4.2. Perfect of *hāyâ*, `be' |
| | 4.3. Nominal clause (verbless) |
| | 4.4. Existential clause with *yēš*. |

| *Irrealis* | 5. Negation of verb clause (any group).[283] |

Longacre seems quite secure with the above taxonomy, and this is borne out by the present writer's own private statistical inference work. He says, "Clause-initial perfects are outranked by preterites but in turn outrank clauses with perfects and preposed nouns."[284] He is, however, able to consider a taxonomy where both the preterite and the perfect are on the storyline band.

> The scheme given here could be alternatively conceived . . . as embodying a story-line band in which the preterite is primary and the perfect is secondary. As long, however, as a cline is presented—a scheme symbolizing degrees of departure from the storyline—it makes little difference whether the perfect is conceived of as in the same band as the preterite or in the next lower band immediately contiguous to the preterite; in either case no element is closer to the primary storyline than is the perfect. At all events, it is a first degree departure from the mainline of the story.[285]

This is of some significance since in the debate over the significance level of the perfect (*qatal*) others have suggested that it says the same thing and does exactly the same thing in places (topicalization and focus) as the preterite.[286] However, Longacre's rejoinder is terse and to the point: "The burden of proof rests with those who want to say that formally distinct forms are ever functionally exact equivalents."[287] He questions the operation of placing the noun (N) + *qatal* as an equivalent to the *wayyiqtol*.

> . . . this sort of an analysis would involve a 'promotion' of the N *qtl* to storyline status. The main difficulty here is the inevitable dependence on a subjective judg-ment: even though the clause is not the usual storyline form, we consider it to be a mainline event instead of a preliminary event. But who is to make such deci-sions once we ride rough- shod over the formal distinctives? I shall insist later in the article that whether or not a N *qtl* be considered as promoted to fill a function

similar to that of the primary storyline, nevertheless, as a secondary storyline it remains qualitatively different from the primary storyline.[288]

It seems that no matter which path is chosen, though, statistically it is impossible to show any form as a functional equivalent in narrative to the *wayyiqtol*.

So, the questions arises: "Do I need to be a Hebrew language expert to do text-linguistics?" No, but it would certainly be easier. My wife and I did a text-linguistic analysis of James several years ago that now appears in my survey notes without exhaustive recourse to Greek. In it we ascertained, going somewhat against the prevailing winds, that James was not, in fact, wisdom literature but more like Old Testament legal literature. What one needs to be able to ascertain is where the leading verb of the sentence is and where there is subordination. Following that, one must be able to determine to some degree of accuracy what kind of subordination is present.

Now, back to biblical narrative: every language has a storyteller's tense. In English, ours is the simple past tense. Hence, we will need to acquire a Bible that is a bit more literal than some of the newer, more paraphrastic ones available. I recommend the NASB, ESV, or the old RSV (white out the marginal notes, please). These will help us to maintain the backbone of the story while keeping the backgrounded material out of the foreground. Background and setting will thus be kept from that which pushes the story forward—the simple past tense of the English language.

So, in conclusion, we see that text-linguistics with a dead language text helps us to establish the rules of engagement for the text. Each text tells us how to read it by the vocabulary it chooses, yes, but more, by the combination of the semantics and syntax it uses. The author has long since passed on and so we have no way to engage him to ascertain more clearly what he wished to communicate to us—save necromancy (which seems an inappropriate application of 1 Samuel 28). Hence, the only way we might engage the author is to know for certain who he was and then get hold of another text—with its own rules of engagement—and delve more deeply into his psyche. With several of the biblical texts this is, of course, impossible and so we must have the faith to believe that the author wrote clearly enough to be understood apart from such sleuthing. For those with a high view of inspiration and God's superintendence over the process and preservation of the text, this will be less of a reach than for those with a low view or no view of inspiration and preservation. For these latter we might simply say that classical philology has always learned the languages first, read and translated the texts second, and then followed with historical inferences from these two prior tasks. Frequently, this has lead to a reciprocal relationship between them; but, the order is usually that which I have given. This is the way it has been done and the text gives us the rules of engagement.

## Participant Reference

One of the more interesting and productive confluences of text-linguistic theory and narrative interpretation occurs with respect to what is called "participant reference." As you will recall from your language studies (including, I hope, English), there are ways to express oneself more powerfully and more benignly. For instance, active voice is more powerful than passive. One still uses passive voice when one desires to distance him/herself from responsibility or association with an idea. Computer grammar checks still flag us when too much passive voice is used. Also, the second person imperative is more powerful than the jussive and so on. This is also the case with respect to participant reference. When someone's name, title, and relationship to persons and matters in question are all mentioned, it is more powerful than simply using the proper gender pronoun. I will give you an edited version of Robert Longacre's hierarchy:[289]

## Participant Reference Resources

First let us list a series of resources from the study of participant reference and from that a few deductions will be given.

1.     Nouns (including *proper names*) + qualifiers such as adjectives, relative clauses (with *'asher*), and descriptive sentences (clauses with *hayah*, "be" or nominal clauses).
2.     Nouns (including proper names) without such qualifiers.
3.     Surrogate Nouns as substitutes for 1 and 2 above, especially by resort to terms for kinship or occupation/role. (Sometimes, especially with minor participants, this maybe the usual level of participant identification, e.g., a relative clause may simply be part of a job or role description.)
4.     Pronominal Elements.
    a.     independent subject pronouns
    b.     object pronouns (*'eth* + pronominal element)
    c.     preposition + pronominal element
5.     Pronominal Object Suffixes on Verbs.
6.     Subject and Possessor Affixes.
7.     Null References, e.g., in regard to objects that are implied in the context but not stated in a given clause.

As you can tell by the italicized Hebrew in the above listing, ascertaining participant reference is more successfully accomplished using Hebrew; however, there are some principles of general linguistic theory and narrative interpretation that can help us: "While the participant reference resources of Biblical Hebrew are, as a whole, of the sort that might be found in any language, there are some idiosyncracies [sic], especially in regard to ranks (4) and (5)."[290]

That is to say, we do not have pronominal affixes in English. So, we have to dumb down a bit in regard to precision and just use what we know about the principles of accuracy. At this juncture I'd like to recommend a book by my former student and longtime friend, Dr. Steven D. Mathewson.[291] In his book *The Art of Preaching Old Testament Narrative*, he offers numerous helpful tips for the person who does not have all the tricks that Hebrew studies afford the expert.

The hierarchy given above helps us to recognize a couple of things: first, the importance of the various participants, and second, what operations participant reference performs. These things help us to keep the main ideas of the story firmly in focus.

## Ranking the Participants

Given the above hierarchy, then, Hebrew narrative should most probably utilize those resources in a manner that betrays certain hierarchically ranked distinctions. The following schema is not necessarily restricted to biblical Hebrew narrative.[292]

1.  Major Participation (the slate of participants for the whole story):
    a.  Central (protagonist)
    b.  Other(s)
    i.  Antagonists
    ii.  Helpers/Bystanders
2.  Minor Participants (participants whose role is restricted only to particular episodes in the story)
3.  Props
    a.  Human
    b.  Animate
    c.  Inanimate
    d.  Natural Forces[293]

## Operations of Participant Reference

Given the above two schematizations for biblical Hebrew narrative in particular and narrative interpretation in general, the following operations (transactions) are carried out within the story with respect to participant referencing:[294]

1.  Introduction into the story, i.e., the first mention of a participant or prop.

2. Integration into the story as central in a narrative (whether main or embedded) or as thematic participant of a paragraph.
3. Tracking, i.e., tracing references to participants through the text so as to keep track of who-does-what-to-whom, and other such considerations.
4. Reinstatement (applicable if a participant has been off-stage).
5. Indication of Confrontation (e.g., at the climax of a story) and/or role change, i.e., flip in dominance patterns (at a denouement).
6. Marking Locally Contrastive Status (accomplished by fronting a noun in the second sentence of an antithetical paragraph).
7. An Intrusive Narrator Evaluation.

Keeping these and other considerations in mind builds a nice bridge between narrative interpretation and text-linguistics. It also appropriately paves the way for more macro considerations with respect to compositional analysis. It will help us focus on what the story is about and the relationship between the characters. This in turn helps us to focus on the overall compositional strategy employed by the writer. A reciprocal relationship between these three studies will help us to understand the movement of the story better, all the while helping us not to misread the message of the story.

## 3.    Narrative Interpretation with Compositional Analysis[295]

In compositional analysis there are several criteria which may be used to determine that relationships exist within or between texts (establishing either inner-textuality or intertextuality). Some of these are, for instance, the "keyword" connection (*gezera sewa*), word-plays (such as *atbash, gamatria, haphak*), and the simple conjoining of certain words or passages (*semukin*).[296] Bar-Efrat offers us categories so as to qualify and quantify the usage of these words: first, the frequency of the word in the Bible; secondly, the frequency of the word in that text/series; and thirdly, the nearness of the words within that text.[297]

The total "mass" or number of such connections is yet another criterion. The connection becomes more convincing as more evidence is accrued for that intended connection.

What weaknesses might cause one to use caution in this method? To begin with, there needs to be clarification in regard to typology. By the word "typology" is meant the author's intended highlighting of an actual relationship between two or more events or objects (e.g., the creation/garden blessing and the fruitfulness of Israel in Goshen).[298] This highlighting was accomplished by intentionally composing the accounts in such a manner as to draw attention to their inter-relationship.

One would need to be convinced by the evidence that such relationships were intended by the author. Much of the reasoning behind it has to do with what may be called the "logically possible alternate." That is, how would a relationship be affected if, for instance, the author had chosen other vocabulary? The "logically possible alternate" does not exist in reality. In reality, what we have is a textual datum. So, in some cases, one must establish a minimum threshold for the amount and kind of evidence. That is, what would be acceptable evidence for the given case? In some cases it might be possible to accept as little as the typological usage of three terms in parallel texts. For instance, the author's use of the same three terms (פרה/רבה/מלא),[299] among other demonstrable relationships, in Genesis 1 and Exodus 1, in such a tight grouping, may establish the idea that Israel in Egypt was fulfilling the edict given to the creatures in Genesis 1.[300] Theologically, then, Israel in Egypt would be recreating or fulfilling some element of the "garden" blessing in Egypt.[301] There are, of course, other examples of ties in these two sections. The concept of "The Land" or "Israel" is one of them.

Compositional analysis does not seem to have been largely accepted in the western hemisphere. Most of the work done in this area seems to be by German scholarship. It is possible that part of the reason compositional analysis has not been accepted has to do with the fact that most scholarship in the United States is still influenced by what may be called British empiricism. For instance, the present writer did his undergraduate work in research branches of psychology called psycho-physics, neuro-anatomy, and physiology. Students trained in experimentation are told that unless they are able to produce results of 97.5 percent probability or greater they have nothing to publish. Obviously, this has not caused the field of psychology to be any less prolific in its literature. But it does cause a noticeable shift in the type of literature produced. Instead of producing articles indicating statistical significance, articles are produced of the "case study" nature. Often this is what is done in the field of compositional analysis. A few examples are cited and the student is asked to accept this as the obvious key to compositional strategy. Only in the face of overwhelming evidence can some people be persuaded to this notion.

By way of illustration, the present writer once took a seminar in which, in the course of the discussion, the students were to be persuaded as to the compositional structure of Genesis 14 (that is, chapter 14 not being intrusive to the broader context of Genesis chapters 13 and 15).[302] The illustration had to do with the connection between מָגֵן\O\O in Genesis 14:20 and מָגֵן\O\O in Genesis 15:1. If that had been all the evidence available, it would have been the logical conclusion that there is here little more than coincidence. In this particular case, one might have wondered whether or not source criticism had more in its favor and that chapter 14 was intrusive. John H. Sailhamer has illustrated the following eleven examples,[303] including not only *gezera šewa*, but also *haphak*, and *gamatria*.[304]

## Observed Textual Ties Between Genesis 14 and Genesis 15

| | | | | |
|---|---|---|---|---|
| 1.[305] | 14:13 | הָאֱמֹרִי *(ha'emōrî)* | 15:16, 21 | הָאֱמֹרִי |
| 2. | 14:13b | בְּרִית *(berît)* | 15:18a | בְּרִית |
| 3. | 14:14b | 318 men | 15:2b | אֱלִיעֶזֶר *('elî'ezer)* = 318 [gamatria][306] |
| 4. | 14:14c | דָּן *(Dān)* | 15:14a | דָּן |
| 5. | 14:15 | דַּמָּשֶׂק *(Dammāśeq)* | 15:2b | דַּמֶּשֶׂק *(Dammeśeq)* |
| 6. | 14:16a | הָרְכֻשׁ *(hārekuš)* | 15:14b | בִרְכֻשׁ *(birkuš)* |
| 7. | 14:18a | צֶדֶק *(tsedeq)* | 15:6b | צְדָקָה *(tsedāqāh)* |
| 8. | 14:18a | שָׁלֵם *(šālēm)* | 15:15b | בְּשָׁלוֹם, *(bišālôm)* |
| | | | 15:16b | שָׁלֵם *(shālēm)* |
| 9. | 14:19b, 22b | שָׁמַיִם *(šāmayim)* | 15:5a | הַשָּׁמַיְמָה *(haššāmaymāh)* |
| 10. | 14:20a | מִגֵּן *(miggēn)* | 15:1b | מָגֵן *(māgēn)* |
| 11. | 14:21 | הָרְכֻשׁ *(hārekuš)* | 15:1b | שְׂכָרְךָ *(śekhorkâ)* |

[haphak רכשׁ *(rkš)* reverses שׂכר *(śkr)*][307]

This amasses evidence that is far more convincing, not only for proving the flaws of source criticism, but also for compositional strategy of the book. In fact, depending how one goes about the process of tabulation, it could be said that this evidence very nearly produces statistical significance. In view of the fact that this evidence is amassed across nine verses, it could be said that eleven cases in nine verses definitely shows statistical significance. The above example is fortunate. It does not seem that there will always be so many examples in such a close configuration. Nevertheless, as will be shown shortly, there are numerous instances where these kinds of relationships can be suggested, if not demonstrated.

For instance and by way of contrast, in the context of the Joseph Narrative, von Rad has seen the need to show some "Wisdom" connection.[308] Bolger, however, has shown a connection between the Joseph Narrative and what transpired in the Garden.[309] Let us now conclude with Eric Bolger's final remarks concerning this topic: "Compositional analysis is the study of the way various units of biblical text have been purposefully combined into a larger whole. The factors or characteristics which establish relationships between these units may be studied to determine the strategy behind a particular author's use of his materials. Such characteristics may be found at a number of different levels."[310]

His desire to clarify, simplify, and consolidate terminology is also to be appreciated. After further discussion, the benefits of his approach will be easily seen.

> The term compositional analysis will be used in this dissertation to refer to the analysis of compositional structure. This terminology has a number of benefits. First, it avoids the theological associations of Child's term, the canonical approach. Thus its nature as an interpretive method rather than as a religiously grounded approach is emphasized. Second, it avoids the identification of the method as merely another step in the process of historical-critical exegesis as suggested in the term composition criticism. Rather than being a logical extension of critical methodology, it will be argued below that compositional analysis is [a] valuable tool for discerning the intended meaning of Scripture, that of the final form of the received biblical text.[311]

The above is also a clue to the direction toward which this discussion is moving. That is, the compositional approach will be adopted as one of the three major parts of the omnibus method adopted by the present writer.

Where might one go wrong in this type of approach? Perhaps there might be the temptation to take weak evidence and posit an unjustifiable relationship. One should also provide evidence to the effect that there was a conscious choice involved in the selection of some words as over against others. Therefore, one should also indicate the ramifications of reverse conditions: that is, if other words (synonyms) had been chosen, how would it have changed the meaning of the text? For instance, as Alter and Polzin use narrative interpretation with the Samuel Narratives, Hans-Christoph Schmitt applies the method of redaction criticism consistently to the Joseph Narrative in his bid to overthrow what he calls classical Pentateuch criticism and establish his version of the supplementary hypothesis, and so I evaluated his work in my dissertation.[312] In that he is looking at the same data as someone involved in compositional analysis or typological exegesis, his examples are useful; in that he goes beyond the bounds warranted by that evidence in attempting to stratigraphically date the text, his results are less helpful.

Finally, then, why is it that these three methods have been chosen to be synthesized? It was desired first and foremost, that the three approaches be textual approaches. This means that there is a conscious avoidance or form-critical approaches,[313] and approaches influenced by von Rad's kerygmatic exegesis.[314] Secondly, it was requisite that the three approaches be recent. The word "recent" may be subject to different interpretations. However, in that all the authors have written their works since 1981, they seem to include the best of recent textual scholarship. The idea "recent" also must be filtered through the grid of the avoidance of methodological adulteration. For instance, in Alter's first chapter, he momentarily leaves a literary approach and moves toward typological exegesis in explaining how Genesis 38 has been woven into the narrative structure as a whole.[315] Up to this point it may be argued that his approach is not primarily textual.[316] It is not difficult to find reverse adulterations in the allegedly textual approaches taken in more recent volumes.

Initially, an attempt was made to find three proponents of the respective methods that were of some equivalence; that is, among other things, writing on the same level. It was decided that this was as futile a pursuit as it was unnecessary. In the first place, the study is a comparison of the proverbial "apples and oranges." Although it might be said that all three approaches are fruit in that they are textual approaches, each one looks at the text in a different way. For instance, extending the metaphor: Schmitt is peeling back the skin of the orange to determine what the orange is composed of, what holds it together, and its provenance; Longacre is attempting to give a complete analysis of the molecular composition of his apple from seeds to stem; and as Davis peels his banana, he is attempting, among other things, to observe how it grew on the tree and its usefulness to the consumer. Secondly, since there are so few recent examples of these three approaches on this particular block of text, it is the contention of the present writer that basically there are only these three to work with.

It needs to be said at the outset that what Hans-Christoph Schmitt is doing in his *Josephsgeschichte*, is not compositional analysis. Schmitt is engaged in redaction criticism. Nevertheless, often the redaction critic and the compositional analyst are looking at the same material and only operate with different presuppositions and move toward different goals. First, before moving on to an analysis of Schmitt, this treatment will present a brief review of the salience of compositional analysis.

According to Georg Fohrer, composition criticism seeks to explain the way an author combines diffuse textual units to create the larger whole.[317] Compositional analysis is designed to answer a series of questions. These might include: What direction has the author taken in combining these units? What function does a particular unit serve within the larger composition? What might be the literary, and/or religious-theological viewpoint of a composition? What is, then, the theological intention of the author himself?[318] Other ways of addressing these questions might be: What large units of text did the author use to construct his final text? How are the units delineated? Generally, what functions do these individual units serve in view of the completed whole? More specifically, what final touches did the author give to his text that enable the reader to determine how the text is to be read and received? Finally, and most crucially, what is the religious and theological viewpoint of the final form of the text?[319]

What then is the difference between redaction criticism and compositional analysis? Compositional analysis is concerned with exploring the "art and manner" of the connection (*Zusammenfügung*) of various passages. Redaction criticism endeavors to explain "the extent and art and manner" of editorial revisions (*der redaktionellen Bearbeitung*). The focus of compositional analysis is, therefore, synchronic. It emphasizes the way an author's work is organized into a unified whole. The focus of redaction criticism, then, is diachronic. It emphasizes the changes various editors have made in the process of combining materials into larger units.[320] Redaction criticism attempts to isolate elements indicating changes through time for the purpose of showing a developmental process in the shaping of the work. Compositional analysis observes elements used by the author that indicate the strategy by which the purpose of the work may be elucidated. Another way of looking at these distinctions is as follows:

> . . . redaction criticism focuses in particular on various revisions (made to units of text or collections of units) which are *not* related to a larger compositional scheme or structure. For example, redactional revisions would range from assorted glosses and changes in the consonantal text or vocalization, to the addition of larger portions of text to existing units, to the combining of sources such as those of the Pentateuch, as long as such revisions appear to have been made *without respect to a broader compositional purpose or strategy*. Whereas such revisions may certainly be theological in nature, that theological perspective has not been integrated into the whole composition. Such revisions are studied for clues as to the redactor's theological interest rather than the theological viewpoint of the author of a composition.[321]

Redaction criticism focuses, then, on things that make for textual discontinuity, whereas compositional analysis emphasizes those things that indicate continuity. Redaction criticism is a method of peeling back layers of textual strata—as in an archaeological excavation—like pulling the layers off an onion to finally arrive at what may be left of the original elements of the text. So far as the biblical text is concerned, the assumptions are that such elements can be proven to be subsequent additions, and that they can be proven to have been made "without respect to a broader compositional purpose or strategy." It may, therefore, be difficult to prove that the final theological viewpoint of the redactor is materially different from that of an original author. Following another line of reasoning, this would also follow from the fact that his supposedly derivable text does not presently exist in its original form.

Part of what is involved in compositional analysis has to do with the delineation of what comprises a text. The analysis of the textual situation must include the determination as to whether or not a unit of text is strategically related to other units as part of a meaningful complex. What, then, becomes of paramount interest is links or parallels between various units in a more complex whole.[322] In the case of biblical narrative in general and more specifically Pentateuch and Genesis in particular, "such units are generally connected to the smaller and larger context of a particular book by repetition of certain words or clauses or by a continuity of subject matter and plot, such that they function as part of the larger unit."[323] An illustration of this has to do with the seam (such as it may be) between Genesis and Exodus. The cataphoric reference at Genesis 50:24 lends itself to an emphatic reference to the return of the Israelites to the land of Canaan—the subject matter of the Exodus. Conversely, some of the backreferences in the book of Joshua (e.g., 24:32 to the proper disposal of the bones of Joseph) tie the narrative so closely together from Genesis (50:25) through Exodus (13:19) to Joshua that many have attempted to posit a single composition—hexateuch. In a sense, at the compositional level, it may be suggested that the reading of Genesis through Joshua functions approximately as promise and fulfillment, at least at the theological level.

John H. Sailhamer, expanding upon the work of Fohrer, has indicated several other crucial elements in compositional analysis for isolating an author's narrative strategy. Relationships exist not only within units themselves, but between contiguous units. Some features that operate internally are: introduction, conclusion, sequence, disjuncture, repetition, deletion, description, and dialogue.[324] The relationship of a particular unit to a larger context is determined by a comparison of the thematic interests of the larger composition to those of the unit in question. Where there is a sharing of terms, ideas, themes, etc., the smaller unit may be understood as theologically related to the whole.

Significantly, there seem to be at least four levels at which this sharing of parallels may transpire. Shimon Bar-Efrat has described these as the verbal level, the level of narrative technique, the level of the narrative world, and the level of conceptual content.[325] First, the verbal level includes elements of words or phrases and their combination. These may be combined to create repetition, systematic variation or other stylistic features. It is at this level that such word plays as *gezera shawa* (keyword), which is the use of a word, even at the "root" level, or a synonym across textual boundaries, *gamatria*, or numerical exegesis, *haphak*, or the reversal of letters in a single word, etc., are observed. Secondly, the level of the narrative technique includes analysis of the narrator's method of conveying the meaning of the text. This includes whether or not the narrator chooses to use report, dialogue, colorful imagery, or mere reporting of fact. Thirdly, the level of the narrative world includes the portrayal of narrated events and characters. Structure at this level may be evidenced "by parallels between the dramatic, spatial, or temporal structure of two or more narratives."[326] Lastly, the final level is that of conceptual content. This emphasizes the themes or ideas in the various narrative units.

When it can be demonstrated that there is a relationship between two units, or a single unit and a larger context at one or more of these levels, it becomes progressively easier to posit a structural relationship between them. At any single level, if a relationship can be shown, then a structural relationship indicating the author's narrative strategy may be suggested. The more levels at which relationships can be demonstrated, the more convincing the relationship at the structural level.

There are several advantages of such an approach to that of classical redaction criticism. The first has to do with the nature of the inferential logic used in redaction criticism. Assumptions include anonymous redactors and editors whose intentions are not always transparent. The result is that, as in most areas of critical thought, there is an extremely complicated hypothetical redactional history of the text. Also, it is difficult to read a biblical work in any form other than the one present. The conjectured forms of the text are not complete but must include supposed deletions. Second, as was noted earlier, the compositional approach is a synchronic approach. It therefore provides the advantage of being justified on the basis of its ability to understand a unified text without making essential a speculative editorial history. Third, there is often grave difficulty in contextualizing a text within a historical framework. The compositional approach has the advantage of treating the text as literature. That is, various units of biblical tradition are given a literary context that potentially supersedes the original context. "A compositional approach provides a means of taking the texts seriously in their final form and of treating the text as bearing meaning apart from specific circumstances."[327] This includes the collateral advantage of not confusing categories between understanding the text and contextualizing its reported events, interpretation and apologetics.[328] This need not necessarily deny that there has been a complicated history of transmission at the diachronic level (possibly including macro-redaction), it simply places the emphasis on the one stage of the transmission available in its unity at the synchronic level: the final form of the text.

Brevard Childs believes that it is this final form of the text that is the key to its own interpretation.[329] It is the shaping process that has led to a "highlighting" of certain elements and a "subordinating" of other elements in the composition. One implication of this shaping is that any emphasis on completely overarching motifs or categories must be resisted if they cause the canonical shape itself to be ignored or relegated to a secondary significance. Such categories might include *Heilsgeschichte*, aesthetics (art), and historical accuracy. Though there will be distance established from any statements questioning the historical accuracy of the biblical text in this book, nevertheless, it can be categorically stated that the making of historical statements and interpretive statements need have no necessary relationship. On canonical shape, Bolger concludes: "To fail to consider the final compositional shape of the biblical text is to risk interpreting it in ways other than those intended by its shapers."[330]

As an orthodox interpreter, then, the present writer has drawn textual clues from 2 Timothy 3:16. This indicates that the text of the Bible is the appropriate starting point for the making of theological statements. It is therefore inappropriate for the interpreter to proceed by the use of systematic categories and historical reconstructions apart from those provided by the text itself. John H. Sailhamer has indicated that meaning of a text is informed by both its sum and its parts. That is, taking his cue from modern text-linguistics, Sailhamer sees that the meaning of a text is understood to be a function of its form and content rather than the subject matter to which it refers.[331] A compositional approach derived from text-linguistics is committed to the self-evident fact that the only access to the events related in the biblical text is that very text itself. It therefore remains imperative that the compositional analyst adheres to the biblical text, for from it are derived both the meaning of the text and the truths and applications which he seeks.

Before discussing Schmitt, perhaps some further explanation of redaction criticism is necessary. John Barton approaches the issue of redaction criticism under the head of form criticism.[332] The question addressed by redaction criticism is, how did the final redactor intend for us to read the text? What redaction criticism does, is to take a small element of classical source theory and attempt by analysis of the seams of the various "texts" to demonstrate why the text was assembled in such a manner. The basic assumption is that if the "texts" are disassembled, they are incoherent. By giving the text a "close reading" the redaction critic attempts to find out how the redactor achieves his effect, why the redactor arranges his material as he does, and what devices the redactor uses to give unity and coherence to his work. In this, several similarities may be seen to what has been described above in regard to compositional analysis. Although it may be said generally that the redaction critic is simply following through on the presuppositions of classical source criticism and form criticism, by simply employing the method and abandoning, ignoring, or suspending judgment on the presuppositions, the exegete is prepared to make something of a transition to compositional analysis.

## Conclusion

By way of concluding commentary, the present writer would like to note several things regarding critical approaches to the biblical text. The redaction criticism Schmitt utilizes to arrive at his version of the supplementary hypothesis includes a series of presuppositions that may not stand up under any kind of scrutiny.[333] First, when he arrives at a conclusion as to which stratum a segment is to be allotted to, has he fulfilled necessary and sufficient conditions to the effect? Let him be given the benefit of the doubt for the sake of argument. Let us say that he has sufficient reason for the allocation of a segment characterized by certain attributes to the Judah stratum, and another with other attributes to the Reuben stratum (or any such alleged stratigraphy [Yahwistic, Elohistic, etc.] with respect to deuteronomistic history). If his system is internally consistent, it could not be said that he had insufficient grounds for his conclusion. However, *if there is any other reason whatsoever* as to why a certain segment contained a particular attribute or characteristic, then it would be inaccurate to say that there were necessary grounds for such a separation. It may be argued that frequently Schmitt argues in exactly such a short circuit. That is, his results may fit the theory, but it still remains an open question as to whether the theory could be proved true.

There is another problem of a general nature. In a significant amount of his argumentation against Redford, Schmitt adopts a historicist stance for the sake of argument. There is a basic problem with forcing these texts into a historical context. One's understanding of the text is made to live or die, as it were, on a comparison between one's historical reconstruction of the times as indicated under determinations external to the text and one's historical reconstruction of the times as described by the text. This problem is further exacerbated by a complicated redactional history presupposing late dates and various revisers from different geographical locations and philosophical/theological perspectives. As to whether or not all these matters can even be sorted out with any reasonable degree of certainty seems questionable.

A third problem has to do with the tacit presupposition of developmentalism. Although Schmitt never overtly makes developmental claims, nevertheless, what he does belies what he believes. For instance, he allocates texts with material including theologized wisdom to the Reuben stratum (similar to E), whereas he thinks the original Judah stratum (similar to J) only contains wisdom materials used in the context of entertainment or folklore. Later still, wisdom in the post-elohist Yahwistic revision stratum (really, post-P) reflects the supposed advancement whereby matters of theodicy are discussed. It is an open question in anthropological circles as to whether religions progress or degenerate or both. It would seem, assuming static intelligence throughout recent history, that very complicated questions were dealt with at every point along the way.

Finally, Schmitt tacitly assumes the presuppositions of the source critical theory in attempting to overturn it. It is not immediately apparent that the methods are significantly different enough to arrive at two such diametrically opposed theories. With source criticism (Schmitt's "classical pentateuchal criticism") one assumes that there are (at least) two complete sources that run parallel through history. They are at some later date combined in what Schmitt calls "a mechanical redaction process"—although he does not embrace such a concept himself. A quick glance at the present writer's doctoral dissertation, Appendix C, should be evidence enough that such a position could not be adopted without further assumptions.[334] The text as we have it does not automatically betray sources. This is where Schmitt indicates that the process had to be very self-conscious and deliberate. With the supplementary hypothesis, there is a single source which goes through several phases of revision. In Schmitt's case, he sees the Judah stratum—a minority of remaining text—as having been read first by the reviser of the Reuben stratum. This redactor reads, interprets, and revises the material deleting from and supplementing his received material in such a way as to achieve his intended theological ends. Subsequently, the post-elohist Yahwistic reviser does approximately the same thing, and so on. In each stage the text is shaped until it becomes the received text, or that which we have now—the final form. The questions remain, nevertheless, as to whether or not there is sufficient information available from the text as it now stands to defend either position against the other. Was it (at least) two separate textual traditions skillfully woven together? Or was it the case that a single textual tradition went through an extensive process of revision? It would be difficult to make a definitive statement either way, given the inferential logic necessary to break away from the final form of the text. It does not seem that critical scholarship, using similar methodology, is able to come to enough of a consensus as to which verses and fragments are to be apportioned to any particular stratum, for the system to be valid. Do the developmental presuppositions hold? It seems that either perspective holds its own developmental presuppositions. It would appear that neither set of developmental presuppositions could be said finally to overthrow those of the other.

In conclusion, it may be seen that redaction criticism as abstracted from its presuppositions is a useful tool to help us determine where there are breaks in the text as we have it. This says exactly nothing with respect to sources that can be stated in anything other than the most risky inferences. What it does help us with is compositional analysis. It shows us changes in stories and episodes. It shows us perspectival shifts as well as changes in emphasis or focus. This compositional emphasis helps us to ferret out such things as themes, development at the ideational level, and application. Wisdom and faith themes are ascertained by using compositional analysis. By looking to the seams of a text, we may find out much more than formal distinctions. We may also find out what it was the writer wanted the reader to take with him after reading the text—application, moralization, an ethical lesson, an expanded or heightened concept of God, and so on. Enjoy the quest!

# Notes

—∕∿∕—

[1] Robert Alter, *The Art of Biblical Narrative* (New York: Basic, 1981), e.g., 159-177, etc., minus the moniker "fiction."

[2] *The Holy Bible: English Standard Version*, ESV (Wheaton, Illinois: Crossway, 2001), 282.

[3] See, for instance, Alan Gardiner, *Egyptian Grammar: Being an Introduction to the Study of Hieroglyphs*, 3rd ed. (Oxford: Griffith Institute, Ashmolean Museum, 1988), 12-15.

[4] Alter, *Art*; Robert Polzin, *Samuel and the Deuteronomist* (Indianapolis: Indiana University Press, 1989, 93); *idem*, *David and the Deuteronomist* (Indianapolis: Indiana University Press, 1993), minus the concept of the Deuteronomist, in my opinion.

[5] On a lighter note, I had a student who wrote the following: "OK Now for some extrospection…I spoke with Charlie today about the Occult and questionable practices in Samuel. It seems that it is treated much too comfortably for the old folks my church. Some examples are: Casting lots to figure out that Jonathan broke his dad's vow. (14:41-42), Picking Saul out of the baggage (10:20), and The whole Endor fiasco. I bring it up because I don't quite know what to make of it. *I expect that Samuel resurgence at Endor will be discussed sufficiently in class…Hey maybe this is when Samuel wrote the rest of 1st and 2nd Samuel. After being dead a while he would have had a chance to get the rest of the story, and he wrote it down then…*" (Brian Beers, Personal Correspondence, September 16, 2003).

[6] Ellisen, Workbook, Part II, 36.

[7] F. Brown, S. R. Driver, C. A. Briggs, *Hebrew and English Lexicon of the Old Testament* (Oxford: Clarendon, 1953), 1028.

[8] Robert Polzin, *David and the Deuteronomist: A Literary Study of the Deuteronomic History*, Part Three 2 Samuel (Indianapolis: Indiana University Press, 1993), 8.

[9] *sic* "deliverances," if you prefer; it is plural. It could be merely abstract, I suppose.

[10] Descendents is lit. "seed." It has the possibility of being either singular or collective plural.

[11] With apologies to Harry Chapin.

[12] Polzin, *David*, 25.

[13] Ludwig Koehler, Walter Baumgartner, *The Hebrew and Aramaic Lexicon of the Old Testament*, vol. 4 (Leiden: Brill, 1999), 1555.

[14] Francis Brown, S. R. Driver, C. A. Briggs, *A Hebrew and English Lexicon of the Old Testament* (Oxford: Clarendon, 1953), 1028.

[15] A point I've often made with respect to pan-Semitic studies: "Hebrew mamas taught Hebrew babies, Hebrew." The point is that they were the vehicles for the conveyance of Hebrew culture through the medium of the Hebrew language. Call me a simpleton if you wish, but, the mamas from Carchemish didn't teach their children anything that could have been understood by either a mama or her baby in Beersheba. Hebrew women knew; and we can only wish we had one here to help us write our grammars and lexicons for us.

[16] This is Prohibition #345 of Maimonides, a twelfth century Jewish philosopher and exegete quoted by John H. Sailhamer. See his *The Pentateuch as Narrative* (Grand Rapids, Zondervan, 1992), 348, 481, 515.

[17] Robert Bergen, "1, 2 Samuel," *The New American Commentary*, vol. 7 (Nashville: Broadman & Holman, 1996), 78.

[18] BDB *Hebrew Lexicon*, 116; used approximately 27 times often times with "sons" hence, "sons of worthlessness."

[19] HALOT 1:133-4; for the adjective, they suggest "ne'er do well."

[20] Bergen, "1, 2 Samuel," 86, n. 47.

[21] Polzin, *Samuel*, 52-3.

[22] Polzin, *Samuel*, 51.

[23] e.g., Wolfgang Schneider, *Grammatik des biblischen Hebräisch* (Munich: Claudius, 1974), 261; "Macrosyntactic signs are words, particles, and expressions which serve . . . to mark out the major divisions of a text. . . . The speaker inserts such macrosyntactic signs in order to highlight for the hearer the beginning, transitions, climaxes, and conclusions of his address. . . . Even if the spoken (colloquial) language is the essential sphere of such macrosyntactic signs, nevertheless its influence can be also observed in the literary, fixed linguistic forms, such as we encounter in the Bible, especially in contexts involving dialogue." Translated into English for us in B. K. Waltke and M. O'Connor, *An Introduction to Biblical Hebrew Syntax* (Winona Lake: Eisenbrauns, 1990), 634.

[24] Note also the unilateral message after "Samuel prayed" in chapter 8. It is also the point where Samuel comes closest to usurping the full prerogative of the "anointed" monarchy. God is the rejected monarch, however, not Samuel.

[25] BDB 710.

[26] HALOT 2:770.

[27] See, for example, Trude Dothan, *The Philistines and Their Material Culture* (New Haven: Yale, 1982), 18-19, 22, 35; *ibid*., 22, "The word *seren*, preserved only in the plural, has been the subject of much research and is thought to be a proto-Greek Illyrian or Lydian word that later entered the Greek language."

[28] Dothan, *Philistines*, 22-3.

[29] In the past, I have used the following outline for the text of chapters nine and ten. Theme: Whether we like it or not and depending upon the empire, each of us has the potential to be either the king or the king-maker. I. Saul's search: Introduction of the king (9:1-14). The meeting between the king and the king-maker is inevitable. II. God's choice for king: Choice of the king (9:15-27). The king-elect experiences many mysterious things in the presence of the king-maker. III. Saul among the prophets: (10:1-16). The king-elect may find a new side to himself after meeting with the king-maker. IV. Saul publicly chosen king: Saul's choice by Israel (10:17-27). The king-elect's acceptance is luminous accolade—the eclipse of the king-maker dark.

[30] From G. D. Vreeland, Ph.D., "Saul: A Life Suspended in Doubt": A Character Sketch for Northwest Baptist Seminary, Chapel Services, May 24,-5, 2001.

[31] Robert D. Bergen, "1, 2 Samuel" *The New American Commentary* (Nashville: Broadman, 1996), 128.

[32] Robert Polzin, *Samuel and the Deuteronomist* (Indianapolis: Indiana University Press, 1989, 93), 92-95.

[33] Polzin, *Samuel*, 101.

[34] Polzin, *Samuel*, 103.

[35] R. Larry Overstreet, "Course Notes" BE512 Old Testament Historical Literature, Northwest Baptist Seminary, Tacoma, WA.

[36] Polzin, *Samuel*, 104.

[37] Polzin, *Samuel*, 104.

[38] Ridout, 105.

[39] This is smooth narration and quote introduction formulae, there is no disjunction "but" as indicated in NASB and other versions (1 Samuel 11:13). It moves swiftly and seamlessly; one might easily imagine that narrative distance and real time are not that far separated here.

[40] My student, Brian Beers, has a rather provocative preliminary study on triple introductions of place names and he will attempt to present that at a future Evangelical Theological Society regional meeting.

[41] I am thankful to the students in my course, BE837 Exposition of First and Second Samuel, for helping me brainstorm this notion and for Brian Beers in particular who not only started the ball rolling but quickly developed the formal presentation while we were in class.

[42] Robert Polzin, *Samuel and the Deuteronomist* (Indianapolis: Indiana University Press, 1993), 108-114.

[43] Robert Bergen, "1 & 2 Samuel" *NAC* (Nashville: Broadman, 1996), e.g., 118, 123, 132, 134, 143, 164, 220.

[44] Robert Bergen, "1 & 2 Samuel" *NAC* (Nashville: Broadman, 1996), 134-5. Here is the translation of the NRSV as quoted in *Ibid.*, 135, n. 34, with a comment from Bergen: "Now Nahash, king of the Ammonites, had been grievously oppressing the Gadites and the Reubenites. He would gouge out the right eye of each of them and would not grant Israel a deliverer. No one was left of the Israelites across the Jordan whose right eye Nahash, king of the Ammonites, had not gouged out. But there were seven thousand men who had escaped from the Ammonites and had entered Jabesh-gilead. About a month later. . ." Other recent versions that include this information are the NEB and NAB.

[45] *Ibid.*

[46] *Ibid.* n. 35.

[47] Robert Bergen, "1 & 2 Samuel" *NAC* (Nashville: Broadman, 1996), 137, n. 41.

[48] Robert Polzin, Samuel and the Deuteronomist (Indianapolis: Indiana University Press, 1993), 72-76.

[49] In the "deuteronomistic literature" *Baal* (singular) is in Jg. 2:13; 6:28, 30, 31, 32; 1 K 16:31, 32, 32, :18:19, 21, 25, 26, 26, 40; 19:18, 22:53; 2 K 3:2; 10:18, 19, 19, 19, 29, 21, 21, 21, 22, 23, 23, 23, 25, 26, 27, 27, 28; 11:18, 18, 17:16; 21:3; 23:4, 5. *Baalim* (Plural) Jg. 2:11; 3:7; 8:33; 10:6, 10; 1 Sam. 7:4; 12:10; 1 K 18:18. *Ashtar* [sic! "*r*" ?] is never mentioned in the singular and may be represented by *Asherah* and *Asherim* (when the idolatrous practice is in focus). There may have been some confusion. In any case, *Ashtaroth* and *Asherim* do appear. *Asherim* appears in Deut. 7:5; 12:3; 1 K 14:15; 23; 2 K 17:10; 23:14. *Asherah* appears in Deut. 16:21; Jg. 6:25, 26, 28, 30;
1 K 15:13; 16:33; 18:19; 2 K 13:6; 17:16; 18:4; 21:3, 7: 23:4, 6, 7, 15. *Ashteroth* appears in Deut. 1:4; Jos. 9:10; 12:4; 13:12, 31 (all place names with Adrei); Jg. 2:13; 19:6; 1 Sam. 7:3, 4; 12:10; 31:10.

[50] Simon Hornblower, Antony Spawforth, *et al.* eds. *The Oxford Classical Dictionary* 3rd ed. (Oxford: Oxford University Press, 2003), 766; Gerald D. Vreeland "The Philistines: Origin, Culture and Conflict," (Th.M. thesis, Western Conservative Baptist Seminary, Portland, Oregon, 1985), 34-35; James D. Muhly, "How Iron Technology Changed the Ancient World, and Gave the Philistines a Military Edge," *Biblical Archaeology Review* 8 (6, 1982): 43; Menashe Har-El, "The Valley of the Craftsmen," *Palestine Exploration Quarterly* 109 (1977): 83.

[51] Apologies to the writers' guild, I forgot to turn off the sound and read the closed captions for the hearing impaired and so I most probably did not get the punctuation quite right. The way the actor plays it, there was more of a full-stop after "Baggins." Regardless, I'm sure all this would have been news to Tolkein. . . .

[52] I really do not want to argue about the "unrealistic" numbers at this point; the point is that both the narrator and the characters sensed that the Philistine military was a very real threat. A huge force in such a narrow strait is a victory waiting to happen for the smaller force. It will work in the next couple of chapters—despite the numbers . . . as it certainly would for the Maccabees.

[53] From Ephraim Stern, ed., *The New Encyclopedia of Archaeological Excavations in the Holy Land*, 4 vols. (Jerusalem: Israel Eexploration Society /Carta, 1993, tables in the back of each volume, e.g.), 4:1529.

[54] I wrote about this years ago: Gerald D. Vreeland, "The Philistines: Origin, Culture and Conflict" (Th.M. Thesis, Western Conservative Baptist Seminary, Portland, Oregon, 1985), 34-37, 44, 63. See also the discussion on the Tabor Oak by Manaseh Har-El, "The Valley of the Craftsmen," *Palestine Exploration Quarterly* 109 (1977):83. Apparently the Tabor Oak burned hotter and so stands of them (*Quercus ithaburensis*) in the highlands were exploited for the manufacture of iron. The older furnaces burned at 1100 to 1200 degrees C;

whereas the Tabor Oak would burn at up to 1530 degrees, the necessary heat for iron production (Vreeland, "Philistines," 34).

[55] 2 Samuel 2:10 (the syntax describing Ish-Bosheth's reign is very much like that used to describe Saul's. However, the manner in which the numeral "two" is used is different, indicating that something has been omitted from the number in Saul's case); 5:4 (In David's case the second indication of years is in the singular); 1 Kings 14:21 (Rehoboam's case matches David's); 2 Kings 8:17 (Jehoram's case likewise), 26 (Ahaziah also); 12:1 (Joash is similar, but there is some intervening material); 15:2 (Azariah's case is syntactically more like the case of David's reign), 33 (Jotham's case is similar to the preceding); 16:2 (The case with Ahaz is the same); 18:2 Hezekiah's case is the same); 21:1 (Manasseh's case is the same), 19 (Amon's case is more like that of Saul: the reason appears to be the numeral "two" requiring the plural of "years"); 22:1 (Josiah's case is more according to the Davidic formula); 23:31 (The pattern is blown with Jehoahaz because of the usage of months instead of years), 36 (The Davidic pattern is resumed with Jehoiakim); 24:8 (with Jehoiachin the pattern reverts to months), 18 (The final instance reverts to the Davidic pattern).

[56] Norman Henry Snaith, ed., *Book of the Law, Prophets and Writings (Heb;* London, The British and Foreign Bible Society, 1958), 442.

[57] Alfred Rahlfs, ed., *Septuaginta* (Stuttgart: Deutsche Bibelgesellschaft, 1979). 523.

[58] K. Elliger, W. Rudolph, *et al.*, *Biblia Hebraica Stuttgartensia*, 5th ed. (Stuttgart: Deutsche Bibelgesellschaft, 1997), 464.

[59] *Ibid.*

[60] Noted in Robert D. Bergen, "1, 2 Samuel," *The New American Commentary* vol. 7 (Nashville: Broadman, 1996), 148 n. 54.

[61] *Ibid.*

[62] This is not the time for a lesson on hermeneutics; but, Luke is writing Scripture here, not Paul and other problems with Paul's speech in this location will be addressed several times in my commentaries on 1 and 2 Samuel. For the record, however, Paul indicates that David, in Acts 13:22, is, "a man after My heart, who will do all My will." Paul is quoting something here; but he is working without the net of a known precedent. We must infer Paul's meaning from 1 Samuel 16:7 and 12. This is a tradition, not a text; and in my opinion there is much in the text that works against the tradition.

[63] Bergen, "1, 2 Samuel," 148.

[64] A "horse acre" is considered by the county to be enough land to raise one horse, or about 8/10 of an acre in my neighborhood.

[65] People have often commented upon the severity of the punishment. "Couldn't he just repay it?" "Did everybody in the family have to die?" The only provisional resolution that I have been able to come up with is this threefold suggestion: perhaps the severity of the times coupled with Jerry's Law of the First Offense along with the complicity of his family members in the crime ensued in what to us, not to them, appeared to be cruel and unusual punishment.

[66] Barry J. Beitzel, *The Moody Atlas of Bible Lands* (Chicago: Moody Press, 1985), 113, map 40.

[67] One of the more intriguing usages of this verse came to me in a rather uncomfortable way: one time I was out trying desperately to keep the wolf away from the door by public speaking. Part of the agreement was that I would be given a free lunch along with my honorarium. I accepted and certain persons were appointed to entertain me and my family. During the course of conversation, we ascertained that the man was, in fact, an American citizen; but his wife was a foreign national. The discussion degenerated to the topic of the American revolution—a matter of some pride in our household. Educational systems elsewhere apparently put a different spin on it from how we were raised—this lady having been an educator in their system. And she quoted us: "Rebellion is as the sin of divination, and insubordination is as iniquity and idolatry" (1 Samuel 15:23a, b). My first thought was, "Yeah, and you're not supposed to return a slave to his master,

either" (approximately, Deuteronomy 23:15). Having been taught manners by my Victorian parents, I kept my peace. Be that as it may, I cannot say that I have ever seen that verse prostituted in such a manner. But regardless of what I think about the United States and her latter-day "divination, iniquity and idolatry," this encounter demonstrates several things. First, grudges can go on for generations, yea, centuries; and just because I like folks from, say, the Commonwealth, for instance, that does not necessarily mean they like me or even want to put forth the most minuscule effort to understand me. Secondly, not everybody thinks that the disassembling of the Commonwealth was a good idea. Thirdly, some people think that drunk, insane, oppressive, Hessians (e.g., George III) were the good guys. Fourthly, I am reminded of the duplicity of those who live, prosper and even thrive off a system they secretly and sometimes outspokenly loathe or seek to overthrow. Finally, and as pertains to our topic here, some people will take any verse of the Bible out and make it walk away to any end they so choose—regardless of context. The context is the direct disobedience to a direct and clear command from God to a specific ruler in ancient Israel. That is what God considers to be like "divination, iniquity and idolatry." Although there are many who would de-legitimize the government of the United States, they would do well to look elsewhere than a contextualized quote imbedded in an eleventh century narrative from a universe away.

[68] e.g., Leviticus 19:26 (different word, same idea); Numbers 22:7; 23:23; (Balaam Narratives and oracles, same word) more precisely, Deuteronomy 18:10 (listed and compared to those who practice human sacrifice).

[69] BDB 1043; HALOT 4:1609.

[70] HALOT 4:1609.

[71] In the past, I have used the following as theme and main points for oratory presentation: (Theme), God's man or woman will be characterized by virtue. 1. God's man or woman will be busy (vs. 1-12). 2. God's man or woman will be gifted—Spiritual gifts, learned skills, natural talents (vs. 13-17). 3. God's man or woman will be winsome—attractive, charismatic, [without any negative connotations] (vs. 18-23).

[72] For a fascinating discussion on 1 Samuel 16 for those who know Hebrew well, see, Robert D. Bergen, "Evil Spirits and Eccentric Grammar," in Bergen, ed., *Biblical Hebrew and Discourse Linguistics* (Dallas: SIL, 1994), 320-335.

[73] Millard J. Erickson, *Christian Theology* (Grand Rapids: Baker, 1983-5), 990-1.

[74] *Ibid.*, 995.

[75] Trude Dothan, *The Philistines and Their Material Culture* (New Haven: Yale, 1982), 19.

[76] Trude Dothan, Moshe Dothan, *People of the Sea: The Search for the Philistines* (New York: Macmillan, 1992), 10.

[77] Ephraim Stern, ed., *The New Encyclopedia of Archaeological Excavations in the Holy Land* (Jerusalem: Carta/Israel Exploration Society, 1993), charts on 1530.

[78] Wolfgang Schneider, *Grammatic des biblischen Hebräisch* (Munich: Claudius, 1974), 231, 261-3; Bruce K. Waltke, M. O'Connor, *An Introduction to Biblical Hebrew Syntax* (Winona Lake, IN: Eisenbrauns, 1990), 54-55, 578-79, 634, 667-68, etc.

[79] e.g., Robert Polzin, *David and the Deuteronomist* (Indianapolis: Indiana University Press, 1993), 165-6.

[80] Robert Polzin, *Samuel and the Deuteronomist* (Bloomington: Indiana University Press, 1989, 93), 177-8.

[81] In the past, I have used the following as theme: Loss of personal integrity leads to loss of leadership integrity and finally to self-destructive behavior and ruin of the institution.

[82] See note 80 above.

[83] Both verbs are in the *niph'al* theme and are, in theory, "passive voice." The first is incompleted action and hence open to the hypothetical slot in which the narrator has David put it. The second is completed action and

illustrative of a historical tense the narrator uses in describing Jonathan as he left the banquet room in a huff. The subject of both verbs ("he") is Jonathan.

[84] Just a note here: Ahimelech was most probably the "high priest." However, because of the thematic thread running through the narrative that Eli's house is doomed, the narrator probably wished to avoid such nomenclature until such a time as Zadok is available for elevation (cf. 2 Samuel 8:17 and 1 Kings 2:35) and Abiathar had been defrocked. Until fairly late in the monarchy, "the priest" functions as either a term for the office of high priest or a title for a specific priest according to the context. It would not appear that the term "the high priest" was used in biblical narrative until Jehoiada's time (2 Kings 12:10). In Leviticus, the term appears to be "the anointed priest" (e.g., Leviticus 4:3, 5, 16; 6:22; esp. 16:32). The term "the high priest" is of course already known in Numbers in regard to the cities of refuge (Numbers 35:25, 28 bis.). The word in this case is the same as that used to refer to Jehoiada. Succession being established, the term (chief or high priest) is unknown in Deuteronomy, Joshua, Judges 1 & 2 Samuel and 1 Kings. However, it is implied in the context by specificity of the office and in the usage of the definite article.

[85] I once did a message under the title of "Four Pitfalls of Christian Leadership." Some of that material will be retained.

[86] For a brief history of the debate between the Jesuits and the Dominicans, the literature, and an excellent discussion on David's conversations with God at Keilah see, Robert Merrihew Adams, "Middle Knowledge and the Problem of Evil" in *The Problem of Evil*, M. M. Adams and R. M. Adams, eds. (New York: Oxford University Press, 1990), 110-125.

[87] See relevant recent discussions in John S. Feinberg, *No One Like Him*, (Wheaton: Crossway, 2001), 325-337, 375-436; Gregory E. Ganssle, ed., *God and Time* (Downers Grove: InterVarsity, 2001), *passim*; William Lane Craig, *Time and Eternity: Exploring God's Relationship to Time* (Wheaton: Crossway, 2001), *passim*.

[88] Private conversation with Donna G. Vreeland, May 18, 2004.

[89] For those who might want to bend their brains farther, I might suggest: William Lane Craig, "'Men Moved By the Holy Spirit Spoke from God' 2 Peter 1:21: A Middle Knowledge Perspective on Biblical Inspiration," *Philosophia Christi*, (1999): 2:1:1:45-82. I might also suggest a discussion that actually includes this material from 1 Samuel 23, Edward Wierenga, "Providence, Middle Knowledge, and the Grounding Objection," *Philosophia Christi*, (2001), 2:3:2: 447-457.

[90] Special thanks go to Dr. Jack Willsey, our systematics guru at Northwest Baptist Seminary for correcting my *haphakh* (reversal) of these ideas. It is good to have someone around that is current in the jargon generator department. See also Feinberg, *No One Like Him*, 378, where the term, *sempiternity*, is defined.

[91] In my New Testament courses, I go at odds with the establishment—you would expect as much—and suggest that our customary definitions of grace are too passive. I suggest, and attempt to defend, that grace is the benevolent power of God toward His people. That is, grace seems to do things and is hence powerful; grace seems to be limited, like the effects of angels to those who will inherit salvation; and His people are those in special relationship to Him by grace through faith.

[92] Robert Polzin, *Samuel and the Deuteronomist* (Indianapolis: Indiana University Press, 1993), 205; the enclosed quotes are, of course, from Kyle McCarter "1 Samuel" in the *Anchor Bible* (Garden City: Doubleday, 1980), 400.

[93] Judges 13:2; 17:1; 19:1; Ruth 1:1; 1 Samuel 1:1; 9:1.

[94] cf. Bergen, "1, 2 Samuel" *NAC*, 209-10: "The term translated by the NIV here as a geographic name literally means "dwellings/habitation" and may refer to a religious compound within Ramah, perhaps even the one mentioned in 9:22."

[95] This "threefold" business here indicated by the temporary insanity of three sets of emissaries, culminates in the threefold attempt to retrieve Elijah, much later in the "deuteronomistic" history (2 Kings 1:9-16) when

fire consumes two of the three companies sent. Apart from the viable historical nature of things, it is excellent storytelling technique!

[96] I am thankful to Mark Steyn, "Now's not the time for Bush to go soft," Chicago Sun Times, May 16, 2004, for this image.

[97] In the presentation of this as a message, I followed the main idea that "integrity is rare in the desert."

[98] Harold S. Kushner, *When Bad Things Happen to Good People* (New York: Avon, 1981).

[99] *Ibid.*, italics, the publisher.

[100] In the past I have used the following for theme and points: Theme: Godless Leadership Is But Another Sorry Tale of Money, Power and Politics. 1. Unchecked Fear Can Lead to Godless Leadership. 2. Godless Places and Godless People Can Mould Us (either by de fault, design or *de facto*?) into Godless Leaders. 3. Deception and Violence Are Characteristics of Godless Leadership.

[101] This is often done with "Abimelech" in Genesis 20 and 26. Nevertheless it could be a case of poponomy, naming after the grandfather—Achish in the second text is, after all, called the son of Maoch; there is no such referent in the first text.

[102] In all this I refuse to accept the conventional wisdom with its obsolete mantras that necessitates multiple authors, strands, strata and trumps each non-falsifiable argument with the hermeneutical slight-of-hand of a convenient redactor from up the sleeve. The story is simply too perfect for that and it works better than the many scenes from the Odyssey. The fact that the story is astonishing means precisely nothing with respect to its being possible. I maintain that it is possible that all Philistia was momentarily struck blind and that the former "incognito" appearance of a nutty David worked. The scenario is far too brilliantly described for the narrator not to have noticed when something drew dissonance to the breaking point. Apart from a predilection for the cynical, one ought to leave a story to its own merits . . . it is someone else's story, after all. . . . Meanwhile back at non-falsifiability: Non-falsifiability with a coherent system shifts the burden of proof or disproof to the cynic. My text, I maintain, is a coherent system and the burden is shifted to the skeptic.

[103] Unless I'm mistaken, this is the kind of thing that Polzin and others call *mise-en-abyme*. However, it needs to be said that the definitions are so opaque, arcane, and esoteric as to defy comprehension by the uninitiated; see, Polzin, *David*, 37-8. That is one of the problems we non-guild people face when trying to play with other peoples' nomenclature: the guild literary Shriners don't want us to know the sacred handshake. . . . Part of it has to do with, as Polzin candidly expresses, the fact that "We have no commonly accepted designation in English for this literary phenomenon. . ."; *Ibid.*, 38. Regardless, it seems to be a manner of telling the story that mirrors what the story is about: Like Jonah's spiritual descent being mirrored by all the "and he went down" verbs in chapter 1 of Jonah. According to my French dictionaries, *Mise en* has something to do with "manner of." *Abyme* is not in any of them and when a Frenchman starts speaking in tongues, all bets are off.

[104] See also, Deut. 10:17, 19 (*bis*); 27:25; Prov. 15:5; 17:8, 23; 21:14.

[105] I owe a debt of gratitude to my colleague and friend, Dr. R. Larry Overstreet for some of these insights. They were derived from personal discussion but are available from his chapel message on May 29, 2003 at Northwest Baptist Seminary. Tapes may be obtained by contacting the school.

[106] Robert Polzin, *Samuel and the Deuteronomist: A Literary Study of the Deuteronomic History* (Indianapolis: Indiana University Press, 1989), *passim* esp. 255, n. 1.

[107] In the past, I have used the following for a theme and main points for 1 Samuel 28 and 29. Theme: When the institution finally crashes to the ground, there will be some bizarre side effects. Points: 1. Leadership, grasping at straws, will entertain bizarre methods to gain information and results. 2. Against all logic, some allies will become enemies—some of those enemies will be protected. Corollary: 3. Against all logic, some allies will remain allies—some of those allies will not be protected.

[108] *Webster's Ninth New Collegiate Dictionary*, 722.

[109] *Ibid.*, 790.

[110] Bergen, *NAC*, 265.

[111] "Renewed, renovated," C. T. Lewis, *Elementary Latin Dictionary* (Oxford: University Press, 1991), 709; e.g., Domitian was supposed to be Nero redivivus.

[112] Robert D. Bergen, "1, 2 Samuel" *NAC* (Nashville, Broadman, 1996), 265.

[113] *Ibid.*, 267, n. 150.

[114] *Ibid.*

[115] *Ibid.*

[116] *Ibid.*

[117] Ronald J. Youngblood, "1 & 2 Samuel," *Expositor's Biblical Commentary*, ed., Frank E. Gaebelein, *et al.* vol. 3 (Grand Rapids: Zondervan, 1992), 778-9.

[118] Robert D. Bergen, "1 & 2 Samuel," *The New American Commentary: An Exegetical and Theological Exposition of Holy Scripture NIV Text*, ed., E. Ray Clendenen, *et al.* (Nashville: Broadman, 1996), 265, n.149.

[119] Again, for chapters 28 and 29, I have used these for the theme and points. Theme: When the institution finally crashes to the ground, there will be some bizarre side effects. Points: Leadership, grasping at straws, will entertain bizarre methods to gain information and results. 2. Against all logic, some allies will become enemies—some of those enemies will be protected. Corollary: Against all logic, some allies will remain allies—some of those allies will not be protected.

[120] "In this figure a negative statement is used to declare an affirmative truth." A. Berkeley Mickelsen, *Interpreting the Bible* (Grand Rapids: Eerdmans, 1963), 193.

[121] Robert D. Bergen, "1, 2 Samuel" *NAC* (Nashville, Broadman, 1996), 272.

[122] D. A. Carson, *Exegetical Fallacies* 2nd ed. (Grand Rapids: Baker, 1996), 139.

[123] See HALOT 1:58, for the broad and not infrequent usage of the term.

[124] *Ibid.*

[125] e.g., Polzin, *Samuel*, 81-83, in my lowly opinion, he handles this particularly well; and defined more broadly, *ibid.*, 86.

[126] Polzin, *David and the Deuteronomist*, 16-17; cf. Polzin, *Samuel and the Deuteronomist*, 223-24.

[127] Polzin, *David*, 17.

[128] *Narrative Art in the Bible*, JSOTSupp. 70 (Sheffield: Almond, 1984).

[129] Hans-Christoph Schmitt, *Die Nichtpriesterliche Josephsgeschichte* (Berlin: De Gruyter, 1980), 199-218; George W. Coats, *From Canaan to Egypt* (Washington, D.C.: The Catholic Biblical Association of America, 1976), 93-96; Claus Westermann, *Genesis: A Commentary*, 3 vols. (Minneapolis: Augsburg, 1984-86), 3: 15-18, 31-32, 46-47, 58-59; Donald B. Redford, *A Study of the Biblical Story of Joseph (Genesis 37-50)*, Supplement to *Vetus Testamentum* 20 (Leiden: Brill, 1979), 254-72.

[130] Robert D. Bergen, "1, 2 Samuel" in *The New American Commentary* E. Ray Clendenen, *et al.*, eds. (Nashville: Brodman & Holman, 1996); Robert Polzin, *Samuel and the Deuteronomist: A Literary Study of the Deuteronomic History* Part Two, 1 Samuel (Bloomington & Indianapolis: Indiana University Press, 1989, 93); *Idem, David and the Deuteronomist: A Literary Study of the Deuteronomic History*, Part Three 2 Samuel (Bloomington & Indianapolis: Indiana University Press, 1993); Walter Bruggemann, "First and Second Samuel," in *Interpretation: A Bible Commentary for Teaching and Preaching*, James L. Mays *et al.*, eds. (Louisville: John Knox Press, 1990; Ronald F. Youngblood, "1, 2 Samuel," in *The Expositor's Bible Commentary*, Frank E. Gaebelein *et al.*, eds. vol. 3 (Grand Rapids: Zondervan, 1992).

[131] Notions such as positivity in interpretation are initially treated below, pp. 25-32.

[132] See for example Shimon Bar-Efrat, *Narrative Art in the Bible*, JSOTSupp. 70 (Sheffield: Almond, 1984; Robert Alter, *The Art of Biblical Narrative* (New York: Basic Books, 1981); Meir Sternberg, *The Poetics of Biblical Narrative: Ideological Literature and the Drama of Reading* (Bloomington: Indiana University

Press, 1985); George W. Coats, *From Canaan to Egypt: Structural and Theological Context for the Joseph Story* (Washington, D.C.: The Catholic Biblical Association of America, 1976); and Claus Westermann, *Genesis: A Commentary*, trans. J. J. Scullion, 3 vols. (Minneapolis: Augsburg, 1984-86), vol. 3.

[133] See below, pp. 21-22, 419, n. 250.

[134] For what follows, I am indebted to Eric Bolger for his groundbreaking work in this area both in personal conversation and in his dissertation proposal for Trinity Evangelical Divinity School, 1992, 2-7.

[135] See Georg Fohrer, *Exegese des Alten Testaments: Einführung in die Methodik* (Heidelberg: Quelle & Meyer, 1983) 143.

[136] Robert Alter, *The Art of Biblical Narrative* (New York: Basic Books, 1981).

[137] Ibid., 47.

[138] Ibid., 51.

[139] Ibid., 52.

[140] Ibid., 60-61.

[141] Ibid., 61.

[142] J. Daniel Hays, "Has the Narrator Come to Praise Solomon or to Bury Him? Narrative Subtlety in 1 Kings 1-11," Paper for NW Region of ETS, Plenary Address, March 1, 2003 *JSOT* 28, no. 2 (2003), 149-174.

[143] Alter, *Art*, 65.

[144] Ibid.

[145] Ibid., 66.

[146] Ibid., 67.

[147] Ibid., 67-68.

[148] Ibid., 69-70.

[149] Ibid., 74.

[150] Ibid., 74.

[151] Ibid., 75.

[152] Ibid., 77.

[153] Ibid., 80.

[154] Ibid., 88.

[155] Ibid., 89.

[156] Ibid.

[157] Ibid., 90.

[158] Ibid., 91.

[159] Ibid.

[160] Ibid., 92-3.

[161] Ibid., 94-5.

[162] Ibid., 95-6.

[163] Ibid., 97.

[164] Ibid., 98.

[165] Ibid., 100.

[166] Ibid., 102.

[167] Ibid., 107-8.

[168] Ibid., 112.

[169] Ibid.

[170] Ibid., 112-3.

[171] Ibid., 114-5; I will discuss the issues involved with foregrounding and backgrounding in the treatment below.

[172] Ibid., 117.

[173] Ibid., 117-8; See below where, with the help of Polzin and Sternberg, I attempt to develop Saul's transparent character and David's opaque nature in the narrative.

[174] Ibid., 118.

[175] Ibid., 120.

[176] Ibid., 121-2.

[177] Ibid., 124-5.

[178] Ibid., 125-6.

[179] Ibid., 126.

[180] Ibid., 127.

[181] Ibid.

[182] Ibid., 129.

[183] Ibid., 129-30.

[184] Julius Wellhausen, *Prolegomena to the History of Israel*, Trans. Black and Menzies (Edinburgh: Black, 1885), 342, with respect to Exodus through Deuteronomy; however, nothing else Wellhausen does indicates that he could produce a "unity" superior to that of the final form—anywhere!

[185] Alter, *Art*, 132.

[186] Ibid., 133.

[187] Ibid.

[188] Quoted in Ibid., 135.

[189] Ibid., 136.

[190] Ibid.

[191] Ibid.

[192] Ibid., 137-40.

[193] Ibid., 141.

[194] Ibid., italics his.

[195] Ibid.

[196] Ibid., 144.

[197] Ibid., 145.

[198] Ibid., 146.

[199] Ibid., 147.

[200] Ibid., 148; following and noting Gros Louis.

[201] Ibid., 149.

[202] Ibid., 150.

[203] Ibid.

[204] Ibid., 152.

[205] Ibid., 153.

[206] Ibid., 154.

[207] Ibid.

[208] Ibid.

[209] Ibid., 155.

[210] Ibid., 155-6, italics his; I need to place a disclaimer here: Alter writes this whole book under the rubric of "prose fiction." That is he feels that the Bible is fiction which may or may not be finally proven to be historical. To him, the issue is virtually irrelevant. However, to those of us that respect the Bible as both literature and history—as true truth—and to those of us who have lived life outside of the ivory tower of the academe, we might note that there is comedy and tragedy in any life worth living. It is almost easier to view these

narratives as real historical, albeit selectively historical, accounts of real people in a real world as depicted by a real narrator narrating a real narrative world. There is certainly nothing that necessarily militates against the historical.

[211] Ibid., 156; However, it is my opinion that the narrative historian can accomplish the same task of crafting characterization by selecting his material. When will he tell the story by "indirect discourse"—merely narrate the story? When will he tell the story through the characters' quotations, monologues and dialogues? The answers to these questions create characterization as readily as the "prose fictional method."

[212] Now there is some privileged information!

[213] Alter, *Art*, 157.

[214] Ibid.

[215] An interesting admission!

[216] Ibid., 157-8.

[217] Ibid., 158.

[218] Ibid.

[219] Ibid.

[220] Ibid., 158-9.

[221] Ibid., 159-163; You should notice that "recognize" is beaten to death in Gen. 37:32-33 and 42:7-8, etc., so much so that our English versions tend to use different vocabulary to avoid the monotony. This recognition also carries forward a motif beginning with Jacob's deception of Isaac e.g., Gen. 27:23.

[222] Ibid., 176.

[223] Ibid; I, of course, concur as long as we realize that the word "fictional" promotes a heretofore unproven assumption. It could be just good prose history.

[224] The blow-hot blow-cold relationships between Samuel and Saul and David and Saul and Jonathan and Saul come to mind here.

[225] The relationship between Saul and Jonathan fits here perhaps.

[226] Ibid. See some of my characterization of Saul below. These texts become all the more profound as we see that they were, in biblical times, dealing with the same issues and personal dissonance as we are in the post, post-modern world.

[227] Ibid. Of course, the fact that some of the long shelf life of these stories is related to truth claims is also important.

[228] Ibid., 176-7; elsewhere he has referred to this as the "monotheistic revolution" so I question the usage of the word "revelation" in the second line.

[229] Taken from Gerald D. Vreeland, Ph.D. Diss. (Deerfield Illinois: Trinity Evangelical Divinity School, 1994), 117-146.

[230] Teun van Dijk's 1979 work is referred to in Robert de Beaugrande and Wolfgang Dressler, *Introduction to Text Linguistics* (London: Longman, 1981), 14.

[231] de Beaugrande and Dressler, *Introduction*, 23, (citing Kenneth Pike, *Language in Relation to a Unified Theory of the Structure of Human Behavior*, [The Hague, Mouton, 1967]); Robert D. Bergen, "Text as a Guide to Authorial Intention: An Introduction to Discourse Criticism," *JETS* 30/3 (1987) 327; F. I. Andersen (*The Sentence in Biblical Hebrew*, [The Hague: Mouton, 1974], 21-24) uses the word "clause" where some text-linguists employ the word "sentence."

[232] de Beaugrande and Dressler, *Introduction*, 19.

[233] Ibid., 3, emphasis theirs.

[234] Ibid., 4, emphasis theirs.

[235] Ibid., 5-6.

[236] Ibid., 7, emphasis theirs.

[237] Ibid., 7, emphasis theirs.

[238] Ibid., 8-9, emphasis theirs.

[239] Ibid., 8.

[240] Ibid., 9, emphasis theirs.

[241] Ibid., 10, emphasis theirs.

[242] Depending upon how one views the textual fabric called Genesis, a decision may have to be made as to whether the Joseph Narrative looks back upon the Patriarchal Narratives in an inner-textual or inter-textual manner. It is not the purpose of the writer to answer such questions at this point.

[243] de Beaugrande and Dressler, *Introduction*, 14-18.

[244] Ibid., 18.

[245] Ibid., 18-19.

[246] Robert D. Bergen, "Text as a Guide to Authorial Intention: An Introduction to Discourse Criticism," *JETS* 30/3 (1987): 327-36.

[247] Longacre, *Joseph*, 14.

[248] e.g., see Gen. 50:25, concerning the disposition of Joseph's remains.

[249] John H. Sailhamer, "Introduction to Hebrew Narrative," (Unpublished lecture for Trinity Evangelical Divinity School, n.d.).

[250] Ibid., 18.

[251] Ibid., 20, n.36.

[252] Ibid., emphasis his.

[253] Longacre, *Joseph*, 15.

[254] Ibid., 15.

[255] Ibid., 15.

[256] Macrostructure is further explained below, pp. 140-42.

[257] As we have already stated, one proficient in *Joseph* will do well in *Samuel* as many of the analogies will apply.

[258] Longacre, *Joseph*, xii; idem., "Analysis of Preverbal Nouns in Biblical Hebrew Narrative: Some Overriding Concerns," *Journal of Translation and Textlinguistics, JOTT* 5 (1992): 209, n.1.

[259] Longacre, *Joseph*, 13-14.

[260] Ibid., 14.

[261] Ibid., 42.

[262] 5a. Language texts are composed of successively smaller organizational units of language; b. Each successively higher level of textual organization influences all of the lower levels of which it is composed.

[263] Longacre, *Joseph*, 42, emphasis his.

[264] Ibid., 43.

[265] Ibid., 43.

[266] Ibid., 43.

[267] Ibid., 42, *sic*; note here also the preliminary textual assumptions Longacre is making about the text's parameters.

[268] Ibid., 54.

[269] Ibid., 59-63.

[270] Ibid., 59.

[271] Ibid.

[272] Ibid.

[273] Ibid., 60.

[274] Ibid.

[275] Ibid.

[276] Ibid.

[277] It may also be of interest to note that there are several subcategories of paragraphs in each type of discourse. Narrative has nine subcategories: sequence, simple, reason, result, comment, amplification, paraphrase, coordinate, and antithetical. Predictive has seven subcategories: sequence, reason, comment, amplification, coordinate, antithetical, and evidence. Expository has seven subcategories: result, reason, comment, amplification, paraphrase, coordinate, and evidence. Also, hortatory discourse has four discourse subcategories: unmitigated, partially mitigated, completely mitigated, and deferential.

[278] Longacre, *Joseph*, 87 (preterite = simple past tense in English).

[279] Ibid., 106 (often in the form "and X will do such and such").

[280] Ibid., 111 (participles, infinitives, nominal sentences [and probably stative verbs]).

[281] Ibid., 121 (any verb expressing mood in English: imperative, exhortation "let us do such and such," or also the third person, jussive force, "let him do such and such." My opinion is that these go in the order of second, first, and third person from strongest to weakest respectively.).

[282] Ibid., 59.

[283] Ibid., 81.

[284] Ibid., 81-82.

[285] Ibid., 82, n. 6.

[286] Nicholas A. Bailey and Stephen H. Levinsohn, "The Function of Preverbal Elements in Independent Clauses in the Hebrew Narrative of Genesis," *JOTT* 5 (1992): 179-207.

[287] Robert E. Longacre, "The Analysis of Preverbal Nouns in Biblical Hebrew Narrative: Some Overriding Concerns," *JOTT* 5 (1992): 216.

[288] Longacre, "Concerns," 214.

[289] Robert E. Longacre, *Joseph: A Story of Divine Providence* (Winona Lake: Eisenbrauns, 1989) 141-2.

[290] Ibid., 142.

[291] Steven D. Mathewson, *The Art of Preaching Old Testament Narrative* (Grand Rapids: Baker, 2002).

[292] Longacre, *Joseph*, 142-3.

[293] Ibid., 143; so in the case of the Joseph story, Joseph is the protagonist whereas his brothers become antagonists. Jacob is reduced to the status of a bystander. Minor participants include the man who found him wandering around near Shechem, the cupbearer and the baker, Potiphar's wife, and the steward in Joseph's house. It is a judgment call as to whether Pharaoh is a major or minor participant. Interestingly, Benjamin, who never speaks, is a human prop, the donkeys animate props, the cloak of Joseph and his clothes grabbed by Mrs. Potiphar inanimate props, etc.

[294] Ibid., 143.

[295] Adapted from G. D. Vreeland, Ph.D. Diss. (Deerfield, Illinois: Trinity Evangelical Divinity School, 1994), 1-4, 13-23. 284-294, 346-350.

[296] These notions are expanded and developed below in the introduction to Chapter 4, p. 289.

[297] Shimon Bar-Efrat, *Narrative Art in the Bible* (*JSOTSuppl.* 70, Sheffield: Almond, 1984) 212; these matters will be further developed below in the introduction to Chapter 4, pp. 289-90.

[298] See below, pp. 16-17.

[299] Left to right: to fill, to multiply, to be fruitful.

[300] The typology may be also extended: שרץ is used in Gen. 1 as well, but not in the blessing. Note also the roots עצם and שרץ are used in Ex. 1:7. The three terms פרה /רבה /מלא are used at the recreation in Gen. 9:7, when God blesses the survivors of the flood. Note also how Abimelech uses the word עצם when he asks Isaac to move away in Gen. 26:16; it seems that soon Pharaoh would be compelled to ask Israel to move away

because they were too mighty for him. This then puts five terms in a tight grouping to connect Exodus with the earlier traditions of Genesis.

[301] J. Sailhamer, "Genesis," in *The Expositors Bible Commentary*, vol. 2, F. Gaebelein, ed. (Grand Rapids: Zondervan, 1990) 279.

[302] Ronald B. Allen, Class Notes for BLS 521 "Genesis," Portland, Or.: Western Conservative Baptist Seminary, Spring 1984.

[303] John H. Sailhamer, "1 Chronicles 21:1 — A Study in Inter-Biblical Interpretation," *TrinJ* 10 NS (1989) 45; idem., "Genesis," in *The Expositors Bible Commentary*, F. Gaebelein ed. (Grand Rapids: Zondervan, 1990) 125.

[304] Gerald D. Vreeland, "The Joseph Narrative — Genesis 37-39: An Analysis of Three Modern Textual Approaches" (Ph.D. Diss., Trinity Evangelical Divinity School, 1994), 18-19. John H. Sailhamer, "Genesis," in *The Expositor's Bible Commentary*, Frank E. Gaebelein, ed., vol. 2 (Grand Rapids: Zondervan, 1990), 125-6.

[305] 1. The Amorite. 2. Covenant. 3. Eliezer. 4. Dan/ "will judge." 5. Damascus. 6. The possessions/with possessions. 7. [Melchi]zedek/righteousness. 8. Salem/in peace/full. 9. Heaven/toward the heavens. 10. Delivered/shield. 11. Possession/your reward.

[306] א = 1, ל = 30, י = 10, ע = 70, ז = 7, ר = 200: = 318.

[307] Sailhamer, *Genesis*, 125; idem., "Inter-Biblical Interpretation," 45.

[308] Gerhard von Rad, *Old Testament Theology*, (New York: Harper, 1962) vol.1, 172f.; Idem., *Genesis: A Commentary*, (Philadelphia: Westminster, 1971) 347-440; Idem., "Josephgeschichte und ältere Chokma," in *Vetus Testamentum Supp.* 1 (1953) 120ff.

[309] Eric Bolger, *The Compositional Role of the Eden Narrative in the Pentateuch*. Ph.D. Dissertation, Trinity Evangelical Divinity School, 197-200; See also John H. Sailhamer, *The Pentateuch as Narrative*, (Grand Rapids: Zondervan, 1992) 221-30.

[310] Bolger, *The Eden Narrative*, 24.

[311] Ibid., 24; bracketed italics are mine.

[312] Hans-Christoph Schmitt, *Die Nichtpriesterliche Josephsgeschichte: Ein Beitrag zur neusten Pentateuch-kritik*, (Berlin: De Gruyter, 1980); also note at the outset his dependency on P. Volz and W. Rudolph, *Der Elohist als Erzähler Ein Irrweg der Pentateuchkritik?* (Giessen: Verlag von Alfred Töpelmann, 1933), particularly the second section by Rudolph exclusively on the Joseph Narrative.

[313] e.g., Westermann, *Genesis*, vol. 3.

[314] e.g., Coats, *From Canaan to Egypt*.

[315] Alter, *The Art of Biblical Narrative*, 10-11.

[316] Ibid., 46.

[317] Georg Fohrer, *Exegese des Alten Testaments: Einführung in die Methodik* (Heidelberg: Quelle & Meyer, 1983), 139-40.

[318] Eric Bolger, "The Compositional Role of the Eden Narrative in the Pentateuch" (Ph.D. Dissertation, Trinity Evangelical Divinity School, 1992), 14.

[319] John H. Sailhamer, "Genesis," *EBC*, 6.

[320] Fohrer, *Exegese*, 143.

[321] Bolger, *Eden Narrative*, 16-17, emphasis his.

[322] Bolger, *Eden Narrative*, 15; Fohrer, *Exegese*, 144-46.

[323] Bolger, *Eden Narrative*, 15.

[324] John H. Sailhamer, "Exegetical Notes: Genesis 1:1-2:4a," *TrinJ* 5 (1984): 74.

[325] Shimon Bar-Efrat, "Some Observations on the Analysis of Structure in Biblical Narrative," *VT* 30 (1980): 154-73.

[326] Bolger, *Eden Narrative*, 23.

[327] Ibid., 28.

[328] See General Introduction "Theory on Reading the Biblical Text" above.

[329] Brevard Childs, *Introduction to the Old Testament as Scripture* (Philadelphia: Fortress, 1979), 76.

[330] Bolger, *Eden Narrative*, 33.

[331] John H. Sailhamer, "Exegesis of the Old Testament as a Text," in *A Tribute to Gleason Archer*, ed. Walter C. Kaiser, Jr. and Ronald F. Youngblood (Chicago: Moody Press, 1986), 279-96.

[332] John Barton, *Reading the Old Testament: Method in Biblical Study* (Philadelphia: Westminster, 1984), 43-59.

[333] It is not the purpose of this book to give an exhaustive refutation of critical methodology and presuppositions; such a presentation would be multiple volume in itself. For several treatments of varying comprehensiveness and acceptance see: J. Orr, *The Problem of the Old Testament* (New York: Scribners, 1908); B. B. Warfield, *The Inspiration and Authority of the Bible* (Phillipsburg, N.J.: Presbyterian and Reformed, 1948) (a series of reprinted articles appearing from 1892-1915, see esp. his treatment on "Inspiration and Criticism") 419-42; S. R. Driver, *An Introduction to the Literature of the Old Testament* (Edinburgh: T. & T. Clark, 1913. 9th ed.), which if taken seriously would render impossible his more realistic work in idem. *A Treatise on the Use of the Tenses in Hebrew* (Oxford: Clarendon, 1892) due to the impossibility of critical dissection cohabiting with the textually static assumptions required for syntax and semantics; P. Volz and W. Rudolph, *Der Elohist als Erzähler: Ein Irrweg der Pentateuchkritik?* (Giessen: Verlag von Alfred Töpelmann, 1933); U. Cassuto, *La Questione della Genesi* (Florence: University of Florence, 1934); idem. *The Documentary Hypothesis, and the Composition of the Pentateuch: Eight Lectures* (Jerusalem: Magnes Press, 1941, 1983); W. L. Möller, *Grundriß für alttestamentliche Einleitung* (Berlin: Evangelische Verlagsanstalt, 1958); R. K. Harrison, *Introduction to the Old Testament* (Grand Rapids: Eerdmans, 1969), 3-82; K. A. Kitchen, *Ancient Orient and Old Testament* (Downers Grove: InterVarsity, 1966), 79-86, 112-38; G. L. Archer, Jr., *A Survey of Old Testament Introduction* (Chicago: Moody Press, 1974), 83-169.

[334] Vreeland, *Joseph Narrative*, 467-75.

Printed in the United States
132842LV00006B/1/A

9 781602 662117